Osterville

Volume I

A History of the Village

By
Paul L. Chesbro

WILLIAM S. SULLWOLD PUBLISHING, INC.
TAUNTON, MASSACHUSETTS

Introduction

Never before has so much material about this village and its people been concentrated in one place. This book, which represents nearly thirty years of research by Chesbro, is an invaluable source of information, and it belongs in the library of every home in Osterville.

Although not a writer by profession, its author has, from the time he was a boy, enjoyed the study of history. Chesbro has attempted in this, his second book, to bring to light numerous facts uncovered during his years of research. Many of the articles are reprints from issues of *The Barnstable Patriot* published between 1830 and 1935, with kind permission from Mrs. Percy Williams. Sturgis Library in Barnstable Village has been another source of valuable knowledge.

Chesbro's first book, a pictorial history entitled "Osterville, A Walk Through the Past," was published in 1979. Its opening chapter, the Rich Letter written in 1877, served as his base of reference. Chesbro's new work provides greater breadth and far more depth. Readers of "OSTERVILLE" will discover how the village was named, learn of land disputes and settlements and how they were arrived at, find news items dated as early as 1830 and as recent as during the decade of the 1940s. Our village hall, schools, library, post office, churches and cemetery are viewed from their inceptions.

We learn of our part in the Revolutionary War, the Civil War, the Spanish-American War and World Wars I and II . . . and celebrations of Memorial and Independence Days. Hour-by-hour descriptions of the 1944 hurricane and its aftermath bring back, to those of us who survived it, vivid memories of the storm's fury.

Organizations, including the Beacon Club, Temperance Society, baseball teams, athletic associations, bands, scouting, drama groups, fire department, the Lincoln Club, as well as our business enterprises — the Factory, coasting trade, boat yards, inns and hotels, and oystering — all are reviewed. Village locales such as the bridges (Bumps River and Oyster Harbors), West Bay, Little Island, Oyster Harbors, Wianno, HI GA HO and Seapuit are highlighted. Countless photographs of people and places illustrate the text.

Chesbro had originally planned to include in this book his histories of old Osterville families, but the resulting size of the book would have made it unwieldy. He is, therefore, publishing "OSTERVILLE" in two volumes, the first to come out in 1988, the second in 1989. Both volumes are books every Osterville resident will want to own. Chesbro's thirty years of dedicated research guarantee the quality of these two new books.

— Andrea Leonard

Dedication
To my mother
Grace P. Chesbro
Who for thirty years has put up with
all of this memorabilia scattered about
her otherwise orderly house.

CREDITS

Above all, I want to first express my sincere appreciation to all who helped me gather information for this book, those who told me their stories, those who loaned me their cherished photographs to copy, and those who gave me their old pictures to keep. I want also to thank Mrs. Carl F. Riedell and Andrea Leonard of Osterville and Miss Sheila Peters of Scottsdale, Arizona, for typing the manuscript. For proofreading, I am again indebted to Mrs. Carl F. Riedell, Andrea Leonard, Townsend Hornor, Sheila Peters, and to Joy Buhler of Harwich. To Charlotte Merrill of Allegan, Michigan, my heartfelt thanks for assisting me in indexing and other details. Thanks are also due to photographers Mark and Adrian Cote who provided copies of many of the pictures used herein.

Paul L. Chesbro

Osterville, 1988

Key to Abbreviations

C.R.	Church Records
F.B.R.	Family Bible Records
G.A.R.	Grand Army of the Republic (Civil War)
G.S.I.	Grave Stone Inscription
inst.	of this month
K. & L. of H.	Knights and Ladies of Honor
m.	married
M.E. Church	Methodist Episcopal Church
O.A.A.	Osterville Athletic Association
O.L.S.	Osterville Literary Society
O.V.I.S.	Osterville Village Improvement Society
Sch. or Schr.	Schooner
U.H.I.S.	Union Hall Improvement Society
ult.	in the last month
W.C.T.U.	Women's Christian Temperance Union
W.R.C.	Women's Relief Corps
Y.P.S.C.E.	Young People's Society of Christian Endeavor

Table of Contents

The Naming of Osterville

Osterville's name believed to be a corruption of Oysterville

For many years what is now Osterville was known as Oyster Island Village, and the present name is undoubtedly a corruption of Oysterville. The large island near Osterville was long known as Oyster Island, then later and for many years, Grand Island, and recently (since 1925) as Oyster Harbors, thus perpetuating the local tradition.

The Indian Paupmunnuke was Sachem of the territory where Osterville now stands; his tribe was the Cotachese, and the rivers or inlet which lie between Osterville and Oyster Harbors was called Skunkomug. Various places in the vicinity were, in the Indian language, Chunkomuck, Skonkonet, and similar names.

Translated into English, these Indian words all spring from the same root, Chunkoo, the Oyster, according to Amos Otis (Genealogical Notes of Barnstable Families), "thus the meaning of the present name, Osterville, is derived from the Indian, although changed and made more prosaic with the addition of the French 'ville.' " In either form, the delicious oysters, which abound in these waters and are still grown here, are commemorated.

From the records of J. M. Leonard

Osterville — By Cornelius Lovell — 1861

Osterville is situated in the southern part of the Town of Barnstable. It was so called from the great number of shell fish called oysters formerly found on its flats. It contains about four hundred inhabitants chiefly engaged in coasting from Albany to Boston. It contains a Baptist and Methodist meeting house and a Hall in which the Universalists hold their meetings. There are two schoolhouses, one situated in District No. 13, the other in No. 19. The former is most new, while the latter is rather the worse for wear. The inhabitants are in general a quiet, generous and well-disposed people.

Osterville by Mathilde Adams

The land along the South Sea was bought of the Indian in 1648 for two copper kettles and some fencing, done with Myles Standish acting for the settlers and Paupmunnuck for the Indians.

Cotocheset was the name of a neck of land containing thirty acres southeasterly from Mystic Landing, and adjoining to Roger Goodspeed's houselot, that Paupmunnuck, in his sale of land in 1648, reserved to the Indians, and this was his place of residence. It was afterward known as the Indian Fields. This name is almost identical in meaning with Kokachoise and was the name of his Sachemdom and the name of the small island and narrows a little distance to the southeast. The tract of country which was Cotocheset, until very recently (1815) known as Oyster Island, is a peninsula bounded on every side except at the northwest by water if Bumps River, a branch of the Chunkomuck or Skunkamug, be considered its northern boundary. At the division of the town into two parishes in 1717, the Skunkamug (Phinney's Mill stream) was made a part of the boundary line. It now separates Wequaquet from Skonkonet. The exact definition of the name is "an oyster bed."

Cotocheset is bounded on the south by Vineyard Sound, called by our ancestors the South Sea; southwesterly, including Great and Little Oyster Islands, by Oyster Bay, inlet or river; and northwesterly by Mistic. The early settlements made by the English were at Sipnesset and Kokachoise in the south. In the north few settlements were made except in the immediate vicinity of the mill privileges. (Sipnesset was a little brook that flows into the bay at Oyster Island landing.)

All the southerly part of Barnstable was called the "South Sea," and the Indians resident there, "South Sea Indians." The earliest settlers at South Sea were John Thompson, who sold his land to John Lovell, Roger Goodspeed, Jonathan Hatch, Thomas Bumpus and Joshua Lumbert. Thomas Bumpus' house was on "Lovell's Way" in Cokachoiset, now Osterville. Samuel Bumpus' house was at Skonkonet, now called Bumps River, and on the road south of Thompson's Bridge. His house stood near the cedar swamp. His house lot and other lands in the vicinity of Thompson's Bridge, laid out to him in 1716, were for one share he bought of his brother-in-law, Samuel Parker, and one of John Howland.

The grant of Jonathan Hatch's land was recorded February 14, 1655, but it is probable that the grant was made and that he removed to South Sea at an earlier date. His lands are thus described: Fifty acres, more or less of upland, with a parcel of marsh adjoining at a place commonly called Sipnesset on ye South Sea, also eight acres of meadow, four at Oyster Island which is very particularly described. One half of his farm he subsequently sold to Thomas Shaw, and then sold the same May 27, 1661, to Mr. John Thompson, who resold to John Lovell about the year 1674.

At this time (1655) there were very few whites settled at South Sea. Roger Goodspeed, who resided at Mistic, was probably his nearest neighbor for several years. At this time oysters were very abundant in the waters in the vicinity of his residence, and many barrels were annually pickled and sent to market.

For many years after the settlement of the town, all the lime used for building purposes was manufactured in the vicinity of Sipnesset from the shells of oysters. Dry wood cut into small pieces was procured and a kiln built of alternate layers of shells and wood; the whole was covered with turf, excepting a small opening at the top and another at the bottom where the fire was set, and the shells converted by the heat into quick lime of a superior quality.

Many Indians dwelt near the residence of Goodman Hatch. The wigwam of Paupmunnuck, sachem of the Massapees, was about a mile distant. He traded with them, visited them, and at times was perhaps too familiar with them. It was policy for him to be on good terms with them. They were his neighbors, and if by his conduct he had excited them to hostility, they had it in their power to do him much injury. Moses Goodspeed, thirteenth child of Ebenezer, and grandson of Roger, inherited the homestead of his ancestor and by purchases made by him and his son, Seth, the latter became the owner of all the lands that were his ancestors', and it is now the property of Henry Goodspeed, a son of Seth.

In 1697, the South Sea men were Thomas Macy; Benjamin, John, and Ebenezer Goodspeed, sons of Roger; John Lovell, and his sons John, James, William and Andrew; John Isham; Thomas Bumpus; Dolar Davis; Thomas Lewis; Joshua Lumbert; John Linnell; John Phinney, Jr.; Edward Lewis; Joseph Lothrop, Jr.; John Lewis; and Edward Coleman. Soon after that date the Hallett, Crowell, Bearse, and Claghorn families settled at South Sea.

Memories of Old Osterville
Written in 1939 by
Mrs. Mary Scott Scudder
Reminiscences of the Early Coming of Summer Visitors to Osterville and Wianno

In the early 1870s, after the sad days of the Civil War were over and conditions had settled down to normal, people began to think of getting away in the summer season from the heat of their city homes to the country, mountains or shore. The thoughts of many turned to Cape Cod.

At the same time, the business of shipping freight by sailing vessels to and from Boston, New York, Hartford, and Albany had begun to decline so that it was no longer profitable; for that reason many captains quit the sea, stayed at home, and helped care for the new-comers. Many opened their homes and found ready response from those who were eager to enjoy the hospitality, good food, and other attractions.

In our own village, Mrs. Susan Scudder, down the lane (now East Bay Road), took boarders. A family by the name of Baldwin is remembered by some of our older people.

To get to the beach for bathing or fishing, the boarders used to hire a man with a horse and lug-wagon (with boards across for seats), who drove them down to the end of the lane, around Phinney's Bay, by numerous fish shanties, on to the beach. Ten or twelve in a load; 10 cents apiece.

There is another name connected with the Scudder Cottage which will be remembered for many years by old and young: Armstrong, of Pittsburgh, Pa. This family had been going to Canada for the summer for a number of years. In the summer of 1904, a drowning accident had occurred, and on that account the family did not feel like going there again.

They talked the matter over with a friend who said she was going to Cape Cod. They asked her to look around for a place for them. Soon they had a reply that she had found a house in Osterville, and the price was $300 for the season, but as it was getting late, they might have it for $150.

They wanted to buy the house but could not get it at that time. The family spent four seasons in Miss Bertha Chadwick's house. One year there was some talk of going to Europe, and the boys said, "What! Not go to Cape Cod!"

In 1910, Mr. Armstrong bought the Susan Scudder Cottage. By friendly association with the village people, they have endeared themselves to all. Their only daughter, Mary Martha, had an outdoor wedding in 1927 on the beautiful grounds of their summer home, to which many of the village people were invited. Mr. Armstrong passed on in 1935, but Mrs. Armstrong and the family still love Indian Knoll and every summer finds them here.

After giving up coasting as master of a vessel, Capt. Nelson Harvey Bearse in company with Jehiel Hodges built boats in a shop on the shore of East Bay for a few years prior to 1885. The Bearses had been taking a few boarders in their home, but about 1890 they remodeled it, calling it East Bay Lodge. They carried it on very successfully until 1917 when it passed into the hands of Brown and Tower, and it is now run by Charles Brown.

There was another family who, like the Armstrongs, after coming here for a number of years, decided to buy a summer house. Major and Mrs. Goodspeed, of Columbus, Ohio, were guests at East Bay Lodge in the late '90s and bought Rev. James Goodspeed's house, next to the Lodge, facing the bay in 1900. They were interested in the life and activities of the village, being especially helpful to the Methodist Church and, later, to the Community Church. Major Goodspeed passed on a number of years ago; Mrs. Goodspeed more recently in 1932.

A sign, hung by the driveway of "The New Crosby House" at West Bay, reads: "Established in 1860." The Old Crosby House started in a small way, but additions and alterations were made as occasion required, until in 1876 it was a sizable hotel. Families came, year after year, to enjoy the bathing over in "the Narrows," the boating in a regular "Crosby" cat boat, the fishing out by "The Beacon," and croquet, which was played even by the men, before golf became fashionable. Capt. and Mrs. Horace S. Crosby made it so pleasant, people were loath to leave. Since the death of Capt. and Mrs. Crosby, the Crosby House continues under other management as the "New Crosby House."

There was a family named Chaplin who were the first city people to come to Osterville, but I do not know the date. I have a book, "Inside Our Gate," written by the daughter, Christine Chaplin Brush*, in which is a lovely account of their arrival in Osterville, perfect strangers, to the house now owned by Mrs. L. Ebling. Mr. Chaplin was a Baptist minister, and the good people of the Baptist Church had supper all ready for them.

There are other families who are cherished in our memories. The Carret sisters who built "Carret House" on Parker Road, now "Engadine Lodge." The Richard Barrows family of Morristown, N.J., who were first at the Carret House, and later occupied the house where Mrs. Elsie Gardner now lives. Deacon George Dexter of Boston, who lived in the house now owned by Mrs. Frank Hagerman. Nichols, Noyes, Halliday, Van Dusen . . . one cannot name them all.

---

*Christine Chaplin Brush was the wife of the Rev. Alfred H. Brush. She died in 1892. Her father was the Rev. Jeremiah Chaplin; her mother, Mrs. Jane Dunbar Chaplin.

Capt. Nelson H. Bearse was the agent who sold to the Gaff family a tract of land on the north shore of Centerville River, west of Centerville Bridge, belonging to Russell Marston of Centerville. The family came from Cincinnati, Ohio, and consisted of Mrs. James W. Gaff, a widow, and four young people. They had been coming to the Cotocheset House, and finally decided to build.

Two beautiful homes were built in the spring of 1888: one for Mr. and Mrs. Thomas T. Gaff, and one for Mr. and Mrs. Charles M. Hinkle. Later, Mr. and Mrs. Daniel H. Holmes and Mr. and Mrs. Gordon Shillito built homes as well.

The estates are known as "The Bluffs." Families who have been employed in various ways on the estates have settled here permanently: Beaumont, Cross, Hansberry, McEacheron, and others.

Only Mrs. Thomas T. Gaff remains of the original family, Mrs. Hinkle having passed on in February, 1939. Mrs. Hinkle and Miss Jean Hinkle have spent most of each year here, the latter being interested in town affairs.

In 1869, Harvey Scudder of Boston, brother to Erastus Scudder, a native of Osterville, interested a Mr. Chadwick of Boston in a plan of developing the land up at the beach for a summer resort, and the Osterville Land Co. was formed. It took quite a few years to raise the money to buy the land from different owners and clear it ready for building. There was no direct road leading to the beach then, but a continuation of the present Bates Street led to Neck Pond through the woods, as now.

The first move was the building of a road beginning at what was James Newton Lovell's Corner (James Allen Lovell's) over the property of the following persons: Erastus Scudder, Cyrenius Lovell, John Lovell, Susan Scudder, James Goodspeed, and George Hinckley. These people lived on East Bay Lane, but owned land inland as far as Neck Pond and Lot's Pond. The town had charge of building this road, now called Wianno Ave.

Mr. Erastus Scudder had charge of building the road running parallel to the beach, now called Sea View Avenue. Johnnie Hinckley got a chance to work on the job, so Scott Scudder, being 12 or 13 years old, asked if he could work. Mr. Scudder thought he was too small, but he said he might try, and he was kept on the job.

The Cotocheset House was built in 1873 by David and Alonzo Lent, Edgar and Arthur DeWitt, Azor D. Hall, Simeon Letteney, and others among whom were some young carpenters from Nova Scotia. It was very up-to-date. Rich Cottage, the bowling alley, and the stables were built at the same time. Following those were Hill Cottage, Chace (now Blodgett), Tolman, Garrison, Wellington, Prescott, Hallowell, Jones, Phelps, and many more, for each new-comer interested some friend. Mr. William Garrison told me that the lumber to build some of the early cottages was brought by vessel from Boston, and rafted ashore from New Harbor. There had been an exposition in 1876 and the buildings had been torn down.

Mr. William L. Garrison came to visit the Wellingtons in 1876 and later built several cottages. One, "The Cones," was built for him by Daniel Crosby and Charles Daniel, who had recently come to Osterville (1879). Mr. Garrison was the one who was instrumental in raising money for our public library in 1881, the dedication exercises being held in the Methodist Church, December 30, 1881. A framed account of the meeting hangs in the library and also a portrait of Mr. Garrison. The library has been a wonderful asset to our village. In 1877 the Osterville Land Co. sold out to Mr. Joseph C. Stevens.

One of the early managers of the Cotocheset House was Mr. P. A. Roberts of Boston. In 1879, Mrs. Thankful Ames was put in charge of the hotel. She visited other hotels, learned how to preside, and was very successful. The old Cotocheset House burned down July 17, 1887, but was immediately rebuilt. Under the cornerstone of the main building is a receptable containing letters, names, and small articles contributed by the remaining guests and sealed in by Mr. Joseph W. Tallman, the mason.

During the early days, the mail for those living at the Beach came to Osterville marked "Cotocheset House," and someone came down to get it. After the fire, a post office was established, and Miss Jennie L. Hinckley was appointed postmistress in 1889. The name "Wianno" was derived from the Indian name Yanno, with the first syllable, Wi-anno.

In 1896, Messrs. Henry B. and Frank A. Day of Boston built a cottage on Sea View Avenue. Ed. H. Fuller of Marstons Mills was the contractor. Each family used it part of the summer. In 1900, Mr. Frank A. Day built another, further to the west. H. S. Fraser was the architect, and Ira L. Hinckley was the builder. Walking down to church, the Days named the woods "The Cathedral Pines." Mrs. Day and family still come to Wianno (1939).

There are several families, sons and daughters of the earliest comers to Cotocheset (Wianno) who still come to Wianno for the summer, not only for the recreational program — boating, bathing, golf, etc., — but for old times' sake, as well.

There was always a friendly feeling between the guests at Cotocheset and the village people, and these families still take an active interest in the welfare of Osterville.

Mrs. Francis Bird, Mr. W. L. Garrison, and Mrs. J. Mott Hallowell serve as trustees of our public library. They have interested others, and every year with the cooperation of the villagers, a rummage sale is held for the benefit of the library and other activities. A substantial amount is raised. A few years ago, Dr. Fritz Talbot was helpful in organizing the "Osterville Historical Society" and is still active, attending meetings and proposing plans for activities.

Land Disputes

I think it was about the 15th day of May 1832 when I saw two or three cattle that Christopher Lovell took in to the pasture on our Dead Neck, and they pastured about in the Necks. I should say one month before my father turned up any cattle, and after he turned up, soon after he, Christopher Lovell, took in more cattle as I was told, to pasture. I saw oxen and other cattle several times on my father's land, and I thought they intended to pasture the Neck peaceably together, but about July, Mr. Christopher Lovell took the young cattle that he pastured at home and put them in the field by the pond. I should think that they were kept in and about said field about three or four weeks, then the next I heard of them they were up in the Neck, and Mr. Christopher Lovell was complaining that our cattle had eaten up a great deal of his hay. I saw them, Christopher Lovell's cattle that he took in, on our land feeding September 19th, 1832, and September 22, while they were pastured in the field by the pond. They were in my Father's field a considerable part of the time, his fence being not more than knee high. I again saw them October 22nd on my Father's March 30th, and I again saw them on the marsh, November the 17th. The young cattle came down out of the Necks.

James N. Lovell
Statement

Hyannis, September 20, 1832

Mr. James Lovell:

Dear Sir:
I received a letter from Mr. Christopher Lovell yesterday with a complaint against you that you have let your cattle destroy his bog on Dead Neck for which he demands satisfaction; therefore you had better settle with him for the same for to save from the expense of suit, I am, Sir,

Gorham Lovell

Osterville, Sept. 22, 1832
To Gorham Lovell Esq.

Dear Sir:
Sir, I received a letter from you today stating that your brother Christopher Lovell had entered a complaint against me for destroying his hay on Dead Neck. I think the fact is that I have the same grounds for making a complaint that he has. For his cattle or cattle that he has taken in has eaten up our hay and he has taken in oxen and young cattle to pasture five or six head and now wants me to pay for it. I think that if the truth was known the balance would stand in my favor. He pastured it from two to four weeks before me. He took his cattle out two or three weeks and then turned them in again.

From your servant,
James Lovell
By James Newton Lovell

Osterville, January 10th, 1833

Received three dollars and twenty-five cents the same being in full from Christopher Lovell's demands against James Lovell on account of said James' cattle damaging said Christopher's meadows on Dead Neck, and the expense of same, also the damage done to the woodland on said Neck, up to this date.

Signed: Gorham Lovell

Mr. Christopher Lovell

Sir:
My Father requested me to write to you to inform you that he has a demand against you for the damages your cattle (or cattle that you took in) has done for the past year on Dead Neck, to his meadow, woodland, and hay. He therefore requests you to call and settle the same to save further expense.

Yours,
James N. Lovell

Osterville, January 12, 1833

Osterville, February 7, 1833
This certifies that sometime in the fall or summer of 1832 I heard Christopher Lovell state that he did not agree with Allen Goodspeed to pasture his oxen on Dead Neck so called or the Neck and was to have no compensation of said Goodspeed for the pasture.
Josiah Scudder, Jr.

I hereby certify that on the morning of May 23, 1833, Mr. Christopher Lovell came to my Father and appeared to be considerably excited. He threatened to tear down my Father's fence on Dead Neck; my father told me he wanted I should watch him. I accordingly went up to Dead Neck and concealed myself near the fence. It was not long before said Christopher came and I saw him tear down the fence. He tore down all except a few posts where it joined him. He was engaged in pulling it down 35 minutes.
Osterville, May 23, 1833
James N. Lovell

I hereby certify that on the morning of May 27, 1833, I saw Christopher Lovell, Samuel S. Lovell, going up into the Neck. Said Christopher and Samuel having threatened to tear down, etc., our fence on the dividing line between our lots, I thought it was best to watch them. I accordingly hastened up to the Neck to see if they did the same. When I first came in sight of them, they were just leaving a pair of bars which they had also mentioned to tear down. I found them taken out. (I had seen them up the night before.) They then proceeded to the fence. Then I saw said Christopher begin to feel of the poles. Soon after I saw Samuel pull up stakes and they both seemed to be hard at work. I then changed my place to the other side of the Swamp. I still saw them at work directly. I saw said Christopher take his axe and went to cutting down the fence. I watch them some time and see them work. I then walk westward around the swamp. I heard cutting all the time. I heard Samuel say: them fine trees, these and some other talk which I could not distinctly understand. Soon after I left them at work and came home there was seven head of my Father's cattle enclosed in his field, and close by where they was cutting down the fence, already to go out as soon as they left. The fence above-described is in the hither Neck, so called, and the west side of the lot of sand that my Mother bought of Russell S. and Thomas S. Lovell's and down by or near the Swamp.

Osterville, May 27, 1833
James N. Lovell

At noon on this 27th of May, 1833, Mr. Robert Lovell and myself went up into the hither Neck to see what the damage was that the said Lovells had done to said fence, and we found that it was mostly torn down and some of it cut up and also found that they had cut Oak and Pine wood on said James' lot and that the cattle had not then got out but nothing to hinder. As we were coming home we met Samuel S. Lovell going up after the fencing stuff with a horse and cart of wood. We turned about and went back. We had considerable talk. I asked him if he tore down the fence to see what he would say. He would not say, but said he knew who tore it down. I asked him if he was going to take the wood and fencing stuff away. He would not say. We then came off and we watched at Mr. Lovell's Shop. He soon came home with quite a large load of the wood and fencing stuff and drove it to his door.
James N. Lovell

1834

May 12	C. Lovell & Nehemiah Parker carted down J. Lovell's fencing stuff.
May 16	I, James N. Lovell, saw Job Childs and horse in my Father's Lot (swamp).
May 19	C. Lovell come to shoot our dog and some difficulty.
July 24	Samuel S. Lovell told me that they was agoing to drive their cows up into the Nether Nake and down after I saw C. Lovell and S.S. Lovell driving 2 cows up.
July 26	The bar was all taken out and let down so that cattle might go upon Ded Nake.
August 2	At a quarter before 9 I saw C. Lovell let down the bars on Ded Nake and on September 8 I saw D. Fuller's colt upon Wm. Blount's marsh on Ded Nake Point.
September 16	D. Fuller's colt folloed E. Berce [Bearse?] off.

The author has found these land disputes most fascinating and believes others will as well. However, the grammatical structure of many of the sentences and paragraphs were written by men who at that time had a limited education. The author has left some the way he found them recorded; others have been changed to make it more understandable by the reader.

Be it known by these present that we the undersigners agree to submit the differences that exist between us in regard to pasturage, fences, wood, and all other difficulties that exist between us, in regard to Dead and Hitter Necks to Jacob Lovell, Henry Lovell, and Ebenezer Parker for three years last past from this date, and agree to abide their judgment, in case we recant from their decision, either of us for so doing we agree to pay the other party Eighteen dollars.

Osterville, September 30, 1834

We hereunto set our hands and seals, this 30th day of September, 1834

> Christopher Lovell
> James Lovell
> Samuel S. Lovell

Attest:
James N. Lovell

Osterville, September 30, 1834

I hold myself firmly bound to James Lovell as surety for Samuel S. Lovell and Christopher Lovell's faithful performance of the above contract as bond.

> Josiah Scudder, Jr.

―――――――――――――

I hereby certify to whom it may concern that when I went up to mow English hay for Christopher Lovell (I think in July in 1832), he wanted I should turn my oxen upon Dead Neck to pasture. He said he wanted to get all the cattle to pasture he could. He further stated that Allen Goodspeed had pastured his oxen on Dead Neck.

> Marshall Hinckley

Osterville, October 3, 1834

―――――――――――――

I hereby certify, to whom it may concern, that I made an agreement with Samuel Lovell and Christopher Lovell to turn my horses on the Neck pasturage, and I turned them up twice, and they stayed there but one or two days each time. It was in May, I think, of this year.

> Signed: Heman Hinckley

Osterville, October 3, 1834

I certify, to whom it may concern, that in June (I think) in 1832, as I was coming off of Oyster Island with my cattle, I turned my oxen out upon Dead Neck, and then came down and made an agreement with Christopher Lovell for them to run there one fortnight. In about a week, I was in Osterville and fell in with Mr. Christopher Lovell. He notified me that my oxen were in the streets and offered to help me drive them back, but I said I wanted them, and I drove them home, and they were there but one week.

> Signed: Allen Goodspeed

Osterville, Oct. 3, 1834

―――――――――――――

I hereby certify, to whom it may concern, that I pastured my horse on Dead Neck one or two weeks in 1832 on Christopher Lovell's wright and I also certify that I pastured my horse three weeks in the Hither Neck in May this year upon Christopher Lovell's wright and made an agreement both times.

> Seth Goodspeed

Osterville, October 3, 1834

―――――――――――――

I hereby certify that in 1832 Mr. Christopher Lovell came to me and wanted I should turn our hiffer (heifer) upon the Nake (Neck), he said he could pasture her there as well as not. I accordingly drove her up as far as General Field and Mr. Christopher Lovell said he would drive her up. He afterwards called and told me that he had drove her up and said he could pasture a great many creatures. She ran, as nigh as I can recollect, from August to September or October. She was there from two to three months.

> Betsy P. Lovell

Osterville, October 4, 1834

―――――――――――――

I hereby certify that in the fall of 1832 Mr. Christopher Lovell and James N. Lovell came into my shop. They soon began conversation about Dead Neck. Said James told said Christopher that he had pastured oxen on Dead Neck the past summer. He said it was an absolute lie he had not, and he further stated that I wrote a lie to Gorman Lovell, Esq. about the oxen, and I think he has repeatedly stated to me that he did not pasture the oxen on Dead Neck.

> Robert Lovell

Osterville, October 4, 1834

I certify that I saw a white horse a number of times in James Lovell's lot on meadow ground at a place called the Lot Swamp. I think it was about the 15th or 16th of May of this year.

Signed: Phinneas Adams

Osterville, October 7, 1834

Objections to Use of Neck Pond for Purpose of Watering Lifestock.

To all persons to whom it may concern as I the subscriber have learnt, that Philander Scudder, as executor of Joshua Lovell's last will and testament, objects to James Lovell and others going to Neck Pond in the usual beaten cartway for the purposes of watering teams and getting water.

I therefore certify that the branch of the road now in use, leading from the main Neck road to the southeastern end of the Neck Pond and then up to the main road again, I have peaceably improved the same over fifty years prior to 1843, and I also have known James Lovell to improve the same road over fifty years prior to 1843 without any molestation whatever. And I will also add that to my certain knowledge it has been an open watering place for anyone that passed to and from the Necks and no person prohibited for more than fifty years prior to 1843.

Signed: Benjamin Hallett

I, the subscriber, certify that my father improved the land now owned by Joshua Lovell's heirs adjoining the east end of neck pond up to the year eighteen hundred and fourteen, that while he improved the same then was the road now in use, that went down to the pond that went into the neck and it was used at that time and has been ever since by James Lovell and all others who went that way as a public watering place, without molestation or objection up to 1843 and I have also myself used it as a watering place and carting water therefrom.

Signed and sealed in Osterville, March 16, 1844
Hansard Hallett

I hereby certify that the watering place at the east end of neck pond so called and road leading to and from the same has been used by the public and is especially by James Lovell for more than forty years previous to 1843.

George Lovell

Osterville, April 25, 1844

I the subscriber certify that I have known and used without objection the above specified road as a watering place and have known James Lovell and all other persons that passed that way to use the same as a public watering place for thirty-five years before 1843.

Robert Lovell

Osterville, March 21, 1844

1847, January 4th — David Fuller and I found the bounds moved. some time in January 1847, Mr. Ewer said it ran north and south from stone. February 15th, Mr. Jesse Crosby, Isaac Ewer went into the Neck, March 1. Mr. Ewer said it was northerly and southerly from Cedar swamp. Tuesday, March 23, 1847, Mr. Isaac Ewer, Freeman Crosby and Reuben West, with Robert Lovell's horse and cart went into the Neck 1/2 past 12 o'clock pm. I went up and watched them and saw them all cutting wood on Harvey Scudder's woodlot and all helped load the cart, and Mr. West went off with the load at 1/2 past one pm. They cut two full rods into Mr. Scudder's lot.

1847, May 4: not more than 5 or 6 days since the bounds again moved. I saw Mr. Ewer go up into the neck and return.

January 25, 1848: I this day saw that the bounds had been moved; that is, the stones taken away from the two trees on the jury line to the south of the great swamp; the marks where the stones lay looked as though the stones had been removed but a short time. I should think I have seen them lay there less than six weeks from this date.

James N. Lovell

Osterville, December 13, 1847

Mr. James N. Lovell called on me this evening and said that Mr. Isaac Ewer has, for the first time of any one, made a claim upon the lower part of the James Lovell's Cranberry marsh and said Ewer also claims the privilege that said Lovell has to drain said cranberry marsh. I will here certify that James Lovell bought the rod wide as the writing states for a drain and paid my father for it, and I also certify, and am willing to swear to the same, that my father has told me that the line between his land and Samuel Holmes', on Isaac Ewer's land, was by the young line through the great swamp, and on the same line from the swamp to the sea shore. I bought of my father, up to that line, and I sold to

Harvey Scudder, up to the same. There were good bounds on the line from the swamp to the heap of stones by the beach hill, of trees marked, and heaps of stones, and I will further state to the best of my belief that Mr. Isaac Ewer, my father, and myself, went through on the young line from the swamp to the shore and examined the bounds. There was then no dispute. It was while I owned the land.

Samuel S. Lovell

Attest: James N. Lovell

———————————

This may certify that I, the subscriber, went with Christopher Lovell sometime in July, 1821, into the Hither Neck, so called, for the purpose of looking at a certain piece of woodland and cleared land with intent to buy, the same being afterwards sold to Harvey Scudder, and I also certify that a part of said land was then planted with corn and that the said Christopher Lovell then showed me the bounds and said it was about 2 rods or 2-1/2 rods wide at the sea shore, thence bounded westerly by James Lovell's fence until it came to the round cedar swamp of Daniel Lovell until it comes to a ditch leading from said swamp to the great cedar swamp until it comes to the jury line, so called, and thence by said jury line to the sea shore; the above said bounds were then plain, being designated by marked trees and stones on the east side from the great swamp to the sea shore, and embraced all the land then under tillage, and I should say about one or one-and-a-quarter acres of woodland and beach.

Signed: Isaac Hodges

Osterville, April 5, 1849

———————————

Establishing Bounds
Division of Fences and Appraisal between David Fuller, Seth Weeks, and Samuel I. Ames

Osterville, March 14, 1843

We, the subscribers, wishing to have a division of fences made between our lands on adjoining what is called the Isham Estate, but now gone, or passed principally into our hands, and we mutually agree to leave the division of fences made between our lands on and the same, if we wish, to James N. Lovell, and agree to abide by his decision, and in case either of us recant from said Lovell decision, for so doing, he shall pay the other party ten dollars for the same.

Signed: David Fuller
Seth Weeks
Samuel I. Ames

Osterville, March 14, 1843

I, the subscriber, have attended to the business as described above and make a division of the first string of fence between Capt. David Fuller and Capt. Seth Weeks, as follows: Capt. David Fuller, beginning at the Northwest corner of his lot, and running southwesterly as the fence now stands, twenty four rods to a stake and stones, and have appraised the fence, as it now stands on Capt. D. Fuller's line, to be worth eleven dollars and 85/100, and Capt. Seth Weeks has the refusal whether to take it or leave it, and the remaining part of the string, leading to the corner near the road being twenty six rods, I determine as Capt. Weeks' part of the fence, and have not appraised it.

The second piece of fence is near the swamp between Capt. Weeks' and Fuller's; I commence at a post marked and run westerly as the fence now stands, eleven rods, which part Capt. Weeks is to make as his part, as is not appraised, and Capt. David Fuller's commencing at the end of the eleven rods at a stake and stones, and running on the same course ten rods into the swamp to intersect the line of other fence. I also have appraised Capt. David Fuller's part of the fence which I consider worth three dollars and 25/100 and it also is left to the option of Capt. Weeks to take it at appraisal or not.

The next piece of fence that I viewed was between Capt. David Fuller's and Samuel I. Ames, the division of the fence being already made. I only appraised Capt. Fuller's string to a post marked and easterly as the fence now stands, fifty one frames of post and rail fence which I appraised to be worth twenty four dollars, fifty two cents, this also Mr. S. I. Ames has the refusal whether to take it or not to, and lastly, I appraised a small piece of fence between Capt. D. Fuller's and S. I. Ames'. Capt. Fuller's part of the fencing stuff is worth two dollars and eighty cents, and Mr. Ames also has the refusal whether to take or leave the same, as it now stands.

Signed: James N. Lovell

Osterville Items

Salt Works at Osterville

In 1812 the manufacture of salt was at its height on the shores of East Bay. Thomas Ames, Seth Goodspeed, George Hinckley, Henry Lovell, Jacob Lovell, Deacon Josiah Scudder Sr. and George Lovell all had vats and windmills at East Bay.

August 26, 1834

A meeting will be held in Centerville Meeting House on Friday next, 29th inst; at which time an address will be delivered by Benjamin F. Hallett, Esq. on the subject of Masons, and Anti-Masons, and delegates chosen to attend the Antimasonic Convention, to be held in Boston, Sept. 10, 1834.

DIED

November 26, 1834

In Osterville, Hannah Occo, a colored woman aged about 70 years.

November 15, 1836

Upon the petition of Oliver Hinckley and others, praying for a road in the village of Osterville, in said town of Barnstable, from near the shop of Robert Lovell, to the shore by the ship yard of Oliver Hinckley, to be laid out, the Commissioners having reviewed the premises and heard the parties, and it being determined by them to be of common convenience and necessity to locate and establish such new highway or common road; it is therefore ordered that notice be given to all persons and corporations interested therein, that the Commissioners will meet at the house of Oliver Hinckley, in Osterville, on Monday the twenty-first day of November next, at nine o'clock am.

December 20, 1837

The Annual Meeting of the Barnstable Peace Society will be held in the Meeting House in Osterville.

October 17, 1838

In Osterville, Lemuel Francis, only son of Lemuel and Mercy Baker Hamblin, aged two years and twenty-four days.

And is it thus — and must we part,
Thou tendril winding round my heart,
Just as I feel a mother's joy,
Oh must thou go my lovely boy?

Why was't thou lent so short a space,
No smile ere meet a parent's face,
Could there no other chastening prove
The strength of our Redeemer's Love?

No t'was the just decree of God
That we should bend beneath his rod
In his own way — to teach the soul
That all events he must control.

Then may I be resigned and still,
And bow submissive to His will,
And own His justice and His power,
That brought me to this trying hour.

To the Selectmen of the Town of Barnstable or to the Overseers of the Poor.

Greetings: We, the undersigners, would represent to your consideration that there is a boy living at Mr. Stetson Jones's by name, Ebenezer Claghorn Childs, and that he is an idle and vicious boy and that it is highly necessary for someone to have the management of him; also that said boy is in the habit of stealing from the neighbors and has once been to jail for stealing; also, Mr. Jones being poor and feeble is not able to support or manage the boy; we therefore pray that you will take the boy into your custody and bind him out to some suitable man which we consider will be a grate benefit to the boy and to our satisfaction.
James N. Lovell and others

Osterville, April 20, 1843

May 27, 1846

Bass begin to make their appearance on the South shore. Capt. Isaac Hodges, of Osterville, seined forty or more one night last week.

December 6, 1853

Narrow Escape — Last Tuesday, three boys belonging to Osterville, named George T. Lovell, David Fuller and Ansel Adams, while outside in a small boat were suddenly capsized, and after remaining in the water about 20 minutes, were picked up when nearly exhausted, by a boat from the schooner Glide which was fortunately in the harbor. Had it not been for the kindness and promptness of Capt. Lovell and his crew, they would all soon have found a watery grave. Too much praise cannot be given them, for their kind exertions in their behalf.

June 27, 1854

Narrow Escape — On the 19th instant, a company of young ladies, at Osterville, whilst enjoying a walk, visited the wharf of Mr. George Hinckley, and whilst there Miss Augusta Lovell, one of the party, sprang into a boat for amusement. Suddenly finding the boat loose from its moorings, she jumped into the water and it was with great difficulty that she was rescued from a watery grave, by the ladies present.

Small Pox at Osterville

December 26, 1854

We learn that two or more cases of small pox now exist at Osterville and several cases of varioloid. The scarlet fever and whooping cough are also prevalent in that village, and the place has been visited during the past season by a severe epidemic of dysentery.

October 9, 1855

In June of 1855 there were 456 people living in Osterville.

February 5, 1856

Was −4° degrees on Monday Feb. 4 1856.

About Osterville

March 16, 1858

Formerly, deer were quite plentiful in this region, but now they are rarely seen. It is, however, a favorite resort for fox hunters, and large numbers have been killed the present season. This village contains about five hundred inhabitants and is quite famous as a summer resort.

February 13, 1866

Freedmen's Meeting — Mr. J. Q. A. Brackett delivered an interesting lecture in Osterville on Monday evening week, and at its close a branch Society of the New England Freedmen's Aid Society was organized by choosing Erastus Scudder, President and William Crocker, Secretary and Treasurer. A canvassing Committee was also chosen, and Osterville will therefore under such management give a good account of herself.

July 24, 1866

Serious Results of Tampering with a Loaded Shell. The Providence Journal says that schooner Seneca, Capt. Dottridge, which arrived at that port Tuesday morning, from New York, while in the latter city took on board a nine-inch shell, and while near Sands Point, on Long Island, about 12 o'clock Friday noon, the mate undertook to take out the powder. He had removed a portion, which was lying in three separate piles on deck, to one of which the cook in sportiveness touched fire. The fire communicated to the powder remaining in the shell, and the explosion which followed tore a large hole through the deck of the vessel, carried away a portion of the rail, smashed the galley, rent the sails, broke the cook's leg, and injured the mate, though not seriously. It was fortunate that there was no loss of life, as two other men were standing near. The cook was left in the hospital in New York. His name is Henry Crocker, and he belongs in Osterville, Mass. His limbs will probably have to be amputated.

March 5, 1867

The beautiful homestead of Mr. Edwin Coombs, in this place, was sold at auction last Tuesday morning to Mr. Harrison Phinney, master carpenter, of this village.

April 2, 1867

Petitions Against A License Law. The following petitions against a license law were presented in the House last week, and referred to the Committee:
    Of Isaac Lovell and 41 others of Osterville.

December 21, 1869

This quiet, pretty village, located a few miles west of its more ambitious and pretentious sister, Centerville, girt round by a sea of waters and evergreen pines, enjoys a seclusion all its own. Being one side of the most travelled highways, its solitude is broken only by the daily advent and exit of the mail coach, or the rattling lug wagon, moving slowly along, bearing to a market the only manufactures of the place, pine and oak wood, or an ambitious peddler with three horse power and team radiant with glistening paint and golden letters, dashing through the long quiet street.

It has been thought appropriate to change the name of this place to "Sleepy Hollow," as it has enjoyed a nap of about the same duration as Rip Van Winkle's. Twenty years ago this place showed signs of life and activity which are not visible now. Then, oftentimes a dozen or eighteen sail of vessels, belonging mostly in the village, were seen in our harbor; cargoes of corn, flour, etc., were landed. In the two shipyards, at either end of the village, the ring of the builder's hammer and cheery saw was heard. Now it is quite an event for even one vessel to drop anchor in our harbor; and the shipyards have lost all semblance of their former use. The reason for this sad decline is comprised in the word Death. That insatiable monster has either whelmed vessel and entire crew, or selecting the captain as his prey, has hurled him from his confident walk on the quarterdeck to an instant watery grave.

Others, and some of our principal men, have gone to the village churchyard never to return. The whole place has felt the loss of our most energetic and best men, and fatherless families and widows are found in almost every other house in the place. The old post and rail fences our great-grandfathers built still show their lengths of mossy rails along the roadsides, and the oldest inhabitant can hardly remember when the last house was built. Thanks to a former generation, we have a few ancient balm gileads and silver oaks for shade trees, but these are fast disappearing before the march of time and fierce gales, and nothing is being planted to take their places. The west end of the village runs down to the borders of one of the best, if not the best bay for boat sailing that can be found on the Cape. Here boatbuilding is carried on quite extensively by Messrs. Horace and Worthington Crosby. Their centreboard sailboats are hard to be beat in speed, and they cannot be beat in honesty of build. Stepping on board one of them at their wharf, we start with a flowing sheet, pass through a beautiful bay, then glide into a

Corner of Main Street and Blossom Avenue looking North. Same location as picture below, forty-five years later, c. 1915.

wide flowing river, past the elegant home of Mr. Perkins of Boston, erected on a high bluff where a few years ago, the pines held undisputed control, and from the brow of which the sunset view cannot be surpassed in beauty. From the river we glide into another and larger bay, and the pretty tree-embossed village of Cotuit stands before us like a picture. If we like a dash of spray, we steer out boldly through a narrow passage and are soon dashing over the waves of the Sound.

Osterville has been the birthplace of some who have become eminent in life, among whom may be named the late Hon. Zeno Scudder, Hon. B.F. Hallett, the present Judge Henry A. Scudder, and others. One who has lately ascended the woolsack showed his remembrance of his native village by sending, on Thanksgiving Day, his check for one hundred dollars, to be distributed amongst the needy here. Such an act speaks volumes, and is worthy of emulation by others who have left these quiet villages and acquired wealth in our cities. When those in our village who have means can unite and start some kind of manufacturing business which will benefit them and give the young men and women employment at home, then our march will be forward and not backward, as now.

___

February 28, 1871

Death, of late, visits us in various forms, and at oft' recurring intervals: Mr. Hinckley, falling in old age by his own hand; Rev. Mr. Colyer, who was killed on the railroad track while kindly trying to aid others, had married his wife here and his remains were brought here and interred. Friday, we carried to the grave Cora, daughter of Mr. Nelson Lewis, who fell in consumption's deadly grasp in the seventeenth year of her age. Saturday morning a little girl, daughter of Rep. Goodspeed, some five years of age and the "pet of the household," died from disease of the brain caused doubtless, by being thrown from a carriage. So death comes, sundering the dearest ties of earth. Our solace is the hope of a blissful re-union.

Long Cottage — Main Street — c. 1870
The oldest house in Osterville.

At the time this photograph was taken, the Alvin Baker Family lived here; formerly, the residence of Hansard Hallett. The house has changed hands many times in recent decades. The chimney of the Samuel Hallett House (later the residence of R. David Hinckley) is visible beyond the trees. At far right, the house of Benajah West can be seen, now the home of Alcott Hallett, Jr.

July 25, 1871

Among the many pretty little towns on the shores of Cape Cod, is the quiet village of Osterville, which like modest merit is likely to be overlooked in the shadow of her pretentious neighbor, Barnstable. Although there is no hotel, most of the private houses are filled with boarders from Boston and New York, who Thursday evening assembled at the house of Mrs. Susan Scudder, to celebrate the silver wedding of Mr. James Goodman, a worthy fellow citizen, one of the leading insurance agents in Boston.

The house and grounds were tastefully decorated with Chinese lanterns, mottoes in evergreen, and the beautiful vines growing so luxuriantly in the surrounding woods. The bride and bridegroom received their guests standing under the marriage bell made of the rarest flowers, and among the appropriate presents was a fish knife. A poem was recited, there was music by some of the best amateur singers.

After a fine supper and a grand display of fireworks, the guests departed, feeling that style and fashion were not necessary to true enjoyment, and wishing when the golden wedding was celebrated "they might be there."

October 17, 1871

To the Hon. County Commissioners for the County of Barnstable.

The undersigned, citizens of Barnstable, in said county, respectfully represent that the public convenience and necessity require that a public highway should be laid out in said Town of Barnstable commencing near the dwelling house of Adeline Lovell and running to the shore and landing place near the dwelling house of Seth Goodspeed in the village of Osterville, following the course of the present way as near as practicable, but widening and straightening the same.

June 11, 1872

Oysters are again being planted in this vicinity with expectation of the realization of handsome profits.

December 22, 1873

Dear Messrs. Editors:

Noticing in the columns of your valued paper a request for locals, I take the liberty of troubling you with a few notes from our (at present) quiet village.

The Cotocheset House seems deserted, save by parties of young people, who patronize the bowling alley connected therewith, it affording them a fine source of amusement.

The new cottage on the bluff is progressing rapidly and its fine appearance adds greatly to the beauty of the settlement.

The Schooner G. L. arrived here from Providence Monday and is now with the Schooner Copia, wintering in our bay.

Amusements are not in abundance here, but we are sometimes favored with an entertainment not to be surpassed by many of our large towns, or even cities. Your correspondent was assured of this fact last evening, by attending the Musical soiree given at the house of Mrs. Esther P. West by her accomplished granddaughter, Miss L. E. Runyon, assisted by the Misses O. J. West and J. L. Hinckley, both highly cultivated musicians. The house was crowded with the youth and beauty of the village, who listened with rapt attention, applauding and often encoring the various pieces. The music comprised many of the latest ballads of the day, together with selections from the great composers.

This evening for a change, we have a Social Hop in Village Hall so you will now see we are still alive in Osterville.

December 30, 1873

Our inhabitants for the past week have been so busy preparing for Christmas festivities that they have thought or talked of but little else; and last evening might have been observed people going in all directions to their several places of entertainment.

The principal attraction was the Methodist Church, where three large trees bore a truly abundant harvest of what seemed strange fruit for cedars; however it seemed just as acceptable, judging by the smiling faces that surrounded one on every side. The presents were in good taste and some of considerable value. Among these might be noticed one from the parish to their pastor, (Rev. Mr. Ewer); also for the hard times, a valuable gift of green backs to the venerable and worthy citizen, Mr. Zenas Weeks, from his numerous friends in this village. Mr. Weeks is one of our oldest inhabitants and a worthy member of the Baptist Church.

Beside this (the grande affair) I might mention some of the smaller but no less attractive assemblies at the private houses. Among these I think I may say a few words of one as a type of the whole. At the house of Capt. William B. Parker were assembled the numerous representatives of the Parkers with their relatives. The children were in good spirits, and as no restraint was imposed on their actions, they seemed to enjoy themselves even more than those at the Church. After all were assembled, a room heretofore closed was opened, disclosing the fact that Santa Claus does not always confine his labors to the Churches. A tree was there and richly it was laden. I sincerely believe if old Scrooge could have looked in and seen the happy faces, the ghosts of Christmas, past, present, and future would not have been necessary to soften his hard heart. Now came the distribution, and no one was forgotten. Truly, Kris Kringle's register must be a wonderful book. But soon the little ones began to tire and their bright eyes to grow small, causing the company to disperse sooner perhaps than the older ones might have wished.

December 30, 1873

There were also family gatherings at the houses of Capt. Nathan West, Capt. Charles Ellis, Mr. Nelson Lewis and others, at all of which I have no doubt happiness reigned supreme.

February 3, 1874

The past week has been devoted by a great part of our population to attending a series of religious meetings calculated to revive the energies of both the organized Churches of this village, and consequently called a revival.

November 30, 1875

We notice the Parker House, so-called, recently bought by James Simonet from South America, is having new bay windows, is being painted, and fixed up generally.

December 7, 1875

On Monday week the citizens of this place were invited to meet at the vestry of the M.E. Church to take action in regard to getting up a course of lectures. Notwithstanding the extreme cold, a goodly number responded to the call, and after due deliberation it was decided to have six or more free lectures, and the following offices were chosen:
President — Asa E. Lovell
Secretary — Lucy A. Lovell
Treasurer — Israel Crocker
Executive Committee — Freeman Lovell, Rev. F.E. Cleaves and Rev. J.W. Fitch.
Committee to Solicit Funds — D.C. Lewis and Jessie L. Hinckley

February 1, 1876

Our boys had out their sleds for the first time this season Wednesday; Thursday the foundation for this fun had disappeared.

February 29, 1876

A party from here went out on Vineyard Sound gunning last week and returned with one hundred and fifty-five "coots." They report these sea fowl very plenty on the Sound.

March 7, 1876

A party from here shot 161 coots on the Sound Saturday.

March 21, 1876

We had a nice lecture Thursday evening. Although it was stormy and dark yet there was a good audience. The lecture was by the Rev. Charles Winchester of Brockton. Subject: Demon Drink. He made all see the Demon, and all see the government say you may have this Demon only give money for duties and license.

April 18, 1876

Our gunners sent a barrel of coots to Boston and cleared five cents per bird. Rather poor investment.

May 2, 1876

Seth Rich and John A. Blossom have sent a lot of willow shrubs to the Vineyard Camp Ground to be set out around the pool.

June 27, 1876

We notice quite a number of removals. Alvin Baker and family have moved into the house with Capt. Samuel Lovell, Capt. Warren Cammett taking the house they left, and Mrs. Russell Lovell taking the one vacated by Capt. Cammett, as the one she occupied is to be sold. Miss Martha M. Hallett has moved into the house with Mrs. Rose Parker, where she intends to keep house.

September 12, 1876

Osterville begins to have the appearance of lonliness. Only about fifty summer visitors are left with us.

October 24, 1876

Osterville is dull at this season of the year, as our summer visitors have all left and it is not time for our young men to get home from their summer's work.

January 30, 1877

We have two ice boats here — one owned by Capt. Charles G. Lovell and others, and the other by John W. Williams. Their speed, with good wind, is said to be about a mile a minute.

January 30, 1877

The slippery times have caused a few accidents here, as elsewhere. On the 22nd inst., Mrs. Austin Lovell and some others were somewhat bruised, and Mr. Henry A. Hodges broke his leg, but it being cork it was soon mended.

January 30, 1877

Five deer were seen near Bump's River Thursday morning — one buck and four does.

February 27, 1877

The ice having taken up the East Bay Wharf, men are at work putting it down again, this time with stone cribs instead of piles.

February 27, 1877

Capt. Ensign Nickerson and Bethuel Adams are together building a house and yard for hens on a large scale.

May 8, 1877

The new road to the shore near the Crosby Brothers' boat house is finished, and the contractors have made a paying job of it.

May 22, 1877

A number of gunners have been here after coots, and in three days during the past three weeks killed about 400. The birds have now left for colder parts.

June 12, 1877

The sweet singing mosquito is with us and has not forgotten how to bite.

November 20, 1877

Our pogie fishermen have nearly all arrived home.

January 1, 1878

Two funerals occurred in our village yesterday (Monday), Squire Josiah Scudder's and Mrs. Hannah Parker's, two of our most aged and respected citizens. Mrs. Parker, who is well known as a nurse throughout this section of the Country, died Sunday morning, after quite a long sickness. Mr. Scudder was struck with paralysis while chopping wood in his woodhouse on Friday afternoon, and died the following afternoon. He was a brother of Judge Henry A. Scudder, and was well known as one of our leading and most intelligent citizens.

January 29, 1878

Winter half gone and no ice in icehouses yet.

January 29, 1878

Capts. J. P. Hodges and N. H. Bearse are having a house built side of East Bay Wharf in which they intend to build boats. We wish them success.

April 9, 1878

Messrs. Hodges and Bearse, having launched their new boat, had a social dance in their shop Tuesday evening.

May 7, 1878

Fourteen of our men have gone to Tiverton and vicinity at Porgy oil works, and some four or five more are to go soon.

December 24, 1878

Mr. Luther Jones, our village butcher, is building an ice house at James West's pond.

January 7, 1879

Our ice houses are being filled with good ice.

January 28, 1879

Scarlet fever is quite prevalent but of a light nature.

April 15, 1879

Summer visitors are expected to be plenty. The Crosby House has all its rooms engaged and the Cotocheset nearly so, with others in private homes.

May 6, 1879

Quite a number of our men have gone to R. I. Porgy Oil works for the season, and more are going the present week.

August 26, 1879

The storm landed many boats high on marshes, but most of them have been launched again in good order. The tide was the highest ever known. At Mrs. Seth Goodspeed's the water was about one foot deep in the barn and pig-sty, so the pig had to take refuge on the platform in the rear part of his quarters. Bath houses, wharf, etc., were washed away and some destroyed. The bank along the shore was badly washed away, and between the Neck, so called, where we want a cut through, the sea washed over all along. H. N. Lovell had quite a dowery left him near his house. Nearly one-quarter of a mile from shore were tons of seaweed and drift stuff, boats, etc. At Capt. J. P. Hodges' two large trees were blown down, and at other places corn was destroyed.

October 7, 1879

Mr. Frank West, Frank Boult and Frank Williams have each come home with the cranberry fever and gone to picking.

October 21, 1879

Cranberry picking is good, and on Wednesday last J. W. W. Crosby picked 200 quarts, Charles E. Lewis 186 quarts, Scott Scudder, 180 quarts, from off Mr. Luther Hamblin's bog.

December 2, 1879

There was a shoot for roosters Thanksgiving Day. Three shots for 25 cents at a mark; the one that put the most shot in the mark took the rooster. Israel Crocker took first, Frank Boult, second.

March 16, 1880

Osterville without ice! is the cry.

June 1, 1880

Miss Cora Parker and Mrs. Ella Lovell have hired the store owned by Capt. Lot Phinney and started a dress and cloak making establishment.

June 1, 1880

The Colorado beetles are thicker than ever before.

June 1, 1880

Our little village is crowded with summer visitors.

September 7, 1880

A new hearse house is being built for our new hearse.

October 19, 1880

Our new hearse has arrived, and looks nice.

November 30, 1880

A deer visited our school house, Thanksgiving Day, coming within 35 yards of it; yet our gunners failed to get him.

January 11, 1881

Horse racing is the order of the day while good sleighing lasts.

March 22, 1881

Mr. Mumps has paid our village a visit — calling upon Miss Abby L. Crosby, Messrs. Zenas West and Frank M. Boult. Expect he will call upon more before he leaves the village. He came from a ball at Cotuit.

April 20, 1881

Mr. George Weeks has gone to the Oil Works at Tiverton, also Mr. Frank Williams and Mr. Howard Lovell.

June 14, 1881

We have two street lamps to light us on our way dark nights; one a present from Capt. O. D. Lovell, in the Square in front of the house of Mrs. George Lovell, the other a present of E. Scudder Esq., placed in front of Village Hall, and now one more is wanted near the Post Office.

June 28, 1881

William O. Crocker and Wallace F. Crocker have each a new carriage to ride in.

September 6, 1881

For the first time, the lighting of a kerosene street lamp in the village of Osterville.

September 6, 1881

A load of stone was driven on our hay scales and broke them down, and the scales will probably now be condemned.

October 11, 1881

Some sixty or seventy pickers go from this village to the various cranberry bogs.

October 25, 1881

The poles are being set for the new telephone line between Cotuit, Osterville, Centerville, Hyannisport, Hyannis, and West Barnstable.

November 1, 1881

The hay scales have been thoroughly repaired.

November 15, 1881

Deer are quite plenty. Horace Whippey killed two in the water, Herbert Crosby one on the Island, N. H. Bearse and J. R. Goodspeed chased one in Vineyard Sound about one mile and got him.

November 15, 1881
    Our telephone line is in working order.

———————————

November 29, 1881
    We of Osterville are a quiet people, and as a natural sequence we enjoyed a very quiet Thanksgiving — but a most pleasant one nevertheless. The "boys" got up a shooting match which excited not a little attention. The prizes (roosters) were taken by Messrs. Wilton Crosby, Herbert Crosby, Israel Crocker and Bradford Ames.

———————————

December 27, 1881
    Christmas was pleasantly observed here, both publicly and privately. A Christmas Tree was erected in the M.E. Church and yielded largely in fruits and happiness to the little ones, as well as those of an older growth. Family trees abounded. One at the residence of Capt. N.E. West bore over two hundred presents, and grandparents, parents, children and grandchildren sat down to a grand supper after it had been robbed of its fruit. Sunday evening a grand Christmas Concert was given at the Baptist Church, which proved to be a most pleasant and profitable occasion.

———————————

January 17, 1882
    No ice as yet. 500 tons wanted at this place.

———————————

February 7, 1882
    Wednesday our telephone refused to work. It was found that it had blown over the chimney of Mrs. Augusta Scudder which was some three or four feet away.

———————————

October 24, 1882
    The Misses Carret are building a large two story house, for the purpose of taking summer boarders, on land purchased of Joseph Coffin, near his house.

———————————

October 24, 1882
    Report says nine new dwellings are to be built the coming winter in this place.

———————————

November 14, 1882
    Singing school commenced Monday evening, Professor Dennis, as leader.

———————————

November 21, 1882
    Some deer killed in this vicinity.

November 21, 1882
    Capt. Nelson Bearse and others have been at work on the road leading from Capt. C. A. Lovell's to the boat house of Capt. O. D. Lovell.

———————————

November 28, 1882
    The officers of the lecture association for the ensuing year are:
    President — W. F. Crocker
    Vice President — A. L. Robbins
    Secretary — Charles N. Scudder
    Executive Committee — Charles F. Parker, Israel Crocker, and Mrs. James A. Lovell

———————————

December 26, 1882
    Skating has been good and well enjoyed the past week.

———————————

January 2, 1883
    And now we have two mails a day, commencing Monday, the year round.

———————————

January 9, 1883
    Crosby Brothers have filled their ice house and Granville Ames has also filled one at Neck Pond, the ice being six and eight inches thick.

———————————

February 6, 1883
    A Lodge of K. & L. of H. (Knights & Ladies of Honor) has been formed in this village under the name of the "Gannett" Lodge, and on Friday evening was instituted by R. H. Harris, D.G.P., of Yarmouth, and the following officers were installed over it:
    Past Protector — Uno H. Hillman
    Protector — Charles F. Parker
    V.P. — Thankful Ames
    Secretary — Frank M. Boult
    F.S. — J. H. Chadwick
    Treas. — I. Crocker
    Chap. — Emily Fuller
    Guide — Wm. H. Bearse
    Guardian — Mrs. Wm. H. Bearse
    Sent. — A. D. Hall
    Med. Ex. — T. R. Clement, M.D.
    Trustees — H. P. Crocker, D. P. Bursley,
                    Wm. B. Parker
    The Lodge starts off under the most favorable auspices, some thirty-seven of our citizens — both ladies and gentlemen — signing the petition for a charter.

February 27, 1883

Mr. Grafton Bassett has put a new meat cart on the route between Hyannis and Osterville, and with such an accommodating driver as Albert J. Bacon we cannot help being pleased.

March 20, 1883

Big colds and whooping cough are raging here now.

June 5, 1883

Potato beetles have arrived in good number.

June 5, 1883

Fresh scup and bluefish are quite plenty and cheap, but most of them are sent to New York and Philadelphia.

July 10, 1883

A fine brougham with its colored driver can be seen nearly every evening driving our streets. I hear it is owned by a Mr. Carret.

July 17, 1883

Mr. Isaiah Crocker and Mr. Robert Evans have each lost a cow.

September 11, 1883

All hands for cranberrying is the call now.

October 2, 1883

Mr. Hiram Gardner has moved his building onto Pudding Pan Hill, so called, and is to have it fixed into a house to live in.

November 3, 1883

Mr. Hiram Gardner has moved into his new house on Pudding Pan Hill so called.

December 25, 1883

A light fall of snow on a hard, icy foundation has made good sleighing on our streets and the "trotters" are being treated to extra grooming and more oats in preparation for the sleighing season.

January 1, 1884

It took three mail bags to hold Christmas presents at the mail Monday of last week, besides a number by express.

May 13, 1884

The town pump is to be located on the street in front of the schoolhouse.

May 20, 1884

Scup are quite plenty.

June 3, 1884

Bluefish are quite plenty, and our fishermen are getting good hauls.

August 26, 1884

A quantity of furniture and other effects supposed to have drifted from the U. S. steamer Tallapoosa, which sunk off Cottage City on the night of the 21st, has been picked up by fishing boats of this vicinity. Among other articles was a course or number of lectures and drawings illustrating the subject of "electricity" written on large sheets of paper with black ink. The author had written and numbered about 115 pages. It is a valuable scientific work which the author would be glad to recover. It is in good state of preservation after having been in the water about forty-eight hours.

The owner can secure the work by applying to Capt. S. L. Boult of this village.

November 18, 1884

A deer was seen on the street near here on Tuesday with two dogs in pursuit.

May 12, 1885

An unknown woman, partially deranged, wandered here and unable to give any intelligible statement of herself was by order of Capt. Lovell, one of the overseers of the poor, conveyed to the Alms House at West Barnstable on Saturday, where she could be cared for until her residence could be ascertained.

September 29, 1885

The high lines among the cranberry pickers from this village are, Oliver Coffin 360 qts. and Joseph C. Crosby 344 qts., one day's picking. They use "Lumbert's Patent Cranberry Picker."

January 12, 1886

Schr. Congress of Bath, Maine, Capt. Willard, from New York for Portland, parted her chains while off Hyannis during the heavy gale and storm of Friday night and came on shore nearly opposite the Cotocheset House. Signals of distress were seen during the forenoon. Citizens of the village gathered in large numbers on the beach, but owing to the severe wind and roughness of the sea, were not able to rescue the crew until the early evening, the wind abating somewhat. Two dories manned by an Osterville crew and a volunteer crew from Cotuit succeeded in reaching the vessel and bringing them all (six in number) safely to shore. They were taken to the Cotocheset House where hot coffee and food had been provided for them. Afterwards several citizens of the village took them to their homes where they were kindly cared for. Many thanks to those Cotuit friends who so readily and quickly responded to the call for help. The Congress was coal loaded and is bilged.

January 19, 1886

Nothing has been done towards discharging the cargo of coal from Sch. Congress ashore at the beach. Mr. Palmer of Bath, chief owner of the schooner, Mr. Swett and Mr. Kemp representing the Insurance Co. of Wellfleet (at which office the cargo is insured) have been here, but have all returned. Capt. Willard and Mr. Palmer, Jr. still remain to care for the vessel.

January 19, 1886

Considerable damage was done at the beach during the late storm; bath houses were destroyed, the beach badly washed away, etc.

February 16, 1886

Boston Tow Boat Co., L. F. Baker, agent, will discharge cargo coal and float Sch. Congress, ashore at Osterville.

March 2, 1886

Messrs. F. L. & C. N. Scudder have bought of the Marine Ins. Co., Wellfleet, the cargo of coal aboard Sch. Congress, ashore near the Cotocheset. They have contracted with Capt. Sturges of Cotuit to freight the same to their coal wharf at the West Bay.

March 9, 1886

Intelligence was received here Saturday of the death of Dr. J. D. Chaplin, a former summer resident of this village. Dr. Chaplin's death occurred in New York on the 5th inst.

March 16, 1886

Milton Crocker and Walter Rich have returned from "Eastman's Commercial College", Poughkeepsie, N.Y., having completed their course of studies.

March 23, 1886

About 150 tons of coal have been landed from the stranded Schr. Congress.

May 4, 1886

A stage driver reports seeing four deer on his trip to West Barnstable Saturday morning.

September 7, 1886

The hearts of Osterville people were made happy last week by the arrival of M. N. Shorey with his Photograph Salon. This gallery has the modern accessories of the day and all photographs are taken by the instantaneous process. Our photographer comes well recommended, having been with one of the leading galleries in New Bedford for a long time. The need of a photographer in our village, especially in this season, is apparent to all, and will fill a want long felt by both old and young.

We wish Mr. Shorey much success, and by his close application to business so early and late, we guess he is having all he can attend to.

February 8, 1887

Mr. Samuel Ames went to Brockton last week and drove down a nice team recently bought there by Mr. Freeman L. Scudder. Mr. Scudder has recently sold to Wilton and Joseph Crosby a horse and buggy.

May 24, 1887

Workmen have been grading the hill near Village Hall the past week.

January 10, 1888

Capt. Joseph F. Adams and Mrs. Julia Phinney have been improving their residences by a fresh coat of paint.

January 24, 1888

Parker and Crocker had their ice house filled the last week; house at Neck Pond filled; house at Lumbert Pond partially full.

May 8, 1888

H. W. Chaplin, Esq., of Boston was in town the most of last week. Mr. Chaplin is having a piazza and dormer window added to his house. Mr. Frank Boult and Mr. Frank Williams are doing the work.

July 17, 1888

On Friday evening, July 13th, Gannett Lodge, No. 610, K. and L. of H. held its semi-annual installation of officers.

A delegation from Bay View Lodge of Cotuit, was present.

After the Degree of Protection had been conferred on two new members, D.D. G.P. John Kendrick, Jr. of South Orleans installed the following officers:

Protector — Frank W. Hodges
Past Protector — Charles E. Lewis
Vice Protector — Mrs. Mercy N. Lovell
Secretary — A. L. Robbins
Financial Secretary — Charles F. Parker
Treasurer — E. M. Parker
Chaplin — Annie A. Hodges
Guardian — Edward M. Lovell
Sentinel — H. P. Crocker

Refreshments, consisting of ice cream and cake, were served.

August 14, 1888

It is estimated that there are between five and six hundred guests at Osterville and Wianno.

August 21, 1888

The Selectmen met on Friday to view the proposed road from Mr. James Goodspeed's Ocean Ave., and decided to lay the road out, and will meet again for that purpose on Thursday, Aug. 23rd.

September 4, 1888

Quite a number went from this place to the horse race at Cotuit on Friday.

September 4, 1888

The hail storm on Monday, 27th, was very severe; several panes of glass were broken in the house belonging to the S.A. Wiley Estate.

September 11, 1888

We see the ladies have very pretty flower gardens, which is a great improvement to the street.

September 25, 1888

Large numbers of black bass are being taken from the David Lewis Pond.

October 2, 1888

The equinoctial storm was very severe here, but did comparatively little damage, blew down some trees, and drove nearly every boat in West Bay ashore.

Fortunately, none were damaged except the Bessie which lost her bowsprit.

October 2, 1888

The Carret and Crosby houses are closed for the season.

December 25, 1888

The old landmarks are disappearing one by one. The old house so long occupied by Mr. A. E. Lovell and his parents has been torn down. It had not been inhabited for a number of years, but there are many in our village who miss it.

January 22, 1889

Mrs. Charlotte Holm is building a large addition to her house to accommodate boarders.

January 22, 1888

There was a slight fire in Parker and Crocker's store on Friday night at about 5 o'clock p.m. A lot of brooms and axe handles that were piled in a rack overhead caught fire from a lamp and if it had not been discovered in season a disastrous fire would have resulted.

March 5, 1889

Mumps have made their appearance in the village.

March 5, 1889

The ice houses have been filled with ice from 4 to 6 inches.

The Town of Barnstable

March 6, 1889

New Buildings and Improvements.

According to the Assessor's figures the valuation of the Town of Barnstable has increased over that of 1887 over one hundred thousand dollars — $117,655.

When we note the active operations that have been going on the past year at Wianno and Osterville, it is not surprising to find that a little "boom" has struck our staid old town. The advantage of the Cape as a summer resort are each year becoming better known and appreciated by personal knowledge by thousands who seek our shores for rest and recreation. Many have become so attached to the beauties of location, ease of access, healthful climate and natural resources for summer recreation and sports, as to become temporary citizens, invest in real estate and build summer residences in which they pass from four to seven months each year. This is particularly the case at Osterville. At Wianno Beach the elegant Cotocheset House was built last year, and we will add right here, that, to increase its capacity, a large addition is now being built to meet the demands of summer guests. The increased assessed valuation in real estate at this point alone is not far from $75,000 and building operations have been going on during the past season which still further enhance our valuation. Property that, a short time go, was considered of little value has increased with the rapidity known only in western corner lots, and activity in real estate is everywhere noted.

To give our readers some idea of the extent of recent building operations in Osterville we will mention, in addition to the Cotocheset House, the names of the following persons who have built costly residences during the past year.

Miss Helen Tinkham
Mr. Milton Leonard
Mr. Thomas Gaff
Miss Mary Gaff
Mrs. Charlotte Holm
Mr. William L. Garrison
Mr. H.W. Wellington
Mr. W.A. Dietricks
Mr. Nelson H. Bearse

In addition to the above, the Crosby House has been enlarged by the addition of one story.

Mr. Geo. S. Dexter's residence, and that of Mr. F. W. Parsons, have each been remodeled and enlarged.

Capt. C.A. Lovell, Capt. D.P. Bursley, Mr. E.B. Lovell, Mr. and Miss Gaff, have each built a stable, and Mr. Wilton Crosby a boat house. Also a half dozen windmills have been erected for supplying private residences with a system of water works.

April 2, 1889

Work has commenced on the new road located near the East Bay.

April 16, 1889

Messrs. Parker and Crocker have dissolved partnership and Mr. Parker will continue the Dry Goods business and Mr. Crocker the Grocery business, having made two stores of one.

April 16, 1889

We have a new society formed among the young people here. It is called the Young People's Christian League, meets once a week, we believe,

at the homes of its members and discusses some subject or person.

May 28, 1889

Mr. Warren Cammett has gone to New York with Joseph C. Crosby in catboat Aurora.

June 11, 1889

Capt. Herschel Fuller and Mr. J. M. Leonard are having their houses painted.

September 24, 1889

H.W. Wellington, Esq. has contracted with Mr. Thos. Pattison to fill and grade the swamp and lot near Messrs. Hinckley & Son's lumber yard, on the new road to Wianno. On the lot will be a fine tennis court.

April 30, 1889

The building movement has extended from Wianno to the village: Captain William B. Parker is having a new barn built by Mr. Bradford of Hyannis; Mr. Israel Crocker is having an addition made to his store by Mr. Owen Jones of Cotuit; Mr. E.C. Alley is enlarging his barn with the help of some of our local carpenters.

May 28, 1889

Horse trading has been quite brisk the past week. Churchill Alley has two new horses, and Henry P. Crocker and William O. Crocker each have one.

October 22, 1889

We see two pretty little ponies driven about our streets by Master Bennie Lancy and Master Arthur F. Lewis, each in a little dog-cart and many of the little ones are happy as they are taken out riding.

October 22, 1889

Mr. Frank Bearse has purchased a nice cow.

October 22, 1889

F.W. Parsons, Esq. has contracted with Mr. Thos. Pattison to grade the marsh on the old Hinckley estate, which will be converted into a cranberry bog, on the upper portion of which will be made a tennis court. Mr. Pattison has just completed the grading of a baseball field for the same gentleman, near the Cotocheset.

November 19, 1889

A petition for a lodge of the Order of Aegis is being circulated here. Among the signers are Mr. and Mrs. Charles F. Parker, Mr. and Mrs. Frank W. Hodges, Rev. Bryant McLellan, Capt. Thomas Pattison, Watson F. Adams, Charles E. Lewis, Frank H. Williams and others.

November 19, 1889

Capt. West, Herbert F. Crosby and Elliott Crosby went gunning over to Barnstable Friday and got forty birds.

January 7, 1890

"La Grippe" has established itself firmly in the village; most of the cases are in a mild form however, but it is an evil that is "bad enough at its best."

January 14, 1890

Pine Bluffs Lodge No. 51, Order of Aegis, was instituted in this place last Tuesday evening by C.S. Burgess D. S.P. of Falmouth. This new order, although not yet a year old, numbers nearly four thousand members and is growing rapidly. It is managed on the same principle as the Iron Hall, with the advantage of being incorporated under the wise laws of Massachusetts and possessing features that make it preferable to that institution. Pine Bluffs Lodge starts in with twenty Charter members and expects their membership to increase to half a hundred ere another year comes around.

Their officers are:

Charles E. Lewis — President
Charles F. Parker — P.P.
Thomas Pattison — V.P.
Frank W. Hodges — Sec.
Frank H. Williams — Treas.
Geo. D. Lewis — Chaplain
C.A. Lovell — Marshall
Frank A. Jones — Guard
E.F. Swift — Sentinel

April 22, 1890

Mr. F. L. Scudder and Mr. Churchill Alley went to Brockton on Saturday. We learn they bought several horses, carriages, etc., while there.

May 20, 1890

Mr. James West and Mr. Ernest Alley have each a nice new horse bought of Mr. Percival; also Mr. Joseph F. Adams, one bought of Obed Baxter.

May 27, 1890

Mr. Israel Crocker and Mr. Henry P. Crocker have each a fine, new order wagon, built by Mr. Milton Leonard.

May 27, 1890

We hear the Misses Carret will not occupy their house the present season, but have rented it to another family.

November 4, 1890

Mrs. Charlotte Holm is occupying her new house, having leased her former tenement to Mr. James Corcoran, who now occupies it.

November 11, 1890

Capt. N. E. West, Herbert F. Crosby and sons of this place and Mr. Charles A. West of Port Jefferson, L.I., spent several days on Sandy Neck last week. They had a fine time, securing 227 birds of various kinds.

January 13, 1891

Ice cutting commenced Saturday at the Factory Pond and Lot Pond.

September 15, 1891

The thieves are busy here as well as at West Barnstable. One lady lost a pie from her pantry, the screen being removed from the window by the thieves, and the same night a cow was milked in the night; evidently the persons were hungry; and some one is taking small fruit from gardens, etc. They may get caught, for people are on the lookout now.

September 22, 1891

Some thirty of the Republican Citizens of Osterville met in the rooms over H.P. Crocker's store on the evening of the 17th for the purpose of organizing a Republican Club. The meeting was called to order by Charles F. Parker, Esq., who was chosen Temporary Chairman, and A. L. Robbins, Temporary Secretary. A temporary constitution was then adopted, under which the following officers were elected:

President — C. F. Parker
First Vice President — H. P. Crocker
Second Vice President — Thomas Pattison
Secretary — J. M. Leonard
Treasurer — Dr. T. R. Clement
Executive Committee — Israel Crocker,
                    Charles E. Lewis,
                    James R. Goodspeed,
                    Clarence L. Baker,
                    Maurice G. Crocker

and the President and Secretary-Ex-Officio.

It was voted that the name be the Osterville Republican Club. The Executive Committee was instructed to inquire into the matter of joining the State Republican League, procure permanent headquarters for the use of the Club and draw up a set of by-laws. The meeting then adjourned subject to a call of the Executive Committee.

October 6, 1891

A coast surveying party have been in the village for four or five days, running their lines in some very curious places, on people's door steps, and one man was somewhat surprised to find one of them in his pig-sty.

October 27, 1891

The first snow of the season fell on Friday morning.

December 1, 1891

Ralph Crosby and Harry Fuller are home from school for a short vacation.

December 15, 1891

The foundations are being laid for another house on the "Schoolhouse Hill," to be built for Miss Maggie Bliss.

December 22, 1891

Fill the children's stockings on Christmas Eve from Parker's grocery for they are selling the best broken candy — 2 lbs. for 25 cents, mixed nuts — 15 cents a lb., and sweet Florida oranges at 25 cents a dozen.

February 2, 1892

The recent cold snap has brought a little hope to the ice companies, although there is no ice fit to cut yet. "Uncle Sam's" Pond was frozen enough last week to give the young people a taste of skating, which they enjoyed to the uttermost.

February 16, 1892

The ice houses are now all filled, and the summer supply of ice is sure.

March 8, 1892

We were quite shut off from communication with the outer world for two days last week, had no mail for 48 hours, and badly blockaded roads. A genuine old-fashioned snow storm.

May 10, 1892

Our Road Commissioner, Mr. Coleman, and his corps of men are working busily on the roads, levelling the two long hills between S.L. Leonard's and the village and putting the roads and sidewalks in good order.

May 17, 1892

The new street lamp at the grocery of H. S. Parker & Co. is very acceptable.

May 28, 1892

Good cooking butter, 22 cents a lb., at Parker's Grocery.

August 2, 1892

Mr. James H. Crocker of Newtown opened a saloon for the sale of ice cream, fruit, peanuts, tobacco, cigars and so called temperance drinks in a new building on land leased by him from Mrs. Mary Weeks, on the Avenue, on Thursday last. His ice cream and cooling drinks were very much appreciated in the heat of last week, and we hear he had a large run of trade.

September 20, 1892

George D. Lewis and Edmund H. Lewis are home from Acushnet for the cranberry season.

October 4, 1892

The Schr. Luella took a load of little neck clams from here last week.

October 18, 1892

Mrs. John Bell has a new parlor organ, and Mrs. H. Foster Lewis a new piano.

October 18, 1892

We hear that Mr. F. A. Dane has recently purchased (for F. L. Scudder and Son) the meadow belonging to Seth Rich, adjoining the West Bay. The Messrs. Scudder have now a nice lot of land with a waterfront, which, we understand, is to be used for a coal yard.

November 15, 1892

The Osterville Republican Club met at the rooms Thursday evening and passed the following:

Resolved, That we are undiscouraged by the defeat and will keep in line and do our best to win victory next year.

The following officers were elected for the ensuing year:

Guide — W.H. Bearse
Chap. — E.S. Alley
Guard — H. Fuller
Sen. — J. Milton Leonard

After the installation ceremony members and invited guests, to the number of fifty, enjoyed a very nice turkey supper. The rest of the evening was spent in playing the national game, whist.

A Subscriber

May 11, 1896

Mr. James H. Crocker is enlarging his ice cream saloon.

James H. Crocker standing in front of his ice cream saloon in the Crocker Block during the 1890s. Later this building became the Daniel Block, named for Robert Daniel who purchased and enlarged it.

August 24, 1896

Mr. Locke of Boston with his family are occupying the Isaiah Crocker Place. Mr. Locke has bought a building on Main St., of J. W. Tallman, and will open a meat market there soon.

September 21, 1896

The severe storm of Saturday morning did considerable damage. Several chimneys were blown down. Six mammoth trees in front of Charles Daniel's were uprooted, their branches falling on to the house in such a way as to nearly imprison the occupants. The hailstones, many of which were as large as English walnuts, made havoc with window panes, breaking about 500 in this village, it is estimated. It was the severest storm of the kind ever known here.

The horse attached to the "Hyannis Bakery" became frightened on Thursday, while hitched to a post, and ran, upsetting the wagon near Mulberry Corner, scattering the food right and left, and clearing himself from all but the front wheels, bolted for F. L. Scudder's barn, where he was obliged to stop. The wagon looked like "a well-done turnover with mince filling."

November 2, 1896

A grand Republican Rally was held on Saturday evening. Crowds of people from this and adjoining villages headed by the Sandwich band marched through Main St. to Village Hall to listen to Hon. Willard Howland of Boston and Judge Grover of Canton. Following this, the crowd proceeded to the large field, used for a bicycle track, where a large bonfire was lighted which presented a grand appearance while the band played several selections. Returning to the Square three cheers were given for speakers, band, etc.

June 7, 1897

The Misses Carret of Boston have opened their house here for the summer.

Aerial view of Osterville in the late 1940s
This photograph was probably taken from the original water tower that was built on Tower Hill. Looking out over the center of the village, West Bay, Oyster Harbors, Cotuit, and Succonessett are visible.

Osterville Village Center — 1940
Aerial view of Intersection of
Main Street and Wianno Avenue

Post Office and Baptist Church, Osterville, Mass.

Center of Osterville Village — Early 1900s

— 1922 —

— 1987 —

Daniel Block — 1930

Center of Osterville Village — Mid-1930s

November 8, 1897

The work of grading the Hall hill is progressing under the supervision of Mr. James A. Lovell.

Farnham Cottage — January 31, 1898
Farnham Cottage which was located on the east side of Wianno Avenue at the present intersection of the avenue and Bates Street. The house, later moved down the avenue and across the street to its present site next to Woodland Avenue, belongs to Mr. and Mrs. William Kittila.

January 3, 1898

The usual Christmas Tree celebration was very much in evidence as was manifested by the large gathering of old and young, who met at the Baptist Church to commemorate this day of all days of the Christian Church, and enjoy the many tokens of the loving and unselfish spirit that pervades this Christmas time. The tree, dressed as it was with the most heterogeneous fruit that tree ever bore, was a thing of beauty. Delighted exclamations from the young people burst upon the ear, as they caught sight of its manifold treasures and eagerly dwelt upon and speculated as to who would be the fortunate recipient of the big doll in the blue dress or the sturdy looking sled bright in its coat of glittering varnish. The evident and unalloyed enjoyment of the children carried the memories of the older people back to their Christmas time and made them enter into the present as children again. Although there were many private Christmas trees in the village, the presents this year were more numerous than at any previous time and none were forgotten. The meeting was called to order at 7 P.M. by the Chairman, Capt. Thomas Pattison, who after addressing the audience, briefly announced the following program:

Original piece entitled, "A Merry Christmas to the Families of Osterville" by Mr. William H. Bennett

Singing, "The Child and the Star" — Frederic Scudder

Recitation — Philip Chadwick
Recitation — Marion Gibby
Recitation — Herman Williams
Recitation — Addie Crosby
Singing, "Merry Christmas" by children

Singing — Old Folks' Choir
Prayer
Roll Call — Mrs. A. A. Cram
Historical Sketch — Rev. James R. Goodspeed
The Early Class Meeting — Oliver H. Crocker
Reminiscences of former pastors
Hymn, Rock of Ages.

January 31, 1898

A small hotel is soon to be erected on land adjoining the Farnham cottage on Wianno Avenue.

February 7, 1898

Nearly all of the ice houses have been filled during the past week, the men working day and night to accomplish their end before the warmer weather came. They are anxiously waiting for another cold wave that the work may be completed.

May 2, 1898

While Mr. W. A. Fuller was making his business trip through this village on Saturday his horse became frightened of some turkeys and ran through the street and into H. P. Crocker's barn, where he left the wagon and some of the meat in a dilapidated condition.

May 9, 1898

Mrs. Charlotte Holm of Charlestown is spending a few weeks here looking after the interests of her house, a portion of which is undergoing repairs at the hands of the young men who lease it for a club room.

Charlotte Holm 1851-1926

September 26, 1898

Mr. Henry Dainty is improving his place by a new barn, having torn down the old one.

December 12, 1898

A new set of Fairbank's scales are soon to take the place of the old ones that have stood for many years in the village centre.

January 16, 1899

Dr. Higgins is having a new office built, corner of Main Street and Wianno Avenue. Mr. E. H. Fuller of Marstons Mills is doing the work.

February 27, 1899

To the Voters of the Town of Barnstable:

I hereby announce myself as a candidate for Road Commissioner. I have the support of the following well-known men of Osterville:

Charles E. Lewis,
J. M. Leonard
N. O. Lovell,
Capt. H. P. Crocker.

I ask the support of all the voters who like a good road and want the Town's money used with judgment.

Your truly,
Owen B. Lewis

April 17, 1899

The new set of Standard Scales have at last been erected in Post Office Square and are now ready for use.

June 5, 1899

The Osterville Pleasure Club had their first outing May 30th, when six of the leading members drove to East Sandwich, Sandwich and Cotuit, taking dinner at Morse's Hotel and supper at Jones' Inn. They arrived home at an early hour and all pronounced it a great success.

June 26, 1899

We are pleased to hear that Mr. B. F. Gibby and family are intending to spend the summer at their former home in Osterville. It will be cheerful to see the corner light up again.

August 21, 1899

We are glad to see the new houses going up in the village, and there is a rumor of others to be erected later. Mr. Frank Williams, Mr. Clarence Baker, Mr. Elliott Crosby and Mr. Harry Tallman are among those who are already at work.

September 11, 1899

Mr. Dainty has closed his house and returned to the city.

1899 — The Dainty Residence, Main Street, previously that of Isham Family, later of Seth Weeks, and more recently of Maurice Allen. Removing the veranda revealed the classic lines of this Antique Cape Cod House.

Dr. and Mrs. Henry Dainty

October 9, 1899

The public telephone has been moved from C.F. Parker's to the store of H. P. Crocker.

October 9, 1899

October Prices for Coal:

Egg and Furnace	$6.25
Stove and Chestnut	$6.50
Franklin	$7.75

October 30, 1899

Work has been commenced on the houses of Walter Lewis and L. W. Leonard.

January 8, 1900

The ice houses connected with the Crosby House and the Cotocheset are being filled from Neck Pond with six inch ice. Capt. Thomas Pattison has also filled his ice house from his reservoir.

June 4, 1900

The heavy frost on Monday night of last week damaged the gardens to quite an extent in this vicinity.

October 8, 1900

Messrs. Harry C. Lovell and Everett Small, Mr. J. W. W. Crosby and wife, Mrs. Ella L. Lovell and Mrs. Ida B. Hall were among those who visited Brockton Fair.

December 3, 1900

One after another the old landmarks disappear. The barn of Mrs. Thankful Small blew down in a recent gale, and the shed of Mr. James A. Lovell has been torn down. These buildings have stood for nearly a century and will be missed along the road.

February 4, 1901

Several houses have been filled with good five inch ice during the past week.

May 6, 1901

Members of the Osterville Pleasure Club have given up their rooms, rented of Mrs. Holm, and have joined the Beacon Club in Crocker's Block.

August 12, 1901

Mrs. Laura Kerbaugh is having her house painted. Capt. N. E. West Sr., has also painted his recently. Mr. Frank W. Hodges has added new blinds to his house.

July 1, 1901

Measles and mumps are quite prevalent just now.

July 1, 1901

Mr. James H. Crocker has opened his ice-cream rooms in Crocker's block.

October 7, 1901

Mr. Harry C. Lovell, Mr. E. Chessman Crocker, Mr. William F. Adams and W. Frank Adams attended Brockton Fair the past week.

November 11, 1901

The tramp accompanied by a dog, who has been in this vicinity for a week or more, was arrested Thursday morning by Officers Ames and Baker, and taken to Barnstable jail.

November 18, 1901

Capt. N. E. West and Mr. Herbert Crosby spent the past week gunning at Sandy Neck.

January 6, 1902

On Sunday, Dec. 15th, during the heavy storm of that day and night, Collier's Ledge Beacon was destroyed. This beacon marks a dangerous ledge of rocks in Vineyard Sound and is a guide for all vessels passing the north channel to and from Boston and adjacent harbors. The destruction of this marine guide mark has been communicated to the Department through the Hon. W. S. Greene and by his efforts we hope to have it replaced during the early summer months.

January 20, 1902

About 2,000 tons of good 8 inch ice has been harvested, and the ice men are happy.

March 17, 1902

Mr. and Mrs. Dainty of Somerville were down to attend the funeral of Mr. George Weeks.

April 14, 1902

A few children in the village are afflicted with whooping cough.

August 11, 1902

We notice with pleasure many improvements along the street, viz., the old barn adjoining what is now the band room has been torn down and carried away. A fine new fence has been built in front of Mrs. Augusta Scudder's house; Mr. Twombly is making extensive alterations in the house and outbuildings on the Dr. Clement estate; Mr. C. A. Driscoll and Mr. Azor D. Hall have each given their houses a new coat of paint.

January 26, 1903

The concert on Thursday evening last was a grand success. The Ladies Club should be commended for their public spirited and unselfish work. Both the work of the "Crosby Orchestra" and the tableaux are worthy of special mention. The subjects taken for the tableaux were effectively presented with colored lights and were much appreciated. The violin solo by Mr. Arthur Wyman was rendered with style and finish, and very enthusiastically received. He was accompanied by Miss Addie L. Bearse and we hope we may be able to hear them again soon.

March 23, 1903

Spring is here with the song of the robin, while the peepers commenced their spring work a week ago. Time to plan that Easter bonnet.

April 20, 1903

Mr. Chester Crocker has given up his business in the barber shop on account of his health. We learn he intends to succeed his father, Mr. James H. Crocker, in the ice cream trade during the summer.

May 18, 1903

Work on the stone road is progressing rapidly.

October 5, 1903

The building owned by Mr. James H. Crocker is being enlarged. The Beacon Club are to have more commodious rooms and Mr. Chester Crocker will have an up-to-date barber and pool room in the building. Mr. A. C. Savery of Cotuit is superintending the work.

November 30, 1903

The work on Crocker's block is completed and the building is much improved in appearance. The Beacon Club have moved into their rooms on the second floor. Mr. Chester Crocker, the popular barber, occupies the whole lower floor, having fitted it up with new billiard tables and all the latest furnishings for his business.

December 21, 1903

Mr. Augustus E. Coleman and Mr. Owen B. Lewis left here on Wednesday last for Newbury, N.H., where they will engage in logging.

January 11, 1904

The Osterville Ice Co., have recently erected a new house, to hold 800 tons, not far from the site of the old one, which has been torn down.

February 22, 1904

New cases of measles are developing every day; old and young alike are afflicted.

March 14, 1904

We are sorry the dancing class is ended, but pleased to know it was a financial success. Few villages can boast of so good an orchestra and with Mr. Ariel Tallman as manager of dances, have had many nice parties.

May 30, 1904

Mr. Clarence Baker, John Adams and Joseph Crosby have spent several days in Provincetown buying oyster needs.

July 4, 1904

Souvenir post cards may be had at Mulberry Corner Store.

January 2, 1905

Mr. Albert D. Williams and Mr. Albert L. Hinckley have gone to Boston to take a course of study to fit themselves for a position as chauffeur.

January 16, 1905

The ice houses are all filled with good 12 inch ice.

June 26, 1905

The tempest on Monday night did considerable damage in our community. The lightning struck the roof of Prof. Jacoby's house at West Bay, passing down through the rooms, shattering a partition between two sleeping rooms, rendering Prof. Jacoby and his little boy unconscious, and leaving them quite deaf for a time. Mr. Ira Hinckley's house on Wianno Ave. was also struck and damaged to quite an extent. Fortunately no one was injured.

November 6, 1905

Miss Minnie Cammett and Miss Mabel Evans have been on a week's visit to New York City, shopping and visiting many notable places of interest. They report a most enjoyable trip.

November 20, 1905

Mr. Thurber and family have moved here from Dennisport, and are living in Mrs. Barbara Whippey's house. Mr. Thurber works for Mr. J. M. Leonard, blacksmith.

December 11, 1905

The buildings, Squirrel Inn and a part of Pine Cottage, have been successfully moved to West Bay and contractor Allen Chadwick, with his men, are busy making the two one large building, to be a Hotel for use next summer.

April 10, 1906

An alarm of fire called out a crowd Tuesday afternoon, to save the property of Mr. Henry Dainty. While burning grass in the field, the flames spread rapidly in every direction and soon reached the houses of Mr. Dainty and Miss Mary O'Rourke, and but for the prompt action of a few who were early on the spot the consequences might have been serious for it was nearing the woods near the public dumping ground that stretch to the border of the village on the north. Fortunately only the field was burned over and no serious results followed.

October 2, 1906

Mrs. Isabel M. Richards has just disposed of her estate at Osterville to Andrew Adie of the Moore Spinning Company of Boston. The property comprises a fine house, stable and several acres of land. Over $30,000 has been expended on this property.

October 30, 1906

Mr. Roland C. Ames and Milton Crocker have gone on a gunning trip to Maine.

November 6, 1906

Miss Aleria Crocker has gone to Boston to take a course of study at Bryant and Stratton's.

February 5, 1907

All the icehouses have been filled the past week with very good ice, and everybody is happy.

April 9, 1907

The new street lamps have been put in position and lighted the past week for the first time. The effort of the Improvement Society, to lighten the dark places of the earth, is commendable. Mr. E.R. Evans has the contract for lighting.

April 23, 1907

Mrs. Hugh Rogers has purchased the house, occupied by the Bearse family, adjoining Mrs. Elizabeth Leonard's estate and expects to occupy it soon.

May 7, 1907

There was a large attendance at the poverty ball on Thursday evening week. Mr. Thomas Pattison and the Land and Harbor commissioners graced the occasion with their presence.

May 14, 1907

Mr. Samuel N. Ames, Mr. Alcott N. Hallett and Representative Thomas Pattison each drive a fine horse recently purchased.

July 23, 1907

Mrs. Carlson and two children, from Jamaica Plain, are visiting Mrs. Charlotte Holm.

July 30, 1907

Capt. Rulon and family of Greenport, L.I. have moved here, having purchased the Suthergreen house, North Main Street.

August 13, 1907

Mr. Lindsay, who with his family has spent many seasons at Wianno, has purchased "Yvery", the estate of Mr. O. D. Lovell with adjoining land owned by Mrs. Cyrenius A. Lovell and Representative Thomas Pattison.

November 5, 1907

Mr. George Berry has hired the Adams house of Mrs. H. Foster Lewis and expects to occupy it this week.

January 13, 1908

Two new pianos arrived in Osterville last week at the homes of Mr. Stephen Bates and Mr. Walter I. Fuller.

January 27, 1908

Owing to the severe storm Friday night, the mail stage was detained at West Barnstable all night. The drifts became impassable.

February 10, 1908

Most of the icehouses are nearly full. The ice is between seven and eight inches thick.

March 9, 1908

We feel proud that our town showed, at the last election, its stand for no license.

April 13, 1908

Mr. Ernest DeWitt and Mr. Dexter Pattison visited Mr. Roy Braley in hospital in Boston.

April 27, 1908

A long-felt want has at last been filled by the opening in our village of a home bakery. Frank W. Hodges and Son, under the firm name of Hodges & Co., are offering a line of food of the same quality and made from as good ingredients as can be found on the tables of Cape Cod's native cooks.

April 27, 1908

Horace S. Parker & Co. are selling the best canned peaches this week for 28 cents.

May 25, 1908

Mrs. Albert Jones and daughter, Mrs. Cordelia Taylor and daughter, and Mrs. Shirley Ames, visited Hyannis, Thursday afternoon.

June 8, 1908

The following streets have been named and sign-boards posted. Main Street from Wm. Coleman's to the bridge toward Centerville; Parker Road from Mulberry Corner to the James Parker estate; Bay Street from Mulberry Corner to West Bay; Wianno Avenue from Main Street to Wianno; West Bay Road from Main Street to West Bay; East Bay Road from Mrs. Thankful Ames' estate to East Bay; Cross Street from East Bay Road to Wianno Avenue; Bridge Street from West Bay Road to Grand Island.

June 15, 1908

Eighteen fire extinguishers have been purchased on the condition that the Village Improvement Society pay half the expense.

June 22, 1908

Five new street lamps have been procured by the Village Improvement Society.

July 6, 1908

Ellsworth Adams is in the employ of Mr. William O. Crocker.

July 13, 1908

The houses of Mr. Elliott Crosby, Daniel Crosby, Ralph Crosby, and the shop of Mr. G. Webster Hallett have been painted.

August 10, 1908

Streets have been sprinkled with petroleum to keep the dust down.

August 17, 1908

Last Monday evening, suspicions were aroused by a young man prowling around the bicycle store and garage belonging to Mr. Carl Lagergren. About 11 o'clock, a dim light was observed in the shop by Mr. and Mrs. Frank Williams. Mr. Lagergren was notified and, with Mr. Williams, went over to the shop. The electric lights were turned on, but the would-be thief made his escape. However, he left his bicycle in his retreat and, as the wheel has been identified, there is but little doubt who the thief was.

August 17, 1908

Winthrop Scudder and Charles Berry started this morning on a trip to New Hampshire on their bicycles.

October 5, 1908

Mr. Fred Dill and Joseph Tallman attended the Brockton Fair this past week.

November 9, 1908

A Democratic rally was held in Union Hall last Monday evening. At the close, Mr. Dalton invited those present to remain for the complimentary dance.

December 28, 1908

Harvey Hallett, Edward Daniel, Ernest DeWitt, and Harold Crosby are home for the holiday.

January 4, 1909

A New Year's dance was held at East Bay Lodge Friday evening.

January 11, 1909

Through the efforts of Mr. Richard M. Winfield and Mr. Edward S. Crocker, enough money has been raised to grade and level about two acres of land at West Bay for a ball field.

February 1, 1909

The children have greatly enjoyed the skating the past week.

February 8, 1909

Ice harvesting began last week.

March 1, 1909

The ice crop here is a failure. Mrs. Thankful H. Ames is filling her ice house with ice from Lowell.

March 22, 1909

The town pump near the corner of Mr. Israel Crocker's Store has had a new base and otherwise improved.

May 3, 1909

Mr. Robert Daniel and Mr. Foster Lewis have improved their lawns by setting out hedges. Several houses have been newly painted.

May 10, 1909

Mr. Arthur Wyman has organized an orchestra. Mr. Wyman plays the violin, Harvey Hallett, slide trombone; Burleigh Leonard, cornet; John Horne, bass viol; Harold Jacobs; piccolo; Edmund Fuller, drums; Maude Baker, piano.

July 26, 1909

More road-oil was put on Main Street Thursday, from near Mulberry Corner as far as Mr. J. Milton Leonard's.

November 29, 1909

A new barber shop has opened in town.

Janury 4, 1910

The skating on Sam's Pond Christmas week was excellent.

January 11, 1910

Nearly all of the ice-houses were filled a week ago.

January 25, 1910

Mr. Walter I. Fuller and Mr. Bernard Lovell started on their meat route for Marstons Mills, Monday morning, but were stuck fast in a snowdrift three times and had to be shovelled out before reaching their destination.

February 15, 1910

Tramps in this place do not remain long. Saturday Samuel N. Ames was summoned, but on his arrival the tramp was gone.

April 12, 1910

Two new lamps have been procured, which will be placed near Mr. Cornelius A. Driscoll's and Mr. William Coleman's.

May 3, 1910

Concrete walks have been made in front of Israel Crocker's Store.

May 31, 1910

Since last fall twelve new houses have been built, to say nothing of those which had had additional improvements made. Surely this is a good indication of prosperity.

June 28, 1910

A new macadam road to Wianno has been completed at a cost of $7,000. Our summer guests will greatly appreciate this, as well as those who have heavy loads to draw to and from the beach.

August 23, 1910

The upper end of Wianno Avenue has been recently oiled.

September 27, 1910

Fuller's market beginning on October 1st will sell for cash only. By doing so, they will be able to give the customer the best goods at the very lowest possible prices.

November 1, 1910

A democratic rally was held in Mr. George Berry's pool room Wednesday noon.

November 1, 1910

Mr. John D.W. Bodfish, the independent candidate for representative, spoke in Union Hall.

November 8, 1910

A few days ago, Mr. Andrew Johnson picked a mess of peas from his garden, and Rev. E. McP. Ames had string beans from his garden. This is what is called intensive gardening.

November 15, 1910

The Study Class met at the home of Mrs. Henry Foster Lewis, Thursday evening. Fifteen were present. Mr. Gould was elected instructor for the next four weeks and Maurice Allen, secretary.

December 13, 1910

The children have enjoyed the skating the last week. Many of the older ones also are renewing their youth.

December 27, 1910

A new engine has been procured by the Ice Co., and if the weather permits, they will soon be cutting ice. A few ice houses have been filled. One of the party recently had a rather cold bath.

January 17, 1911

The Ladies Aid met with Mrs. Freeman Adams Thursday afternoon. The following officers were elected for the ensuing year: President, Mrs. John Bell; Vice President, Mrs. Israel Crocker; Secretary and Treasurer, Mrs. W. Scott Scudder.

March 14, 1911

Judging from the last election, some of our citizens need to wake up, or they will someday find the town voting for license.

March 14, 1911

Summer is coming! Robins have been seen.

March 14, 1911

Not a lady here was at the polls last Monday. Even upon matters in which they are eligible to vote, they did not exercise their right.

May 2, 1911

Mr. George Berry has sold his barber shop to Willis F. Nute of Boston.

May 16, 1911

Miss Addie G. Crocker, who was graduated from the Deaconess Hospital and confirmed as a deaconess, is at home, and has been assigned to work for a church in Boston, and will begin her labors in July or early in autumn. She is one of Osterville's promising young ladies.

May 30, 1911

Winthrop Scudder and Charles Berry are taking a trip on their wheels. They will stop in Boston over Memorial Day.

June 6, 1911

Mr. Sawyer's horse ran away the other day, causing some damage and a little excitement.

September 5, 1911

In spite of the week's storm a large number of Osterville people attended the Barnstable Fair.

Main Street c.1900
Left to right: Building at left is believed to be Oak S. Crosby's restaurant, mentioned in the Rich letter written in 1877. The building was later owned by Joseph W. Tallman, Sr. Next small building is Lagergren's Garage. Beyond it, the steeple of the Baptist Church can be seen.

October 17, 1911

Mrs. Everett P. Childs and Lincoln Baker on Wednesday afternoon, while coming out of Bernard Ames' yard, by accident pulled the wrong rein, the thill striking the tree, throwing them both out, Mrs. Childs cutting her face which required three stitches taken. Lincoln Baker was rendered unconscious and remained so for over an hour.

December 19, 1911

Mr. and Mrs. James Allen Lovell and Mr. and Mrs. G. Webster Hallett went to Boston last week in Mr. Lovell's touring car. Mr. Lovell has disposed of the car he has driven for some time and purchased a brand new car. The car is handsome and very strong.

January 16, 1912

There will be a neighborhood meeting in Osterville near the close of the month. Preachers and Christian workers will be invited. Short addresses from all the preachers. The meeting will be an all day service.

January 16, 1912

The ice houses are being well-filled in spite of the cold weather; many men have worked hard for several days, getting the good clear ice for the summer trade.

February 27, 1912

The Men's Club party and entertainment gave much satisfaction to all who were present. Men danced with men, and ladies with ladies. the night was disagreeable, but many were in attendance.

October 15, 1912

A Progressive Republican rally was held at the barber shop of Mr. Willis Nute last week. Quite a large company gathered to listen to the speakers.

November 12, 1912

Mr. Jesse Murray and Gerald Chadwick have been stopping for several days at the Plains, hunting. They had good luck and found an abundance of fowl and partridge.

December 31, 1912

Mr. Frank Allen, who runs the auto truck for Mr. Everett P. Childs, went to Boston last week, taking the truck to be overhauled. Mr. and Mrs. Thornton Adams and Miss Daisy Jones went with him.

November 11, 1913

Mr. Frank Allen of South Braintree was the weekend guest of Mr. Norman Williams. The patrons of the Star Theatre very much enjoyed the duets Saturday evening by Mr. Allen and Mr. Williams.

January 5, 1914

Messrs. Karl Chadwick and Leon Hinckley have passed examinations and entered the U.S. Navy for a four years' enlistment. We admire their courage and feel proud to know that two of our young men have entered the employ of "Uncle Sam" and wish them every success in their new life.

January 19, 1914

The ponds in the village all froze over the past week during the cold snap, and the ice men hope to harvest soon; Mr. Harold Crosby and Mr. Parsons having already filled their houses.

February 16, 1914

Wednesday night and Thursday was the coldest period ever known in Osterville within the memory of any living resident, the temperatures being 15 below zero Thursday morning and hovering around zero all day.

March 16, 1914

Post Office block and the house and buildings adjoining have been treated to a new coat of paint and look much better. Mr. Ed Fuller and men have done the work.

June 22, 1914

Mr. Eben Harding is living in the room over the tailor shop.

August 10, 1914

The summer season is at its best in our village at the present time and judging by appearances it is a busy one. Fifty-two autos were counted passing a certain point on Main Street in a half-hour one afternoon recently.

September 14, 1914

The Scudder coal vessel made a quick trip to New Bedford recently, leaving in the morning and returning at night loaded.

January 4, 1915

The committee on the Village Christmas Tree wish to thank Messrs. Warren Codd and Albert Hinckley for the nice tree furnished, and also all others who had a share in the work.

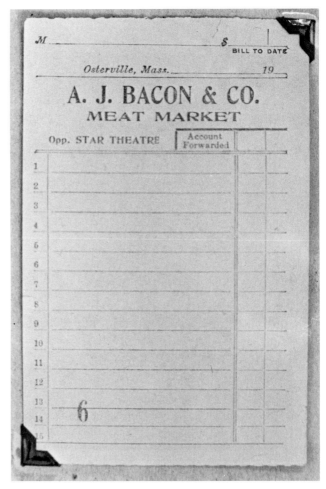

Billhead — A. J. Bacon, & Co. Meat Market

January 4, 1915

The Osterville Ice Co. began cutting ice Monday. A splendid quality of clear 6½ inch ice was housed.

April 5, 1915

The Disagreeable Four held a dance Thursday evening, and all reported a good time.

September 20, 1915

Mr. & Mrs. William O. Crocker and Mr. and Mrs. Arthur Wyman and little daughter are enjoying a very pleasant vacation at Cobb's camp, Forestdale. Mrs. George B. Fuller is in Mr. Crocker's store and newstand during his absence.

December 15, 1915

Messrs. Carroll Crosby and Verner Childs have gone to New Hampshire for a two or three weeks' hunting trip.

January 24, 1916

Ice has been cut on some of the ponds in the village and at the beach.

At the time this picture was taken, the first building on the left was owned by Joseph Tallman, Sr.; next beyond was central garage owned by Carl Lagergren; the spire of the Baptist Church rises from beyond. Crockers Store is seen back of the buggy. On right is Carrie Rich's Ice Cream Parlor. c. 1900.

March 6, 1916

It is understood that Mr. Albert J. Bacon has left Mr. I. Crocker's store and will open a meat business for himself on Main Street.

April 24, 1916

Several of the grown people are suffering from the pinkeye.

July 24, 1916

The Town pump in this village is being replaced.

September 4, 1916

Mr. George B. Fuller and Mr. and Mrs. William O. Crocker enjoyed a very pleasant sail recently with Capt. Roland C. Ames in his fine catboat, the ALICE.

September 18, 1916

Mr. Adrian Chadwick and Mr. Owen B. Lewis are in the employ of Mr. Allen Chadwick, who is building a new house for Mr. Edward S. Crocker.

October 9, 1916

The Osterville Ice Co., having sold all the ice they housed last winter, are buying it in Hyannis to supply their customers. Mr. W. S. Scudder is carting it from there in his auto truck.

November 27, 1916

A number of our citizens have attended some of the Billy Sunday meetings in Boston and speak of him as being a wonderful man, and all right.

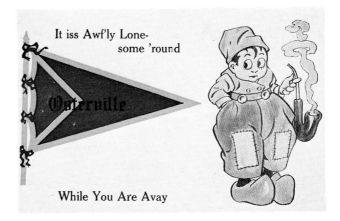

It iss Awf'ly Lonesome 'round Osterville While You Are Avay

December 4, 1916

Our village hunters had lots of sport and quite good luck during the open week, three or four deer being killed by them.

December 18, 1916

The annual meeting relative to the village Christmas tree was held at the library. Mr. W. P. Hodges was elected clerk, and Mr. Albert Hinckley, chairman of the meeting. Motion was made and carried that the tree be held Christmas night, Monday, December 25 at seven oclock.

Following are the committees: Christmas tree, Boy Scouts; to set and take town tree, Boy Scouts; to call off gifts, Ralph Crosby, Charles E. Lewis, Maurice Crocker; to decorate tree, Mrs. O.C. Coffin, Mrs. W.P. Hodges, Mrs. Jennie Boult, Mrs. Hattie Crosby, Mrs. Robert Daniel; to cut gifts off tree, Walcott Ames, Joseph Tallman, Jr., Herbert Hinckley, Jesse Murray; to distribute gifts, Jessie Boult, Isabel Lewis, Alma Crosby, Hilda Lagergren, Hazel Ames, Annie Nute, Eleanor Taylor, Agatha Crocker; entertainment, Mrs. Minnie Bates, Mrs. Dora Braley, Walter I. Fuller, E.H. Fowler.

December 25, 1916

Mr. Hugh Rogers had the faithful dog he has owned for some years shot last week on account of old age.

January 8, 1917

Karl Chadwick and Guy Jones have gone to Springfield to work for H. L. Handy & Co., meat packers of that city.

January 11, 1917

Messrs. John W. Williams and Charles Coleman have each lost a horse the past week.

March 12, 1917

Mr. Charles M. Jones has resigned the position he has held with Messrs. H. S. Parker & Co., for quite a number of years, and entered the employ of Mr. Walter I. Fuller. Mr. Karl Chadwick is in the employ of Messrs. Parker & Co.

April 16, 1917

Monday evening week, nine passengers for this village arrived at the West Barnstable station to find there was no means of conveyance waiting, so they telephoned to expressman Coleman, who said he would try to meet them at Lombard Home. This he succeeded in doing with his truck and the party, consisting of four ladies and five gentlemen, after being very nicely entertained at the home, reached their destination in safety about nine o'clock.

July 2, 1917

Messrs. Albert Coleman and Russell Evans each have a new horse purchased recently of parties in Plymouth.

July 30, 1917

The Scudder hay scales are being repaired.

July 30, 1917

Edward Tevyaw had the misfortune to fall off his bicycle recently and break one of his arms, but is recovering as fast as can be expected.

August 13, 1917

East Bay Road has been rebuilt and is now a very fine road to ride over.

August 20, 1917

One of the finest turnouts in town is that of Mr. Andrew Adie, who is daily seen driving his handsome thoroughbreds through the town while the bugler at intervals heralds their arrival.

January 21, 1918

The W. C. T. U. held a social at the home of Mr. and Mrs. J. W. Tallman on Wianno Avenue last Monday evening. A pleasant time was enjoyed playing games, reading and singing. Refreshments consisting of war bread and punch were served.

February 25, 1918

Messrs. Arthur Wyman and Frank Allen have entered the employ of Mr. G. W. Hallett.

September 2, 1918

William F. Adams visited his aunt, Mrs. Cora Lewis, on Wednesday, arriving on the morning train and returning in the afternoon to Camp Upton, N.Y. He expects shortly to leave for overseas.

October 7, 1918

The school, churches, library and all other public places will be closed for another week, at least, or until further notice from the Board of Health.

December 2, 1918

A gunning party consisting of Messrs. J. Milton Leonard, Frank B. Gardner, Forrest Burlingame, Herbert Hinckley and Maurice Crocker are enjoying a vacation on Nantucket.

December 16, 1918

A meeting was held in the library Tuesday evening to make arrangements for a village Christmas Tree which will be held Christmas Eve at 7:00 P.M. The officers for the year are:

Chairman, Mary L. Crocker; Secretary and Treasurer, Alice Coombs. The following committees were chosen: Hire Hall, Mary L. Crocker. Decorate Tree, Addie Coffin, Alice Coombs, Anna Williams, Fannie Robbins. Entertainment: Blanche Daniel. Call presents: Maurice Crocker, Harry Lovell. Cut presents: Leonard Tallman, Howard Scudder, Harold Crosby, William Crosby. Distributing: Charlotte Boult, Jessie Lewis, Mary Shields, Grace Crocker, Lillian Tevyaw, Dorothy Cahoon, Olive Scudder, Eleanor Taylor, Annie Nute, Elsie Chadwick, Agatha Crocker and Helen Whiteley.

Master of ceremonies: J. M. Leonard.

January 6, 1919

Our little village has seemed under a cloud of gloom for the past week. Sickness, death and sad hearts are in many homes.

There is a lesson for us in each life that has passed on. With Earl DeWitt we think of a happy home life, a devoted husband, a tender thoughtful son, a kind and obliging neighbor.

With Watson Stockman, a man untiring in his care and devotion to an aged, crippled mother; lonely, discouraged and unable to work, yet brave to the end.

With William Bennett, our aged Civil War Veteran, a genial, kind, sympathetic man, one whose motto was loyalty to his wife, friends, home, church, and his country.

January 13, 1919
     Carmen Butler is ill with the influenza.

October 20, 1919
     Messrs. Walter I. Fuller, Ernest Jones, Leo Beaumont, George and Carl Burlingame are among those who reported for Boston police duty in that city the past week.

November 3, 1919
     Donald Coffin and Edwin Lagergren arrived home from their trip to California on Monday.

After the Flood — 1920
     This picture was taken from the present Armstrong-Kelley Park looking toward the home of Everett Fuller which formerly stood at the corner of Old Mill Road and Main Street.

January 12, 1920
     The ice company has its three ice houses filled with 7 to 9 inch ice.

January 12, 1920
     Our young people have enjoyed very good skating on Joshua's pond the past week.

January 19, 1920
     Our church and school bells were rung for five minutes on Friday noon in the celebration of constitutional Prohibition which went into effect on that day.

July 26, 1920
     Two young ladies from New York passed through our village on Monday on a tramping trip from Woods Hole to Provincetown.

Jananuary 17, 1921
     An epidemic of measles is in town.

In the early 1920s, this building stood on Main Street where, until 1987, the Flower Boutique was to be found, just down the hill from the Baptist Church. In center, Constable Harry Lovell; others unknown.

January 17, 1921
     Skating on the ponds has been enjoyed by the young folks of the village the past week.

March 7, 1921
     Many new cases of measles and whooping cough have developed the past week.

August 1, 1921
     Prayer meetings have been well attended considering the extreme heat.

August 29, 1921
     These cool nights make us anxious about frosts. Cranberries have received much damage already from worms.

October 17, 1921
     There is not so much activity at Mulberry Corner. Robbins' laundry has closed for the season.

November 28, 1921
     Several cases of scarletina are reported in the village.

December 19, 1921
     Messrs. E. S. Crocker, J. M. Leonard, S. J. Wardwell and Frank Gardner spent a recent week in Nantucket on a hunting trip.

January 2, 1922
     Mrs. Andrew Adie and daughter Miss Rosamond Adie, of Chestnut Hill and Wianno, have returned from abroad. Miss Adie completed her work with the American Committee for Devastated France Nov. 1, and since then has been traveling in Italy with her mother.

January 23, 1922

All the ice houses are filled with good, clear, seven to nine inch ice.

February 13, 1922

A slight accident occurred in Post Office Square Wednesday afternoon when a Reo truck side-swiped a Ford car. No one was hurt, but the smaller car was quite badly damaged.

April 10, 1922

Mr. Harold Crosby of the Crosby House entertained 42 guests over the weekend. Seapuit Club was also filled to its capacity.

April 24, 1922

During the tempest Tuesday night a transformer in front of Charles Lewis' home was struck, plunging every electrically lighted home from the golf links to Centerville into total darkness.

May 29, 1922

Warren Codd is demolishing his barn and will erect a new garage on the old site. Frank Boult is also about to build one for himself.

June 3, 1922

Elliott Crosby and Harry Tallman have both purchased new cars.

July 3, 1922

Glad to see the improvement to the sidewalk in front of Mr. Gardner's and Mr. Alley's. We hope the good work will continue farther, in fact, the whole length of the street.

July 17, 1922

Blueberries are in the market.

July 24, 1922

Messrs. Everett Small and Chessman Crocker have just added electric lights to their houses, making another bright place on North Main Street, cheering the "traveler along the way".

September 18, 1922

Parents are entreated to try and use their influence in getting their children to attend Sunday school. Many older people remember the things they learned in their childhood more keenly than the things of the present. It is nice, therefore, to store the young mind with the things that are worthwhile.

October 23, 1922

Mr. Albert J. Bacon spent the weekend with his sister in Boston enjoying some of the evangelistic meetings. He is selling out the contents of his market, planning to have a rest and change this winter.

December 4, 1922

Russell Lewis and Elmer Whiteley recently enjoyed a few days' visit in Boston.

December 11, 1922

Electric light poles are being erected on Parker Road, which must be a pleasant sight to those who have waited so long for lights on that street.

December 18, 1922

While turning the corner near William Coleman's Sunday week, the car driven by C. D. Parker skidded and crashed into a tree, nearly demolishing the machine. Mr. Parker and the chauffeur escaped injury.

January 8, 1923

The snow storm Wednesday night was served with a high wind. So large were the flakes they looked like little snowballs. The snow was heavy and it was hard for autos to get to the early train next morning.

March 5, 1923

The Washington pie sale Feb. 22, under the supervision of Mrs. Mary Scudder, Mrs. Addie Coffin and Mrs. Preston Fish, was so successful that $116 was taken and more is to be handed in later.

March 19, 1923

Quite a number from this village attended the poverty ball recently held in Marstons Mills. First prize for the men, a Gillette razor, was won by George Burlingame.

March 26, 1923

Walter I. Fuller and Stuart Scudder sang at the Men's Social in Sandwich Thursday night.

June 4, 1923

Mr. Raymond Pierce has moved his family into the store owned by Mrs. Lewis, which he has arranged as a dwelling house. Mr. Pierce is running the ice cream parlor owned by Carrie R. Williams.

June 18, 1923

Large loads of trunks are arriving daily, so we know our summer guests are soon to be with us, and we extend a cordial welcome.

***

July 16, 1923

Lillian Tevyaw, Ruth Horne and Bernice Chadwick are employed at Pierce's ice cream parlor.

***

August 6, 1923

A spark from the chimney at Roscoe Hinckley's house set fire to the shingles on the roof. The fire was quickly extinguished. There was quite a little excitement for a while.

***

September 10, 1923

Victor Adams and Lincoln Baker motored to Boston Saturday. Mr. Adams has a position as a teacher of a school in Peabody.

***

September 24, 1923

Four hydroplanes passed over the village Wednesday, creating quite a whizz and whirr in the air.

***

October 15, 1923

Last Wednesday seemed to be Peddlers' Day.

***

November 5, 1923

Chester Crosby and Delton Hall are recovering from an attack of the measles.

***

November 12, 1923

Mr. and Mrs. Cecil Goodspeed have returned from their wedding trip and are receiving many congratulations and gifts. A goodly sum of money was presented from the fellow-workmen of the Daniel Bros, showing their good wishes and esteem for the young people.

***

March 3, 1924

There are several cases of "pink-eye" in the schools.

***

April 7, 1924

Quite a number from Osterville attended the medicine show at Cotuit Wednesday evening.

***

July 3, 1924

Raymond Pierce has opened his ice cream parlor on Main Street.

Cecil Goodspeed — c. 1908

***

January 15, 1925

The boys and girls have been having a fine time skating the past week.

***

February 19, 1925

Several of the children in the village are confined to the house with chicken pox.

***

July 2, 1925

Miss Hope Adams and Miss Imogene Leonard are home for the summer.

***

August 13, 1925

Stanton Parker and Loomis Kinney have gone to Camp Devens for the month of August on their vacation.

***

Sixth Fairway and Seventh Tee — Wianno Golf Course — 1920s

41

October 1, 1925
Ernest Jones, Rawson Ashley and George B. Fuller took a trip to New York the past week, going by way of the Mohawk Trail.

January 28, 1926
William Hodges has resigned his position as janitor of the public school. Frank Jones has taken his place.

March 11, 1926
Property is changing hands almost every day. It is reported that there is to be a chain of stores on Main Street. It is also said that George Lewis has sold his house at Joshua's Pond.

March 25, 1926
A building is going up beside the A & P store, which we understand is going to be used for a Union Telegraph station.

April 8, 1926
Work has begun on land recently bought by J. J. Gallagher on Wianno Avenue. This will make a fine development when finished.

July 1, 1926
The silver cup won by the Osterville Girl Scouts at their meet in Harwich is now on exhibition in the Osterville Library.

July 22, 1926
The new house of Dr. Chute is progressing rapidly and it is hoped it will be ready for occupying by fall.

October 28, 1926
Misses Inez Swift and Helen Nute are attending school at the Hyannis Beauty Parlors.

February 10, 1927
Among those who attended the Sportsman Show in Boston were Messrs. Maurice Crocker, Walcott Ames, Herbert Hinckley and Thornton Adams.

March 3, 1927
The new block on Main Street is rapidly nearing completion.

March 17, 1927
Mrs. Byron Tevyaw was found unconscious on the lawn of the Community Church Monday night where she was attending a meeting. Feeling faint, she went out and was later found by someone. She was taken to the home of her brother, Forrest Burlingame, and a doctor summoned. She later was removed to her home where she is confined to her bed. At present writing Mrs. Tevyaw is improving under the skillful treatment of Dr. W. D. Kinney.

March 31, 1927
The friends of Albert J. Bacon were surprised to learn of his death in Forestdale recently. Mr. Bacon was a resident of this place for some years and was well known here, having been employed at I. Crocker's meat market and later being in business for himself.

August 11, 1927
Both officers, Chester L. Baker and Harris C. Lovell, are occupying new traffic stands, which were donated by residents of Osterville.

August 18, 1927
Edward Crosset entertained a party of sixteen on the yacht "Betty R" Sunday. Among the distinguished guests were Secretary of the United States Treasury, Mr. Mellon.

September 15, 1927
A severe electrical storm, accompanied by rain in blinding sheets and considerable wind, swept over this village Sunday. A bolt struck the house of Stuart Scudder.

January 26, 1928
Robert Cross, J. Milton Leonard and Cornelius Driscoll will leave for New York on the steamer Metapan bound for Kingston, Jamaica and Panama for a pleasure trip. They will also stop at South American ports.

February 23, 1928
Roscoe Hinckley is confined to his home with a severe cold.

May 17, 1928
Don't forget the military whist at the School house May 24.

L. to R., J. Milton Leonard, Robert Cross, Mr. Robbins, (a friend of Mr. Cross), and Cornelius Driscoll. c. 1928.

May 17, 1928

In the novice typewriting County contest at the Barnstable High School Saturday Miss Elaine Tallman won the first place with 44 words per minute, 8 errors. Honorable Mention went to Eleanora Lagergren with 34 words, 13 errors. The cup was awarded to Barnstable High.

May 24, 1928

Daniel Bros. have the contract for building a new house for Edward Gould, Jr., on Eel River Road.

June 21, 1928

It is about time the officials placed a cop at Crocker's corner. The traffic is each day growing exceedingly dangerous at this point. Officer Lovell was obliged to leave his post at Mulberry Corner several times and clear out a mix-up in Post Office Square.

July 19, 1928

In three hours Sunday 920 cars passed the Osterville Fruit Store by actual count.

July 26, 1928

Over eleven hundred cars passed the Osterville Fruit Store in three hours by actual count Sunday. The traffic was unusually heavy, a constant stream of cars coming from the four corners at this point. It is felt by all that the little park at Mulberry Corner should be done away with. It is a most dangerous place and we fail to see why the Highway Department does not do something about it. Saturday

there was more grinding of brakes as cars coming all ways nearly crashed into each other while the officer was off his station. A car driven by Mr. Babcock from the Wianno Club crashed into an ice truck owned by Jesse Muray which was parked near the Fruit Store and damaged both cars to some extent. Fortunately no one was injured. It is astonishing how people take that corner without slowing up. We sincerely hope the town will take some action before some terrible accident happens.

November 15, 1928

Mrs. Roscoe Hinckley is driving a new car, the gift of her sister.

Hoover Parade in Osterville — 1928

With the enthusiasm born of victory, a crowd of Hoover rooters from Osterville got together almost spontaneously, piled into 39 cars, and held an impromptu Hoover victory parade. A bugle corps from a girl scout troop led the march, and the line wound its way around the streets of Osterville, then headed for Hyannis, where it learned it was the only group in the district showing an active enthusiasm.

The cars that formed the nucleus of the parade were decorated with Hoover pictures, braided ribbons, flags, and tinsel. As they proceeded through the streets and toward Hyannis, they were joined by new cars whose drivers caught the spirit and wanted to take part.

The idea for a parade first entered the head of Mrs. Chessman Crocker, who assumed charge. Other drivers, whose cars bore decorations and figured brilliantly in the parade, were Lauchlan Crocker, of Marstons Mills, Norman Williams, Willis Crocker, Harding Joy, Capt. Thomas Collins, John Lewis, and George Rankin.

January 3, 1929

Work at the new block on Main Street presents a scene of activity as big trucks daily unload lumber and brick. The work is progressing steadily as weather permits.

February 14, 1929

Walcott Ames, Herbert Hinckley, Stuart Scudder, Bernard Ames and Forrest Burlingame attended the fight in Boston Thursday night.

February 21, 1929

The old Rich cottage which has been moved back is to be put in repair and rented to Jean Henner.

February 21, 1929

A car from Leonard's Garage was reported stolen yesterday while the driver stepped into the barber shop.

June 27, 1929

Joseph Eldridge, 16, regular messenger boy at the Osterville Western Union office, was bitten by a dog owned by George Burlingame while carrying a message at 9:30 this morning according to a report made by the police department at Hyannis. The injury is not considered serious and Eldridge was able to remain on duty after receiving treatment.

July 4, 1929

Work on the Daniel Block is being carried on rapidly. A sign extending the whole length of the building is being erected, on which the signs for the individual stores will be painted. The interior of the various stores and the Post Office are being renovated. The fine cement pavement between the stores and street adds much to the comfort and convenience of pedestrians.

July 25, 1929

Elaine Tallman, Fred Wetherbee, Evelyn Williams, James Goff, Marjorie Fuller and Roy Bronson, with Mr. and Mrs. Walter Fuller, enjoyed a sailing party one night last week. After the party refreshments were served at the Fuller residence. A very delightful time was had by all.

August 1, 1929

Mrs. Addie G. Crosby has gone to Boston to consult a specialist about her eyes.

August 15, 1929

We are glad to see that the police have at last stopped boys from riding bicycles on the sidewalks. It is a dangerous practice, and some narrow escapes from being run down have been experienced. Now let them get busy and stop some of the crazy driving throughout Main Street.

August 22, 1929

Is our new drug store meeting your needs, or do you go to Hyannis to spend your money as in the past? Osterville is gradually waking up to her responsibilities and needs. The next thing we hope to see located here is a bank. Who will be the pioneer in this movement? One is certainly needed.

September 12, 1929

The Hyannis Trust Company have petitioned the Board of Bank Incorporation for authority to maintain a branch office in Osterville. A hearing on the petition will be next Wednesday.

September 26, 1929

John Banks has a new Ford Coupe.

October 3, 1929

Rummage Sale money allotted to activities were:

$300 to Osterville Public Library
$100 to District Nursing
$100 to Girl Scouts
$25 to Flower Mission Work, W.C.T.U.
$25 to Tree Fund, Christmas
$25 to Union Hall

The committee met with Mrs. J. Mott Hallowell Saturday afternoon to disburse the money. At the close of the meeting tea and cakes were served. Our summer friends deserve the grateful thanks of the recipients.

October 17, 1929

Main Street is again a scene of activity as ground is being broken for the new branch bank of the Hyannis Trust Company. Daniel Bros. have the contract and we may expect to see it in operation by spring.

October 31, 1929

Williams Bros. are opening a new hardware store in the Pattison Block, Osterville, where they will carry a complete line of hardware, paint, oil burners, ranges, cabinet heaters and the usual variety found in an up-to-date hardware store. The store is well-lighted and attractively fitted with steel tables with glass tops, steel shelving and combinations, combining good taste with wearing qualities and convenience. This new venture will prove a notable addition to the thriving village of Osterville.

November 7, 1929

Bernard and Walcott Ames, Stuart Scudder, Jesse Murray, Herbert Hinckley, Forrest Burlingame and Walter I. Fuller have returned from Pittsburg, Maine, where they went on a gunning trip. At the first outlying camp they hired a guide and penetrated ten miles into the interior on foot over a road which defies description. The boys were game and finally reached their destination in the forest primeval where they led the life which is dear to the hearts of most men. They took along a radio, checkers and cards. When they were not seeking the wild denizens of the forest, they got in touch with the outside world or soothed their jaded nerves with a game. They returned with a new zest for the winter's work. We have not been privileged to view their trophies of the chase, but we understand they have enough souvenirs to go around among their friends. Porcupines are adorned with a most accommodating number of souveniers.

November 21, 1929

Tremors from the earthquake shock were felt in various parts of the village. Dishes rattled on shelves, doors swung back and forth and things seemed real spooky for a while in several homes. Many thought it might be a heavy truck passing but were disabused of that idea as the tremor lasted a few minutes.

November 21, 1929

Sverre Bjerke will leave here Thursday for New York where he will take the boat for his home in Norway. We understand this is the first time Mr. Bjerke has been home in about eight years. He will probably return in February, as he plans to spend two months there. Mr. Bjerke is a general favorite and his friends wish him a happy visit and return.

January 23, 1930

Mr. and Mrs. Merton H. Bates and Mr. and Mrs. Burleigh Leonard enjoyed Monday in Boston at the Auto Show.

January 23, 1930

Delton Hall and Chester Crosby, we understand, will attend the motor boat show in New York next week.

The Horn of Plenty c. 1925-1930
Located on Wianno Avenue. In 1987, this building is the location of La Shack. Standing in front is Ruth Horne.

February 6, 1930

Cornelius Driscoll, J. M. Leonard and Robert F. Cross started last week for a three week trip to Havana. Other points of interest along the route will be visited.

February 27, 1930

Leonard's Garage was broken into some time Sunday night.

March 13, 1930

The directors and officers of the Hyannis Trust have issued invitations to the opening of their branch at the new bank building on Saturday afternoon between the hours of two and eight. The new office will be open for business on Monday, the 17th.

April 3, 1930

Mrs. James Mott Hallowell is in town for a few days enjoying her summer home.

April 10, 1930

Work of straightening the road near Twombly's Corner was begun Monday.

May 8, 1930

Misses Harriet Alleman and Helen MacLellan have moved into the old Scudder homestead on Main Street which they recently purchased and have their business office there we understand.

May 15, 1930

Citizens of the village were roused from their slumber Saturday night by a sharp fusillade of firearms and the boom of a heavy gun. It was later learned that a government boat was chasing a rum runner outside the cut and endeavoring to capture her. Whether she was hit in any way was not learned, but she proved smart enough to outwit her pursuer.

May 15, 1930

Mrs. Andrew Adie, a summer resident here, who has been around the world, left the steamship Columbus at San Pedro, California, and is now visiting her daughter.

October 30, 1930

The Western Union Telegraph office is closed for the season. The Newsstand will attend to telegrams.

November 27, 1930

Some petty thief broke into H. S. Parker's grocery store Wednesday night and took a small sum of money, cigars and cigarettes. The break was made through a rear window.

Aerial View of Main Street's intersection with Blossom Avenue — c. 1940. Loop in left foreground is at the rear of Midway Garage.

c. 1911 — Ross Cowling at the Hay Scales

Left to right in picture: Blanche (Lovell) Daniel, Rachel Daniel, Dora (Robbins) Lovell — Blanche's mother, Ruth Horne, Edna (Crosby) Horne — Ruth's mother, Mrs. Attaresta Johnson — Dora's sister, and Mr. Andrew Johnson.

When this picture was taken, this was the home of Mr. and Mrs. Andrew Johnson. The house stood where the parking lot of the House and Garden Shop is now and was called "Robbin's Nest." c. 1910.

L to R — Isabel Lewis, Margaret Cross, Josephine Cross. Seated on ground — Elliott Lewis. This photograph was taken at the Barnstable Fair — c. 1909

Left to right, bottom row of three: Henry Small, Bernice Chadwick, Pauline Chadwick; back row of two: Mrs. Everett Small and Elsie Chadwick. c. 1918.

Left to right, standing on ground: Elvira Lewis, Dorothy Rankin, Elva Crocker. Standing on running board: Pauline Chadwick, Bernice Chadwick c. 1922.

Seated L to R — Blanche Lovell,
        Georgiana Daniel.
Standing — Edna Crosby.

Seated L to R — Wilton Crosby,
        Roland Ames.
Standing — Warren Lovell.

Seated L to R — Wilbur Crosby,
        Freeman Adams.
Standing — Nathan West, Jr.

Left to right: Mrs. Richard Lewis and Harry Tallman standing in front of the old Osmond Ames home on Bay Street, c. 1900. This house had formerly been the home of Nymphas Hinckley. In later years it ws owned by Mr. and Mrs. Frank Hansen.

Left to right, seated: Joseph Crosby and Frank H. Williams; standing: Henry P. Leonard.

1. Ida (Bacon) Hall, 2. Abbie (Crosby) Williams, 3. Ella (Scudder) Lovell, and 4. Jennie (Hinckley) Boult.

1. Minnie Bates, 2. Merton Bates, 3. Frances (Lovell) Fuller, 4. ?, and Addie Bearse.

47

Left to right: Jennie Fuller and
Myrtle Crosby

Florence Adams and Duncan Wetherbee
— c. 1890s

Left to right: Sarah H. Boult, Ella Lovell,
and Addie Bearse.

Left to right: Alice (Jones) Ames, Addie Bearse,
Minnie (Jones) Bates.

Souvenir Mug of Osterville — c. 1900

The Village Hall

Barnstable, Wednesday Night, October 14 or 15, 1803, at the proprietors' meeting held in their house in Lovell's Neighborhood, so called, met by order of the Committee, Nehemiah Lovell, Samuel Holmes, and Benjamin Hallett, or those that was at home to fix on the establishment of their house for the future and not to be altered.

1. First, voted and chose Capt. Nymphas Hinckley, moderator.

2. Secondly, voted and chose Nehemiah Lovell, proprietor, clerk.

3. Thirdly, voted that every share holder have a vote and as many shares as a man owned, so many votes he had.

4. Fourthly, voted that all business in future of said proprietors' house for repairs or every other business, except a private school, shall be elected by the majority of votes after a meeting being warned and due time by the above committee or an other chosen.

5. Fifthly, voted that thee house shall never be opened for a private women's school unless the proprietors neglect or don't get a man's school.

6. Sixthly, voted that the house shall be free for the town school for the district if the town or selectmen will give the old school house to thee proprietors of the new as they own it now.

7. Seventhly. The pews to be drawn by lot.

8. Eighthly, voted that the house shall be free for a private day school for all that live in this district paying their part of the tuition if they don't own any shares, all that send out of the district to pay two cents per head per week for the benefit of the house.

9. Ninthly, voted that the above be abiding and binding Regulations until Every owner shall consent to alter it.

10. Tenthly, voted to dismiss the meeting at half past eight o'clock at night, finished all the business of the house, and drew the pews as they stand on the other side.

Attest: Nehemiah Lovell, Proprietor and Clerk

The regulations for the future government of the house as drawn and reported by the Committee chosen for that Purpose

Article 1. The above named House shall be called the Village Meeting House.

Article 2. The Baptist Society shall improve the house one half the time in each month if they wish untill the Methodist Society shall wish to improve the house as shall be hereafter stated.

Article 3. The Congregational Society shall improve the house one half the time in each month they wish, untill the Methodist Society shall wish to improve the house as shall be hereafter stated.

Article 4. The Methodist Society shall improve the house one sixth part of the time in each month when they wish by giving timely notice to the above named Societys.

Article 5. When the Methodist Society wish to improve the house as stated in Art. 4, and the above Societys, Baptist or Congregationalist do not supply the house with a Minister of their own order, their one half of the time each, the Methodist Society shall improve that part of the time when the above named Societys do not improve, if the deficiency in the above named Society does not amount to their part of the time, it shall be granted by the Society which is not deficient if it does not amount to more than one twelfth of the time. Reference to be had, at all times and by each Society, to the original Constitution of said house.

Article 6. If either of the above named Societys do not supply the house with a minister of their own order, the other Society shall have the privilege of said house if they wish, in preference to any other, by applying to their Committee, hereafter to be made choice of.

Article 7. A person shall be chosen annually to take care of the house, keep the keys, open and shut, also sweep when necessary, also light said house when there is evening meeting held by either of the above named Societies, this office shall be put at Auction, which the lowest bidder will have.

Article 8. Three wardens shall be chosen, annually, and Swann, whose duty it shall be to suppress all disorderly conduct in any person in time of public worship, and attend to all the duty which the law of this Commonwealth requires of them.

Article 9. All expences for oil and taking care of the house or any other necessary charges accruing to said house shall be paid by each Society in proportion as they occupy said house.

Article 10. A Committee of three persons shall be chosen annually in each Society to see that the aforesaid regulations are complied with, and shall act as the executive of the Societies to admit into said house such ministers as they shall think proper when not occupied as aforesaid stated.

Article 11. These regulations shall not be altered within the term of twenty years to come which will close November the Seventh in the year 1851.

Josiah Scudder
George Lovell
Oliver Hinckley
Committee

A Copy
and C _____ sed
Attest James N. Lovell
March 7th, 1843

April 17, 1844

After a warm debate, growing out of an article in the warrant, in relation to the interest which the town holds in a meeting house in Osterville village, the town voted not to relinquish their right in the house, but that hereafter, all religious denominations, without distinction of sect or party, shall hold meetings in the house.

September 12, 1849

An Association of Ladies in Osterville, purpose holding a Rustic Fair, in the "Old Village Meeting House" on Thursday, 20th inst; commencing at 2 and closing at 9 o'clock pm. Their object is, to raise funds for procuring Window Blinds and new Hymn Books for the Baptist Church in the village.

Useful and fancy articles, and refreshments will be exhibited for sale. Admission, 10 cents; children half price. If a storm on Thursday, the next pleasant day will be chosen.

By order of the Committee,
Mrs. A. Lovell
Mrs. I. Scudder
Mrs. P. Scudder
Mrs. H. Crocker
Miss B. P. Lovell

A copy by James N. Lovell, December 28, 1853
Barnstable, November 19th, 1853

We the undersigned Proprietors and Pew Holders of the Village Meeting House in Osterville agree by our signatures to have said house put at Auction and Sold to the highest bidder for cash, and the amount of sales divided equal with each pew holder, also the land belonging to the same, and we appoint Capt. Hansard Hallett our agent to set the time of such sale, and give a deed of said house and land in our behalf.

Isaac Hodges	Thomas Ames
Joseph Robbins	Robert Lovell
Samuel Crosby, Jr.	Alvan Crosby
Lewis Crosby	James Lewis
Benjamin F. Crocker	Tirzah Crosby
Isaac Ewer	Oliver Hinckley
Daniel Crosby	Timothy Parker
Heman Isham	James Lumbert
Samuel Crosby	Nathaniel Hinckley
Lot Hinckley	Josiah Scudder
George Hinckley	Asa Crosby
Mary Ames	George Lovell
Andrus Bearse	Zilpha Lovell
Warren Hallett	James Lovell
James N. Lovell	Philander Scudder
Henry Lovell	Joshua Lumbert

Dec. 28, 1853 after due on 7 days notice, Mr. Luther Hinckley sold the house and land, this day to Mr. Josiah Ames, the highest bidder for $200 dollars.

December 30th, 1873

There will be a Grand Ball at Village Hall in Osterville, on Thursday evening, January 1st. Music: Smith and Walker's Quadrille Band of Middleboro. Oyster supper furnished by A. Backus. Manager: E.C. Robbins; Floor Director: C.G. Lovell, H.P. Crocker and A.L. Robbins. Tickets: $1.50. Ladies are cordially invited.

February 17, 1874

Tuesday evening Mr. Barney Gould "the world-renowned pedestrian," lectured in Village Hall at the request of a number of our citizens. He was introduced to the audience by Dr. Fuller of this place and commenced by saying he had traveled through nearly every state in the Union including the "State of New Orleans." After giving an amusing account of his adventures while travelling through the country, the lecturer touched on the popular subject of women's rights, and then religion, closing his remarks by saying, "if a man did as he would be done by he had religion enough." He then indulged in a little "tripping of the light fantastic" for the amusement of the

BARNEY GOULD

E. G. Perry, in writing of Barney Gould in his book, "A Trip Around Cape Cod," copyright 1898, describes the man as follows: "He was probably of good stock, — possibly descended from a Pilgrim fallen from grace, for he had intelligence, wit, honesty and energy, carrying express matter always on foot, before there were other expresses here, over and even beyond the Cape, without loss or delay to his patrons. A well-authenticated instance is mentioned where, commissioned to deliver a mattress at Hyannis from Middleboro, he walked to Hyannis, procured a wheelbarrow, wheeled it to Middleboro, and then trundled barrow and mattress back to the Cape town again."

younger portion of the audience, and at 9 o'clock departed with his better half (whom we understand always accompanies him) for Mashpee, where he is to lecture.

We were pleased to notice that altho' a large company of the young people were present, the attendance of even a single justice of the peace was not required to preserve order.

February 23, 1875

Such a length of time has elapsed since I acted as newspaper correspondent that I hardly know how to open a letter to such an august personage as the public press; but it seems as though in such dull, cold and icy times anything of interest that occurs in our different villages should be chronicled for the amusement and pastime of your readers, so I attempt once more to enact the role of reporter.

While the conversation among the older portion of the company congregated each evening at the groceries seemed, for the past week, to turn to the severely cold weather, the younger people were gathered in small groups apparently discussing very important questions, and by glancing at the wall, you might have noticed the cause of these deliberations, for there was posted a finely printed notice (from the Patriot Press) of a "Variety Entertainment at Village Hall," and Wednesday evening the grand affair came off. Your correspondent arrived at the Hall about seven o'clock and found it nearly full, and as no seats were reserved for members of the press, was obliged to press his way through the crowd, and at last found a place which, though too near the stage to be fashionable, answered the purpose of seeing and hearing very well.

The entertainment opened with a fine quartette called, "Friends we come with hearts of gladness," and they might have added, we hope you will have the same ere we finish our entertainment, for they certainly strove to make the evening pass pleasantly. Then followed Reading, Tableaux, Singing, Farces and Negro Minstrels, all well enacted. We think that in reading Miss Jessie L. Hinckley carried off the palm. Her reading of the poem "High Tide," being better than is often heard from an amateur elocutionist. In Tableaux, a representation of one of Rogers' Groups, "The Dying Soldier," was probably the finest, although "Slim Jim's Courtship", with the accompanying singing, provoked the most laughter. In singing, Miss Runyon and Mr. Robbins' several duets were excellent, and the concluding quartette, "Silver Threads among the Gold", was very fine. The Negro Minstrels, with their ballads and jokes, reminded one of the palmy days of Morris Brothers, and Billy Morris himself could hardly have surpassed Mr. Azor D. Hall in the "Darkey Photographer."

Altogether it was truly a variety entertainment in the full sense of the word. The programme was repeated with a slight variation on Thursday evening, but owing to the postponement from Wednesday evening on account of the storm, the music engaged for a dance after the exhibition could not come. They had, with the assistance of our "home band", a "little time", as the managers expressed it, but soon dispersed to their homes to either shudder in their dreams over "Bluebeard's Secret Chamber", or laugh when awake at the remembrance of "Slim Jim's Courtship", or "Scene in the Dentist's Office", and one and all to regret that what had been looked forward to so long could now only be referred to as in the past.

February 15, 1876

Wednesday evening a concert was given at Village Hall by Messrs. Maynard and Hatton. The singing was good.

August 1, 1876

Our annual Fair and Tea Party will be held at Village Hall on Thursday afternoon and evening, August 3rd. Every endeavor will be made to make it an agreeable and pleasant occasion for all.

January 1, 1878

Our young people between the ages of 12 and 20 participated in the pleasures of a Pound Party at Village Hall Thursday evening. Each participant contributed a pound of something to make up the feast, and contributed his or her mite towards defraying the expenses of the Hall. An economical as well as good time was had.

September 9, 1879

The Village Hall is having an addition put on. Quite an improvement.

December 2, 1879

A "hop" at the Hall Thanksgiving evening was well enjoyed by quite a large party. Music was furnished by Mr. Hiram Weeks, who played the violin and by a number of ladies of the company who took turns at the organ.

December 30, 1879

Thursday evening another tree, at Village Hall, to which all were invited. At six o'clock the curtain arose amidst the ringing of sleigh bells and burning of powder, noise, etc., when the audience saw Capt. Horace. S. Lovell in his sleigh, with robes and fur cap, looking as though he came from the cold, with a full load of good and pretty things. The tree was also well loaded with presents, and after being introduced as the Santa Claus of the evening, Mr. Lovell proceeded to distribute them, making all look bright and happy. After all the presents had been distributed, cake and coffee were freely dispensed. At different houses there were family trees loaded, and good, bright, happy times with in but rather stormy without.

February 8, 1881

There was a masked Ball at Village Hall last Friday evening. We were not present, but heard it was a success.

August 30, 1881

That cheap ball at Village Hall, Monday evening week, was a good time for 25 cents, and ice cream thrown in.

November 29, 1881

A neck-tie party and dance at Village Hall, Thursday evening. Coffee, cake, and a good time enters into the programme.

December 20, 1881

The citizens of Osterville met at Village Hall and organized for a course of lectures, to commence as soon as they can get some one to lecture.

February 27, 1883

There was a skating party at Village Hall last Wednesday evening and Thursday evening there was a fancy dress ball.

March 6, 1883

There is talk of a new hall for this village.

March 27, 1883

A new floor is being laid at Village Hall.

Osterville Improvement Association — August 1883

"Pro Bono Publico"

To the Summer Guests of Osterville, and Others.

As a means of accomplishing the several improvements which have been the topic of considerable conversation this summer, and also to provide for the maintenance of these and such others as may hereafter be made, it has been suggested that a desirable way in which to facilitate these ends will be to propose a general union of cottagers, hotel guests, proprietors, and such villagers as can be interested, in an organization which may be called the OSTERVILLE IMPROVEMENT ASSOCIATION.

The wants to be provided are a good wharf, and a plank from wharf to hotel and cottages. Later on may be considered, provided the funds raised will warrant, a playground, shade trees where needed, and a casino.

To obtain the funds to provide and maintain these, it is proposed:

1st. that the association shall be organized on a business basis;

2nd. that a thousand shares, at $10.00 each, shall be offered for subscription;

3rd. that guests, cottagers, land-owners, hotel proprietors, and all resident parties interested, shall be invited;

4th. that subscribers shall be entitled to one vote for each share of stock owned;

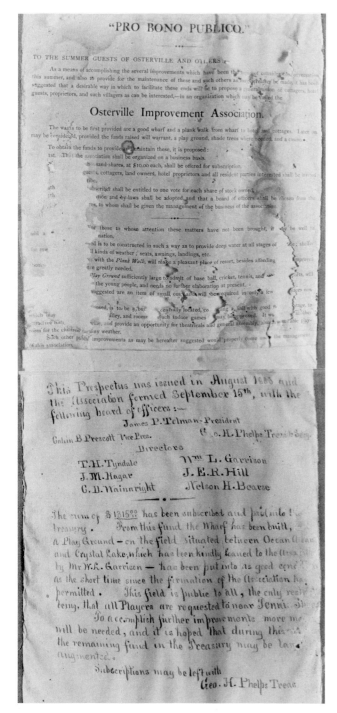

"PRO BONO PUBLICO."

TO THE SUMMER GUESTS OF OSTERVILLE AND OTHERS:—

Osterville Improvement Association.

5th. and that by-laws shall be adopted and that a board of officers shall be chosen from among the subscribers to whom shall be given the management of the business of the association.

For those to whose attention these matters have not been brought, it may be well to add a note of explanation.

The Wharf is proposed to be constructed in such a way as to provide deep water at all stages of the tide; shelter for row and sail boats in all kinds of weather; seats, awnings, landings, etc.

The wharf, in conjunction with the Plank Walk, will make a pleasant place of resort, besides affording much improved boating, are greatly needed.

As envisioned, a Playground sufficiently large to admit of baseball, cricket, tennis, and other field sports, will be much appreciated by the young people, and needs no further elaboration at present.

The shade trees suggested are an item of small cost and will be required in only a few open places now without any shelter from the sun.

Another item proposed, is to be a building, centrally located, connecting a hall with good stage, to which may   alley, and rooms for such games as may be approved. It would be another attractive feature of Osterville, and provide an opportunity for theatricals and general assembly, also an admirable playroom for the children in rainy weather.

Such other public improvements as may be hereafter suggested would properly come under the management of this association.

This Prospectus was issued in August 1883 and the Association formed September 15th, with the following board of officers:

James P. Tolman — President
Calvin B. Prescott, Vice Pres.
Geo. H. Phelps, Treas. & Secy.
Directors:
T. H. Tyndale
J. M. Hagar
C. D. Wainwright
Wm. L. Garrison
J. E. R. Hill
Nelson H. Bearse

The sum of $1315.00 has been subscribed and paid into the treasury. From this fund the Wharf has been built, a Play Ground — on the field situated between Ocean Avenue and Crystal Lake, which has been kindly loaned to the association by Mr. W. L. Garrison — has been put into as good condition as the short time since the formation of the Association has permitted. This field is public to all, the only restriction being that all Players are requested to wear Tennis Shoes.

To accomplish further improvements more money will be needed, and it is hoped that during this season the remaining fund in the Treasury may be largely augmented.

Subscriptions may be left with
Geo. H. Phelps, Treas.

May 20, 1884
A colored troupe "The Texas Jubilee Singers" — gave one of their entertainments in Village Hall, Wednesday evening, to a good house.

September 2, 1884
Rev. O. L. Ashenfelter will preach in Village Hall next Sunday afternoon at 3 o'clock. His sermon will be an examination and discussion of the doctrine of the atonement of Jesus Christ.

July 15, 1884

Rev. O. L. Ashenfelter will preach a sermon text Sunday afternoon in Village Hall to show that the sun and moon did not stand still at the command of Joshua, with some remarks upon the fallibility of the Bible.

_____

March 20, 1888

Rev. Mr. Pitblado of Brockton lectured at Village Hall on Thursday evening on "Men and Women for the Times" to a full house, giving a very enjoyable lecture.

_____

September 4, 1888

The Boston Ideal Co. played "Uncle Tom's Cabin" at Village Hall on Monday night to a full house.

_____

January 21, 1890

A Citizens' Meeting has been called at Village Hall, this Tuesday evening at 7:30, for the purpose of nominating a candidate for Selectman, and etc., The call says: Believing it is full time that Osterville was represented in this matter, the committee would urgently request a full attendance. The call is signed by Thomas Pattison, Frank Boult, J. M. Leonard, Austin Lovell, William B. Parker, Henry P. Crocker, Israel Crocker, Committee.

_____

January 28, 1890

The caucus at Village Hall was called to order at 7:30 p.m. A.L. Robbins was elected chairman and C.F. Parker Secretary. There were about 150 persons present. S.L. Leonard moved that all voters of the town present should have the privilege of voting. After much discussion participated in by S.L. Leonard, T.R. Clement for and Thomas Pattison against it, the motion was voted down. Balloting for Selectman then commenced. Thomas Pattison, F.W. Hodges and H.P. Crocker were nominated by the chair to sort and count ballots. An informal ballot was then taken, with the following result:

C.A. Lovell had   52 votes
William B. Parker had   29 votes

Mr. Parker then withdrew and the ballot was made formal and on the motion of Mr. Parker, unanimous, amid great applause.

_____

July 8, 1890

Village Hall is being newly painted, improving its appearance.

September 23, 1890

Village Hall has a new square grand piano purchased through Mr. Thomas C. West of New Bedford.

_____

March 1, 1892

The Masque Ball given in Village Hall, Osterville, on the evening of Feb. 23rd, was in every way a grand success. The music furnished by Dobson's Orchestra of Whitman, was so greatly enjoyed that not until 3 A.M. did the dancers confess themselves weary and ready to cry, enough. Among the dancers might have been seen "Uncle Sam," (Mr. L. Willis Leonard), treading a measure with "Topsy," (Miss M. I. Cammett); A "Spanish Cavalier," (Capt. H. P. Crocker), dancing with a gorgeously costumed "Pocahontas," (Miss Jennie Fuller); his Satanic Majesty, (Mr. M. G. Crocker), with the "Queen of Clubs," (Miss Isa Leonard); a Turk, (Mr. Ralph Crosby), with a Scotch Lassie, (Miss Frances Lovell), and so on in sublime and ridiculous (dis)order.

The most elaborate costumes were worn by Mrs. Belle Annand, a gown of white satin and brocade, with pearl ornaments; Mrs. Daniel Crosby as a Gipsy Queen and Miss Myrtle Crosby in pink satin, lace and flowers as May Queen; and Mr. C. F. Parker as a Prince; Mr. A.D. Hall in suit of white and silver. Tastefully and prettily dressed were: Mrs. J. M. Leonard, Queen of Spades; Miss Olive Fuller, Dawn; Mrs. George Williams, ivy trimmed gown; Mrs. J. A. Lovell, fancy dress, spangled; Mrs. S. H. Bates, Mrs. C. F. Parker, Miss Ethel Crosby, Peasant Costumes; Miss Emma Matthews of Yarmouth, "Columbia;" Miss Mary R. Lovell, Miss S. H. Boult, Kate Greenaway dresses; Mrs. A. D. Hall and Mrs. Wilton Crosby in blue and silver fancy dresses. Mr. J. A. Lovell, Mr. E. S. Crocker, Mr. Henry Leonard as clowns, and Mr. Geo. Williams as a giraffe-necked individual, caused great laughter; also Mr. E. S. Alley, who played girl so successfully as to deceive all the gentlemen. And tho last mentioned, the supper served during intermission was by no means the least enjoyed feature of the evening; on the contrary, we shall long wish for such another.

_____

June 6, 1893

There was a fine variety show here on Friday evening in the hall. The gentleman and lady, together with their troupe of animals, consisting of a donkey, a St. Bernard dog, a trained monkey, an Irish setter, a pug dog, and a trained goat, stopped over Saturday night and Sunday at Mr. Frank A. Danes'.

November 14, 1893

At the variety show performance, which has been held for several nights in Village Hall, the plush album prize, which was given by vote of the audience, to the handsomest woman in town, fell to Mrs. Fannie A. Robbins. The prize of a fine, large, well cured "Cape Cod turkey" for the homeliest man in town, fell to Mr. David B. Fuller.

October 9, 1894

Go and see the great Kickapoo Indian Medicine Co., in Village Hall, Wednesday evening, Oct. 10th, for one week. A grand concert by a host of star artists. Free to all adults.

December 4, 1894

The Village Hall is being altered and improved in the interior, and is to have new windows put in.

December 25, 1894

There is a fine new Steinway piano in Village Hall.

January 8, 1895

The Crosby Orchestra of seven pieces gave a dance in Village Hall the evening of the 1st inst; which was the event of the season, although but about thirty couples participated. The music was well worth listening to and many spectators who did not dance, availed themselves of this opportunity to hear some first-class music. The same music will give an assembly at Centerville Thursday evening, and we have no doubt that when it becomes known that we have an organization in our midst, capable of giving us better music than we have been in the habit of getting from Middleboro, Brockton or Bridgewater, the Crosby Orchestra's engagements will fully equal their time to fill them.

January 15, 1895

All are cordially invited to attend the "Clam Chowder Social" to be given by the Osterville Improvement Society in Village Hall, Jan.17th P.M. Chowder served from 8 to 9. Tickets: 75 cents.

January 22, 1895

The dance and supper in Village Hall on Thursday night was a very pleasant one. The music was furnished by the Crosby Orchestra.

May 6, 1895

George M. Baker's three act drama "My Brother's Keeper" will be presented in Village Hall on Friday evening by the young people of this place, which promises to be a very pleasant entertainment. In the cast are Messrs. Warren M. Hodges,

William F. Adams, Ariel H. Tallman, Thomas F. Matthews, Henry M. Parker, Misses Blanche Lovell, Ellen E. Crowell, Georgia H. Daniel.

Old Village Hall, c. 1890
    Standing, left to right: Fannie Robbins, Sarah H. Boult, Edna Crosby, Abbie Crosby

January 29, 1896

On New Year's night the O.V.I.S. gave a very enjoyable entertainment in Village Hall which called out a full house. The programme consisted of instrumental music by Miss Addie Bearse; a farce entitled "Hiring Help"; instrumental music, Miss Cross; a monologue, Mrs. Lucy Leonard; needle race by three gentlemen; solo, Miss Littlefield; tableau reconciliation; after which there was a sale of useful and fancy articles, concluding with a lunch of cake and coffee. The audience then disbanded with the exception of the young people, who stayed to trip the light fantastic to the inspiring music of Prof. Backus's Orchestra of four pieces.

We understand it is the intention of combined talent, of the two above named societies, to give a dramatic entertainment, not only in Osterville but also in Hyannis and Cotuit, in the near future, the stage management of which will be under the direction of Mr. G. Webster Hallett and the general public need no other guarantee that the entertainment will be of a high order.

New Village Hall, c. 1897-1898

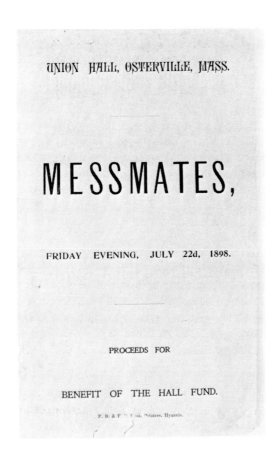

UNION HALL, OSTERVILLE, MASS.

MESSMATES,

FRIDAY EVENING, JULY 22d, 1898.

PROCEEDS FOR

BENEFIT OF THE HALL FUND.

F. B. & F. Co., Printers, Hyannis.

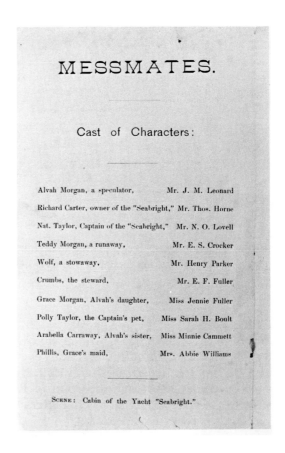

MESSMATES.

Cast of Characters:

Alvah Morgan, a speculator,	Mr. J. M. Leonard
Richard Carter, owner of the "Seabright,"	Mr. Thos. Horne
Nat. Taylor, Captain of the "Seabright,"	Mr. N. O. Lovell
Teddy Morgan, a runaway,	Mr. E. S. Crocker
Wolf, a stowaway,	Mr. Henry Parker
Crumbs, the steward,	Mr. E. F. Fuller
Grace Morgan, Alvah's daughter,	Miss Jennie Fuller
Polly Taylor, the Captain's pet,	Miss Sarah H. Boult
Arabella Carraway, Alvah's sister,	Miss Minnie Cammett
Phillis, Grace's maid,	Mrs. Abbie Williams

SCENE: Cabin of the Yacht "Seabright."

Mr. Nelson O. Lovell; Aids: Mr. G. Webster Hallett, Mr. Ariel Tallman, Mr. J. Milton Leonard. Supper will be served in lower hall. Proceeds for reduction of debt on Hall.

May 5, 1902

The annual May ball given by the Ladies of the Union Hall Improvement Society, Thursday evening, May 1st, was a complete success, both socially and financially. The unexcelled music rendered by the celebrated Ferguson Orchestra of Bridgewater was greatly enjoyed and appreciated by the many spectators and more than select party. The grand march, escorted by the manager, Mrs. J. Allen Lovell, followed by her six aids — Mrs. M.G. Crocker, Mrs. George Williams, Mrs. Charles Hall, Miss Edna Crosby, Mrs. J. M. Leonard, Mrs. Wilton Crosby — was much complimented, being something entirely new and original. All were gowned in sweet, fairy-like costumes, carrying wands and forming figures which were very attractive. The supper was enjoyed by all, being the most appetizing of any that this Society has ever served. How soon may we look forward to another of the same kind?

December 21, 1903

There promises to be a large attendance at the grand Christmas Ball in Union Hall on Friday evening when the Osterville Orchestra of 8 pieces will furnish music. Mr. Harry Tallman, assisted by Messrs. Robert Daniel, Ernest DeWitt, Ralph Crosby and Walter Fuller, will manage the floor.

January 25, 1904

A grand Leap Year Ball will be given by the U.H.I.S. in Union Hall, Osterville, Friday evening, Feb. 12th. Music by Crosby's Orchestra. Manager, Mrs. Daniel Crosby; aids, Miss Frances Lovell, Miss Esther Crocker, Miss Georgie Daniel, Miss Addie Bearse, Miss Blanche Lovell. Dance tickets, 50 cents; supper tickets — 35 cents; spectator tickets, 15 cents. Grand March, 8:30.

August 8, 1904

A hurdy-gurdy party will be given in Union Hall on Wednesday evening.

May 22, 1905

There will be a grand ball in Union Hall on Tuesday evening, May 30th, at which Nickerson's Orchestra of five pieces, will furnish the music. Mr. Nelson O. Lovell will be the manager.

November 13, 1905

There will be a meeting in Union Hall at 7:45 o'clock P.M., Thursday evening, November 16, 1905, for the purpose of forming a Village Improvement Society. All ages will agree that such a society has a large and broad mission in our community, and only with the united effort on the part of all can the best results be attained. It is earnestly hoped that this meeting will be largely attended by both old and young, ladies and gentlemen.

November 20, 1905

Thursday evening a meeting was held in Union Hall and a Village Improvement Society organized.

November 27, 1905

A meeting of the Directors of the Osterville Improvement Society was held on Thursday evening, and plans and methods were discussed as to the best means of obtaining results for helping the appearance of the village. A committee was chosen to solicit members, and it is hoped that every man, woman, and child called upon will join, and so contribute towards the funds. Entertainments will be given during the winter, and all contributions will be most gladly received by the Treasurer, Mr. H. S. Parker.

July 10, 1906
Village Improvement Society

The Osterville Village Improvement Society, that was organized last winter, is in a flourishing condition and the results of its good work are manifest in many directions.

The old hay scales, that have been an eyesore for so many years, have become a thing of beauty. Several of our squares have been graded and set with trees and shrubs, but above all the general interest taken by nearly all our citizens to do what they feel able to in the way of improving and keeping their home grounds neat is to be commended in the highest terms.

The first visit to judge the places for the prize offered by Mr. Forster for the best kept places in Osterville was made last week. There will be several other visits during the summer and points will be kept of all places which come up to a certain standard. These points are divided into five parts: 1st, the front yard; 2nd, the rear yard; 3rd, the walks; 4th, the gardens; 5th, general. Under each head there are twenty points, making a hundred points to each visit. The places getting the highest number of points win the prizes.

Remember it is just as important to have a well kept yard as it is a well kept house and many more people see and criticise it.

Whatever you do outside will not only make you happier but will also make your place an attractive element in what we hope will be one of the prettiest villages on the Cape. Let all, whether they care to enter the contest or not, get into the spirit of home improvement.

In judging the places no energy will be spared to make a fair distribution of the prizes. It is the desire of Mr. Adams that you shall not have the opportunity to criticise his work, and he will do everything in his power to make it impossible.

February 6, 1906

The Whist Party and Cake Walk under the auspices of the Osterville Improvement Society, in Union Hall, Thursday evening, was pronounced a success by those attending.

Masquerade Ball

February 19, 1907

It was the general opinion of all who witnessed the Masquerade ball, given by the O.V.I.S. in Union Hall, on the evening of Feb. 8th, that not since our hall was dedicated has it shown such an array of beauty, color, lights and costumes.

Although the weather in the morning was threatening, the night proved both fair and mild, and at an early hour could be seen on the streets many queer objects, all wending their way toward the scene of attraction.

The hall was appropriately trimmed for the occasion, the huge order of dances on the wall suspended by a merry couple in a dancing figure.

The music was furnished by Ferguson's Orchestra and the concert at eight o'clock was very much enjoyed, both by dancers and the many spectators on the stage. At 8:30 o'clock the march was formed, led by Mr. N. Hastings Allen, as knight in armour, and Miss Minnie I. Cammett, as queen of the garden.

The circle was large and all entered into the spirit of the music, making it a merry party. The costumes were exceptionally pretty, and some very unique ones as well, among them being Miss Molly Bearse and Miss Ruth Barnet, as seven footers.

Miss Myrtle Crosby — dwarf
Miss Sarah Boult — Dutch girl
Miss Mary Norton — maid
Miss Margaret Daniel — sailor maid
Miss Marcia Hallett — morning star
Miss Christine West — night
Miss Zora Coffin — old fashion costume
Miss Genieve Leonard — sunflower
Miss Angeline Childs — peasant girl
Miss Marjerie Leonard — red riding hood
Miss Maud Baker — red riding hood
Misses Hannah Whelden and Lillie Baker — twin babies
Miss Christie Ames — old fashion girl
Mrs. Ivy Leonard — apple Mary, a figure of New York
Mrs. Horace Parker — four-leaf clover
Mrs. Marjorie Suthergreen — peasant

Mrs. Blanche Daniel — Samantha
Mrs. Anna Small — queen of hearts
Mrs. Hattie Crosby — Automobilist
Mrs. Margaret Swift — cards
Mr. Henry Parker — dude coon
Mr. Harry Tallman — Turk
Mr. Elliott Crosby — sailor lad
Mr. Joe Tallman — happy Hooligan
Messrs. Shirley Evans and Harold Crosby — clowns
Mr. Chester Baker — Jew
Mr. Dexter Williams — Chinaman
Messrs. Jack Driscoll and Arnold Bearse — ghosts
Messrs. Abbott Robbins and Bob Daniel — twins
Mr. Henry Leonard — black domino
Mr. Wilber Jones — fancy costume
Mr. Earl DeWitt — old man

A supper of salads, cold meats, cake and coffee was served at intermission in the lower hall. At the hour of two the party broke up, each one feeling ten years younger in spirit, and that it was an evening well spent. A handsome sum was realized for the O.V.I.S.

April 30, 1907

Don't fail to attend the phonograph concert in Union Hall tomorrow evening and hear, not only the best, but some of the latest records. It will be a first class entertainment. Remember it is given for the benefit of Mr. Taylor who has been sick for a long time. Come one, come all, and lend a helping hand.

August 27, 1907

Marie Grosse, the celebrated dancer, will appear in Union Hall on the evening of Labor Day, next Monday. Madame Grosse's hurdy gurdy parties are as usual — attractive and on a holiday should draw a large crowd.

January 13, 1908

The Village Improvement Society Officers:
President, Walter I. Fuller
Vice President, Owen B. Lewis
Treasurer, Mrs. E.M.(Edith) Crosby
Secretary, Stephen Ferguson
Board of Directors: Mrs. Ariel H. Tallman, Abbott L. Robbins, Miss Molly H. Bearse, Walter S. Scudder, Rev. E. McP. Ames, Chester A. Crocker, Charles Daniel, F.W. Parsons, Henry P. Leonard, Stephen H. Bates.

January 20, 1908

Union Hall Association President J. Milton Leonard; Vice President, Mrs. E.M. (Edith) Crosby; Clerk, Abbott L. Robbins; Treasurer, Henry M. Parker.

January 27, 1908

At the meeting of the Village Improvement Society, Wednesday evening, which met with Mr. Owen B. Lewis, nine directors were present. Mrs. William D. Kinney and Mrs. Freeman Adams were elected directors in place of Mr. Stephen Bates and Mr. J. Milton Leonard, who resigned.

February 10, 1908

Village Improvement Society met. Their main topic of discussion was concerning the lighting of our streets.

February 17, 1908

Village Improvement Society met; they voted to procure new street lights.

March 23, 1908

Village Improvement Society gave an entertainment in Union Hall. Potato Race: Donald Coffin and Carroll Crosby. Donald won. Pie Contest: Walcott Ames and Edwin Lagergren. Walcott came out ahead.

March 23, 1908 — Masquerade Party

Quite the most attractive dancing party of the season in Osterville was the masquerade given under the auspices of the Osterville Village Improvement Society, an organization whose membership includes many of the first ladies of the village, at Union Hall, Friday evening, March thirteenth.

Mrs. Daniel Crosby was mistress of ceremonies and was ably assisted by the aids, Messrs. Maurice G. Crocker and Ernest DeWitt. Mrs. Crosby was most beautifully gowned in white lace and silver gauze over pink taffeta and wore silver ornaments in her hair.

A concert preceded the dancing given by Fogg's orchestra of Rockland, and at eight-thirty the grand march was formed and it was an interesting spectacle with its representations of different nationalities and periods.

Mrs. Nathaniel Hastings Allen and Mr. Azor D. Hall led, and about twenty-five couples were in costume. Mrs. Allen was dressed in the period of '75, and in every detail, black silk dress, large bonnet with lace veil and small black silk parasol, was the dame to the very life. Mrs. Walter Fuller was in a similar costume, and was a sweet picture of the olden days. It would be hard to say who would have captured the prizes had there been any awarded. One of the most unique and fetching, was the costume worn by Mrs. Harry Tallman, a carnival costume of white, trimmed in gilt sequins and black silk diamonds appliqued in a striking design. Miss Mabel Evans surely looked the part of the "Gypsy Queen" in her oriental dress of red and yellow, and her many rare old jewels were much admired. Mrs. Kinney was very chic in her riding costume, and Miss Maud Baker looked unusually pretty in a white gown appliqued in shamrocks. Mrs. Horace Parker was an excellent clown, and Miss Belle Williams, as "Red Riding Hood" and Miss Alice Jey as "Morning" were prettily dressed.

Among the gentlemen were many unique costumes, the cleverest being the three teddy bears, whose make-ups and antics greatly amused the on-lookers. They were represented by Messrs. Fred Dill, Jack Driscoll and William Baker. Mr. Harry Tallman was a capital hobo and one could almost imagine him having tramped the length of the Cape. Mr. Walter Fuller was also a tramp and a very good one. Mr. William Bearse was surely a slick darkey in his suit of black with yellow satin waistcoat and yellow hat, a most correct costume for the cakewalk. Mr. Nathanial H. Allen and Mr. Azor D. Hall wore Dominos. Mr. Chester Baker dressed as a Turk. Mr. Edward Crocker was most realistic as Bridget, and was quite a revelation to all upon unmasking.

Supper was served at intermission and a bountiful supply of good things awaited the dancers.

June 1, 1908

Village Improvement Society met to consider the advisability of placing fire extinguishers in one or more places in town.

June 29, 1908

A hurdy-gurdy party was held in Union Hall Friday evening.

November 16, 1908

Report of the President of the Osterville Village Improvement Society: In compliance with the provision of Article 6 of our constitution, I wish to submit the following report of the year's work.

First, I wish to thank my associates, the board of directors, for their faithful attendance and harmonious cooperation in all our work.

During the year we have added five street lights to those already located. Sign boards showing the names of the principle streets have been placed on lamp posts and buildings. A new grass plot has been made in the western part of the village and shrubs planted. Main Street has been kept clean through the village and the weeds and rubbish removed. Through the cooperation of householders and property owners, eighteen fire extinguishers have been placed in residences throughout the village, and it is hoped that as many more will be added in the near future. That these extinguishers do very effective work was practically demonstrated at two fires during the past year, and the directors should be commended for having made this protection possible.

In making these expenditures, we have endeavored to practice wise economy, and while we have drawn heavily from our treasury, we have been able, through our own efforts and donations from interested friends, to refund a large proportion of the money drawn out, as the report of the treasurer will show.

The cooperation of the whole village in making this, in reality, a society of improvement, is very noticeable throughout our whole community. Lawns are better-kept, houses are being painted, and a general air of improvement is apparent.

Respectfully submitted,
Walter I. Fuller

December 14, 1908

At a meeting of the Village Improvement Society, Mr. Abbott L. Robbins, Mr. Azor Hall, and Mr. W. Scott Scudder have been appointed general managers in the fire department.

January 18, 1909

The Union Hall Association elected the following officers:

President — J. Milton Leonard
Vice President — Mrs. Edith M. Crosby
Clerk — Abbott L. Robbins
Treasurer — James A. Lovell
Trustees: Nathaniel H. Allen, G. Webster Hallett and Charles E. Lewis

---

February 22, 1909

There will be a Washington's Birthday Ball in Union Hall this evening.

July 19, 1910

The Village Improvement Society appreciates the gift of ten dollars from Mr. Alfred Jones.

November 22, 1910

Officers elected for the Village Improvement Society for the ensuing year: President, Mr. Abbott L. Robbins; Vice President, Mr. Walter Scott Scudder; Secretary, Miss Olivia Phinney; Treasurer, Mrs. Henry Foster Lewis; and the Board of Directors: Mrs. Nathaniel H. Allen, Mr. Ralph Crosby, Miss Gertrude Nanson, Mrs. Everett F. Fuller, Mr. James Horne, Rev. E. McP. Ames, Mr. J. Milton Leonard, Mr. Andrew Johnson, Mr. Walter I. Fuller.

November 15, 1910

The amount in the Village Improvement Society treasury as of this date is $154.18.

January 17, 1911

The annual meeting of the Union Hall Association was held last Tuesday evening. The following officers were elected: President, J. Milton Leonard; Vice President, Mrs. Edith M. Crosby; Clerk, Mr. Abbott L. Robbins; Treasurer, Mr. James A. Lovell. Mrs. Samuel N. Ames was elected trustee for a three year Term.

January 17, 1911

The Musical Ravens presented an evening of entertainment at Union Hall on Thursday evening.

April 25, 1911

A special meeting of the stockholders of Union Hall Association met Wednesday night to consider the lighting of the hall. It was voted to light by acetylene gas, and Mr. G. Webster Hallett has the job of installing same.

January 30, 1912

The local entertainment, given by the Osterville Village Improvement Society last Wednesday evening, was certainly up to their standard and apparently well received by the audience. Where all performed very creditably, it is needless to particularize, but anyone who listened to the program could not fail to speak in glowing terms of the mixed quartette composed of Annie Crosby, Hester Bell, Wilson Scudder and Verna Childs.

These young artists were recalled several times and delighted the audience with their fine singing.

Mr. Arthur Wyman as a violin soloist is without doubt unexcelled on Cape Cod; at least his performance at this concert proved his ability.

March 4, 1913

The most brilliant event of the season was the Grand Ball, held in Union Hall February 21st under the management of the Messrs. Harold Crosby, Joseph W. Tallman, Jr., Bernard Ames, Norman Williams, and Harvey Hallett.

At nine o'clock the grand march was formed and led by Mrs. George Williams and Norman Williams.

An excellent supper was served at intermission. The new piano just purchased for the hall, which arrived the day before the ball, gave great pleasure.

January 19, 1914

The annual meeting of the Osterville Village Improvement Society was recently held at the home of Mrs. H. Foster Lewis, when the following officers were appointed: President, A. L. Robbins; Vice President, W. I. Fuller; Secretary, Miss Olivia M. Phinney; Treasurer, Mrs. Cora A. Lewis. Directors: S. H. Bates, Mrs. S. Frank Braley, Mrs. Frank Boult, Mrs. Minnie Allen, J. W. Tallman, W. S. Scudder, J. M. Leonard, and Mrs. Charles M. Crosby.

April 27, 1914

A very pretty masquerade party was held at Union Hall on Friday evening last. The affair was private and was given by some of our local young men under the leadership of Mr. Merton Bates. Music was provided by Wyman's orchestra in the usual able manner. At intermission refreshments of cake and orangeade were served.

The following is a list of those present in costume:

Harold Crosby — clown
Henry Whiteley — Frenchman
Carroll Crosby — clown
Isabel Lewis — clown
Jessie Boult — clown
George Berry — milkmaid
Hazel Thurber — Italian peasant
Hazel Ames — Pocahontas
Dorothy Berry — Japanese lady
Marie Adams — Red Riding Hood
Josephine Crosby — tennis girl
Merton Bates — bathing girl
Wilton Crosby — Turk
Wilson Scudder — Santa Claus
Marion Goodspeed — American girl
Sarah Alley — Italian peasant
Emily Crosby — Spanish lady
Elliott Lewis — Irish horrible
Blanche Swift — housemaid

February 22, 1915

The "Agreeable Eight" are planning a masquerade party for the near future. To comply with the law, invitations have been sent out, and anyone who wishes to attend masked and has not received an invitation can obtain the same by notifying Mrs. H. P. Leonard, or any member of the Agreeables.

March 15, 1915

The much talked of masquerade ball, given by the Agreeable Eight, occurred last Friday evening in Union Hall. This originally was intended as simply a local affair to afford a social evening, but so popular did it become that it was really a very pronounced society affair.

There were some three hundred persons in attendance, nearly all in costume and en masque, including many from surrounding villages, Hyannis being especially well-represented.

The grand march was led by the Agreeable Eight and their husbands as follows: Mr. and Mrs. Ralph W. Crosby, Mr. and Mrs. Walter I. Fuller, Mr. and Mrs. Henry P. Leonard, Mr. and Mrs. Horace S. Parker, Dr. and Mrs. William D. Kinney, Mr. and Mrs. Harry Tallman, Mr. and Mrs. Everett F. Fuller, and Mr. and Mrs. Ariel Tallman. These were costumed as clowns, and to say that the assembly presented a very varied appearance is to put it mildly. Many of the costumes were exceedingly handsome, and the party is one long to be remembered.

May 31, 1915

The Annual Meeting of the Osterville Village Improvement Society was held at the Baptist vestry on Monday evening. The following officers and directors were elected:

President: A. L. Robbins

Vice President: Walter I. Fuller

Sec. and Treas.: to be filled by Board of directors

Directors: Mrs. Frank Braley, Miss Gertrude Nanson, William P. Hodges, Mrs. Minnie Allen, W. Scott Scudder, Albert Hinckley, J. Milton Leonard, Mrs. Edith M. Crosby, Rev. Charles H. Cook, Rev. D. B. Nelson.

The following committees were chosen: Committee to solicit new members: Miss Gertrude Nanson, Rev. D. B. Nelson. Seventeen new members were added at the meeting.

Committee on housing of fire engine — Rev. Charles H. Cook, Walter I. Fuller, Harris Lovell.

Upon the suggestion of Mr. J. Milton Leonard, who was a former committee of one on this matter, it was voted that the present committee look into the matter of having accommodations made in the new school building when completed to house the fire engine.

Committee to confer with selectmen in regards to cleaning up cemetery — A. L. Robbins, Walter I. Fuller.

Committee on street lights — Rev. D. B. Nelson, Mrs. Edith M. Crosby, Charles M. Jones.

Anyone who has a street light out of repair, or who does not care for the light to be in front of their house enough to light it, please notify anyone of the committee.

Committee on grass plots and shrubbery — W. Scott Scudder, Walter I. Fuller.

Committee for clean-up day was called for by the chair to be filled by volunteers and nearly all present responded.

The Boy Scouts volunteered to help in this work and as far as the correspondent knows Saturday, May 29, was the day named. Let us all help to make our village cleaner by at least keeping our own yard and in front of it as clean as possible. To sum up the whole meeting — with cash on hand of about $33 clear of all bills, a good board of directors, backed up as it seemed to be by an enthusiastic body of village people, it seems that the O.V.I.S. is starting on the most efficient year of its existence. When the next annual meeting is held we hope that the president will not have to report as he did this year "little work done through lack of interest," but rather shall his report be, "much work done, interest keen and still growing." Let's get together and pull together to make our village the "village beautiful" so we can always say with pride, "I live in Osterville, second to none on the Cape for its general appearance, and the public spiritedness of its people."

W. P. Hodges, Secretary protem

August 13, 1917

Union Hall has been wired for electric lights by Mr. Herbert L. Hinckley.

August 27, 1917

The colored dance in Union Hall on Thursday evening was well-patronized. Officer Chester L. Baker was in attendance and saw that good order was maintained.

September 17, 1917

There was another colored dance in Union Hall Friday evening.

January 14, 1918

The stockholders of Union Hall held their annual meeting last Tuesday evening and with the exception of treasurer re-elected the old board of officers to serve anothe year. Mr. J. Milton Leonard was chosen treasurer.

Masquerade Ball

February 16, 1920

Strange and unfamiliar forms flitted through our quiet streets on Tuesday evening, February 3, wending their way steathly, or openly defying recognition in their various disguises, their objective being the grand annual masquerade ball held in Union Hall.

The building was ablaze of light. The decorations consisted of red, white and blue festooned about the hall in a very pretty arrangement by Mrs. Lillie Parker and Mrs. Ivy Leonard, who are most artistic on interior decorating. Fogg's orchestra of Brockton furnished the music and too much cannot be said in praise of it. Delightful selections, splendid time, and of quality which did not tire, and they were generous with their encores. The dancers couldn't seem to get enough, and everyone enjoyed themselves hugely.

There were some very pretty and most amusing characters, but lack of space forbids mention of all. A fine concert preceded the grand march which was led by Harold Crosby and Mrs. Myrtle Black, after which dancing continued until intermission, when a fine supper of cold meats, delicious salads, cake and coffee were served in the basement by a corps of waiters.

The affair was under the management of the ladies of the U.H.I.S. which is a guarantee of its success.

The committees on arrangements were as follows:

Supper: Mrs. Edith Crosby, Mrs. Addie Coffin, Mrs. Nancy Childs, Mrs. Mathilde Adams.

Invitations: Mrs. Ella Lovell.

Decorations: Mrs. Lillie Parker, Mrs. Ivy Leonard.

Floor Manager: Harold Crosby.

About $250 was taken in at the box office which will net a goodly sum to the Hall Circle.

List of those in costume:

Arthur Wyman — kid
Fred Nute — dude
Olive Scudder — domestic science
Violet Oates — child
Vivian Sherman — Grecian
George Burlingame — colored
Beatrice Burlingame — Liberty
Myrtle Black — tourist
Maurice Allen — sailor
Eleanor Taylor and Annie Nute — twins
Stuart Scudder and Mrs. Stuart Scudder — riding teacher
Mansfield Crocker — dude
Isabelle Lewis - dairy maid
Mrs. Byron Tevyaw — Camp Fire girl
Roger Higgins — sailor
Raymond Pierce — farmer
Lillian Tevyaw — Japanese
Ernest Jones — Indian
Lillian Pinson — Indian
Parker Leonard — bedtime
Wilson Scudder — colored
Claire Parker — clown
Agatha Crocker — clown

Edna Marchant — Red Riding Hood
William Crosby — Scottish
Mrs. Elliott Crosby — knight
Alice Coleman — old fashioned girl
Mrs. Roscoe Hinckley — ghost
Mr. and Mrs. Chester Huggins — ghosts
Charlotte Boult — fashion
Irving Coleman — chef
Albert Williams — sailor
Grace Crocker — BoPeep
Arthur Coleman — Happy Hooligan
Joseph Swift — sailor
Mrs. Joseph Swift — Red Cross nurse
Roscoe Hinckley — Uncle Sam
Ellen Hansberry — Japanese
Josephine Cross — Japanese
Everett Small — hobo
Dora Braley — Spanish lady
Harold Crosby — bedtime
Gertrude Bacon — clown
Elise Parker — clown
Norman Crosby — band leader
Lucy Sawyer — Red Cross
Elliott Crosby — clown
Annie Nickerson — old fashioned girl
Shirley Evans — dude

Masquerade Ball

April 4, 1921

About 300 people responded to the invitations to the masquerade ball which was held in Union Hall on Tuesday evening.

The music was furnished by Riordon's Orchestra of Brockton, this being the first appearance in Osterville of this famous orchestra. Everyone present enjoyed the privilege of hearing it.

Mr. Harold Crosby was floor manager and B. D. Leonard and Joseph Tallman, Jr., were aids.

The grand march formed at 8:30. The leaders were Mr. and Mrs. J. W. Tallman, Jr., Hawaiians; next in line were Mr. Burleigh Leonard, as Oh-how-wise; Mrs. Burleigh Leonard, queen of hearts; Miss Winifred Campbell, Japanese; Maurice Allen, I. B. Smart; Mansfield Crocker, dude; Miss Charlotte Boult, Spanish maiden; Walcott Ames, clown; Mrs. Stuart Scudder, flower girl; Mr. Stuart Scudder, ghost; Fred Nute and Miss Vivian Sherman, continentals; Miss Josephine Cross, shamrock; Hallett Gardner, Huck Finn; Elise Gardner, Becky Sawyer; Virginia Fuller and Imogene Leonard, popcorn twins; Polly Lewis, Irish lad; Hope Adams, Irish lassie; Mr. Abbott Robbins, English count; Mrs. Minnie Allen, winter garden girl; Maxine Peak, night and day; Phyllis Peak, clown; Genieve Bearse, gypsy; Nason Lewis and Richard Cross, maids; Merton Bates, the red lady; Mrs. Lillie Parker, colonial dame; Miss Edna Suthergreen, chorus girl; Leo Lewis, sailor boy; Miss Marion

McKinnon, French maid; Rachel Daniel and Ethel Parker, colonials; Eleanor Cross, fairy; Mr. and Mrs. Jordan, Clara Mayall, Gene Baker, Irving Coleman and Mrs. Gladys Whitney, clowns.

A supper of cold meat, salad, cake and coffee was served at 11 o'clock by the ladies of the Ball Circle, and a goodly sum was realized for the hall.

December 19, 1921

A meeting was held in the library Wednesday evening to make arrangements for a village Christmas tree. It was voted to have the tree on Christmas eve, Saturday, Dec. 24th, at Union Hall, 7:30 o'clock. The following officers were elected:

Chairman — Mrs. Maurice Crocker
Secretary-Treasurer — Mrs. Alice Coombs
Committee to hire hall — Mrs. Maurice Crocker
To produce tree — George Lewis and sons
Decorate tree — Mrs. Oliver Coffin, Mrs. Ralph Williams, Mrs. Elliott Crosby, Mrs. A. L. Robbins
Cut presents — Walcott Ames, Walter Fuller, Harry Tallman, Ralph Crosby, Mansfield Crocker, George Williams
Call presents — Harris Lovell, J. M. Leonard
Distributing — Charlotte Boult, Jessie Lewis, Grace Crocker, Lillian Tevyaw, Elsie Chadwick, Annie Nute, Eleanor Taylor
Program Committee — Mrs. Max Crosby, Mrs. Jesse Murray, Mrs. Robert Daniel
Put up tree — Norman Williams, Willis Crocker, William Whiteley
Master of Ceremonies — W. P. Hodges

April 24, 1922

A ministral Show that can pull off a two-evening entertainment is surely some ''show'', and those who witnessed last week's performances know that it was a good show and then some. Osterville is rarely blessed in having a ''circle'' comprising such good voices. When this circle is assisted by the products of nearby villages and is backed by Osterville's own Crosby orchestra, it simply leaves nothing to be desired. The costumes also were worthy the occasion. The program shows at a glance what a fine list of numbers was presented, and when the ''aggregation'' was hailed into business by Everett Small and his horn, and kept moving by Interlocutor Victor Adams, and the jokes were some of Osterville's best, the affair is known to have been of the A1 sort. The songs, too, were of the catchy kind. We know of more than one of the audience who has been humming snatches of them ever since. The second part of the program included a solo by Mr. Stevens, who always likes to lend a helping hand, or voice, we should have said. A dance by Miss Harrison of

Hyannis, who is an artist in her line of fancy dancing and shimmying, is a delight to the eye. The program follows:

PART I

Opening chorus
Dapper Dan — Verner Childs
Plantation Lullaby — Walter I. Fuller
Witch Hazel — Ralph Williams
My Sunny Tennessee — Geo. Silva, assisted by B. D. Leonard
Old Fashioned Girl — Norman Williams
I Want My Mammy — Stuart Scudder
I Ain't Got Enough to Pass Around — Wilson Scudder
Tucky Home — John Hanlon
I Ain't Nobody's Darling — E. S. Crocker

PART II

Duet, cornet and trombone — Wilson Scudder, Bertram Ryder
Dancing — Miss Harrison, Hyannis
Solo — Henry A. Stevens, Hyannis
Trio — Scudder Brothers

December 18, 1922

A meeting was held in the library Thursday evening to make arrangements for a village Christmas tree. Officers elected: Chairman — Mrs. Edith M. Crosby, Secretary — Katherine E. Hinckley. Voted to have the tree at the hall on Saturday evening Dec. 23rd at 7 o'clock. Committees:

Procure hall — Katherine E. Hinckley
Procure tree — George Lewis and Mr. Duffin
Decorate tree — Mrs. Fanny Robbins, Mrs. Addie Coffin, Charlotte Boult, Ethel Parker, Grace Crocker, Jessie Lewis.
Call off — J. M. Leonard and Harry Lovell
Cut off — Walter Fuller, Everett Fuller, Harry Tallman, Leonard Tallman
Master of Ceremonies — Wm. P. Hodges
Program — Mrs. Mary Crocker, Mrs. Blanche Daniel, Mrs. Max Crosby, Mrs. Jesse Murray
Put up tree — Norman Williams, Mr. Duffin, Willis Crocker
Disposing of tree — George Lewis
Distribute presents — Charlotte Boult, Ethel Parker, Jessie Lewis, Grace Crocker, Elsie Chadwich, Lillian Tevyaw, Dorothy Cahoon

---

January 27, 1927

The entertainment in Union Hall Friday night under the auspices of the Community Men's Club was largely attended. The program consisted of George Warwick, noted humorist and chalk artist of Boston, who delighted his audience with his skill. Mr. Warwick uses the same easel that he carried with him to the battle line in the World War, where he entertained the boys with his unusual talent. After seeing and hearing him, we have no doubt that Mr. Warwick did his bit in upholding the morale of our boys. He was assisted in the program by a quartette of young men, Dr. Chute, Stuart Scudder, Walter I. Fuller and Fred Scudder of Hyannis, who rendered several selections which were greatly enjoyed. Sverre Bjerke gave a piano accordian solo and responded most kindly to several encores. Mr. Bjerke improves at his every appearance on the stage and is striving hard to master the instrument of which he is very fond. Thomas Milne, who was chairman of the committee, extends thanks to J. M. Leonard who very kindly stepped into the breach made by the tardy arrival of the quartette and helped entertain the crowd with his apologies and remarks. Milton is a good sport and is always ready to fill in, no matter what the requirements are.

May 17, 1928

All roads led to Union Hall on the evening of May 11 when the Union Hall Improvement Society gave their 30th anniversary May ball, which is always looked forward to with much interest. Mrs. Minnie Allen acted as general manager, assisted by the ladies of the Society who proved fully equal to the occasion. A delightful party resulted. Chet Copp's orchestra furnished excellent music. A comfortable crowd was in attendance. Nothing occurred to mar the serenity of the occasion and everybody seemed to enjoy themselves. At intermission all repaired to the basement where refreshments of cake and ice cream were served. The tables were prettily decorated with flowers and favors. Fancy caps were presented to each guest. The prize waltz was won by Miss Eleanor Cross who was most charming in yellow tulle and silver slippers. Terry Rogers of Hyannis was her dancing partner. The grace of Miss Polly Lewis and Homer Sears took the foxtrot prize. Miss Lewis' vivid beauty was enhanced by a red tulle gown and silver slippers.

February 27, 1930

The Masquerade Ball which was held in Union Hall, Feb. 21, was largely attended. Chet Copp's orchestra furnished music. Supper was served in the basement consisting of cold meats, salads, cake and coffee. The hall was decorated in red, white and blue crepe paper very attractively under the direction of Miss Rachel Daniel, a student of Arts and Crafts School in Boston. The Grand March was led by Oscar Lagergren and Frances Sprague in Spanish costume of black and orange. The handsomest costumes were said to be those worn by Mr. and Mrs. Albert T. Chase of West Yarmouth, who represented George and Martha Washington in colonial costume. Mrs. Robert Daniel was chairman of the committee, assisted by Mrs. Ella Lovell

and others. Mrs. Edith Crosby had charge of the supper. The prizes for best costumes were awarded Mr. Lagergren and Miss Sprague.

Osterville Union Hall
by Sarah Hallett Boult, (1863-1960)

The very earliest years of our Hall were its balmy days; built on Hall Hill as a central gathering place for the first small group of families known as "Lovell's Neighborhood," it was primarily and prominently the "Meeting House" in the days when "Uncle Zack" shocked the community by walking out of meeting, for at that time everybody worshipped together.

In 1803, the hall became "School House" as well, until 1826.

Soon a group organized as Baptists, then another group as Methodists, also a group as Universalists, all holding their separate "services" under the one roof, until, during the 1830s the Baptists built a church for themselves. Then in the 1840s the Methodists withdrew and built their church, leaving the Universalists alone.

By 1850, a Social Center was needed, for the settlement had become a village, having its name on a map. Accordingly, the pews were removed to make room for parties, exhibitions, and even dances.

As needed, repairs and alterations were made to keep up with growth of the village, because now it was apparently becoming a real summer resort.

By 1890, signs of age and overwork were plainly seen, and something new was strictly due and was done.

The entire village joined in the new "Hall" idea, so there was much discussion as to ways and places, ending with the same old hill as most central and, best of all, without price or ownership. A committee of supervisors was chosen, and the present plan accepted for the larger building to cover the old foundation.

The old hall, so long associated with every important event, was regretfully removed, and building begun on the new one. All the builders helped build and everyone else helped as best they could with shares being valued at $5.00 each.

Dedicated as "Union Hall" in 1897, having a basement, "supper room," and kitchen, a roomy and well-planned stage, there was never a year without local "minstrels," concerts, or amateur plays with appropriate lights and scenery, and right now I could recall a dozen familiar names of our local "actors" as good as many of the prominent "Stars of the Screen" today.

After 40 busy years, the small group of caretakers were glad to relinquish the Hall to the Horticultural Society, who made good use of it up to and through World War II, after which they transferred it to the present owner, the Osterville Veterans Association.

History of Osterville Schools

East District School, West District School,
School, Dry Swamp Academy,
Elementary School on West Bay Road

An Extract from the Town of Barnstable Records, Book 4th, Page 67

Article 13th in the warrant: To know if the Town will allow the 11th School District to dispose of the Old School House for their use as a new one is built in said district as appears by the request of more than ten freeholders. Dated this first of March, 1804.

in Town Meeting, March 6th, 1804.

Article 13th: Voted that the 11th School District have Liberty to sell the Old School House in said District, Provided they allow the town school to be kept in the new building (without any expence or rent) which was lately erected for that purpose.

Adjourned to 2 of April.
Book 4th, Page 70

Of Barnstable, An extract of Po
5th Vollum Page 226
March 13, 1826   In the Warrant:
Article 18th: To know if the Town will cause the 13th School District in said Town, to be Divided. Also Liberty to Sell the School House in the said district, agreeable to request.

A committee chosen:
Nymphas Marston
viz: Chipman Hinckley
Eliza Crocker

The committee reported leave to divide said district.

Report of Committee Respecting 13th School District

The committee chosen to examine into the expediency of dividing the thirteenth School District (being the Osterville District) report that the number of scholars in that district is too great to be conveniently or usefully instructed in one school and that the inhabitants are nearly if not quite unanimous in wishing a division and this committee are therefore of opinion that it is advisable to divide said district and that line of division should be as follows. Beginning at the south line of the twelfth school district thence running south to the gate on the west side of Samuel Crosby's farm thence running through his farm as the road runs (passing to the east of his house) and so on. The road runs through the farm of Benjamin Hallett (passing to the east of his house) till it come to the highway near Charles Boult's house then crossing the highway leaving said Boult house on the east side of the line and running as the road runs by the east end of Zacheus Howland's house and so on as the road around his land till it comes to the gate which is across the road leading to Desire Parker's and thence from said gate running in or on south southwest course till it comes to the Sound. This line will divide this district into two parts as nearly equal as is necessary and as the committee have reason to believe will be satisfactory to the inhabitants thereof.

Town of Barnstable
Nov. 6, 1826
Chipman Hinckley

Osterville, January 21, 1843

Agreeable to notice being given in the 13th and 19th school district of Barnstable (both in the village of Osterville) for the voters to meet at 6 o'clock P.M. in the west school house (so called) to take into consideration the laying out of a burying (ground) back of the Baptist Meetinghouse, or of enlarging fencing to the old burying ground, and act thereon; many of the voters agreeable to the notice assembled on the above date. Capt. George Lovell called the meeting to order.

Voted and chose George Lovell, moderator and James N. Lovell, secretary.

After talking the subject over, it was motioned and voted to enlarge the old burying ground. That we draw a request to the Town of Barnstable to be inserted in the warrant for the approaching town meeting, to be held in February, for the town to enlarge the burying ground, to right the gravestones, sod the graves, clear the bushes, and to fence the whole in a proper manner, and all present to sign the request, and it was signed by George Lovell and 32 others.

Voted that we choose a committee of five to survey the ground and allot a portion of the same to each family and reserve sufficient for strangers as they may deem expedient.

Voted and chose a nominating committee to select the above committee, consisting of Isaac Scudder, George Lovell, and Josiah Scudder.

Voted to add one more to the locating committee which makes six; the nominating committee reported the following, viz., David Fuller, Isaac Hodges, George Lovell, Samuel A. Wiley, Lot Hinckley, Robert Lovell.

Voted to accept the report of the Committee, and they were severally voted in.

Voted that when this meeting adjourns, it adjourns to meet, when the location committee notifies them to meet, to hear their report.

Voted that the clerk see that the request is sent to the Selectmen to be inserted in the Town Warrant.

Voted to adjourn.

Attest: James N. Lovell
BARNSTABLE

Osterville, March 15, 1845

Agreeable to a notice given by George Lovell, and David Fuller, for a call for the voting of the 13th and 19th School Districts of Barnstable in Osterville to meet the above date in the Old Meeting House to take into consideration the uniting of the two School Districts. Accordingly, several met.

George Lovell called the meeting to order; on motion Voted and choose Capt. Isaac Hodges, Moderator; voted and choose James N. Lovell, Clerk. The object of the meeting was then stated by George Lovell and others. On motion of Isaac Scudder to try the minds of this meeting; all those in favour of uniting the two school districts will hold up their hands. Voted: 7 in favor in the East District; 4 in favor in the West District. Those opposed to uniting, 3 all of the West District, viz. Lot Hinckley, Ira Hinckley, and David Cammett. Voted that we adjourn to meet here next Wednesday evening, which will be the 19th of March instant.

March 19, 1845, agreeable to adjournment, quite a number meet from the 19th district. The Moderator called the meeting to order.

Voted that the union meeting for annexing the 13th and 19th School Districts be dissolved.

Voted that the 19th School District will continue their meeting with the same officers.

Voted that we now choose a committee whose duty shall be to cause a legal School Meeting to be notified in the 19th District for the purpose of raising money to build a new school house.

Voted that this committee consist of three.

Voted that the Moderator nominate the committee. He accordingly nominated Edwin Scudder, Philander Scudder and George Lovell.

Voted that the committee be accepted.

Voted that we adjourn to some future time.

Barnstable, Mass.   To James N. Lovell, one of the legal voters of the town of Barnstable, and an inhabitant of the school District Number Thirteen in said town:

Greeting: In the name of the Commonwealth of Massachusetts, you are hereby directed to notify and warn all the inhabitants of said District, qualified to vote in elections in said town, by leaving a written notice at the place of residence of each of the said inhabitants seven days at least before the twenty-fourth day of March instant; to meet at the "Village Meeting House" in said District on Monday the said twenty-fourth instant, at one of the clock in the afternoon, to act upon the following articles, as follows, to wit:

Article First   : To choose a Moderator.
Article Second : To choose a District Clerk
Article Third   : To know if said United District will raise a sum of money to build a school house.
Article Fourth : To know if the District will choose a committee to expend the money so raised, in locating and building said house.
Article Fifth   : To know if the District will empower the building committee to borrow money to purchase said location and build said school house if the District fail to raise the requisite sum.
Article Sixth   : To know if the inhabitants will take measures to so alter the "Village Meeting House" as will be convenient for our town school in connexion with our village school house.
Article Seventh: To prescribe the mode of warning future District meetings.

Given under our hands, this tenth day of March, in the year eighteen hundred and fifty-one.

Hereof, fail not to make due service of this warrant according to law, and return of the same at the time and place of the meeting aforesaid

Daniel Bassett
Robinson Weeks : Selectmen of Barnstable

Barnstable, March 13, 1851

By virtue of the within warrant, I have notified and warned all the voters in School District No. 13, according to law, to meet as specified within at the time and for purposes therein named, by giving personal notice to many of them, and by leaving at the last, and usual place of abode of each of all the others, a written notification, expressing therein time and place and purposes of the meeting.

Attest: James N. Lovell

March 24th, 1851. According to the within legally notified meeting the inhabitants assembled, as within specified, James N. Lovell called the meeting to order by reading the warrant, and the following business was transacted:

1st, voted by ballot, to choose George Lovell, Moderator;

2nd, voted by ballot to choose James N. Lovell, Clerk for the 13th School District of Barnstable, and he was duly sworn, by George Lovell, Esq.

3rd, it was moved and seconded that the 3rd article be dismissed from the warrant. Voted that the third article in the warrant be dismissed.

4th, Voted on motion that the 4th article be dismissed from the warrant,

5th, Voted on motion that the 5th article be dismissed from the warrant,

6th, Voted on motion that the 6th article be dismissed from the warrant,

7th, Voted on motion that the 7th article be dismissed from the warrant,

8th, And lastly, voted on motion that we adjourn without delay.

Attest: James N. Lovell, Clerk

Sent Geo. Marston
a copy January 13, 1853 JNL

From Report of the School Committee of the Town of Barnstable
For the School Year 1867-8

District No. XII
Summer Term — Principal Department
        Asa E. Lovell, Teacher
        Primary Department
        Cynthia N. Lewis, Teacher
Winter Term — Principal Department
        Asa E. Lovell, Teacher
        Intermediate Department
        Olive L. Parker, Teacher
        Intermediate Department
        Helen A. Scudder, Teacher
        Primary Department
        Eugenie Lovell, Teacher

Miss Lewis evinced an earnest desire to promote the best interests of her pupils. Experience will enable her to make higher approaches toward her own standard of excellence. Miss Parker, to whom we have several times favorably alluded, was much troubled, during most of the term, with ill health, and was obliged to resign her position some three weeks before the close of the term. Her health imperatively demands rest, but we can trust she is not permanently laid aside from the actual duties of the school-room. Very few can long hold the position of a *teacher* and not impair the health. The performance of duty yields a reward known only to the faithful in any department of life. Miss Scudder's connection with the school was too brief to decide as to her capacities for teaching. She indicates, however, a promise of success. Miss Lovell, of the Primary department, gave to her duties energy and application, and the little ones did well under her training.

Wages of teacher per month:	
summer term, principal department	$47
summer term, primary department	15
winter term, principal department	66
winter term, intermediate department	30
winter term, primary department	15
Whole number of scholars:	
summer, principal department	42
summer, primary department	35
winter, principal department	41
winter, intermediate department	23
winter, primary department	24
Average Attendance:	
summer, principal department	38
summer, primary department	28
winter, principal department	35
winter, intermediate department	17
winter, primary department	18
Visitors:	
principal summer and winter	60
intermediate, winter	16
primary, summer and winter	37

Freeman S. Hodges, Henry A. Hodges, Lillie F. Hodges — of same family — and Covil A. Allen have a clearance, — not absent, tardy, whispered, or excused before the close of the session; and Olive S. Parker was excused once only; Ellen C. Wiley, Eliza A. Goodspeed and Willis H. Waitt, absent only from sickness; Clifford F. Lovell absent only a half day; otherwise the above were up to the standard. Lillie Runyon was a member of the school the latter half of the term and has a spotless record. Willis H. Waitt, though for some weeks a severe sufferer from the effect of poison, has an unblemished record during the winter term. Perhaps some parents would be a little surprised could they see the exact standing of their children. Absence, tardiness and parental fault-finding are usually very closely united.

A.E.L.

Osterville School 1861
Friends, parents, committee one and all.

1. You who so patiently today,
   Have heard us all rehearse.
   Pray listen while I give our names
   In short impromptu verse

2. We are a very happy band.
   Assembled for instruction;
   Throughout this pleasant term, we've met
   With scarce an interruption.

3. Miss E. F. Linnell first appears
   Among our scholar's names;
   Beside her, on the self same bench,
   We find Miss Mary Ames.

4. Miss Addie Lovell, next we see,
   Who in our school is better;
   Upon her right search not in vain
   For studious Henrietta.

5. See Chloe Coleman next in front,
   Who sits with Nettie West;
   Our parents must decide for us
   Which one of them is best.

6. In order, next, Miss Adams comes
   Called Helen E. by name.
   Miss Susan West sits side of her,
   Their ages are the same.

7. Miss Isabella Boult just now
   Our special notice claims;
   In front is Mary Hathaway,
   And Hattie Coffin Ames.

8. Next Isabella Williams comes,
   Her lesson she enjoys;
   Miss Ellen Coleman is the last.
   Sorrow we'll call the boys.

9. Cornelius Lovell, first we rank,
   Industrious and kind;
   Joe Linnell sits in front of him
   And Alton is behind.

10. S. Leland Goodspeed next we see,
    We greet him with our cheer;
    Blithe William Henry Fuller's seat
    Is by him very near.

11. And Jimmie sits in front of both,
    Frank Hodges sits beside him;
    E. Channing Bacon studies hard
    We know for we have tried him.

12. Next Willis Bacon we observe
    And William Coleman's name;
    Then Johnny Williams, faith lad
    Who seldom merits blame.

13. Next Freeman Hodges, claims a word,
    And Henry A. his brother;
    May they good children always prove,
    And kindly love each other.

14. But let me mention Nellie's name
    Before I tell the rest;
    She sits in school, just at the right
    Of studious John P. West.

15. Next Warren Lovell's name we see
    Then Robert P's we call;
    And for now our list of names is full
    For we have mentioned all.

16. But stop one more I should have named,
    And certainly have told ye:
    Our teacher who presides oer us,
    His name is A. M. Folger.

17. Now parents, teachers, friends and all,
    Next time we'll harder try;
    We thank you for your interest
    And bid you all good-by.

February 22, 1876

Friday was last day of school. About 50 visitors and a good exhibition of scholars in Grammar School were present, Miss Eunice Whelden, teacher, to whom as well as scholars we would give praise. Speeches were made by Dr. Geo W. Doane of School Board, Asa E. Lovell, Esq. and Erastus Scudder, Esq.

April 11, 1876

Our schools began Monday, April 10th, with the same teachers as before. We notice some improvements have been made around the school house that were very much needed.

May 16, 1876

That new fence around the school house is a decided improvement.

October 3, 1876

The schools are closed and now for Newtown and the Cranberry bogs. The start in the morning is a sight worth seeing. Some seventy boys, girls, and older people, leaving in wagons, carryalls, etc., with sometimes as many as eighteen in one vehicle! There has been but one accident thus far, that of Churchill Alley, son of Joseph Alley, who fell from a wagon Friday morning, the wheels passing over him, but fortunately no bones were broken.

October 2, 1877

Our schools closed Friday for the usual cranberry vacation, and now for the bogs, both old and young.

April 1, 1879

Our schools commenced Monday 31st ult. Miss Ellen F. Crocker of Barnstable teacher the Grammar School, and Mrs. Hannah Whippey the Primary.

October 19, 1880

Our school house looks better with its new coat of paint.

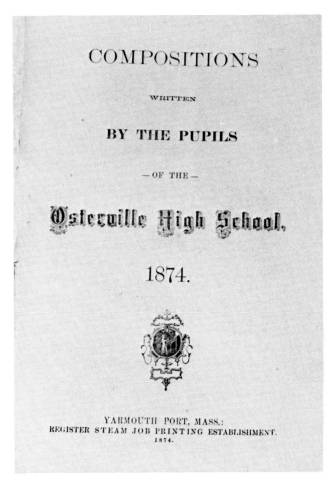

COMPOSITIONS

WRITTEN

BY THE PUPILS

—OF THE—

Osterville High School,

1874.

YARMOUTH PORT, MASS.;
REGISTER STEAM JOB PRINTING ESTABLISHMENT.
1874.

In 1874 Osterville had its own high school.

March 13, 1883

The schools of this village close on Friday next.

July 17, 1883

Our schools came to a close Friday, and now for a long vacation.

October 23, 1883

Our schoolhouse received a new coat of shingles on its roof before the school opened, which was on Monday, 22nd inst; the grammar taught by Mr. Zemira Baker and the primary by Miss Bertha Lovell.

November 27, 1883

The measles have been plenty among the children, and as a consequence our schools are poorly attended.

March 25, 1884

Our school closed 14th inst. for two weeks. They gave an exhibition and closed with a spelling match Saturday evening at Village Hall, Miss Mary T. Lovell taking the prize, a box of stationery. The same teachers will be employed next term.

March 25, 1884

Our teachers, Mr. Zemira Baker and Miss Bertha Lovell, had the closing exercises of their schools at the Hall, Saturday evening on account of the storm. It was well attended by both parents and friends. The declamations were very good, both as to the selection and rendering. They were given by Masters Ernest Bearse, Frank P. Bearse, Adrian Chadwick, Charlie Daniel, Everett Small, Richard Lewis, Charlie Coleman, and Harry Lovell, and Misses Lina P. Ames, Florence Rich, Carrie M. Rich, Eloise Goodspeed, Etta F. Lovell, Frances H. Lovell, Hattie Earle, Lillie Backus and Bessie Cammett, and a dialogue by Grace Small, Charlie Hall, Freeman Adams and Ralph Crosby. these were interspersed with songs from the girls in the Grammar department, and three from the girls and boys in the Primary department, under the leading of Miss Mary R. Lovell. The "Round" afforded the audience much amusement. After an intermission of ten minutes there was a grand spelling match, which was participated in by a large number of the older folks. Miss Mary T. Lovell won the prize, a writing desk. Both teachers are deserving of much praise.

April 1, 1884

Our schools are to have three weeks vacation on account of ill health of Mr. Baker, our principal.

August 12, 1884

The following pupils were perfect in attendance, deportment, and scholarship in the Osterville Primary School:

Harry G. Fuller
Blanche Lovell
Harris C. Lovell

October 11, 1887

The Osterville Grammar School will soon begin its next term with Mr. William Crocker as principal. Mr. Crocker accepts the position left vacant by the resignation of Mr. F. E. Chapin, who has taken a more remunerative school in New York.

March 7, 1888

Roll of Honor — Osterville Primary, Miss Bertha Lovell, Teacher.

One Term: Louise Adams, Myrtle Crosby, Charles Daniel, Kate Daniel, Robert Daniel, Mabel Evans, Susie Greene, Jennie Fuller, Bennie Lancy, John Horne, Grace Small, Ariel Tallman.

Two Terms: Edna Crosby, James Horne, Georgiana Daniel, Thomas Horne, Blanche Lovell, Etta Lovell, Arthur Lewis (late once).

April 3, 1888

Schools commenced on Monday with the same teachers — Mr. Crocker and Miss Lovell.

October 2, 1888

The Osterville Primary school will open Monday, October 8th, in charge of the same teacher.

December 25, 1888

The public schools completed the school year last Friday. Supt. Somes examined the candidates for promotion from Primary School with the following result.

Necessary to pass; 70 percent:
Kate Daniel — 97 per cent
Abbie Lovell — 96 per cent
Nelson Bearse — 96 per cent
John Horne — 96 per cent
Blanche Lovell — 94 per cent
Etta Lovell — 94 per cent
Fred Bearse — 94 per cent
Emily Crocker — 86 percent

March 6, 1889
Extra

Roll of Honor — Perfect in Attendance
Osterville Primary, No. 13. Bertha Lovell, Teacher.

Perfect for one year: Myrtle Crosby, Arthur Lewis, Etta Lovell.

Perfect for two terms: Louise Adams, Emily Crocker, James Horne, Blanche Lovell, Georgiana Daniel, Kate Daniel, Albert Hinckley, Augustus Coleman, Ariel Tallman.

Perfect for one term: Eugene Crocker, Roy Crocker, Everett Fuller, Fred Hammond, Charles Daniel, Robert Daniel, Jennie Fuller, Bennie Lancy,

Lester Lovell, Henry Parker, Edna Crosby, Mabel Jones, May Weeks, Lizzie Coleman, Warren Hodges, Abbie Lovell.

Osterville Grammar, William H. Crocker, Teacher.

Perfect for one term: Carrie Rich, Harry Fuller, Harry Tallman, Robert Daniel, Roy Crocker, Thomas Horne.

Perfect for two terms: Charles Coleman.

October 1, 1889

Our schoolhouse looks remarkably nice in its new coat of paint, and we hear its neighbor, the Baptist Church, is to be renovated outside and in. The work has begun under the supervision of A. L. Robbins.

March 11, 1890

Miss Bertha Lovell began teaching in 1883. Mr. William H. Crocker in 1887.

October 21, 1890

Grammar School in this village commenced Monday, 20th inst; teacher, Mr. Farwell of Brockton.

March 24, 1891

Our village schools closed Friday of last week. The Grammar School will begin its next term April 6 and the Primary April 13. The following pupils of the Primary School have been perfect in attendance the last three months: Arnold Bearse, Lizzie Coleman, Warren Hodges, Hannah Lewis, Ariel Tallman, and Mabel Evans.

July 7, 1891

The Osterville Primary School held its graduation exercises Friday afternoon. By invitation of class of '91, some sixty people were present, and the school was addressed by Rev. Robert Graham, and Capt. William Parker of the School Committee. The following is the program:

Greeting — Bertha Chadwick
A Strange Boy — Augustus Coleman
Temperance Birds — Edgar DeWitt
Time — Lillian Pattison
Being a Man — James Horne
Song, Children's Day — School
The Kitten and the Mouse — Frank Crosby
A Little Boy's Complaint — Ariel Tallman
The Bird's Song — Lucy Crocker
Spring — Lillie Swift
A June Morning Lesson — By six little ones
The Best Beauty — Lester Lovell
Little People — Annie Fuller
A Little Boy's Speech — Willie Hodges
A Question — Mary Hinckley

How She Counts — Gertrude Adams
Song, Jenny Wren — School
A Little Too Pert — Mabel Jones
The Bond of Hope — Lizzie Coleman
Two Sides of The Question — Lovell Parker,
 Teresa Daniel
Little Bo Peep — Edna Crosby
A Chain of Maxims — School
Two Temperance Boys — Andrew Crosby,
 Shirley Ames
Song, Hot Mud Pies — School
Women's Rights — Margaret Daniel
Growing, Hannah Lewis, The Elevens,
 Mary Hinckley
Albert's Question — Albert Coleman
Grandma's Glasses — Bessie Till
The First Letter — Josie Crocker
Vacation Days — Florence Adams
Two Temperance Voters — Edgar DeWitt
 and Teresa Daniel
Song, The Clock
Reminding the Hen — Lovell Parker
When In a Bay — Warren Hodges
Flo's Letter — Bertha Chadwick
Stars and Stripes — School
Valedictory — Ellen Crowell

The following scholars are promoted to Mr. Farwell's School: Florence Adams, Herbert Crosby, Mabel Evans, Augustus Coleman, Mabel Jones, Lester Lovell, Ellen Crowell, Ariel Tallman.

Roll of Honor — Florence Adams, Hannah Lewis, Willie Hodges, Mary Hinckley, Bertha Chadwick, Andrew Crosby.

The lesson prizes were awarded to Grade 1: Florence Adams; Grade 2, Edna Crosby; Grade 3, Hannah Lewis.

June 21, 1892

The schools in our village closed Friday, 17th. In the Grammar School the graduating class, consisting of Jennie Fuller, Katherine B. Daniel, Abbie Lovell and Thomas Horne, had 95 per cent.

June 21, 1892

About sixty people assembled in the Primary School-room Friday afternoon to attend the graduating exercises. Misses Lucy Crocker, Edna Crosby, Margaret Daniel and Master Ellery Jones are to enter the Grammar School, Grade V, having most satisfactorily completed the work of our public school course to that point. Miss Lovell received several very pretty presents from the same little people, who had so attractively decorated the room and carefully prepared the afternoon's entertainment. At the close of the program, prizes were awarded for scholarship, deportment and attendance; and the school most kindly addressed by Superintendent Hallett and Committee Parker.

Program
Song, Come and See How Happily — School
The Little Brown Bird — Bessie Till
Recitation, In June — Albert Coleman
Suppose — Lillian Pattison
Oscar's Opinion — Oscar Johnson
Recitation, Little Robin Redbreast — Frank Adams
Recitation, The New Moon — Andrew Crosby
Solo, Little Children Love Each Other
 — Edna Crosby
Summer — Earl DeWitt
The Holiday — Frank Crosby
Dialogue, Pet and the Fairies — Bertha Chadwick,
 Hannah Lewis, Mary Hinckley
How to Make Up — Mildred Pattison
Be Polite — Shirley Ames
Solo, The Rain Drops — Walter Fuller
The Falling Star — Teresa Daniel
Little Tots — Minnie Bell
A Summer Song — Lillie Swift
The Dandelion — Edna Crosby
A Foolish Mouse — Edgar DeWitt
Dialogue, The Metals — James Horne, Josephine
 Crocker, Warren Hodges, Lovell Parker
The Children's Hour — Lucy Crocker
The Motherless Turkeys — Margaret Daniel
Sixty Years Ago — Hannah Lewis
What Charley Saw — Lovell Parker
The Merry Month of May — Gertrude Adams
Baby Logic — Josephine Crocker
Seven Times One — Walter Fuller
Of Course He Did — Lizzie Bell
Warren's Opinion of Grandmothers
 — Warren Hodges
Recitation, Memory Gems — School
The Lazy Little Cloud — Bertha Chadwick
A Disappointed Farmer — Ernest DeWitt
Luck — Willie Hodges
A Spring Story — Mary Hinckley
Days of June, Recitation and Chorus — School.

July 26, 1892

Mr. John B. Holland of New York City has presented our Primary School, in charge of Miss Lovell, a flag 6 × 15 feet. This flag will be raised with appropriate public exercises at the opening of the school in September.

January 10, 1893

Out of a total of 24 scholars enrolled in the Grammar School the following have not been absent during the term: Louise Adams, Alma Johnson, Willie Adams, Bennie Lancy, Arthur Lewis, Lester Lovell, Henry Parker. Gussie Coleman and Ariel Tallman have been absent one day only.

Dry Swamp Academy — c. 1901

1. Guy Jones 2. Leon Hinckley 3. Wesson Fuller 4. Malcolm Crosby 5. Alphonse Beaumont 6. James Hansberry 7. Donald Coffin 8. Margerie Leonard 9. William Thompson 10. Shirley Evans 11. Elmer Taylor 12. Marion Whippey 13. Edith Alley 14. Beatrice Hinckley 15. Bertha West 16. Marie Adams 17. Ellen Hansberry 18. Thomas Chadwick 19. Zora Coffin 20. Hannah Whelden 21. Addie Crocker 22. Addie Crosby 23. Christie Ames 24. Burleigh Leonard 25. Alice Jey 26. Frederic Scudder 27. Philip Chadwick 28. Oscar Chadwick 29. Ernest Jones 30. Wilbur Small 31. Owen Coleman 32. Gerald Chadwick 33. Dexter Pattison 34. Albert Williams 35. Robert Bell 36. Harry Bell 37. Herbert Hinckley 38. Herman Williams 39. Jeanette Crosby 40. May Adams 41. Edith Jones 42. Marion Whiteley 43. William Whiteley 44. Genieve Leonard 45. Aleria Crocker 46. Mildred Taylor 47. Olive Adams 48. Edward Daniel 49. Isabel Williams 50. Sadie Whippey 51. Harvey Hallett 52. Horace Whippey 53. Thornton Adams 54. Henry Whiteley 55. Marie Hansberry 56. Maude Baker 57. Addie G. Crosby, Teacher 58. Joseph Daniel 59. Carroll Crosby 60. Walter Mahoney 61. Winthrop Scudder 62. James Corcoran 63. Norman Williams 64. John Daniel 65. Earl DeWitt 66. Frank Adams 67. Beatrice Adams 68. Mary Whelden 69. Miss Content Jenkins, Teacher 70. Joseph Tallman, Jr. 71. Marcia Hallett 72. Christine West 73. Mary Baker 74. Daisy Jones 75. Joseph Swift 76. Bernard Ames 77. John D. W. Bodfish, Teacher.

Town for the best drawing of a design for the School Report cover. Brief mention was also made to the faithful cooperation of Miss Bertha Lovell who resigns her position at the close of this term. She enters upon her new life with the best wishes of all who know of her faithfulness during her long term as teacher in the Osterville School. She is the recipient of a beautiful silver fruit basket, the gift of the three schools, in loving appreciation of her work.

October 1, 1900

Mr. John D. W. Bodfish of West Barnstable has been elected Principal of the Osterville Grammar School and will enter upon his work Monday, Oct. 8th.

February 8, 1904

By order of the Board of Health the schools are closed for an indefinite period, owing to the many cases of measles, which have developed rapidly.

March 14, 1904

After four weeks of vacation on account of measles, our schools have begun, and both teachers and scholars seem pleased to begin their work again.

June 12, 1906

Graduating class of 1906 — Christie Ames, Carrie Dodge, Frederic Scudder and Burleigh Leonard.

June 4, 1907

Several cases of scarlet fever are in our village and the Board of Health has ordered the schools closed awaiting further development.

December 17, 1907

Whittier's birthday will be observed in the Osterville schools Tuesday.

BARNSTABLE PUBLIC SCHOOLS.

Report of ....

.... Class.

F B & F F GOSS, HYANNIS.

For the Month of	Reading	Spelling	Arithmetic	Writing	Drawing	Deportment	Absent	Tardy	Dismissed	Signature of Parent or Guardian.
SEPT.										
OCT.	B	A	A	A	B	B	0	0	0	M A Baker
NOV.	B	A	A	A	B	B	4	0	0	M A Baker
DEC.	B	A	A	A	B	B	0	0	0	M A Baker
JAN.	B	A	A	A	B	B	6	0	0	M A Baker
FEB.	B	A	A	A	B	C	0	0	0	M A Baker
MAR.	A	A	A	A	B	A	½	0	0	M A Baker
APR.	B	A	C	A	B	A	½	0	0	M A Baker
MAY	B	A	A	A	A	4¼	0	0		M A Baker
JUNE	B	A	A	A	A	A	0	0	0	

A means Excellent; *B*, Good; *C*, Fair; *D*, Poor; *E*, Very Poor. [OVER]

Third grade report card of Shirley Evans, a pupil at Dry Swamp Academy when Mrs. Addie Crosby was his teacher.

June 1, 1908

A nut from one of the back wheels of the large school barge was lost Tuesday on the return from Hyannis, causing much inconvenience to its occupants.

June 15, 1908

Class motto for graduating class was "Work and Win."

September 21, 1908

The Grammar School opened Monday, September 14. Mr. Ferguson's room has 31 pupils, 21 boys and ten girls; Miss Phinney's room, 34 pupils, 23 boys and 11 girls; Mrs. Crosby's room 21 pupils, 14 boys and seven girls. We observe that the boys are conspicuous in Osterville.

December 14, 1908

Many pupils have been absent from school the past two weeks on account of chicken-pox.

May 31, 1909

Memorial Day in the Schools. Sunday afternoon the scholars will meet at the school and, with the band, go to the cemetery to decorate the graves of our honored dead.

November 29, 1909

Last Tuesday, near Mr. Ariel Tallman's, while the teamster was putting on the rubber boot, the horses swerved, and the school barge collided with a tree; six window lights were smashed and the top of the barge broken off. Another barge was procured, and the gentler sex arrived at school none the worse for their fright. The boys, either from shattered nerves or some other reason, thought best to take a holiday.

February 15, 1910

Last Monday was the coldest day of the season, 5 degrees below zero. Mr. Gould's and Mrs. Crosby's rooms were dismissed in the forenoon as it was impossible to get the rooms warm.

May 10, 1910

The children of Mrs. Crosby's room and Miss Phinney's hung their teachers' May Baskets the past week.

June 21, 1910

1910 Graduates: Horace Crosby, Ellen Hansberry, Beatrice Hinckley, Cecil Goodspeed, Stuart Scudder, Leon Hinckley, Leo Beaumont, Dorothy Berry, Karl Chadwick, Marion Whiteley, and Carroll Crosby.

June 28, 1910

High School graduates from Osterville: Christie Ames and Frederic Scudder.

December 13, 1910

Owing to the snowstorm, the public school had a recess Wednesday afternoon. This was greatly enjoyed by the school children as for the first time this season, their sleds were taken out of the store room and employed on the various hills.

Many of the older ones also enjoyed the snow, and cutters and sleighs glided along the streets.

June 20, 1911

Those graduating from the 9th grade were Howard McCabe, Genieve Fuller, Verner Childs, Burton L. Chadwick.

September 12, 1911

The schools opened today with the following teachers: Mr. Lewis Shiefe, Grammar School; Miss Olivia M. Phinney, Intermediate; Mrs. Addie G. Crosby, Primary.

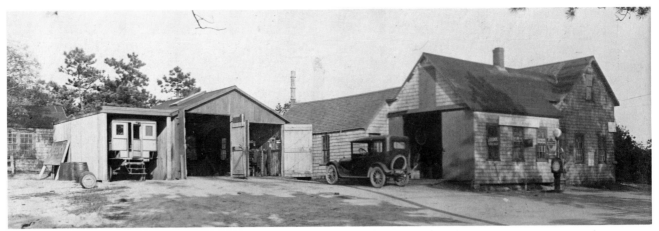

The School Barge "Osceola" — 1920

Pupils entered the school barge "Osceola" via the steps and door at the rear and were seated along the sides of the bus, which was kept in the shed at Leonard's Garage when not in use. The wooden building at the corner of Main and Pond Streets was destroyed by fire and replaced by one of concrete construction during the early 1920s.

February 20, 1912

The school children of the 4th and 5th grades, Miss Phinney's room, were on a sleigh ride to Hyannis Saturday afternoon to see the moving pictures.

June 18, 1912

The graduates from the 9th grade were Victor Adams, George Berry, Elwood Johnson, and Bertil Lagergren.

April 1, 1913

Roll of honor for the Osterville Intermediate School, January 6 to March 28: Irving F. Coleman, Evelyn G. Jones, H. Arthur Coleman.

November 30, 1914

The twenty-thousand dollar public school building, of which our village has been so proud for about two years since its completion, was completely destroyed by fire on Tuesday evening last, November 24, 1914. Mr. Frank Allen, who was passing by the building on this evening, saw what

We feel both glad and sad to-day
And scarce can hide the rising tear
We're glad for changes on life's way
Yet sad to part from schoolmates dear

School Souvenir, 1915, showing Mr. Fred Cargill, teacher.

he thought was fire in the building. He, by telephone, notified the center of the village and an alarm was immediately rung in, and in a short time the men of the village responded, and the work of trying to save the building began. While every man did his duty faithfully, and the fire extinguishers and chemical engine of the village were brought into play, the fire was under so much headway, it was impossible, with the means at hand, to check it.

Third Grade 1913-1914

Left to right, bottom row: Carlton Small, Alfred Lagergren, Elmer Whiteley, Mary Thurber, Howard Lewis, Dorothy Cahoon, Ruth Horne. Middle row: Kenneth Jones, Kenneth Lovell, Levi Gomes, Ethel Parker, Mary Cabral. Back row: John Shields, Grace Crocker, Chester Crosby, Edith Cahoon, Charlotte Boult.

Elementary school children on the steps of the new Osterville School Building which was destroyed by fire in 1914.

After the building was seen to be doomed, attention was turned to saving surrounding buildings. Had the wind remained southwest where it was when the fire broke out, with a stiff breeze blowing, no doubt a good part of the center of Osterville would have been wiped out; but before the fire broke through the building, the wind canted more to the westward, and the sparks were driven toward Mr. James A. Lovell's estate, and the attention of everyone was centered on the saving of his buildings, and those in line with them. Here is where the very efficient work of the men came in, and everyone worked with a will, and their efforts were rewarded in that not another building was destroyed.

Mr. James A. Lovell's house was on fire several times; also the houses of Mr. James Shields and Mr. G. W. Hallett, and Union Hall, and it is said, fire caught on the roof of the hearse house at the cemetery, a good half-mile away. At every place needed was a man or men who, at the risk of being burned themselves from the flying sparks, were ready to extinguish the flames as soon as started, and in this way, saved one of the prettiest parts of our village from destruction.

The fields and roadways from the building to Union Hall were a mass of flames and the great miracle is why other buildings were not destroyed.

It seems to be impossible to definitely discover the cause of the fire or to place the blame, but the general opinion seems to be an overheated furnace.

December 7, 1914

Men are at work getting the old schoolhouse ready for the children so that school can be opened as soon as possible.

1916 — Osterville Elementary School constructed to replace that which burned in 1914.

February 8, 1915

Rumor has it that the new school house is to be built by Boston contractors. The plans show a fine building, well-suited to our village, and it is said the building is to be one story, concrete block, slate roof.

August 7, 1915

The work on the new schoolhouse is progressing rapidly and it looks as though it would be a building to be proud of.

February 7, 1916

The school children have left the Dry Swamp Schoolhouse and have gone into the new one.

September 10, 1917

Our village teachers, the Misses Violet A. Oates, Lucy H. Nutter, Elizabeth F. Alden and Mr. Mitchell are stopping with Mrs. H. Foster Lewis.

July 1, 1918

Among the graduates from the Barnstable High School on Thursday were Isabel Lewis, Hazel Ames, Margaret Cross and Jessie Boult of this village.

June 30, 1919

Graduating from the 9th grade: Jessie Lewis, Charlotte Boult, Howard Lewis, Mary Shields, Leslie Nute, Truman Lewis, Edward Ashley, Ethel Parker and Chester Crosby.

June 21, 1920

Members of the class of 1920 receiving diplomas were Grace Crocker, Lillian Tevyaw, Agnes Shepard, Delton Hall, Kenneth Jones, Carlton Small, Alfred Lagergren and John Shields.

The class presented their teacher, Mrs. Isadore Eldredge, with a gift of a five dollar gold piece.

Mrs. Maurice Crocker was the organ accompanist.

June 28, 1920

The pupils of Mrs. Whittemore and Miss Perrin enjoyed a picnic to Craigville on Saturday. The school barge, Osceola, was engaged to convey them to and from their camping place.

_____

June 28, 1920

Agatha Crocker, Josephine Cross and Curtis Hinckley were the Osterville graduates from the Barnstable High School.

_____

July 2, 1923

Graduating class from B. H. S. from Osterville were — Charlotte Boult, Ethel Parker, Jessie Lewis, Leslie Nute, Mary Shields.

_____

February 11, 1924

Since the ninth grade has been abolished in the schools of the town, Principal Quimby of the Osterville school has started to get as many of his eighth and ninth grade pupils ready for high school in the fall as possible. Honor roll for January in seventh and eighth grades — 90 percent and above in all studies: James Shields, Webster Small, Inez Swift, Adenia Hodges, Lillian Childs, Helen Mac-Quade, Albert Hinckley.

July 10, 1924

The date for the opening of school given last week was a mistake and should have read Sept. 8. Mr. Quimby has several pupils to tutor for the summer, and any parent desiring such work should let him know at once.

_____

August 28, 1924

An electric clock system has been presented to the Osterville school by Edwin H. Coffin and Orville L. Bearse, class of 1883. Osterville and the Town of Barnstable are certainly indebted to these gentlemen for the gift.

_____

March 26, 1925

The Hinckley Electric Light Co. is installing lights in the grammar school here.

_____

June 28, 1928

Parents and friends attended the graduation exercises at the Barnstable High School at Hyannis, Thursday evening. Among the graduates the following were from Osterville: Ira Hinckley, Edmund MacQuade, Henry Fuller, Elaine Tallman, Miriam Ames, Marion Parker.

The Osterville
Free Public Library

December 17, 1878

The young folks have formed a society called the Osterville Literary Society. They chose Rev. H.M. Dean President; Miss Ellen Wiley, Vice President; Miss Ellen Crocker, Secretary. They intend to meet once a week, and sing, declaim, read, etc., for general improvement. All over 16 years of age are invited to join.

June 10, 1879

Some six months ago, a number of the young people of this village conceived the idea of starting a literary society. This was done. Their numbers have rapidly increased until the O.L.S., as it is called, includes nearly all the young and a large part of the older portion of the community. A few weeks ago this society came in possession of what has been known as the "Osterville Public Library." This Library has quite a history. Some six years ago Mr. Stewart Chaplin, a Boston gentleman, whose many generous deeds have placed him high as a public benefactor, made the village a present of a large number of valuable books which, under his personal supervision, reached nearly six hundred volumes. For some unaccountable reason the villagers refused to accept his gift, so Mr. Chaplin has kept possession, and as owner and librarian has done much for the people of Osterville, which we trust is duly appreciated. Not having the necessary time to attend to it, now that the books are in so great demand, he very wisely turned it over to the O.L.S. Once a quarter this Society elects its officers who for the next quarter, June to September, are:

> President — Wallace F. Crocker
> Vice President — Mrs. Josephine West
> Secretary — Mrs. Helen Crocker
> Treasurer — Mr. Roland C. Ames
> Librarian — Mrs. Ella Lovell
> Executive Committee — Rev. T. P. Briggs, Miss Cora A. Parker, Miss Lizzie S. Small.

January 6, 1880

New Year's night there was a happy gathering in the Village Hall to celebrate the first anniversary of the Osterville Literary Society. In the enforced absence of the President, Mr. C. G. Lovell, Mrs. Watson Adams, Vice President, called the Society to order, when followed music and readings. After this, 86 persons, consisting of the Society and a few invited guests, sat down to a tempting collation. When this had been well attended to, the Vice President again called to order and introduced Rev. S. Hamilton Day as toastmaster for the evening. He spoke of the success of the Society, and the profit which all had obtained from its sessions, of the revival of literature in America the past few years, and that a nation's literature indicated the type of a nation's civilization, contrasting, in this respect, England and Russia. He then spoke of literature as ideas and of the power of ideas, concluding with the remark that we expected some ideas this evening, but hoped that whoever spoke would remember that none of us were in condition to be violently agitated. He then introduced successive toasts and their respondents: "Osterville," Mrs. Josephine West, "O.L.S.," Miss Ellen Wiley, "Our President and other officers," Mrs. Granville Ames, "Our Seamen," Capt. Wm. Parker, "The Gentlemen," Mrs. S. H. Day, "The Ladies," Mr. Wallace Crocker. All the addresses were neat, wise and witty. The climax seemed reached, when, at the call of a lady speaker, rousing cheers were given for the O.L.S. The company then arose, after which young and old participated in games which the most fastidious could join. All declared the occasion a splendid success.

September 7, 1880

The Osterville Literary Society met after two months' vacation, last Thursday, at the home of Daniel Crosby, and the following officers were elected for the ensuing quarter:

> President — William H. Bearse
> Vice President — Daniel Crosby

Secretary — Charles G. Lovell
Treasurer — Wallace Crocker
Ex. Committee — Mrs. S. H. Day, Misses Hattie
S. Parker, Cynthia N. Lewis.

December 14, 1880

The Osterville Literary Society met in Village Hall, last Thursday evening, President presiding at the meeting. The following were elected officers for the ensuing quarter:

President — Mr. Daniel Crosby
Vice President — Mr. Frank Boult
Secretary — Miss Lizzie Small
Treasurer — Mr. Wallace Crocker
Editor — Mrs. Daniel Crosby
Committee on Music — Mrs. Wilton Crosby
Committee on Literary — Mrs. Granville Ames

Programme for the evening comprised music, singing, reading of papers, address, and select reading by members of the O.L.S.

September 24, 1881

The foundation for a new Reading Room and Library is being laid between Mrs. Lucy Lovell's and Capt. Austin Lovell's. This is a present from William Lloyd Garrison, assisted by village people. It is to be a nice, large building, and will cost, when completed, about $3,000, we hear.

December 6, 1881

Osterville Public Library expects to be opened Christmas.

Dedication of the Osterville Public Library

An Account Printed in the
Boston Evening Transcript,
January 18, 1882

About six months ago the design of erecting and furnishing a public library in and for the village of Osterville was mentioned to a few of the citizens. As the word was carried from one to another, interest increased and a subscription paper was opened.

The design originated with Mr. William L. Garrison, who headed the paper with a subscription, to which smaller sums were added by the citizens and kind friends from different parts of the country.

On the evening of Friday, December 30, 1881, appropriate dedicatory exercises were held in the Methodist Church, opposite which the new public library is situated.

The exercises were in charge of Mr. Garrison, upon whom all the responsibility of the enterprise has rested. At seven o'clock the people began to gather and at half-past seven the church was com-

Osterville Free Public Library — c. 1910

fortably filled. At that time Mr. Garrison went forward, and, after announcing the object of the meeting, asked for music from the choir and assembled audience. All heartily united in singing "America." After the hymn had been sung, Mr. W. L. Garrison, in a modest, tender, and kind but witty address, gave the history of the library — from his first thought of it until the design was finished. He clearly set forth its purpose and usefulness, gave a financial statement, and commended the institution to the use and care of the people. He then called upon Rev. Mr. Scott, pastor of the Baptist Church, who was the first to encourage him, and who, he was sure, would not desert him then.

A brief, earnest response was given in the address which followed. Mr. G. B. F. Hinckley, of Providence, R.I. a native of this village, being called upon, drew a lesson from Roman history to show how the villages of the Massachusetts seacoast were being "Bostonized," and declared his native place well "garrisoned."

Rev. Mr. Grant, of the Methodist Church, spoke briefly and well in reply to the call of their chairman.

Last, as the occasional speaker, Mr. Herman W. Chaplin, of Boston, gave a clear, logical, didactic address in which he, as a summer resident of the village, repudiated the idea of its being "Bostonized," and showed by numerous examples in each profession and department of business that Boston and New England are greatly indebted to those whose early life has been spent in Cape Cod villages. After this address it was voted, as the sense of the meeting, "that the building dedicated ought to be called 'The Garrison Public Library and Reading Room.'" Gracefully and modestly, Mr. Garrison declined to have his name so used; and the institution is to be, and be known as, the "Osterville Public Library." After the exercises at the church, the library was opened for inspection. The building and furnishings, of the "Queen Anne" style, are neat, substantial, and beautiful. Dictionaries, atlases, gazetteers, and encyclopedias (both Zell's and "American") are in the reference library in the reading room. Here also are the leading monthlies and daily and weekly papers (more than twenty in number). In the library, for circulation, there is a complete set of Harper's Monthly and a judicious selection of other works. A vote of thanks was given to Mr. Garrison, "for his gift and for his kindness, liberality, and interest in the place of his summer home." The exercises ended by singing the poem written for use at the dedication of the library. The library and reading room were opened to the public on Monday, January 2, 1882, Rev. E. B. Hinckley being the librarian.   E. L. S.

POEM

The dream of the designer's brain,
Like seed that ripens into grain,
Under the builder's cunning hand
Has grown into the fabric planned.

Here knowledge opens wide her door,
And freely spreads her ample store,
With garnered Wisdom's lettered page
Embracing every land and age.

Here, when our days of toil and strife
Depress us with their narrowing life,
Escape unto our souls is brought,
Into the world's domain of thought

Here, when rebellious at our fate,
Communion with the good and great
Will from the Present's grovelling care
Uplift us to a clearer air.

We dedicate, with heart and voice,
This building of our love and choice;
And may its influence reach afar
As streams the light from Evening's star.

January 31, 1882

The third anniversary of the Osterville Literary Society, held 17th inst., of which we gave a brief report last week, was a very pleasant affair. The introductory address of toastmaster Capt. William B. Parker was rich in humor and historic interest, as were also the speeches which followed. We take pleasure in the given entry of the poem written for the occasion by Mr. Cornelius Lovell, 2nd, of New York, and read by Miss Lucy C. Coffin.

June 6, 1882

Mrs. George Lovell presented the Osterville Library with a large Bible on her 83rd birthday.

June 20, 1882

The Trustees of the Osterville Free Public Library publish the following circular:

The undersigned Trustees of the Osterville Library, while thankfully acknowledging the

William Lloyd Garrison

Through the efforts of Mr. Garrison, early summer residents at Wianno supported the development of the Osterville Free Public Library during the later years of the 19th Century. To this day, the Wianno community continues its generous concern for our library and other worthwhile village activities.

---

many contributions they have received, earnestly solicit additional donations of money and books.

Cost of Land	$ 125.00
Building	1,583.27
Furniture, fuel, etc.	368.27
Insurance, 5 yrs.	29.50
Books	234.56
Subscriptures to Magazines and Newspapers	$ 75.40
Librarians' Salary, 1 year	200.00
	$2,625.00
Money contributed to June 1	1,841.55
Remaining debt	$ 783.45

At present the Library has only about six hundred volumes, and is sadly deficient in History, Biography and standard works of Fiction. The Reading Room is well supplied with books of reference.

It gives us pleasure to state that the use of the opportunities offered has exceeded anticipation. The love of reading has been stimulated, especially among the young people.

The comfort and good taste of the building has attracted favorable notice beyond the limits of the town, and it is hoped that summer visitors, who are cordially welcome to its privileges, will interest themselves in its welfare by adding new volumes to its shelves and helping us to free it from debt.

W. L. Garrison, G. H. Hinckley, J. P. Tolman, Anna D. Hallowell, H. W. Chaplin, C. F. Parker, Thankful Ames, Trustees.

April 17, 1883

Thursday evening, at the Hall, there was a Broom Drill and Concert for the benefit of the Public Library.

July 17, 1883

A Fair! — In aid of the Osterville Library
and
Reading Room
will be held at the
Village Hall,
in Osterville,
on the afternoon and evening of
Friday, July 27th, 1883.

Contributions of all kinds are solicited and may be left at the Library or with either of the undersigned.

As the privileges of the Library are free to all, summer visitors included, it is hoped that a general interest will be manifested to repeat the success of last year, and ensure for the year to come the necessary means of support.

W. L. Garrison, J. P. Tolman, H. W. Chaplin, Thankful Ames, G. H. Hinckley, Anna D. Hallowell, C. F. Parker.

July 3, 1883

The Osterville Public Library has received a gift of one hundred shells of different varieties from a lady friend at Florida.

July 31, 1883

At the Fair Friday there was a good attendance and a pleasant time was enjoyed. The proceeds for the benefit of the Library, were $300.00.

October 9, 1883

The people of Osterville are proud of their Library building, and its contents, and well they may be. The building would be an honor to any town, and at no distant day the Library itself will be all that can be desired. It is growing. Rev. E. B. Hinckley is the librarian, and he is just the man for the place.

December 25, 1883

On Thursday evening the Osterville Literary Society met, as usual, and after transacting the usual business of the meeting enjoyed the following interesting programme: Music by the Band — Reading by Mrs. Ella Lovell — Music by the Band — Reading by Miss Mary R. Lovell — Singing by a chorus of mixed voices — Music by the Band — A debate — Question — Resolved that a dam is happier at high than at low water. Affirmative, Mr. Zemira Baker; negative, Mr. Charles E. Lewis. After an animated discussion the question was decided in the affirmative.

February 26, 1884

Our library has received fifty new books from H. W. Scovell, Esq., of Waterbury, Conn. He is entitled to the thanks of our entire community for his kind remembrance.

April 15, 1884

The question in relation to having the public library open on Sundays is being agitated.

May 20, 1884

The second year of the Osterville Free Public Library ended with 1883. The success of the first year was confirmed, both as regards the use of the institution and the appreciation with which it has been sustained. The following statement covers the receipts and expenditures for 1883.

Expenses

Librarian's salary	$200.00
Subscriptions to Newspapers and Magazines	80.20
Fuel, oil and expenses	67.23
Repairs, printing, etc.	30.35
Binding magazines	27.80
New books	9.70
	$415.28

Receipts

Balance on hand January 1, 1883	$ 12.33
From fair, entertainments, and donations	495.85
	$508.18
Deduct expenses	415.28
Balance on hand January 1, 1884	$ 92.90

July 21, 1885

A pleasant entertainment was given at our Village Library, on Friday evening last. The Misses Carret of Carret House, furnished a beautiful "Night Blooming Cereus," for exhibition. About one hundred and twenty-five visited the Library, from 8 to 11 o'clock to watch its development, and all must have been amply repaid by witnessing its loveliness.

We are pleased to know that our Library is proving so attractive to strangers, as well as highly appreciated by the village people. Over two hundred and fifty books are distributed each week, and an average of twenty avail themselves of the privileges of the Reading Room daily.

A picnic for the benefit of the Library will be held at Mrs. Granville Ames' grove on Saturday, July 25th, at 2:30 P.M. All are cordially invited both to attend and contribute either to the refreshments table or fancy articles. Articles for either may be left at the Library. The Excelsior Band will be in attendance and a good time is expected. A carriage way will be open from Mrs. Ames' house to Crosby's pond direct.

August 23, 1887
The pretty Queen Anne Library at Osterville was a very attractive sight on the afternoon of Aug. 19th, when the ladies of the Library Aid Society held its annual fair and lawn party. The interior was decorated to the sale of useful and fancy articles, while cakes, ice cream, and fruit were served in booths upon the lawn. The building and grounds were made most effective in the evening by a brilliant illumination. Thanks are due the summer residents who so generously contributed for the success of the fair, and to the Excelsior Band for their enjoyable concert. It is estimated the net receipts will equal $275.

February 5, 1889
The Sewing Circle in aid of the annual Library Fair has commenced its meetings. Mrs. Mary S. Lovell, who has for several years been its President has resigned and Mrs. William Parker was elected to that office. Miss Bertha Lovell still continues as Secretary and Mrs. Herschel Fuller is Executive of Fancy Work Committee.

November 19, 1889
The Osterville Lyceum has reorganized with the following officers:
President — William H. Crocker
Vice President — Thomas Pattison
Sec. and Treas. — Charles F. Parker

December 24,1889
The Osterville Lyceum is thriving and the debates are lively and spicy.

February 11, 1890
At the last meeting of the Osterville Lyceum the following officers were chosen:
William H. Crocker — President
A. L. Robbins — Vice President
George D. Lewis — Sec. and Treas.
Ex. Committee — A. L. Robbins, Walter I. Rich, and J. Milton Leonard.

The question, Resolved, that to the civilized world, fire is of greater importance as a power than water, was participated in by the following persons. Affirmative, Capt. Wm. B. Parker, D. B. Fuller, H. P. Crocker, and A. L. Robbins; negative, Charles E. Lewis and Rev. E. B. Gurney. The question was decided on the merits of the argument in the negative by both judges and audience.

Question for Thursday evening February 13th: Resolved, that civilization has increased human happiness. Affirmative: Charles F. Parker, Esq.; negative, Capt. Herschel Fuller.

January 27, 1891
Perhaps the most popular place in our village this winter is the Lyceum. There has been a good attendance every evening and most of the debates have been spirited and interesting. Mr. Abbott L. Robbins, the President, has few equals in our village as a presiding officer and Mr. Maurice G. Crocker, our Secretary and Treasurer, is too well-known to need any puffing on my part. Rev. F. H. Corson, Capt. Thos. Pattison, H. P. Crocker, Herschel Fuller, Prof. E. W. Farwell and Wm. B. Parker are but a few of the many who have taken hold in such an earnest way that our Lyceum is the leading topic of the day.

April 21, 1891
The startling drama, "The Woven Web" is to be presented in Village Hall on Tuesday and Wednesday evenings of this week, for the benefit of the Osterville Library, by the best of our local talent. Let there be a crowded house both evenings, and thus help along a worthy cause. There will be a dance after the second evening's performance.

June 23, 1891
The Free Public Library of Osterville has received donations from the Lyceum of $14.00, and from the Dramatic Club $30.00, these amounts to be expended in the purchase of new books. The Library has depended for its support upon the annual fair, but the amount realized has been barely sufficient to pay current expenses, leaving no

surplus to be expended in books. The additions to the Library, therefore, have come chiefly from donations of friends and the $44.00 recently contributed is very welcome.

December 15, 1891

The Osterville Lyceum met at 7:45 with the President in the Chair. The subject for discussion: Resolved, "That a hermit is preferable to a dude." This was discussed with great animation by the following gentlemen: Messrs. J. M. Leonard, C. E. Lewis, Thomas Pattison, M. G. Crocker, G. B. Stearns, Owen B. Lewis. Subject for next week: Resolved, "That a woman is as capable of holding any position as a man." Affirmative, C. A. Lovell, Jr., negative S. H. Bates.

January 5, 1892

The last session of our lyceum was a most interesting one. It was called to order by the President, when the following programme was carried out:

Piano solo — Miss M. Lincoln
Recitation — Capt. E. Banett
Reading — Mrs. E. Chadwick

The question, Resolved, "That capital punishment should be abolished" was decided in the negative. The following gentlemen participated in the debate: C. A. Lovell, Sr., S. M. Stearns, Thomas Pattison, C. E. Lewis, M. Crocker, F. W. Hodges, S. Bates, J. M. Leonard and W. B. Parker. The question for next week is, Resolved, "That nature is a greater educator than art." Aff. — F. W. Hodges. Neg. — F. H. Corson.

September 6, 1892

The Osterville Library is the recipient of a fine steel engraving of the late Hon. Henry Scudder of Washington, D.C. As Judge Scudder was a native of this village and retained to the last a strong love for the home of his youth, Mrs. Scudder's gift is most appropriate. It will speak to the generation of today in the well-known words:

"Lives of great men all remind us,
We can make our lives sublime;
And, departing, leave behind us,
Footprints on the sands of time."

April 10, 1894

There will be a Turkey Supper, for the benefit of the Osterville Public Library, served in Village Hall, Osterville, from 6 to 7:30 P.M., Tuesday, April 10th. Admission to entertainment including supper, 25 cents.

August 12, 1895

Our annual Library Fair will be held at Village Hall, Aug. 15 at 3 P.M. Admission: ten cents. There will be a large and attractive sale of fancy articles, ornamental china, cake, ice cream, confectionery and lemonade. Entertainment in the evening. Contributions of money and articles of use and ornament are solicited as well as the generous patronage of the public.

March 9, 1896

The Library Aid Society gave a Turkey Supper in the Hall on Thursday evening. A short entertainment followed the supper, consisting of tableaux, music by Crosby's Orchestra, contra dance, Virginia Reel by ten young ladies "looking backward."

July 20, 1896

The Osterville Public Library will celebrate its 15th Anniversary on the afternoon and evening of July 24th. There will be a large and attractive display of fancy articles, including china, glassware, etc. There will also be cake, ice cream, confectionery and lemonade for sale. The entertainment for the evening will consist of "The History of the Library" by Mr. William Lloyd Garrison, songs by Miss Coffin and Miss Margaret Dietrick, reading by Mrs. Freeman Adams. Contributions of money, articles of use or ornament are solicited, as well as the generous patronage of the public. Admission: 10 cents.

December 13, 1897

The following ladies are officers of the Library Aid Society:

President — Mrs. Daniel Crosby
Vice President — Mrs. William Parker
Sec. and Treas. — Mrs. Lillie DeWitt
Committee — Mrs. Herschel Fuller, Mrs. Joseph Tallman, Mrs. Abbie Williams.

This Society will hold an attractive Christmas Sale Wednesday evening, Dec. 15th at the Library. Ice cream and cake will be on sale.

April 13, 1903

There will be a sale of ice cream and cake at the Library on Wednesday evening, April 15th, at 7 o'clock.

November 6, 1905

The Public Library is to have furnace heat this winter. Mr. J. W. Tallman is doing the work. It is a much needed improvement.

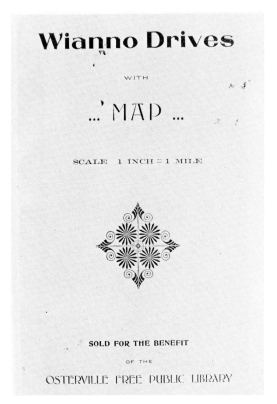

Driving the quiet lanes of Wianno helped raise funds for the Library.

Commemorative plate featuring the Osterville Public Library c. 1900.

November 19, 1907

The Public Library is to be enlarged and made convenient to accommodate the large number of books. Work is already begun on the addition which will be on the north side of the building.

July 6, 1908

The Public Library sign has been newly painted through the generosity of Mr. William Coleman.

"This little sock we give to you
   Is not for you to wear.
Please multiply your size by two
   And place therein with care,
In pennies or in cents,
   Just twice the number that you wear,
(We hope it is immense.)
   So if you wear a No. 10,
You owe us 20, see?
   Which dropped within our little sock
Will fill our hearts with glee.
   'Tis all we ask, it isn't much,
And hardly any trouble,
   But if you only have one foot
We'll surely charge you double.
   So don't forget the time and place,
We'll answer when you knock,
   And welcome you with open arms,
But DON'T FORGET YOUR SOCK."

Sock to be filled and returned to
   Mrs. Maurice Crocker,
         Public Library,
            Osterville, Mass.

On or before Sept. 1st, 1916, for the benefit of the Free Public Library, Osterville, Mass.

July 30, 1917

The public library is wired for electric lights.

April 7, 1919 — Drama

"The Time of His Life," a comedy in three acts, given for the benefit of the Osterville Public Library in Union Hall, March 27 and 28, drew crowded houses both nights. The cast was as follows:

Mr. Bob Gray — Ed Daniel; Mrs. Bob Gray — Lillian Parker; Tom Carter — Walter I. Fuller; Mrs. Peter Wycombe — Myrtle Black; Mr. Peter Wycombe — Albert Hinckley; Dorothy Landon — Beatrice Tallman; Mr. James Landon — J. M. Leonard; Uncle Tom, the colored butler — E. S. Crocker; Officer Hogan — A. L. Robbins.

The opening number was the overture Crusade by the Crosby orchestra of 16 pieces.

The parts were assigned most appropriately and each portrayed his character finely. Mrs. Parker and W. I. Fuller were leading man and lady, and were most natural and easy in their acting.

Mr. Fuller's part was especially hard, as he took two totally dissimilar characters. Albert Hinckley, whose health was of the utmost concern to himself and a source of trouble and annoyance to all with whom he came in contact, kept the audience in a gale of laughter, while Edward S.

Crocker delighted the audience in his impersonation of Uncle Tom, the colored butler.

Mrs. Black, with her calm and unruffled manner, made an ideal aristocrat, while Mrs. Beatrice Tallman, the niece of Peter, was most charming.

Edward Daniel, the alert young businessman and husband of Mrs. Gray, was very good. J. M. Leonard, the dignified father of Dorothy, let forth his pent-up rage and showed how he resented the indignities thrust upon him.

A. L. Robbins, as Hogan, made an excellent officer. Between acts a duet by Uncle Tom (E. S. Crocker) and his double, Uncle Tom, (Walter I. Fuller) brought down the house.

The lovely costumes of the ladies in their various roles added much to the attractiveness of the drama.

December 4, 1922

The Gypsy Cantata for the benefit of the Public Library, under the direction of Miss Jean Hinkle and Mr. Walter I. Fuller, will be held in Union Hall, Dec. 22. The Crosby orchestra has kindly consented to play at this time.

March 19, 1923

"Bar Haven", the drama given at Union Hall Thursday and Friday evening for the benefit of the library, was a great success. Characters:

Capt. Hiram Hoppe, an old fisherman
— J. Milton Leonard

Hardy Stone, his helper — Walter I. Fuller

Leo Bradley, in search of an heir
— C. Roscoe Hinckley

Gideon Graham, a wealthy rascal
— Logan J. Massee

Rev. John Wesley Wiggins, parson at Bar Haven
— Wm. Hodges

Cy Brackett, fishing for fish and Arbella
— Ed Crocker

Mrs. Wardell, of "The Manor" — Myrtle Black

Florence Wardell, her daughter
— Charlotte Boult

Kate Wardell, who comes into her own
— Beatrice Tallman

Spray Hopper, the captain's daughter
— Lillian Parker

Arbella Wortendyke, between the devil and the deep sea — Myrtle Tallman.

January 1, 1925

The addition to the Public Library which is under way will greatly improve its appearance, and also makes the children's room much larger. Adrian Chadwick and Richard Lewis are doing the work.

Miss Katherine E. Hinckley, Librarian 1917-1956

October 23, 1930

Mrs. Francis Bird of East Walpole has presented the Osterville Public Library with a new heating outfit which has been installed by G. W. Hallett & Son.

Ladies and Gentlemen:

On very short notice I have been requested to say a few words to you of the past and future of the Osterville Public Library, for which this splendid musical entertainment is given this evening. I understand that my principal qualification for this undertaking is that I am old enough to remember as far back as the beginning of the Library, which was away back in 1873. At that time there were here members of the Chaplin family, one of the very first families who discovered the beauty and desirability of Osterville as a place to spend the summer months.

This family with the assistance of Mr. Hallett, who was a descendant of the once nationally famous Osterville man, the Hon. Benjamin Hallett, gathered together a small number of books and placed them in a room in the dwelling house occupied by Mrs. Thankful Ames, who was appointed librarian and who later became the popular proprietor of Cotocheset Hotel at Wianno. This small beginning was open to the public; it was popular and proved its usefulness. More and more books were added to the collection and it soon outgrew its limited quarters and moved to a then vacant room in the old school building. A retired minister, Reverend E. B. Hinckley, then became librarian, and the library continued to grow in the size of its collection of books and usefulness.

The summer population of Wianno and the village took a great interest in its welfare and about 1879 or 1880, under the leadership of Hon. Wm. L. Garrison and a number of others in both Wianno and Osterville, it was decided it was time the Library should have a home of its own.

Mr. Garrison headed a subscription list, and through his untiring efforts, sufficient funds were soon obtained to purchase the land and build a suitable building. A corporation was formed, and the building erected, and in 1881 dedicated with elaborate exercises in the M.E. Church, just across the street from the new building. Mr. Garrison had charge of the exercises and opened the meeting with an interesting address. Other speakers were Reverend Mr. Scott of the Baptist Church, Reverend Mr. Grant of the Methodist Church, Professor G. B. F. Hinckley of Providence, a former Osterville boy. The principal address of the evening was by Heman W. Chaplin, Esq., of Boston, a member of the Chaplin family, who started the little collection of books which was the foundation of our present splendid Osterville Public Library, of which we are all so proud.

Such, my friends, is a very brief and inadequate sketch of its past, given almost from memory, except for a few important dates gathered from a recent article published in a local paper. Very much more might be said had I a little more notice of the fact that I was to speak on this subject on this occasion.

Its past has been a splendid record of improvement and success. Its present gives us a splendid library well stocked with hundreds of books on all subjects by the ablest writers the world has produced, an adequate reading room well equipped with magazines of all kinds, from the students' weekly and daily papers well suited to all ages and all classes. And what of its future? Shall it continue to expand and improve its usefulness? I hope and believe it will.

And now I have a few words to say to that younger generation of the village, who cannot remember as I do the time when we had no library, with no such advantages as are now available to you and your children, when books were few and many now in our library were far beyond the reach of most of us. I sometimes wonder if these advantages, like a good many other blessings which come to us without much effort on our part, are appreciated, or if we accept them as something we ought to have and which is therefore ours by right. But if we were asked the question why ours by right, we could hardly answer satisfactorily even to ourselves.

I have said that Mr. Garrison and other summer residents played a large part in making it possible to have our present library. This is true, but I can also remember that in the past the village people played their part, especially in its support, not only by contributing whatever their means would permit, but every year the young people would be busy getting up something in the way of entertainment to raise money for the benefit of the library, but it is some years now since I have heard of any such activity among our young people of today, and I can't but feel that they should try to do something along these lines as their contribution toward the support of this important village institution. I feel that this entertainment tonight is a step in the right direction and the Band deserves great credit for setting an example which I hope others will follow to show those who carry the burden of the support of our Library that we are willing to do our part. I am requested by the Trustees to express to you, Mr. Teal, and the members of your Band their sincere thanks for your splendid concert as a contribution to help support the Osterville Public Library.

J. M. Leonard
1937

Osterville Post Offices

July 31, 1860

The people of Osterville and Centerville are much gratified at the restoration of the daily mail between those places and West Barnstable. The revenue derived from those offices is not, perhaps, more than one-half enough to defray the expenses of that mail route.

July 18, 1876

Osterville is to have two mails a day through the summer season. The first arrived Saturday evening, but by mistake we received the Cotuit Port instead of Osterville mail.

September 12, 1876

Our evening mail comes no more this season. We miss it.

September 14, 1886

A new Post Office has been established at the Beach, "Wianno," for the months of June, July, August, and September. Miss Jennie L. Hinckley has been appointed Postmistress.

April 5, 1887

Saturday evening's mail due at 7:30, arrived on Sunday at 11:30 A.M., delayed on account of the severe storm.

October 30, 1888

New letter boxes have lately been added to the post office.

October 16, 1906

The new post office building in Crocker's block is completed and was opened to the public for the first time Monday, Oct. 8th. Upon the arrival of the evening mail the Osterville Silver Band, stationed on a balcony above the office, gave a concert for an hour to the large crowd gathered in honor of the event. Later in the evening the Beacon Club, who have rooms in the same block, entertained a few guests who have been especially interested in this move of the office to the center of the village. Miss Frances H. Lovell is still the popular postmistress, and is ably assisted by Miss Mildred Pattison.

July 23, 1912

The post office at Osterville has been advanced to an office of the third class. Mrs. Charlotte L. Parker has been appointed by President Taft, and she has been confirmed by the Senate as postmistress.

September 10, 1912

The Citizens of Osterville were surprised last Wednesday morning to find that the Post Office had been robbed in the night and about $1,000 consisting largely of stamps had been stolen.

It was fortunate that it was near the first of the month, and the Postmistress had just sent her returns to Washington. The thieves had first cut into the lock at the front door, and then bored several holes into the safe and used explosives. The door of the safe was blown the full length of the room and found lying at the other end of the room.

As yet, no clue is found to the thieves. Osterville is now large enough to have a policeman at night to be on the lookout for suspicious strangers and loafers on the streets.

April 29, 1913

The new addition at the post office is nearing completion. We will have a fine post office when it is finished.

July 31, 1916

Electric lights are being put in the post office in this village.

April 16, 1917

No school on the 9th, owing to the very severe snowstorm. No evening mail was received in this village although it arrived at West Barnstable nearly on time.

February 25, 1918

Mrs. Charlotte Parker, Mrs. Robert Daniel, Messrs. S. N. Ames and Harris C. Lovell attended the hearing of the post office safe-blowers in Boston last Wednesday.

Beacon Club

January 20, 1896

Noticing in a recent issue of the Patriot an account of the several clubs in Hyannis, the thought has occurred to me that perhaps it might be of interest to some of your readers to know that there has recently been organized in Osterville a social club under the name of the Beacon Club of Osterville, the officers of which are:

President — J. Milton Leonard
Vice President — G. Webster Hallett
Secretary — Charles E. Lewis
Treasurer — N. H. Allen

For the present the Club makes its headquarters in Village Hall, but it hopes soon to move into more comfortable and cosy quarters in the unoccupied part of Mr. James Crocker's store, where two large rooms are being fitted up for its use. The Club numbers, among its members, some of our foremost and well-known businessmen and we understand it is the intention to put in a billiard table and have the rooms, which will be handsomely furnished, open to members and their friends at all times.

March 9, 1896

The Beacon Club met on Saturday evening for the first time at the new rooms in James H. Crocker's block. A turkey supper was served to a few invited guests.

February 8, 1897

The dancing school, which has been held during the winter under direction of Prof. E. B. Fish, closed with the Exhibition Ball on Thursday night. A turkey supper was served during intermission at the Beacon Club rooms, Osmond Ames, caterer. Those who attended report a very good time.

March 15, 1897

The Beacon Club will present the drama "Messmates" on Thursday and Friday evenings of this week, at Village Hall. The following is the cast of characters:

Alvah Morgan, a speculator . . . Mr. J. M. Leonard
Richard Carter,
    owner of the "Seabright" . . Mr. Barnard Hinckley
Nat Taylor,
    Captain of the "Seabright" . . . . Mr. N. O. Lovell
Teddy Morgan, a runaway . . . . . Mr. E. S. Crocker
Wolf, a stowaway . . . . Mr. B. L. Ames
Crumbs, the steward . . . . Mr. E. F. Fuller
Grace Morgan,
    Alvah's daughter . . . . Miss Jennie Fuller
Polly Taylor,
    the Captain's pet . . . . Miss Sarah H. Boult
Arabella Carraway,
    Alvah's sister . . . . Miss Minnie Cammett
Phyllis, Grace's maid . . . . . . Mrs. Abbie Williams
    The drama will be followed by a social dance.

May 2, 1898

The Beacon Club, assisted by friends, are to give the drama "Rio Grande" in Union Hall on Tuesday and Wednesday evenings of this week. The cast includes some of our best amateur performers, and the success with which the "Messmates" was presented last season guarantees a fine performance on these occasions. Let there be a crowded house. The entertainment is for the benefit of the Hall.

May 16, 1898

The drama "Rio Grande," was presented at our new Union Hall on the evenings of the 3rd and 4th insts., and drew large and appreciative audiences. It was given also at Cotuit and West Barnstable with equally successful results. The fine acting of the persons presenting this play merits extended notice for it is rare that better and more realistic acting is given on the amateur stage. Following is the cast:

Retta, Segura's Niece . . . . Miss M. H. Bearse
Sophia, Lawton's Daughter . . Miss M. I. Cammett

Mamie, A New York Belle .... Mrs. M. G. Crocker
Mrs. Biggs,
    the Judge's Guiding Star ..... Miss S. H. Boult
Jose Segura,
    a wealthy Spanish-American . Mr. J. M. Leonard
Col. Lawton,
    Commanding the Garrison .... Mr. N. O. Lovell
Capt. Paul Wybert,
    a Junior Officer .... Mr. E. F. Fuller
Judge Biggs,
    an Enthusiastic Citizen .... Mr. P. H. Hinckley
Lieut. Cadwallader,
    a Holiday Soldier .... Mr. E. S. Crocker
Jonnie Bangs,
    a Dime Novel Desperado .. Mr. N.S. McKendrick
Corp. Casey, An Old "Vet" .... Mr. Vincent Cross

The piece had a peculiar interest at this time, when our relations with Spain are so disturbed, as the principals were Spanish-American. The impassioned character of the Spanish girl, who hesitates at nothing (where her affections are enlisted) was admirably portrayed by Miss May H. Bearse as Retta, and the depth of passionate love and despair, hate, grief, and remorse, with virtue triumphing over them all, was a part that required much study and thought. Mr. J. M. Leonard, as Jose Segura, the wealthy and landed proprietor and Spanish gentleman, was given with most excellent taste. The slow, stealthy movements of the Spaniard was in all his actions, and his costume was perfect. Mrs. M. G. Crocker, Miss Boult, and Miss Cammett were well adapted to their parts, and caused pleasure and surprise at their finished efforts. Mr. E. S. Crocker, in the character of Lieut. Cadwallader, was intuitable and received the applause he so well merited. Messrs. Lovell, Fuller, Hinckley, McKendrick and Cross were each and all perfect in their several parts. Special credit is due to Mr. N. H. Allen, the Stage Manager, for the very complete and efficient manner in which the play was presented.

The Osterville Orchestra, under the leadership of Prof. J. H. Backus, rendered some very enjoyable music during the evening. We understand the play will be given again under the same management at Osterville during the coming summer, and we advise all who desire to see a first-class performance to avail themselves of the opportunity.

_____

March 5, 1900

We notice that by some inadvertence your local correspondent failed to notice the Osterville celebration of Washington's Birthday. We refer to the masquerade and fancy dress ball, given under the auspices of the Beacon Club of this place,

which was one of the most enjoyable and prettiest parties that have been given in this vicinity for many years. The committee on dancing, Messrs. C. F. Parker, N. H. Allen and A. D. Hall, secured for music Ferguson's Orchestra from Bridgewater, who cannot be excelled for perfect dance music, and who in good natured generosity responded to every encore, making the programme long enough to suit the most exacting. The supper was under the direction of a committee composed of Capt. H. P. Crocker, J. M. Leonard and E. S. Crocker, whose names are a sufficient guarantee for good fare. The costumes were many of them elegant but our space forbids us to particularize. In spite of the bad weather and roads quite a number were present from the surrounding villages, and only the storm prevented the crowding of our usually ample hall beyond the bounds of comfort. We think the thanks of the community are due to the enterprise of the Beacon Club whose members have thus once more given the public a chance to enjoy an unusually pleasant evening.

_____

October 22, 1900

"Beacon Club" was the scene of a hot bicycle contest, a few evenings ago, between Mr. Edgar Swift and Capt. H. P. Crocker. Capt. Crocker made the fastest time, but in his hurry to reach the starting point, Mr. A. D. Hall was struck by his wheel and slightly hurt. We congratulate Mr. Hall on his narrow escape.

_____

July 24, 1905

Early Thursday morning, Mr. Joseph W. Tallman discovered a fire at the Beacon Club rooms. It had been smouldering several hours and had burned through the balcony floor and to the roof of the piazza below. It is supposed to have caught from a cigar end thrown into sawdust.

_____

October 25, 1909

The Beacon Club has in preparation a grand Thanksgiving Ball which promises to be the event of the season.

_____

February 5, 1917

Electric lights have been installed in the Beacon Club rooms. The Club has bought a fine piano from Mr. Oliver C. Coffin.

_____

February 19, 1917

The Beacon Club gave a dance in Union Hall last Thursday evening.

Date: 1895

By Laws of the Beacon Club

Article I Name: This club shall be called the 13 Club of Osterville. Amendment adopted Dec. 7, 1895, reads as follows: Name: This Club shall be called The Beacon Club of Osterville.

Article II Officers: The officers shall consist of a President, Vice President, Secretary, and Treasurer to serve three months.

Article III Duties of Officials: *Section 1:* The President shall preside at all business meetings, appoint all committees, cast his ballot on admission of members, in case of a tie vote on a question shall cast the deciding vote, and shall have power to call special meetings at any time. *Section 2:* The Vice President shall officiate for the President in his absence. *Section 3:* The Secretary shall keep accurate minutes of the proceedings of all business meetings and keep a correct account between the Club and its members, receive all moneys due the club and pay the same to the treasurer. *Section 4:* The treasurer shall receive all moneys due the Club from the Secretary, giving receipts for the same, and pay all drafts drawn on him by the Secretary by vote of the Club.

Article IV Entrance Fee and Dues: The entrance fee shall be ten dollars. The yearly dues shall be five dollars, payable quarterly, in advance. Amendment to Article IV, dated Jan. 5, 1901. Entrance fee shall be five dollars instead of ten dollars.

Article V Membership: Any respectable male white person who has attained the year of 21 shall be eligible to membership. Amendment to Article V: If under 21 and over 18 years of age, by the written consent of their parents.

Article VI Election of Members: When a person is proposed for membership, his name and the name of member proposing him shall be posted in Club room at least one week. Then he shall be balloted for, and if no more than two black balls cast, the candidate shall be declared elected. Amendment: 1902: His admission fee shall accompany the application, "but if the applicant is rejected, his admission fee shall be returned to him."

Article VII Quorum: A quorum shall consist of not less than a majority of the members of the club. Amendment: A quorum shall consist of five members. Adopted in 1896.

Article VIII Business meetings: Every Saturday night shall be a business meeting of the club.

Article IX Restrictions: No liquors shall be kept in the Club Room and no gambling allowed.

Article X Suspension: Any member three months in arrears for dues shall be suspended and any member four months in arrears shall forfeit the privileges of the club. Amendment adopted 1897: When a man is three months in arrears for dues, the secretary shall post his name in the Club Room, and if at the expiration of thirty days his dues remain unpaid, the secretary shall notify the club to that effect and he shall cease to be a member of the club.

Article XI Invitation of friends: Members shall have the privilege of inviting friends to the club.

Article XII Amendments: These By Laws can be amended or added to by vote of the club. Amendment adopted 1896: These By Laws can be amended or added to by vote of the club, but any addition or amendment shall be posted in the Club Room a week before being acted on.

Article XIII Payment of Entrance Fee: Immediately after a candidate is elected, the secretary shall notify the same, and his entrance fee shall be paid the first time he attends the club. Amendment adopted 1901: Anyone voted in as a member of the Beacon Club must pay his entrance fee within two weeks of the date of his acceptance.

Article XIV Honorary Members: Any non-resident of Osterville may become an Honorary member of the club by the payment of ten dollars. He shall be exempt from the payment of all dues and, except for participating in business meetings, shall be entitled to all privileges of the Club room: Amendment: *Section 1:* Non-residents of Osterville shall be eligible to honorary membership in the club by having their names duly proposed and posted in the club room at least one week before action is taken, and if elected, shall be required to pay $10, said election to be by Ball Ballot, as for regular members. *Section 2:* Nothing in Section 1 of this article shall be construed to apply to summer residents or visitors of Osterville and Wianno who shall only be eligible to regular membership or by card. *Section 3:* Summer residents and visitors of Osterville may obtain a card entitling them to all the privileges of the club (except a voice in a business meeting) for the term of six months by a majority vote of the club at any regular meeting, on the payment of $3.00. Adopted July 11, 1896.

Article XV Quarterly Reports: The secretary and treasurer shall on the last meeting of each quarter make a report as to the financial standing of the club. Adopted 1896.

November 23, 1895: According to vote of a previous meeting 12 gentlemen met at Village Hall. Meeting called to order by J. M. Leonard. Report of a previous meeting read and accepted.

Voted to organize as a club. Voted that a committee be appointed by the chair to retire and bring in a list of officers subject to approval of the meeting.

The following names were brought in and accepted by the meeting:

President — J. Milton Leonard
Secretary — Charles Lewis
Treasurer — N. H. Allen

Voted that a committee of three be appointed by the President to bring in a list of By Laws at the next meeting. Committee appointed: Charles Lewis, G. W. Hallett, N. O. Lovell.

Voted to accept Capt. H. P. Crocker's office for temporary quarters.

Voted that a committee of two be appointed to see with how little outlay the temporary quarters can be fitted up. Committee: N. H. Allen, H. P. Crocker.

Voted that G. W. Hallett be a committee to confer with Mr. J. H. Crocker and hire his room.

Voted that N. H. Allen be authorized to confer with Mr. James H. Crocker in regards to alterations in Club Room.

Nov. 1895: Voted that the club have an Oyster Stew at the next meeting, and that each member pay his proportionate part of cost.

Dec. 1895: Report of Committee in regards to the buying of gavel and ballot box heard, and Secretary instructed to buy the same.

Jan. 11, 1896: Rent ordered paid for club room, $8.75.

1896: Committee on furnishing reported that the club room would be ready for occupancy March 8, 1896.

Voted that the members of the Vagabond Troupe be invited to the opening of the Club Room, Saturday night, March 7th, and that they and each member of the club have the privilege of inviting one friend.

March 1896: Voted to buy a lounge for the clubroom.

1896: Balance on hand, $87.37.

1896: Voted that J. M. Leonard buy 200 cigars, 100 of 3 cts. straight, and 50 each of two other kind.

1896: President H. P. Crocker, Vice President G. W. Hallett, Secretary Nelson Lovell, Treasurer N. H. Allen.

1896: May: Voted that the committee on cigars buy 500 cigars and 500 cigarettes. Voted to have a whist party and lunch next Saturday evening, members requested to invite one lady.

1896: Voted the committee be instructed to buy 100 Easterbrook & Eaton best fives.

1896: Committee on 4th of July Celebration reported that "the Club keep open house on the 4th of July, and that every child in the village be treated to ice cream."

Sept. 1896: G. W. Hallett, Pres. Committee formed to purchase stove of one G. W. Hallett.

Oct. 1896: Paid Warren Lovell $1.00 a week as janitor.

Nov. 28, 1896: Voted that the club have a gauder spread one week from tonight.

Dec. 18, 1896: Voted that the club extend an invitation to Mr. and Mrs. O. D. Lovell for the upcoming ladies' night.

Dec. 1896: Committee on desk report the desk bought.

Dec. 1896: Wilton Crosby, V. P. Voted that the club give a progressive whist party December 31, and each member invite one lady.

Jan. 1897: Bill for cigars of $16.65 ordered paid.

Jan. 1897: The name of Thomas Pattison was ballotted for membership and was declared unfavorable.

1897: Voted that we discontinue the old way of selling cigars and that they be kept under lock and key and J. Milton Leonard have the selling of them and be authorized to deputize someone else to act in case he leaves home.

March, 1897: Voted to tender the use of our club room to the O.Y.C. for the purpose of entertaining the Legislative Committee on Harbors & Lands.

March, 1897: Committee be appointed by the chair to buy three lamps of H. P. Crocker, price not to exceed $6.00. Wilton Crosby, President.

April, 1897: Committee be instructed to buy two checker boards and checkers. *Resolved* that any member of the club who has a key to the club and desires another, shall be required to pay 25¢ for a duplicate to be furnished by the club. E. S. Alley, Pres.; J. A. Lovell, V.P. *Voted* that Warren Lovell be hired to paint and put in the screens. $21 bill for cigars. J. M. Leonard, Secretary. Bal: $105.12.

Oct. 1897: Voted that G. W. Hallett make some smoke screens for the lamps. J. A. Lovell, Pres.; N. O. Lovell, V.P. 1898.

1898: Voted that a committee of three be appointed to procure a flag and not use over $3. Voted that the same committee have the letters forming Beacon Club gilded and put up on the front of the Beacon Club Room.

1898: Voted that the president confer with the janitor to see if we could not have better service.

The resignation of J. M. Leonard as a member of the Cigar Committee was accepted. Oct. J. M. Leonard to be a committee of one to get the old stove repaired or get a new one. N. O. Lovell, Pres.; Charles Lewis, V.P.; E. S. Alley, Sec'y.; C. F. Parker, Treasurer.

Nov. 1898: Voted that the O.V.I.S. have the use of the club room every Tuesday afternoon.

1899: J. M. Leonard, Pres. Bill of Chester L. Baker for rent of stove and poker, $3.15, ordered paid.

1899: Voted to see what action the Club will take on moving the adjoining buildings. Voted to let Mr. James Crocker do as he likes with it. Feb: Voted to buy spittoons. May: Miss Minnie Cammett donates lamp shade. Charles Lewis, Secretary. Azor Hall to procure three windows for club room. Edgar Swift, V.P. N. H. Allen, Pres.

1899: Voted to rent upper room to Osterville Ice Co. for their meetings.

1899: Voted to have a stag supper for members only.

1900: Edgar Swift, Pres.; C. Lewis, V.P.; C. F. Parker, Treas. Jan.: Voted to loan club dishes to Christian Endeavor Society. Club to have masquerade ball on the 22nd of Feb. Committee: C. F. Parker, N. H. Allen, A. D. Hall. Music restricted to five pieces. Supper to consist of cold meats, hot rolls, cake, coffee, chocolate. Vegetables?

1900: Voted to find out how many would join the club if fee reduced to $5. Bill of H. S. Parker for $19.70 rendered. Voted that the bill be paid and Mr. Parker be requested by the secretary to present his bills quarterly or semi-annually. May: Voted to authorize the secretary to procure a suitable case for cigars. Motion was made twice that the pres. and sec. have the only keys to cigar case. Was declined each time. Warren Lovell, Pres.; H. P. Crocker, V.P.; C. F. Parker, Treas.; Nelson Lovell, Sec. Bill for 500 cigars, $17.50. Committee formed to secure a telephone connection to Hyannis to get the results of Presidential election. Dr. Higgins made an honorary member. James Rogers paid 75¢ a week to keep Club Room clean. Club room to be rented for $1 week for a children's Dance School. C. F. Parker, Treas.; H. P. Crocker, Pres.; N. E. West, V.P.

1901: J. M. Leonard, Sec., paid for 200 cigars, $7.00. Voted that Mr. Wilton Crosby order a keg of beer to be used Feb. 22, 1901. Edgar Swift, cigar chairman, Pres., N. E. West, Jr., N. H. Allen, Sec. Laid carpet on floor. Charles Lewis, Pres.; H. P. Crocker, V.P.; Voted to purchase an extension table. Paid 28¢ for ice. Purchased a water cooler. V.P. Everett Fuller; J. M. Leonard, Pres.

1902: Robert Daniel, Sec.: Voted to buy a dozen armchairs. Charles Daniel, Pres.; James A. Lovell, V.P.; Charles Lewis, Sec.; N. O. Lovell, Treasurer. A bill from Willard Robbins for 50¢ for washing clubroom floor was presented and was laid aside. Sec. R. W. Crosby, Sept. 20, 1902, Voted to take account of stock of cigars. Type of cigarettes: Perfection, Abdallah. Charles Lewis, Sec. Type of cigars: Jackson Squares, N. B. M., Manifold, Hoffmanettes.

1902: Everett Fuller, Sec. Rent for club room July 1st, '02 to October 1st, '02, $15.00. Club room cleaned and papered, 1902, Nelson O. Lovell, Sec. Also H. S. Parker, Sec.

Jan. 1903: Pres. J. A. Lovell; V.P. W. W. Stockman; Sec. J. M. Leonard; Treas. N. O. Lovell. Quarterly rent: $15.00. Bill for $15 for cigars ordered paid. Club asked to relocate by Mr. Crocker. Club to hire new room of Mr. William Crocker for $100 per year. Lease must be for four years. Voted to have a spread on the Opening Night in the new club rooms and that the members of the Osterville Silver Band be our guests on that evening. Club furniture to be restored. Janitor to receive $50 a year. Pack of cards donated to the club. Club to install telephone.

1904: Treas. Nelson O. Lovell; N. E. West, Jr., Sec. Voted to keep cigar case open. No gambling allowed in the club room. James A. Lovell, Pres; Watson Stockman, V.P.; N. E. West, Jr., Sec.; N. O. Lovell, Treas. Mary Jey was paid $1 for cleaning club room windows. Ernest Jones was paid 25¢ for putting wood in club room. Bill of $7 for best V. cigars ordered paid. Voted to rent a piano for club room for six months for $20. Charles Daniel, Sec. Janitor authorized to oil floor. Secretary to buy 4 dozen glasses and 2 doz. soup plates for the club. Shortage in cigar account of $5.99. Janitor fee, $50 per year.

1905: Telephone rented for $15 a year to be paid quarterly. Voted to hold a masquerade Ball. Committee: James A. Lovell, floor manager; Nelson O. Lovell, Supper Committee; Azor D. Hall and N. H. Allen, Invitations; N. H. Allen, Decoration Comm.; H. Manley Crosby, Music Committee. Voted to have floor washed. Net proceeds from ball $62.84. Voted to purchase a clock for the club room. Room rent $25 per quarter. Edgar Swift appointed Cigar Committee Chairman. Purchased four cords of wood, room painted, purchased two rocking chairs and one card table. Bill for four cords of wood, $20. William Coleman did the work. H. Manley Crosby offers club a piano. Club subscribed to the following magazines: Cosmopolitan, Pearson's Recreation, National Hunters, Red Book. Total $4.50.

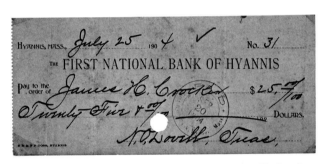

Check written in 1904 by N. O. Lovell to James H. Crocker, owner of the building which is now the Daniel Block where the Beacon Club rented rooms on the second floor.

1906: J. A. Lovell, Pres.; W. W. Stockman, V.P.; C. J. Daniel, Sec.; N. O. Lovell, Treas. Sec. ordered to buy 12 packs of cards. John W. Lewis janitor now. Paid $4.16 a month. Charles Daniel, Pres.; A. D. Hall, V.P.; N. E. West, Sec.; J. A. Lovell, Treas.

1907: Secretary, Owen B. Lewis. Voted to have piano tuned. Voted to burn coal during the winter months due to the high price of wood.

1908: N. E. West, Jr., Pres.; A. D. Hall, V.P.; J. A. Lovell, Treas.; Chester A. Crocker, Sec. Voted that the Sec. put a new handle on the club axe. Owen B. Lewis to work out his back dues as janitor.

1909: Dance held; netted $54.83.

The Beacon Club meeting rooms were on the second floor of this building which may be recognized as the Daniel Block. c. 1910.

1910: Frank Gardner, V.P. Voted to buy 12 chairs. Club to purchase nine spittoons.

1911: Pres: Frank Gardner; V.P.: Edgar Swift; Sec: Charles Lewis; Treas: J. A. Lovell. Voted to put a sink in club room. Lester Lovell, Sec.

1912: Ralph Crosby, Pres; V.P., Edgar Swift; Sec., Con Driscoll; Treas, J. A. Lovell. George Williams to install billiard table for three month's trial. Charles Lewis, Pres.; M. G. Crocker, V.P.; N. E. West, Jr., Sec.; J. A. Lovell, Treas.

1913: Seems that Charles Gifford now owns Daniel Block. Maybe Crocker sold out.

1914: Club to relocate, to rent two rooms in school house. Janitor to receive $1.75 per week. Club to move back into former meeting place.

1915: Pres., Ralph Crosby; V.P., Everett Fuller; Sec., Fred Scudder; Treas., H. P. Leonard. Looking for a cheaper janitor.

1916: E. F. Fuller, Pres.; Charles Lewis, Sec.; Chas. Daniel, Treas.; V.P., Edgar Swift. On motion of Lester Lovell it was voted to give a dance for the benefit of the Club. Voted to see if a suitable lot of land could be purchased to build a club house. Pres. E. F. Fuller; V.P. E. F. Swift; Sec. N. E. West;

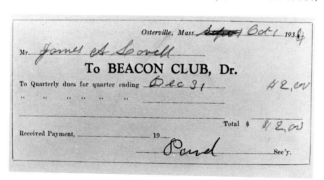

Notice of Dues James A. Lovell, October 1, 1934.

Treas. O. C. Coffin. Voted to see how many members would take out a $20 bond to purchase land for a new club house.

1917: Club room to be wired with electric lights. Voted to purchase a piano from Mr. Oliver Coffin for $50, to be paid for $15 down, and $5 a month until paid for.

Presidents of Beacon Club
1896-1917

J. Milton Leonard
Henry P. Crocker
G. Webster Hallett
Wilton Crosby
Ernest S. Alley
James A. Lovell
Nelson O. Lovell
N. Hastings Allen

Edgar Swift
Warren Lovell, Jr.
Nathan E. West, Jr.
Charles Lewis
Charles Daniel
Frank Gardner
Ralph W. Crosby
Everett Fuller

Vice Presidents of Beacon Club
1896-1917

G. Webster Hallett
Wilton Crosby
James A. Lovell
Nelson O. Lovell
Charles Lewis
Edgar Swift
Henry P. Crocker

Nathan E. West, Jr.
Everett Fuller
W. Watson Stockman
Azor D. Hall
Frank Gardner
Maurice G. Crocker

Secretaries of Beacon Club
1896-1917

Nelson O. Lovell
J. Milton Leonard
Ernest S. Alley
Charles Lewis
N. Hastings Allen
Robert Daniel
Ralph W. Crosby
Everett Fuller

Horace S. Parker
Nathan E. West, Jr.
Charles Daniel
Chester A. Crocker
Owen B. Lewis
Lester Lovell
Cornelius Driscoll
Frederic Scudder

Treasurers of Beacon Club
1896-1917

N. Hastings Allen
Charles F. Parker
Nelson O. Lovell
James A. Lovell

Henry P. Leonard
Charles Daniel
Oliver Coffin

Osterville's Movie Theatre

Star Theatre

The Star Motion Picture Theatre brought Hollywood to Osterville in 1912 or 1913 (no one seems quite sure). Frank Williams, a village carpenter, was its builder, owner, and manager, and he constructed his pride on the property of the old Seth Rich Estate which had stood next door.

A Barnstable Patriot clipping announcing the opening noted that "the house seats 300, with raised seats, which gives all an unobstructed view. Its woodwork is of cherry color, red side walls, high green steel ceiling, and the building is lighted with electricity, making an attractive interior."

The Star, in fact, became just the third building in Osterville to be electrically lighted. A generator on the premises produced the power, with reasonable reliability for the lights as well as for the projection equipment.

The theatre itself was set back from Main Street, standing quite solitary in uncluttered Osterville. Barn-like, it was built of steel, similar to a Quonset hut, with a right and left front entrance, and two rear side exits. A row of lilac bushes, salvaged from the Rich Estate, lined a path from the street to the right entrance over which burned a bright bare-bulb electric star. When the Pattison block was built in 1927-28, a wooden covered ramp was added giving the theatre street frontage and forming a tunnel to the seating area. Karl Chadwick of Parker Road, nephew of owner-builder Williams, recalls that the "tin building did pretty well in those days because the pictures were silent. But the acoustics couldn't be good when sound came. The electric plant was under the supervision of Mr. Bernard Ames. Presiding at the piano with her usual good taste was Miss Dorothy Ames, who was assisted by the Osterville Orchestra. The singing was done by Mr. Walter I. Fuller in his usual good voice and Mr. John Horne was the projectionist."

Mr. Chadwick remembers the Osterville Orchestra was "an amateur orchestra of seven or eight pieces that was pretty good." Arthur Wyman, a left-handed violinist, led the group, and his wife assisted on the piano.

The Star ran three shows a week: Tuesday, Thursday, and Saturday nights, with a new program each evening. Nearly every show consisted of a "two-reeler," double feature, and still advertisements were often flashed on the screen during reel changes. Admission price was 10 cents.

Mr. Fuller, presently of West Bay Road, who sang between reels on opening night, recalls the old Star had a wood stove in the hall to "take off the chill in cold weather; in the summer the doors were opened to cool off the inside. Young boys used to stand across from the theatre and watch the show through the open doors."

"It was the only real evening entertainment in Osterville," Mr. Fuller said. "It marked the beginning of a new age; there was something for the public to go to nearly every night, and pretty nearly every night, it was jammed."

The porched building, with its ICE CREAM sign hung outside, was Carrie Rich's Ice Cream Parlor which was located on Osterville's Main Street at the south end of the structure now known as the Pattison Block. To the right is a sign advertising SIMPSON SPRING BEVERAGES. To the right of that, and above, partially hidden by the tree branch, can be seen the sign reading STAR. This marked the entrance to the STAR MOVIE THEATRE. c. 1915.

October 28, 1913

Miss Dorothy Ames has left Mr. Frank Williams' employ as pianist at the Star Theatre, and we understand has gone to New York to take advanced studies in music. Miss Christine West has taken her place at the Star.

Star Theatre
    The Star Theatre on Osterville's Main Street occupied the site of the present Designer's Walk. c. 1913-15.

August 10, 1914
    Mr. Chester Huggins is employed at the Star Theatre evenings as usher.

December 7, 1914
    Messrs. John Horne and Norman Williams have leased the "Star Theatre" for a term of three months from the owner, Mr. Frank Williams.

Mr. Frank Williams and Karl Chadwick — Mr. Williams was the original proprietor of the Star Theatre.

Atlantic & Pacific Tea Co., the drug store, and the Community Theatre occupied most of the Pattison Block on Osterville's Main Street in the 1920s.

The Osterville Baptist Church

July 11, 1838

Scarcely can be imagined the sensation produced in the peaceful inhabitants of a small country village on first having their ears saluted with the sound of the church-going bell. An instance of this has lately been realized in the neat little village of Osterville. The spirited and enterprising people of this place have been determined that their splendid little edifice should no longer be destitute of that which adds much to the grandeur and beauty of any country seat. Upon the highest eminence in their village, where lately has been erected a fine and elegant church, they have suspended a bell, and there, where once by the aborigines the sabbath was spent unheeded, and where relics of Indian festivities yet may be seen, now are assembled, at the toll of the sabbath bell, a company for public worship.

July 4, 1839

The church voted to hold a fast on the first Monday in the year to pray for a revival in the Church. C. R.

January 19, 1864

Rev. A. E. Battell, having resigned his charge in Middleboro, has accepted a call to the pastorate of the Second Baptist Church in society in Barnstable, (Osterville). On a recent evening many of the church and people met to give their pastor a reception visit at the old family mansion of the late Dea. Benjamin Hallett, well known as one of the first Baptists in this place, whose house was ever open to the hospitality of Christians. After the decease of Dea. Hallett, this place was fitted up by his son, the lamented Hon. B. F. Hallett, as his summer residence. It is now the property of the grandson, Henry L. Hallett, esq., of Boston, who has very generously permitted the occupancy of an appropriate part of the house as the pastor's present residence, free of rent. This besides being a great convenience and help to the pastor, is a

material assistance to the church in their efforts to sustain the cause of Christ. Here it was, says the Watchman and Reflector, the people came to greet their pastor with hands full of provisions in variety, and other useful articles. In these gifts the pastor's only child was kindly remembered. All these tokens of interest by an affectionate people are truly most gratefully acknowledged.

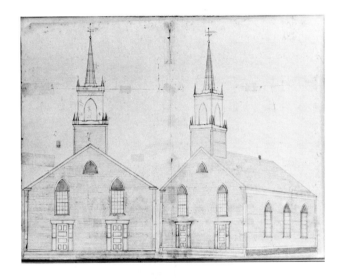

Architectural Plans of the Osterville Baptist Church — 1837
Exterior   Interior

Sterling Silver Communion Set gift of Adeline Hallett Lovell in memory of George Lovell. Reed & Barton Silver Co. — 1865

Poem

For the dedication of the
Baptist Parsonage in Osterville
September, 1875

I stayed just as long as ever I could
In our cottage up in the wood.
Not *exactly* within the minister's fold
Nor *quite* like being "left out in the cold!"

I heard with joy of your grand "house warming."
The very *sound* was truly charming,
As it would be to you, if only you knew,
Up in the woods, the winds how they blew!

Not being able to share the good time,
The best I can do is send this poor rhyme,
To express our thanks for the kind invitation
To join the dear friends in this dedication.

"Where there's a will, there's (always) a way";
Knowing this, they continued to pray.
"The place was too straight, but still they would wait,
And now, God has opened wide the gate!

In His own good time, in His own good way,
Because His children continued to pray,
Each "bought a beam" on every side,
Saying, let us pray on, the Lord will provide."

Visitors came, and saw the need,
Gave good help, and the "God speed."
The house sprang up, the minister cried,
"Hold, 'tis larger in, than all the outside!"

In this "gem of a house" under the eaves
Now lives this good pastor, whose name is Cleaves.

And his name truly seems to say
That with his people he means to *stay*.

Look all around, and you see the trace
Of his wife's hand in every place,
Showing refinement, love and care.
She would make a sweet home anywhere!

May the blessing of God on this house be shed!
By His wonderful grace may you all be led,
Till the "house not made with hands" is given
To a happy company met in Heaven.

F. L. Scudder

November 2, 1875
Completion of Baptist Parsonage

You may have been made acquainted with the fact that we have for some months past been actively engaged in erecting a parsonage for the benefit of the Baptist Society in this place. Upon its completion (and by the way "it is a gem of a house") we contemplated a "house warming." Of what nature it should be we could hardly determine: whether it should be social, dedicatory or festive, select or general, and finally agreed that all who had facilitated progress in any way, come in mood and manner which suited them best, and enjoy for a brief season the "feast of season and the flow of soul." At an early hour on the delightful evening of Oct. 18, the house was filled. Prayer was offered by the Rev. Mr. Fitch, of the Methodist Church; reading of scriptures by the pastor, Rev. F. E. Cleaves. An original hymn, by Mrs. Cleaves, was then sung by the Church choir, assisted by Sabbath School scholars, and the young people of the village. We then listened to a very carefully prepared report of the building committee, by A. E. Lovell, Esq. We find by the report that we are indebted greatly to friends abroad, whose absence we deeply regret. Mrs. Adeline Lovell then favored us with facts and reminiscences of the past, so replete with earnest zeal and kindly interest as to make us forget that she had passed her three-score-years and ten; followed by "Our Past, Present and Future," by Mrs. E. G. Lovell; then a Poem by Mrs. Harvey Scudder, of Boston. Toasts and sentiments were offered, and met with ready response, interspersed with singing, until the lateness of the hour admonished us that we must soon separate, when to our astonishment we found that the best had been reserved for the last, as our pastor presented us with the chronicles of The House of the Priest.

Rev. Thomas Pearl Briggs
Pastor 1879-1880

March 26, 1889

The Baptist Society have a new organ (exchanging the old) for their Church, also new lamps for chandelier and pulpit.

December 24, 1889

An event of considerable local interest, as evidenced by the large gathering, was the re-dedication of the Baptist Church in this village, Sunday, the 15th inst. The dedicatory sermon was given by the Rev. Dr. Eaton of Boston and he was supported by Rev. Mr. Jacelyn of the Congregationalist Church at Centerville, and the Rev. Mr. Shaw from the Baptist Church at Hyannis; also the pastor of the church to be dedicated, Rev. Mr. McLellan. The audience room was well filled with a congregation from this and surrounding villages, for combined with the attraction which such an array of talent would ordinarily have had, was the interest and curiosity felt by all to see the great improvements that (it was whispered about) had been made inside the church and which, it was said, more than balanced what had been done outside, and truly the public were astonished at the transformation that had taken place in so short a time, a transformation that had changed that unattractive, barn-like structure, into one of the most attractive and comfortable audience rooms on Cape Cod. Instead of the dark, dull painted walls, seamed with the cracks of years, the eye fell with a sense of relief on smooth, newly plastered walls and ceilings tastefully covered with paper just suited to the building. The old galleries had disappeared, one having been removed and the other closed from the Auditorium to be used hereafter for a vestry. The large box stoves that have always given us a taste of true extremes of climate, were also gone, and an even temperature pervaded the house, the air being tempered by a new furnace in a new cellar below. The baize-covered door shut noiselessly behind us and our feet press a new carpet of tasty design, covering the entire floor, including the altar, where is the old speaker's desk that looked as if it were an altar that had been used for sacrificial purposes until the wood had taken its color from that use, gone and in its place a tasty desk of hardwood finished in its natural color, cushioned with crimson plush backed by chairs for three speakers of a pattern and with trimmings to match, while the pews of similar wood and design, were cushioned crimson red. The only fault that could be found, if any, was that they were so comfortable that they might induce a sense of repose and so impair the effect of the eloquence that was sure to flow amid such surroundings; and how has all this been accomplished in so short a time? Well I think one and all, owing to the energy and perserverance of the pastor, Bryant McLellan, who, when he announced that he wanted a thousand dollars to fix the church, was laughed at and who has expended about $1,700, $1,400 of which were already subscribed and another hundred contributed by the congregation at that time so pleased were they with the work that had been done. In the evening the house was again filled and the audience entertained, both in listening to the clergy (now reinforced by the Methodist preacher, Rev. Mr. Gurney), and hearing the laity some of whom clearly remembered and related how they attended the former dedication. Two new chandeliers, (one over each side of the church), aided by the old one in the center, fully succeeded in shedding light. The people may well be proud of their church and have to thank first their pastor, who has labored both bodily, mentally and untiringly, recorded by Mr. Abbott Robbins as master builder; J. W. Tallman as mason; Mr. Bates as painter and Mr. Gibley as paper hanger, each with several assistants, while the people did all that they were able to help matters along. We are sorry to hear that Mr. McLellan is confined to the house with a severe cold, but we hear the wish expressed on every side that at least he will recover in season to preach Sunday, as everyone feels it would be a great disappointment to both him and them were he not able to occupy the church he has so thoroughly renovated and beautified, and which he is not by any means the least attraction to those who flock there weekly to listen to him.

July 15, 1890

The Y.P.S.C.E. of this place, aided by the societies at West Barnstable, Hyannis, Cotuit, and Centerville, will hold a social meeting in the Baptist Church, Tuesday evening, opening with a praise service (from Gospel Hymn No. 5) at 7:45 o'clock. The exercises will consist of singing, recitations and addresses, principally by the visiting societies and clergymen present. All are cordially invited.

February 24, 1891

The bell of the Baptist Church has been sent to Boston to be recast.

May 10, 1892

Workmen have been repairing and improving the steeple of the Baptist Church, and it now presents a very attractive appearance with its new gilt balls, vane and letters to mark the points of the compass.

February 26, 1895

The Baptist Church will observe the 60th anniversary of its organization in this village on the evening of March 4th. The public are cordially invited to be present.

September 23, 1895

A fine new Estey organ has been placed in the Baptist Church.

August 2, 1897

Rev. W. A. Rice (colored) will deliver a lecture in the Baptist Church Tuesday evening. Subject: "Slavery as it was." He will sing plantation songs and relate incidents of his life as a slave for 18 years. A collection will be taken for the benefit of the school he represents.

December 6, 1897

Santa Claus will plant a Christmas Tree in the Baptist Church this year, and he hopes every family in the village will heartily co-operate with him and make it the success it has been in the past when he visited in the old Village Hall.

January 3, 1898

An interesting Christmas Concert was given by the children at the Baptist Church Dec. 19th. The room was beautifully decorated with holly and evergreen and a large crowd gathered to listen to the children who were assisted by the choir, and by the pastor, Rev. Benjamin T. Livingston, who sang a solo that delighted everyone. Especial mention should be made of the verses composed and recited by Master William Hodges. They showed marked talent and he should be encouraged.

August 29, 1898

On Thursday evening, Sept. 1st, Rev. B. T. Livingston will be publicly ordained in the Baptist Church.

January 1, 1900 — Christmas Festivities

On Christmas Eve at the Baptist Church a concert was given in which nearly all the children of the village had a part. Notwithstanding the inclement weather, the Church was well filled and the children did their part well, assisted by the choir. Rev. E. M. Antrim of the Methodist Church and Rev. Mr. Corbett of Newton addressed the audience. It is expected that Mr. Corbett will preach again in the Baptist Church Jan. 7th.

Christmas Day was ushered in by a sunrise prayer service at the M. E. Church and other services were held there during the day.

September 23, 1901

Memorial Services in honor of the late President McKinley were held in the Baptist Church Sunday morning. The sombre decorations relieved by the national colors were striking in effect. A large crayon portrait of the President was suspended from the ceiling above the pulpit, while at the rear of the room and on the front of the pulpit were other smaller likenesses. Palms and asters were used in the floral decorations. The entrances to the Church were draped in the national colors, while a life-size portrait framed in black was suspended between. The services were conducted by the pastors of the two churches. Rev. Mr. Miner of the Methodist Church delivered the address, which was listened to with absorbing interest and made a deep impression on all who heard it. A chorus of fourteen voices sang "My Jesus as Thou Wilt," "Nearer My God to Thee," "Lead, Kindly Light" and "America". In the evening at the Methodist Church Rev. J. Robbins spoke to the people on "The Real Source of Individual and National Greatness," taking as a text, Luke 10:27.

Osterville Baptist Church — 1900

February 13, 1905

Rev. Mr. Hood of Newton Center preached in the Baptist Church, Sunday, 5th. The evening service was especially interesting. Mr. Walter Fuller favored the congregation with a solo, while Mr. Arthur Wyman played a violin obligato. He also assisted the full choir in leading the chorus singing. Mr. Wyman has kindly offered to assist in the Sunday evening service in the future, which will afford additional pleasure to the congregation.

The Rev. Charles Cook, pastor of the Osterville Baptist Church — 1914-1915 (Note old watering trough for horses)

August 12, 1913

Rev. B. T. Livingston has broken ground for a summer residence on his lot near Rev. Charles N. Hinckley's home. Rev. Mr. Livingston and family are held in high esteem by the people of our village and we are glad to see that they at least intend to spend their summer vacation with us. Mr. Adrian Chadwick and Mr. Willis Crocker are to do the work which insures a good job, as both are first-class workmen.

August 19, 1918

It is understood the Baptist Church is to be wired for electric lights.

Commemorative cup featuring center of Osterville with the Baptist Church in the background — early 1900s. Property of Mrs. Chester Wyman.

Rev. Benjamin T. Livingston, 1869-1948
Pastor of church from 1898-1900
"A Lofty Soul who Lavishly Shared the Presence of Christ"
Heaven is nearer because he lived.   G.S.I.

In Memoriam
of our late Friend and Sister in Christ

Mrs. Deborah Knox Livingston
by Rev. John A. Thompson

Full three months have passed away,
  And yet it seems so near
Since she was seated at her desk
  So full of hope and cheer.
No more, alas, will she return
  To fill her place again,
But green within her sisters' hearts
  Her memory will remain.

O, it was hard to feel it true,—
  So sudden was the call,—
Just like a bolt from out the blue,
  That morn the news did fall.
Each sister looked as if she'd lost
  The dearest friend she had,
From every eye there fell a tear,
  And every heart was sad.

Oftimes I've thought 'twould better be,
  If we no friends could claim;
Then death would leave no aching hearts,
  Or sorrow in its train.
For when you part with one so dear,
  It seems you've lived in vain;
A shadow o'er your life is cast
  Forever to remain.

True friends are like the rarest gems,
  No value is too high.
Too late we learn to know their worth,
  'Tis only when they die.
But she was loved when in our midst;
  And now she's mourned sincere.
Until that day we follow her,
  We'll keep her memory dear.

Deborah Knox Livingston, 1874-1923
"A Soul Aflame for Christ and Righteousness"
World Wide She Served

G.S.I.

Be strong and of a
good courage;
be not afraid, neither
be thou dismayed:
for the Lord thy God
is with thee wither-
so ever thou guest.

Joshua 1:9.

Mrs. Deborah Knox Livingston:

Became National Director of Citizenship, W.C.T.U. at age 48. Born in Scotland, the daughter of Mr. and Mrs. James Knox, Mrs. Livingston came to the United States early in her life. Educated in Providence and New York schools, she taught school in Rhode Island. A personal friend of Frances Willard, she became an advocate of the Prohibition Cause, and allied herself with this great movement. She was a brilliant speaker and possessed a charming personality.

On Sunday morning, August 5, 1923, God came very near to us and took to himself the beloved mother of our household. We sorrow with that hope which waits for the dawning of the resurrection morning. Letters, flowers, and telegrams were received, and I wish to express for myself and the family of our sincere appreciation for the very kind sympathy expressed. "God is our refuge and strength." May you share the blessings of peace and comfort so richly bestowed in this hour of our grief.

Benjamin T. Livingston

In 1888, looking from Tower Hill toward the village center. At left is Crocker's Store, then the Baptist Church; at right is Dry Swamp Academy. The photographer stood on Osterville's highest elevation, then called Liberty Pole Hill. Ships in Vineyard Sound were visible from the hilltop.

Catholic Church

July 12, 1892

There were two barge (horse-drawn) loads and nine two-seated carriage loads of people from here who attended services in the Catholic Church at Hyannis on Sunday.

July 25, 1904

A social party for the benefit of the new Catholic Church in Osterville will be given in Union Hall on Wednesday evening.

August 1, 1904

The foundation is being laid for the new Catholic Church in the village on Wianno Ave.

Catholic Church, c. 1910

The Roman Catholic Church in Osterville began as a mission church of St. Francis Xavier of Hyannis, just prior to the turn of the century, and continues to grow to this day. Mr. and Mrs. Charles Daniel, who came to Osterville in 1879 to work for the Garrison family of Boston, are believed to have been the first Roman Catholic family to settle in Osterville. At her Bay Street home, Mrs. Daniel held weekly classes for her own children and those of the Beaumont, Baker, and Hansberry families. Later, and before the turn of the century, others of the Catholic faith came to the village to work for those who were constructing homes along Osterville's waterfront.

Services were held at Union Hall during the summer months by The Reverend Cornelius McSwiney, who in 1882 became the first pastor of St. Francis Xavier in Hyannis, and later by The Rev. Daniel Doran who succeeded him in 1902. Once a month during the other seasons, the Daniel family hired a horse and carry-all to take as many of their ten children as could fit to attend services in Hyannis.

The land for the present church site was purchased in 1903 for $400 and consisted of 1¼ acres on Wianno Avenue. Construction of the original Church of Our Lady of Assumption was commenced in 1904 and completed in 1905 when the building was dedicated.

Rev. Doran remained pastor of the church through 1912. In 1913, Rev. Mortimer Downing came to replace him. During the days of his early ministry, services were held every other week in Osterville, as the church still remained a mission of the Hyannis Church.

Under the leadership of Rev. Downing, the church was remodeled and enlarged in 1916, and again in 1926. The Osterville church was established as a parish in 1928; at that time, Rev. Edward Killigrew became pastor. Also in 1928, the church purchased the present rectory and surrounding land from Agnes Till. Rev. Killigrew continued as pastor until 1938.

In 1938, Rev. Thomas J. McLean was named pastor of the church. During his ministry, the Missionary Cenacle was established on East Bay Road in the house which had been built in 1829 by Captain Shubael Baxter; the Cenacle was closed in 1966.

Additional land on Wianno Avenue, opposite the church, was purchased in 1940 for increased parking.

In 1960 and 1961, with the growing population of Roman Catholics, many of whom had come from industrial cities within driving distance of Osterville, the Church of Our Lady of Assumption was once more enlarged and basement rooms remodeled for use of parishioners' meetings. Roman Catholicism has grown to be the largest religious denomination in this area.

Congregational Church

September 6, 1859

Congregational Society at one time owned the Meeting House or Hall. Sold it to Universalist Society.

September 6, 1859 — Good News from Osterville

Osterville is a small village in the broad town of Barnstable, on Cape Cod. A few remaining members of a Congregational society in that village desired to sell their meeting house, as there was not a sufficient number of them left to continue public worship. There was in the place a Universalist Ladies Sewing Society that had accumulated some funds, and by an effort just in character with live Universalist women, they succeeded in adding enough to their funds to purchase the meeting house. Brother T. Bordon, of Hudson, N.Y., who was recently on a visit in that region, preached there a few Sundays ago, and they will continue to have preaching occasionally. But this is not all. Such sisters, and their husbands, brothers and sons, of course, have the spirit of their religion in them, and will make that house their Sabbath home when they do not have preaching. They will meet there, sing praise, read the word, pray, exhort, hold Sunday School, Bible Class, etc., in which course they will find every Sabbath a season of refreshing from the presence of the Lord.

St. Peter's Episcopal Church

July 6, 1903

Next Sunday the new Episcopal Church will be opened for services at Wianno — Osterville. This Church is intended primarily for the summer residents of Wianno as it has been found that there are many who would attend the services of the Episcopal Church if they were provided. The new Church is situated on the main road between Osterville and Wianno and is not far from the shore. It is a simple frame chapel somewhat after the style of St. Mary's Church, Barnstable. The plans were drawn by Mr. Lawrence Hill, Architect, of Boston, and Mr. Chester Bearse of Centerville, has been the contractor. It will hold about 115 and has cost with furnishings about $3,000. The opening services will be held at 11 A.M. and will be the usual service of the Episcopal Church. The Rector of St. Mary's Church, Barnstable, the Rev. J. C. Ayer, Jr., Ph.D., under whose direction the Church was built, will preach. The Rev. James P. Hawkes of Dedham will have charge of the services during the larger part of the summer. There will be service every Sunday at 11 A.M. and other services will be announced later.

Episcopal Church — c. 1910

A Brief History of St. Peter's Church

St. Peter's was founded in 1903 as a summer chapel in the Episcopal Diocese of Massachusetts. Within our Town of Barnstable, St. Mary's Church was founded in 1893, and St. Andrew's summer chapel in Hyannis Port in 1898. So it was perhaps not surprising that a few years later another summer chapel was founded in this section of the Town of Barnstable, completing the third end of a triangle. Today St. Peter's Parish serves people from the southern half of the Town of Barnstable — Wianno, Osterville, Centerville, Cotuit, Marstons Mills, Hyannis Port (some of whom attend St. Andrew's summer chapel when it is open, and St. Peter's during the winter).

The immediate neighborhood of St. Peter's Chapel when it was founded in 1903 — the village

of Osterville, and the section of it on the water known as Wianno, where the Chapel was built — was very small indeed. At the end of the last century a number of summer residents began coming regularly to Osterville, heavily from Boston and Pittsburgh, but also from a wide range of other cities. The small frame Church was built soon after the Chapel was organized. It was enlarged and the Parish House added in 1981 — if you look on the wall of the front pew on your right as you face the altar you will see the markings where the stairs to the old altar were. The new additions happily kept the main body of the old Chapel and the Tower as they had been since 1903.

No one alive remembers the earliest years of the summer chapel. The Rev. J. Cullen Ayer was

March 20, 1877

History of the Methodist Church in Osterville

by Rev. A. M. Osgood

I am not able to furnish anything like a complete history of the Methodist-Episcopal Church of Osterville, there being but very imperfect records of reference. A few items is all we can present.

The first class was organized about 1829, Oliver Hinckley, leader. It numbered about ten members. This place was then one of the preaching appointments of a large circuit. Edward T. Taylor, late of Boston, and for many years pastor of the Boston Post Society, was among the first who proclaimed the glad tidings of salvation, as understood by the followers of John Wesley, to the people of this vicinity. Following him have been many of our most devoted ministers. In 1847, under the pastorate of the writer our Church edifice was erected, at a cost of about $2,500. The sermon of dedication was by Robert Hatfield, then of Sandwich, now of Philadelphia. It was paid for and the sittings made free for all the people. This we considered a great acquisition, and we rejoiced over it with heartfelt joy.

Hitherto our Sabbath services had been held in the schoolhouse and old meeting house, now village hall. In 1848 Osterville became a distinct charge and Rev. John B. Hunt was the stationed minister. Following him our records give the names of Nahum Tainter, John Tasker, J. B. Washburn, B. K. Bosworth, J. C. Allen, John B. Hunt. Again, John Collier, John W. Willett, E. H. Colby, Henry D. Robinson, Edward Edson, Edward B. Hinckley, E. M. Anthony, Charles N. Hinckley, S. P. Snow, C. H. Ewer, J. W. Fish, and A. M. Osgood. Hannah D. Parker's name dates upon our Church record 1823, which is the earliest entry now living. Father Oliver Hinckley and his venerable wife commenced their Church life in 1829. He is in the 85th year of his age; Sister H. a few years his junior. God is still their love and shield. This life will not have been a failure. Greatly will they be missed when the Master shall have called them home.

Whole membership at this date, 68. The conference minutes for the present conference gave 40 scholars in Sunday School, 11 teachers, 200 volumes in library; George H. Hinckley, superintendent.

Our Church edifice is commodious, and in good repair. It is furnished with a good bell, cabinet organ, and vestry. We have a good parsonage. And the society is free from debt, which in these times is a fact of much importance.

Four ministers have gone forth from this Church: Rev. Edward B. Hinckley, Charles N. Hinckley, James R. Goodspeed and George B. Hinckley. The two last named are local preachers.

It is the earnest prayer of the writer, that the future history of this Church may be such as shall honor God, and greatly bless this whole community.

July 2, 1878

Thursday evening last the young folks held a M.E. strawberry festival at Village Hall. Proceeds about $30.00.

July 4, 1882

Strawberry Festival at the Hall last Thursday evening, by the M.E. Society, consisting of strawberries, ice cream, cake, candy, singing, readings, declamations, etc. They cleared about $30.

January 6, 1885

A watch night service was held in the M.E. Church on Wednesday night.

March 24, 1885

An interesting Missionary Concert was held in the Methodist Church on Sabbath evening.

November 10, 1885

Desirable improvements have been made in and about the pulpit at the M.E. Church, giving it a very tasteful appearance. A new stove has also been put in the Church.

March 2, 1886

A series of religious meetings are being held in the M.E. Church every evening. The pastor, Rev. L. B. Codding, is assisted by Capt. Howland of New Bedford. The latter spoke in the M.E. Church last Sabbath morning and in the Baptist Church in the afternoon. The M.E. Church was crowded in the evening with sitters in the aisles. All the meetings have been well attended. Some have for the first time professed saving faith, and many of the Christian people have found great peace. Both societies, the Baptist and Methodist, work together with great unanimity. A number of earnest Christian workers are present from Centerville every evening. Capt. Howland will speak in the M.E. Church next Sunday morning on "The Special Duties of the Holy Ghost" and in the evening on "Sowing and Reaping."

May 18, 1886

At the M.E. Church Rev. C. N. Hinckley spoke last Sunday from the text, "I must preach the gospel to other cities also." Since he came here as a preacher three years ago, much has been accomplished for the good of the Church. The debt of more than a thousand dollars has been paid, and a healthy increase of the Church body and Sunday School is plain to all. Not the least of the legacies which this Church has received during the pastorate now closed is the good name by Mr. Hinckley. The breath of malice and slander is silent, and no word or deed of his needs any defense.

October 26, 1886

Oct. 3rd was a happy day in the little Methodist Church here. A band of young converts were called to the altar and received the solemn rite of baptism and the right hand of fellowship into the Church, having joined the Church militant. We hope to see them follow their Lord, going about doing good and making the world the better for their living in it, and then when He calls them, to join the Church triumphant above and walk with Him in white.

February 7, 1888

Rev. Mr. Newell's subject for next Sabbath morning at the Methodist Church, as announced, "What will you do with Christ?"

February 21, 1888

Revival Services have been held at the Methodist Church the past week, to be continued during the present week.

June 5, 1888

Rev. Dr. Gallagher, P.E., occupied the pulpit at the Methodist Church on Sabbath morning. Mr. Oliver Hinckley, in his 97th year, was present at the service.

March 5, 1889

Revival services will be held in the M.E. Church each evening next week. Rev. G. M. Hamlen and wife of Fall River will assist the Pastor.

May 12, 1891

The Methodist Church here will be reopened Thursday next, May 14. Dr. L. B. Bates of East Boston will preach both afternoon and evening. A tower has been added to the Church, a furnace placed under it, new carved oak pews, new antique oak pulpit set, new carpet, new clock in oak case, new chandeliers, new oak rails for altar and singing seats have been placed inside, and the whole building painted without. The clock is the gift of Mrs. Alice Young of Provincetown, and a memorial window is to be placed in the Church by the relatives of Oliver Hinckley, one of the founders of the Church. Within a year about $2,000 has been expended on the Church and parsonage.

Re-dedication of the Methodist Church

May 19, 1891

Thursday, May 14th, the day appointed for the re-dedication of the Methodist Church in this place, was bright and clear, all that could be desired. The church was very prettily decorated for the occasion with plants and flowers. At the afternoon service the house was comfortably filled with our own people and friends from adjoining villages. The services opened with an anthem by the choir, after which Rev. F. H. Corson, the pastor, read from the Discipline the usual Dedication Service, and Rev. James R. Goodspeed read the Scripture lesson. Prayers were offered by Rev. Mr. Thygeson of W. Barnstable. After the singing of a hymn by the choir and congregation Rev. L. B. Bates of East Boston was introduced, a formality hardly necessary, so well-known is he. He said this was the 205th dedication in which he had taken part, not only in the Methodist denomination but among Baptists, Congregationalists, and others. He was glad to be so mixed up with other denominations for he expected to be in Heaven. His sermon was based on words found in II Kings, 6-6,7. "And the iron did swim. And he put out his hand and took it." This young man was poor, so poor that he had to borrow an axe. But he had a good character. Some people have plenty of money but no character. In his trouble he went to the prophet. In our day the minister is the one to go to in trouble. A pamphlet has been prepared by some infidels on this very subject, asserting that it was no miracle that the iron swam but that the stick which Elisah threw in was a magnetic stick and attracted the iron. When a tree having such a quality can be found then it will be time to believe it. The discourse was full of grand thoughts forcibly expressed. At the close of his address he proceeded in a very happy manner to raise $160, to which $20 was added by collections. Rev. J. N. Patterson of Cotuit pronounced the benediction. The exercises of the evening opened with a praise service led by the choir, accompanied by Mr. E. S. Crocker on the cornet. The lecture by Mr. Bates, entitled "Fourteen Thousand Miles in an Hour," was listened to and enjoyed by a full house. Many thanks are due all who helped make the day what we feel it was, a success.

July 7, 1891

The tongue of the Methodist bell which disappeared about this time last year, was discovered early yesterday morning hanging to a tree in front of the Church.

October 24, 1893

Sunday, Oct. 29th, will be observed as "Old Folks' Day" at the Osterville M.E. Church. The exercises will consist in the regular morning service at 10:30. Songs of "ye olden times" will be rendered by the united choirs of the local churches, also a sermon specially prepared for the "Old Folks" will be delivered by the pastor. The public generally are cordially invited.

November 20, 1894

Last Friday evening the Y.P.S.C.E. and their friends to the number of seventy-five held a "Poverty Social" in the vestry of the Methodist Church. Selections from poetry and song, together with short sketches on "Bells," furnished an interesting programme for the evening.

A pleasing feature of the evening was a "Tune Test." One of the party played parts of different tunes running them together, the company writing down the names as they were played. The prize for the most complete list, a bunch of chrysanthemums, was presented to Miss Littlefield.

Some interesting word games were played and refreshments were served, consisting of crackers and water from which the social took its name.

December 25, 1894

The Rev. O. E. Johnson will have a special New Year's Service in the M.E. Church Dec. 30th. All are cordially invited to attend.

February 5, 1895

At the Fourth Quarterly Conference of the M.E. Church last week the members gave the pastor, Rev. O. E. Johnson, a unanimous invitation to return to the village for his fourth year.

March 25, 1895

Next Sunday, March 31st, will be the last Sunday of Rev. O. E. Johnson's pastorate in our village.

January 4, 1897

The week of prayer will be observed under the auspices of the Y.P.S.C.E. Services will be held every evening in one of the Churches. You are cordially invited to attend and friends from adjoining villages are urged to attend if possible.

September 6, 1897

The M.E. Sunday School and friends went on a picnic Tuesday in Garrison Grove, on the bank of South Bay. A good time was enjoyed by all, young and old. Ice cream, with refreshments plenty, was served. About 60 or 70 enjoyed the day in the grove.

November 22, 1897

The Methodist-Episcopal Church of this place will celebrate its fiftieth anniversary next Saturday and Sunday. A recital of song and literature will be given at 8 o'clock Saturday evening by Samuel J. Mac Watters, assisted by Mrs. L. C. Twombly. Admission: 25 cents. At 10:30 Sunday morning, Rev. G. A. Grant will preach the anniversary sermon, which will be followed by a special Sunday School rally. In the afternoon, at 2:30, there will be given a short history of the Church, and brief addresses by former pastors. The older members of the Church will furnish the music at this meeting. The choir will lead in a song service at 7:30, after which Rev. George A. Sisson will preach the evening sermon. All friends of the Church will be cordially welcomed at these exercises.

The following was the program at the Sunday evening service, held at 7:30 o'clock:

Songs for the Young People.
Prayer.
Solo, Fear Not, O Israel — Mr. Mac Watters.
Singing — Choir.
Sermon — Rev. G. A. Sisson of North Dighton.

The singing was first-class, and the preaching of a higher order. The house was full to overflowing.

The young pastor, Rev. G. M. Fowles, is an ardent, faithful worker in the Master's cause. The work has progressed under his administration and the Church has been quickened.

History of Church

December 6, 1897 — Fiftieth Anniversary

The Methodist Episcopal Church of Osterville celebrated its Fiftieth Anniversary on Saturday and Sunday, Nov. 27, by very pleasing exercises, viz.:

Saturday evening a Literary and Song Recital was given by Mr. S. J. Mac Watters of Boston. Mr. Mac Watters was greeted by a full house and all spoke in praise of the entertainment. The following was the program at the Anniversary Service, Sunday morning, at 10:30 o'clock:

Organ Prelude.
Hymn, Watchman, Tell Us of the Night.
Prayer — Rev. Edward B. Hinckley.
Duet, The Home Land — Mrs. Twombly and Mr. Mac Watters.
New Testament Lesson — Rev. Mr. Hinckley.
Hymn, I Love Thy Kingdom, Lord.
Sermon — Rev. G. A. Grant of Middleboro.

At the Sunday School Rally Day exercises, after singing by the School and Junior Epworth League, a Miss from one of the classes, Genieve Crosby, came forward and repeated the following poem, written by Mr. William Bennett:

Mr. Fowles, you are welcome
To our hearts and Sabbath Home,
Old and young extend this greeting,
We are glad that you have come.

You are welcome to our labors,
For there is work to do;
Welcome to our joys and sorrows,
All these things we'll share with you.

While you tell the blessed story
Of a Saviour's love for all,
May God's richest, highest blessing
On your labors freely fall.

We, the little children, greet you,
As God's messengers of grace.
Will you give us, Mr. Fowles,
In your heart a snug, warm place?

We will ever love and cherish
Our dear pastor from this day,
And with these words of heartfelt welcome
Accept from us this small bouquet.

Mr. Fowles was taken completely by surprise. He is a great worker in the Sabbath School, and his labors are appreciated by our people.

On Sunday afternoon, at 2:30 P.M., the following program was rendered: Singing, "Merry Christmas" by children. The rendering of the program was very commendable and was highly appreciated by an enthusiastic audience and reflected great credit upon the committee, who so ably performed their duty. After the program, the many presents were distributed by the different committees and all wended their way homeward, filled with pleasant memories of the happy and enjoyable anniversary of Him who taught Peace on Earth, Good Will to Men.

M.E. Church, Osterville, Mass.
by Rev. George M. Fowles, 1897

The first Methodists of this village were members of the church at Marstons Mills. In 1829 a class numbering about ten was organized at Osterville with Oliver Hinckley as leader. The members of this class still retained their connection with the church at the Mills, and attended preaching services there, until 1846, when thirty-two withdrew from that church and formed a separate organization at Osterville. Services were held in the old Meeting House until the following year, when a church building was erected at a cost of $2,500, all of which was provided for before dedication. A. M. Osgood was pastor. Robert M. Hatfield of Sandwich preached the dedicatory sermon.

In 1848 Osterville became a district charge, and John B. Hunt was stationed here as preacher in charge. During his pastorate the parsonage was built and furnished.

In 1858, while J. W. Willett was pastor, a bell was purchased and placed in the tower. The vestry was built and furnished in 1862, while H. D. Robinson was stationed here.

The first organ was placed in the church in 1869, during the pastorate of Charles N. Hinckley. This was replaced by the present organ in 1888, while E. B. Gurney was pastor. In 1890 the entire church was remodeled and refurnished at a cost of about $1,600, all of which was paid. F. H. Corson was pastor.

An historical sketch of this church would not be complete without special mention of the labors and liberality of Oliver Hinckley and his wife. Both were converted in 1828, and under the ministry of Enoch Bradley. Both were members of the first class formed in Osterville. Their home was the home of the Methodist preachers for over half a century. Father Hinckley, from the time of his appointment as class leader in 1829, until his death in 1888, was an effective member of the official board. This church has been especially blessed in having loyal devoted Christian workers on the various boards. Of the original board of trustees, John A. Blossom served thirty-one years; Josiah Scudder, Jr., thirty years; George H. Hinckley, forty-four — all of which time he was secretary. Oliver Crocker is the only surviving member of that board. He has completed fifty years of official service, and for the last thirty years has been President of the Board of Trustees. Four ministers have been raised up in this church: E. B. Hinckley, C. N. Hinckley, James R. Goodspeed and G. B. Hinckley. The last-named was a local preacher.

At the present the membership is not as large as it once was, but Methodism still has a loyal band of workers here. Several of the first members of the church have been spared to bless the present generation with their devotion and their prayers. All things considered, our church is prosperous now, and is looking forward to better things in the future. In closing this sketch we wish to state that of late years the church has found a number of friends and helpers among the summer visitors. One of these deserves especial mention. Mrs. J. W. Gaff, a noble Christian woman, by her influence, her presence at the church services, and her liberality, is a great help to the church and an example of a Christian abounding in good works while away from home to spend the summer season.

Trustees and Stewards — Oliver H. Crocker, President; James R. Goodspeed, Secretary and Treasurer; Mrs. A. A. Cram (R. S.), James West, Bethuel Adams, Freeman Scudder, H. Foster Lewis, W. Scott Scudder, Albert Crocker, Edmond H. Lewis, Francis A. Dane, Martha W. Crocker, Emma C. Cammett, Mary Scudder, Cora Lewis, Augusta H. Scudder.

Pastors

1847 — A. M. Osgood
1848 — John B. Hunt
1849 — Nahum Tainter
1850 — John Tasker
1851 — J. B. Washburn
1852 — B. K. Bosworth
1853 — J. C. Allen
1854 — John B. Hunt
1855-56 — John Collier
1857-58 — John W. Willett
1859-60 — E. H. Colby
1861-62 — H. D. Robinson
1863-64 — Edward Edson
1865 — Edward B. Hinckley
1866 — E. M. Anthony
1867-69 — C. N. Hinckley
1870-71 — S. P. Snow
1872-73 — C. H. Ewer
1875-76 — J. W. Fitch
1876 — D. C. Porter
1877 — G. H. Butler
1878 — E. S. Fletcher
1879-80 — S. H. Day
1881-83 — G. A. Grant
1884 — W. W. Hall
1885-86 — L. B. Codding
1887 — C. H. Dalrymple
1887 — E. F. Newell
1888-89 — E. B. Gurney
1890-91 — F. H. Corson
1892-94 — Oscar E. Johnson
1895 — G. A. Sisson
1896 — O. A. Farley
1897 — George M. Fowles

January 3, 1898

Revival meetings were held in the M.E. Church every evening of last week. Rev. C. H. Taylor of New Bedford assisted the pastor. The attendance and interest in the services were very good, and we believe they have been helpful to all who attended them. The pastor of the Church received a substantial Christmas gift in the form of a number of bank notes. Such gifts not only show the spirit of the givers, but they are also exceedingly practical in present times.

October 3, 1898

The hour for Sunday services at the M.E. Church has been changed from morning to afternoon, members of M.E. Chapel, Centerville uniting with them.

January 2, 1899

Successful Gospel Services have been held in both Churches during the past week, conducted by Pastors Antrim and Livingston. On Wednesday evening, Mr. Mc Millan, pastor of the Church in Mashpee, spoke. Mrs. Livingston also had charge of one service.

June 12, 1899

A very interesting Children's Day Concert was given on Sunday evening in the Methodist Church. The program, "Peace or War," prepared especially for the Board of Education of the M.E. Church, was well carried out in every detail.

November 13, 1899

During the month of November Rev. E. M. Antrim of the M.E. Church will hold special evangelistic services every Sunday evening.

December 11, 1899

The Y.P.S.C.E. held a Lemon Social Tuesday evening at the home of Mrs. William Freeman. Each guest brought a lemon, which was given to a committee, who labeled the fruit and laid it aside for further use. An exceedingly interesting program, interspersed with games that called for exercise of brain, made the evening pass quickly, and all pronounce this as "one of the best." At the close of the evening, when the lemons had served their purpose, reports were brought in of the number of seeds, and prizes awarded to Miss Marcia Hallett, who had the most, 22, and Mrs. Owen Lewis, whose lemon contained not a seed. Cake and lemonade were served.

January 15, 1900

The revival meetings were held for two weeks at the M.E. Church by the pastor, assisted by Rev. C.P. Hiller and Rev. Mr. Philip Frick of Boston. Rev. T. J. Everett, Presiding Elder for this District, preached two evenings. His talk will long be remembered by the thinking people. Miss Etta F. Lovell presided at the organ; her singing was fine, and a great help.

The Baptist Church had their meeting Sunday nights at 6 o'clock. Their pastor and people came for a Union meeting. Eight or ten have been converted, and the Churches revived. Mr. Antrim is an earnest worker in his Master's cause.

Mrs. Augusta H. Scudder, over 80 years old, was at most every meeting with her smiling face and her words of cheer for all. She seems to say it is our duty as Christians to plan great things for God, and do the very best we can to carry them out, regardless of the obstacles that we meet, and God will do the rest. We need to give the best we have to God.

January 15, 1900

At the close of the special revival services in the M.E. Church, in which both churches united, the Christian Endeavor Society continued the work by holding cottage prayer services during the past week. These services have been well attended, and we trust productive of much good.

March 5, 1900 — Out of Debt

Sunday, March 4th, was a day of great rejoicing and thanksgiving at the M.E. Church. There has been a debt of $150.00 on the Church for several years, and last October jugs were given out to gather in the offerings. March 4th was set apart as the day to bring the jugs. When they were opened it was found that with other subscriptions, $80.00 had been collected. That seemed a good deal to be thankful for, and the Doxology was sung. Then came the greatest surprise of the day when a letter was read from Major W. F. Goodspeed, enclosing a draft of $150.00. More than twice the amount of the debt was raised. The duet by Mr. Walter I. Fuller and Mrs. Antrim added to the interest of the occasion. Next Sunday the notes will be burned.

December 11, 1905

Evangelistic services have been held in the M.E. Church this week in the charge of Rev. Mr. Plaxton, assisted by Rev. Mr. Scrivener of Cotuit and Rev. Mr. Natino of the Baptist Church.

April 23, 1907

Rev. E. McP. Ames and family, who have been in Stoughton for two years, are at the Methodist parsonage, Mr. Ames having been appointed pastor here for the coming year.

September 24, 1907

We regret to learn of the sudden death of Rev. Oscar E. Johnson of Middleboro. Mr. Johnson was pastor of the M.E. Church here some years ago, and made many friends who will mourn his departure and extend sympathy to the bereaved family.

April 20, 1908

The Epworth League held a poverty social in the vestry Friday evening. Many were dressed in their old clothes and caused much merriment.

May 25, 1908

Officers of the Epworth League were elected:

President	Dexter Pattison
1st Vice President	Miss Addie Crocker
2nd Vice President	Mr. W. Scott Scudder
3rd Vice President	Miss Mildred Pattison
4th Vice President	Mr. Frederic Scudder
Secretary	Mrs. George Lewis
Treasurer	Mrs. Maurice G. Crocker
Organist	Miss Christie Ames

July 13, 1908

The evening service at the Methodist-Episcopal Church will be held Sunday at 6:45 on the lawn.

March 1, 1909

Revival services are being held in the Methodist Church.

May 24, 1909

The Methodist Sunday School has recently organized into a Temperance Society, the majority of the members signing the pledge.

August 23, 1910

Miss Addie Crocker and Miss Marion Childs gave their Sunday School classes a picnic at Aunt Tempy's Pond, Thursday afternoon.

March 28, 1911 — A Farewell Sermon

Rev. E. McP. Ames of the Methodist-Episcopal Church leaves for South Manchester tomorrow morning, where the Annual Conference is to be held. He has been stationed at Osterville for four years and in connection with his charge has also supplied the Methodist churches at Marstons Mills and Centerville. He has served this church the longest of any minister in the over 60 years of its history. Only three others subsequently had remained three years.

In his farewell sermon, he made reference to the splendid work done by the Sunday School and of their increase in average of over 35 per cent. The increase in church membership has been over 40 per cent. The salary was raised the past year, $104., through the efforts of the Epworth League, so that the church has paid more, by $236 this year, for salary, than four years ago.

Total expenses of the church for the past four years, over $4,300. Not bad for a little membership of from 37 to 52. Mr. Ames, on his three charges, has preached over 685 times, conducted over 350 prayer meetings, officiated at 35 funerals, and ridden hundreds of miles on his bicycle.

He has been connected with the Village Improvement Society as one of its board of directors for the past three years and with much feeling, at the close of his sermon, thanked not only the church members, but his many friends for all their kindnesses.

Rev. George A. Grant

Rev. E. B. Gurney

Rev. G. M. Fowles

Rev. O. E. Johnson

June 6, 1911

Rev. W.T. Johnson of the M.E. Church preached that evening from Jonah 3:2 "The Story of Jonah and the Great Fish." Jonah was no myth, but a reality. The God who created fish originally could easily prepare one for this emergency. The Bible cannot be bisected. It is all the Word of God, given by inspiration. Mr. Johnson was listened to with close attention. The male chorus led by Mr. Walter I. Fuller sang several selections.

December 10, 1912

A business meeting of the All Around Class was held for the purpose of re-organizing. The following officers were chosen to serve until the semi-annual election in January: President, Mr. Henry Whiteley; Vice President, Mr. Oscar Chadwick; Secretary, Miss Genieve Leonard; Treasurer, Mr. Oscar Chadwick; Chaplain, Rev. W. T. Johnson.

February 11, 1913

The Lincoln Anniversary program entitled, "The Red Road," or Christ First, was given in the Methodist Episcopal Church Sunday night to a large and attentive audience. The music was rendered by a large chorus choir, with Mr. Arthur Wyman, violinist, and Mr. Edward Crocker, cornetist. The music was fine.

November 15, 1915

Don't forget the debate Tuesday evening at the Methodist vestry. Subject "In order to safeguard the National Peace, the U.S. should increase her military defense."

Chairman of the meeting, Mr. Fowler, our Grammar School teacher. Judges: Messrs. Charles Lewis, J. M. Leonard, and Ralph Crosby.

The affirmative side will be opened by Mr. George Lewis, the negative by Mr. William Hodges; affirmative colleague, Mr. Albert Hinckley, negative colleague, Mr. Walter Fuller. The debate is open and free to all men and women alike.

March 8, 1915

The Junior League held a business and social meeting Saturday afternoon in the Methodist Episcopal vestry. The following officers were elected for the coming six months: president, Truman Lewis; first vice president, Annie Nute; second vice president, George Thurber; third vice president, Olive Scudder, fourth vice president, Gerald Gross; secretary, Elsie Chadwick; treasurer, Dwight Lewis; organist, Irma Cook.

March 22, 1915

"Buy your own cherries," a temperance song and story service, was given in the Methodist Church Sunday evening. This took the place of the sermon in the regular union service for that evening.

Methodist-Episcopal parsonage located on the northwest corner of West Bay Road and Wianno Avenue now location of Post Office — c. 1890s.

116

Methodist-Episcopal Church — early 1900s.

August 30, 1915

The Methodist Church is having a kitchen built on to the vestry. Mr. Ed Lewis and Mr. Foster Lewis are doing the work. They have also put a new floor in the vestry.

September 23, 1918

The electric lights which have been installed in the M.E. church were used for the first time on Thursday evening and gave much satisfaction. As has been stated, they were given as a memorial for the late Mr. Josiah and Mrs. Augusta Scudder by their son, J. Porter Scudder and his sons.

January 17, 1921

Don't forget the thimble party to be held in the Methodist-Episcopal vestry on Tuesday afternoon from 2 until 5 o'clock.

July 17, 1922

There is a great improvement in the Methodist-Episcopal churchyard since the trees are all cleared away.

August 13, 1923

Memorial services for our beloved President Warren G. Harding were held in the Methodist church on Friday from two to three P.M.

Osterville's unpaved Main Street c. 1910. Note horse and buggy in front of Horace Parker's store, left; the Methodist Church with its bell tower; and at far right, the gas lamp on the green where the flag pole now stands in front of The Village Country Store.

Osterville Community Church

by William P. Hodges

There seems to be a great amount of agitation in our little village over the new Community Church movement, and after hearing pros and cons on the question, the writer believes a few words in defense of our present church system are in order.

In the first place, what is the matter with the way the churches have been carried on for the past few years under the name of "Community Church," or, in other words, is not the union of the old established Methodist and Baptist churches of our village a success?

Out of respect for the old members of these two churches, some of whom have gone to their reward above, and all of whom have worked and given in many cases more than the "tenth" to keep the churches open, I am loath to say the old established churches are no longer competent to carry on the religious work of the community.

Those outside the church roll who have always given, I believe, because they considered the churches an asset to the village, I understand now say that they no longer care to give unless they can have a voice in the workings of the church.

Has the day come when the church, in order to keep its doors open, has got to put in the background, baptism, change of heart, and has got to forget the words of Christ which we have heard since childhood, "Thou must be born again?" and swell its members by the mere singing of a covenant saying, in part, "I believe in Christ and promise to uphold the Community Church," but does not repeat the commandments of Christ, above quoted?

These words are written by one not a member of any church, so I am not writing from a selfish point of view, but I feel that the organization now being formed in Osterville would not be upheld by the old church members who have gone and for whom I have every respect. We may be living in a new advanced age, but I cannot conceive any change in the teachings of Christ which have lived through the ages.

If the time is ripe to form a moral church and to lose sight of many of the teachings of Christ which have been the backbone of religion, then I say the new movement is all right, but let's call black, black, and white, white.

When such a church is formed, we must have a man preach to us morality and not religion, or I believe the new movement will be a failure. And I also do not believe we have any right to call the organization the Osterville Community Church, but we must call it the Osterville Community Moral Church.

The above words may seem by some to be far from right, but they are sincere and are written after requests from some who are not in favor of the new movement.

Union Services

January 10, 1893

Union evangelistic services are to be held in the M.E. Church during the week commencing Monday, Jan. 16th.

September 22, 1902

A union service in memory of our late President McKinley was held Sunday evening in the Methodist Church. The pastor, Rev. C. H. Priddy, gave an able discourse on the life and influence of the President. The hymns used were those sung at the funeral a year ago, a quartette rendering the song "Beautiful Isle of Somewhere." Rev. Mr. Spidle of the Baptist Church sang "By the Beautiful Gate." A collection was taken for the McKinley Memorial Fund.

January 18, 1909

The Sunday evening Union services have proven more successful than the most optimistic anticipations. January 10th, the preacher requested the congregation, which numbered 160, to rise and signify by doing so, that from this time they would take no part in raffling or lottery.

August 29, 1911

At the Union Service of the Methodist and Baptist Churches, held at the Methodist Church Sunday evening, Rev. J. Cullen Ayer of the Episcopal Church spoke. The rain kept many away. Those who were there were well repaid for coming by a very practical sermon from the text, "There is none other name under heaven given among men whereby we must be saved."

Temperance Society

September 11, 1833

Temperance Meeting at Osterville. Sunday evening last at 5 o'clock a meeting of the friends of Temperance was held in the Meeting House of Osterville, which was very fully attended by citizens of that place, Cotuit, Hyannis, etc. The services were introduced by singing and prayer from Mr. Richard Thayer. An address on the subject of temperance was delivered by Benjamin F. Hallett, of Boston.

———————————

March 3, 1842

The friends of Temperance assembled in the Baptist Meeting House for the purpose of forming a Temperance Society.

The meeting was called to order by Rev. Mr. Leland. Isaac Scudder was chosen Moderator and Charles Bearse, Clerk.

A Pledge was then presented for the consideration of the meeting by Mr. Leland and after some discussion was adopted.

Fifty-four persons then signed the pledge. It was then voted that a committee of three be appointed by the chair to draught a constitution and Ira Leland, Isaac Hodges and Josiah Scudder were appointed.

Voted that a committee of three be appointed by the chair to nominate officers for the society and Oliver Hinckley, Cornelius Lovell and Joseph Robbins were appointed. The constitution was then handed in by the chairman of the committee chosen for that purpose. Each article was acted upon separately and the whole unanimously adopted.

The committee appointed to nominate officers for the Society reported for:
>President — Hansard Hallett
>Vice Presidents — James N. Lovell
>>Samuel A. Wiley
>Secretary & Treasurer — Charles Bearse
>Directors — David Fuller, Nelson Lovell
>>Austin Lovell, Warren Thomas

Voted that the secretary be and hereby is authorized to purchase a book suitable in which to keep records of the society and that a collection be taken at a future meeting to defray the expense. Voted to adjourn.

———————————

February 14, 1843

Voted and chose as Directors:
>Robert Lovell
>Freeman Lovell
>Alexander Bacon
>William Blount

Voted that we invite Henry A. Scudder to lecture to this Society in this house next Thursday evening at ½ past 6 o'clock p.m.

———————————

February 13, 1844

Voted that a paper be circulated for subscription to raise a sum of money sufficient to supply each family in the village with a Temperance journal.

———————————

February 17, 1845

Voted that it shall be the duty of the directors or standing committee annually to wait on any member that may act disorderly and report at the next annual meeting.

———————————

February 10, 1846

Out of 184 in the village who had signed the pledge all had lived up to the pledge, except one.

———————————

January 30, 1847

Voted that Warren Thomas be expelled from the Osterville Temperance Society for improper conduct.

February 23, 1847

A petition was then read to the meeting to procure petitioners to the Massachusetts legislators for a law to be made that it be imprisonment to violate the license law.

January 29, 1848

One fact it may be well not to omit is that the gentlemen like to have temperate wives for 23 of the ladies belonging to this society have married since its commencement in 1842.

February 10, 1857

Voted that there be a standing by-law that the annual meeting be opened by prayer by some clergyman if one can be had. If not, by someone that may volunteer.

February 9, 1858

Voted that in the opinion of this Society the town agent for the sale of spiritous liquors should so far report in detail at the annual town meeting as to give the names of each purchaser and the amount purchased.

February 7, 1861

The following is the report of the secretary:

Ladies and Gentlemen:

This Society was formed March 3, 1842. And I think there is no question but it has done a great amount of good, for since its formation there has 356 signed its pledge and think you that this number would have been as temperate as they have been were it not for their voluntary resolutions to abstain from intoxicating draught by manfully signing the pledge?

But I am sorry to say that in years past there has been several instances, whose desire or thirst or some other power has prevailed over their good resolution and they have returned to their cups, and to inebriation of course; the only safe way is to touch not, and taste not. I also think those that have received the beneficial influences of temperance should not relax in their efforts to keep the demon intemperance from our village. It is I fear on the increase around us. I was told a short time since by Mr. Timothy Crocker of Hyannis that in his village on Sunday there was a man or person belonging in this village, helped into his carriage he being so drunk he could not get in.

This thirst for the ardent is not dead for at the last funeral which I was tolling the bell two sleighs drove to my house and tried to get something as I was told that might have turned their sleighs sunny side up before their arrival at home, there was no accident from what they received.

James N. Lovell

February 10, 1862

Assembled in the Methodist vestry. The President Deacon Robert Lovell called the meeting to order.

February 10, 1862

There was a complaint made against one of our number that live in Boston — Jesse G. Lovell who had broken the pledge. After discussion it was moved that his name be erased from the pledge which was carried unanimously.

February 10, 1863

Miss Clarissa Lovell procures 80 new signatures to the temperance pledge.

February 8, 1864

Meeting held in Methodist meeting house. The report of the secretary —

My report is that we have done nothing as to the activity of our society since our last annual meeting but I believe its moral influence has as a general thing been good. I have known of but one instance of any of its members being led astray by the intoxicating cup. That person did live in this village but now lives in a neighboring one. His name is Thomas Lewis. On the 16th of last December he brought rum to Robert Evans and had a very bad drunken time and like to have killed each other and I therefore recommend that his name be erased from the pledge.

James N. Lovell

The committee appointed by the Temperance Society of Osterville at their annual meeting, held Monday evening, February 12, 1865, in the vestry of the M.E. Church, to prepare resolutions of respect to the memory of Mr. James N. Lovell, late secretary of said Society, respectfully submit their report.

Whereas it has pleased Almighty God, Our Heavenly Father, to remove from us by death our beloved brother, James N. Lovell, late efficient secretary of the Osterville Temperance Society, therefore:

1) RESOLVED, that the members and officers of this Society are admonished by the dispensation of Divine Providence in the decease of our faithful secretary, Mr. James N. Lovell, in the 62nd year of his age and the 23rd year of his service in our cause, of the brevity of time, the uncertainty of life, and the great importance of faithfulness unto death in the discharge of our obligations to our neighbors and ourselves, and the great principles of righteousness and temperance.

2) RESOLVED, that we are encouraged by the good example of our late secretary to patient continuance of the profession and practice of temperance unto the end.

3) RESOLVED, that we present to his bereaved family and relatives our united assurance of tender sympathy in their great affliction and our earnest hope that their loss is his gain.

4) RESOLVED, that we will endeavor to serve our generation by following after our late esteemed and respected secretary in the plain and safe paths of temperance, until it shall please the Supreme Ruler of the universe to summon us to the general assembly of the upright in Heaven.

5) RESOLVED, that these resolutions be entered in the records of our Society, and a copy of the same be presented to the bereaved family of our deceased friend and brother, James N. Lovell, late Secretary of the Osterville Temperance Society.

Respectfully submitted,
E. B. Hinckley

December 14, 1875

The first snow put in an appearance on Wednesday last, as did also Dr. Charles Jewett, who delivered a fine temperance lecture to a full house.

March 14, 1893

The Young Women's Christian Temperance Union, organized in our village in January, held its first regular meeting Feb. 28, in the vestry of the M.E. Church. The officers of the Society are:

President — Mrs. A. H. Scudder
Vice Presidents — Miss M. T. Lovell
Miss May A. Adams
Sec. and Treas. — Miss Etta Lovell
Supt. of Loyal Temperance Legion — Miss Bertha Lovell

March 21, 1893

Co. C., Barnstable Division of Massachusetts Loyal Temperance Legion, held its first public meeting at the schoolhouse, March 11th. The officers are:

President — Henry Parker
Vice Presidents — Alma Johnson
William Hodges
Secretary — Bennie Lancy
Treasurer — Albert Hinckley
Ushers — Arthur Lewis, William Adams
Chorister — Miss Etta Lovell
Leader — Miss Bertha Lovell

Thirty-nine members being present, the meeting was formally opened by the President, who then called upon the leader to direct the members in the presentation of the following interesting program.

Responsive Scripture Reading with Pledge.
Song, We'll Never Touch a Single Drop.
Secretary's Report.
Treasurer's Report.
Reading, Two Classes — Alma Johnson.
The Dead March — Warren Hodges.
Telling Fortunes — Bertha Chadwick.
Recitation, Temperance Town — Lovell Parker
Recitation, A Wildwood Lesson
— Hannah Lewis.
Song with National Motto.
We Mean to Live All Right — Edgar DeWitt.
Recitation, 'Tis True as Truth — William Hodges
Dialogue — Girls and boys.
My Pledge — Ernest DeWitt
What it Does to our Stomachs
— Albert Hinckley
Recitation, We Ought to Sign
— Andrew Crosby.
Recitation, Never Swear — Oscar Johnson.
Reading — Warren M. Hodges.
Closing song and collection.

A course of Temperance instruction caused quite an interest among the scholars of our schools, and it is hoped the keeping of the triple pledge regarding the use of profane language, tobacco and alcoholic liquors may be productive of much good in the future.

Women's Christian Temperance Union (The W.C.T.U.)

January 8, 1923

The social of the W.C.T.U. (Women's Christian Temperance Union) was held in the Methodist-Episcopal vestry Monday evening, Jan. 1st. A large number were present. The president opened the meeting with scripture and prayer and singing of a few hymns from Songs of Hope, with Miss Olive Scudder as organist. After a little business Mrs. Crosby gave the meeting into the hands of the social committee who had a program of songs, readings by Mr. William Hodges from Joseph Lincoln's writings and by Rev. Robert VanKirk, a spelling match and other interesting games mixed with fun. A collation of doughnuts and hot coffee was served by Mrs. VanKirk assisted by several young boys as waiters.

March 3, 1927

Monday night the Women's Christian Temperance Union held a recognition service in the Community Church in honor of Mrs. Addie G. Crosby, past president of the Deborah Knox Livingston Union for 12 years and who recently resigned on account of failing health. Mrs. Mary Scudder succeeded her.

January 19, 1928

Mr. and Mrs. J. W. Tallman, Mr. and Mrs. W. Scott Scudder and Mrs. Dora Braley of the W.C.T.U. attended Monday's session at the Barnstable Court to witness the trial of liquor cases, but the cases were continued until next week. As far as it went, it was interesting to those who had never witnessed any court proceedings.

March 1, 1928

A petition has been circulated among the members of the W.C.T.U. (Women's Christian Temperance Union) to protest against the bill which is coming before the Senate and House, which legalizes games of chance and lotteries. Mrs. W. S. Scudder has secured over 30 names and sent them in.

April 5, 1928

The Loyal Temperance Legion of Osterville recently organized under the leadership of Mrs. Helen Chadwick and made its first public appearance Friday evening, March 30, at the Community Church.

November 1, 1928

The Women's Christian Temperance Union held services of a patriotic nature in the Community Church Sunday evening. President Mrs. Mary Scudder presided and carried out a program entitled "Service of Induction into Citizenship." This service was non-partisan, simply being solemn exercise intended to impress the privileges and duties of citizenship upon those who are about to assume the duties of voting. Scripture by Mrs. Scudder and prayer was followed by that grand old song, "Who is a Patriot?" sung by the Messrs. Scudder and Childs, Miss Sarah Boult, Mrs. Fred Dill, and Mrs. Mary Scudder. Singing by congregation, March of Allegiance.

J. M. Leonard explained the way to mark the ballot for the benefit of new voters and stressed the importance of doing one's full duty in voting, not only for President, but for other candidates of our particular party. It is not enough, as some think, to vote for just President if we wish to make our party strong and vital. Mr. G. W. Hallett talked on one of the referendum questions, Sunday sports, and give his views on what it would mean to commercialize our Sabbath.

Stuart Scudder sang a solo, "Vote No on Election Day." Mrs. Dora Braley read a poem, "An American Boy to His Father." Miss Sarah Boult read an article on the importance of one vote which has played oftimes a great part in the destinies of men and nations. Your vote and my vote should be a part of our religious duty towards the well-being of ourselves and our fellowmen. Let no obstacle stand in our way of casting our vote if it is humanly possible to do so on the 6th of November.

Remarks from Mrs. Scudder and Benediction, Mr. Arthur Duffin.

October 17, 1929

The annual W.C.T.U. memorial service will be held at Hillside Cemetery Sunday at 3 P.M. for the purpose of honoring the late Mrs. Deborah Knox Livingston and other promoted members. The graves will be decorated with flowers and green. Mrs. Mary Scudder, president of the local Union, will be in charge. Let all members try to be present on this occasion in memory of the one whom all loved and who organized our Union.

Hillside Cemetery

At the Town Meeting held February 6, 1843, the petition from the inhabitants of Osterville for the enlargement of their burying ground near Josiah Scudder's was, by a vote, referred to the Selectmen. The Selectmen notified the inhabitants of Osterville to meet them on the premises on Wednesday, the 19th of April, 1843, at 9 A.M. to examine the premises. The parties met the said 19th day of April, but came to no conclusion owing to the high price that was asked for the land that was necessary for the enlargement of said grounds.

But at the Town Meeting held November 13th, 1843, the Selectmen made a verbal report, viz., that it was highly necessary for the burying ground to be enlarged or a new one laid out. Also that Capt. George Lovell asked quite too much (as they thought) for the land wanted for enlargement, also that a larger amount of land could be bought for less money on the opposite side of the road. Which report was accepted by a motion being made and seconded. That the town purchase two acres of land on the opposite side of the road, for fifty dollars, of Josiah Scudder, for a new burying ground which motion was put and accepted by the town.

And accordingly, to their notice, the Selectmen, viz., Nathaniel Hinckley, Thomas B. Lewis, and Daniel Bassett, met the parties on the ground on December 1, 1843, and laid out a new burying ground opposite the old one, the lot or ground being about eighteen rods square, and two acres, and sold the building of the fence around the same to the lowest bidder.

Many of the inhabitants were not satisfied. They accordingly petitioned the town again, in January 1845, for an enlargement of the old burying ground, which was granted as can be seen on the next page and the plan. November 14, 1845.

Voted at an adjourned meeting of the Town of Barnstable held February 11, 1845.

Voted that David Fuller and others, petitioners, be authorized to remove the fence on the northerly side of the old burying ground in Osterville and enclose in addition thereto, so much land as George Lovell will give the Town a deed of, for the consideration of one dollar. George Lovell, accordingly, gave a deed of the land, March 13, 1845.

July 27, 1846

Baptists agreeable to a notice being given in the meeting house yesterday for the people to meet in the old meetinghouse this evening to make arrangements to lay out the enlargement of the old burying ground. Several citizens, accordingly, assembled and discussed the subject, and on motion, voted and chose a committee of four to lay out said ground into lots. Voted and chosen by nominations:

David Fuller
Oliver Hinckley
James N. Lovell
Josiah Ames

May 16, 1871

Early in March the people of this village assembled in Village Hall effected an organization giving it the name of "The Osterville Burial Ground Association", adopted a constitution and elected officers. The object of the society is the improvement of our cemetery. Some $230 in money and labor have been subscribed for this purpose, most of which has been expended under the superintendence of the executive committee of the society, more especially that of Capt. I. P. Hodges who has evinced fine taste and judgment in the improvements in and about the graves.

Within the year death has been busy in the ranks of our aged. Two have recently left us. Mr. Blount was an Englishman by birth and was a carpenter on board the Guerrierre when captured by the Constitution, made this country the home of his adoption; he has been a resident of this village, we judge, some fifty years or more.

Mr. Goodspeed was a master shipbuilder and pursued his calling in this village many years. He represented his native town one or more terms in our State Legislature.

The Old Burying Ground in Osterville with the enlargement as laid out above. Survey'd and plotted August 10th, 1846.
By: David Fuller
James N. Lovell
Josiah Ames

October 24, 1876

A new tomb is being built in the cemetery for the benefit of the village at the town's expense.

November 10, 1885

Much needed new fences have been put up in front of the cemeteries in this place. The cemetery grounds have also been greatly improved by the removal of briars, etc. This is a movement in the right direction. Our cemeteries should always present a neat and tasty appearance.

May 17, 1892

The Osterville Cemetery has been much improved by a neat wire fence in place of the old one of posts and rails, which was no longer serviceable.

May 29, 1905

A new fence is being built around Hillside Cemetery. A great improvement.

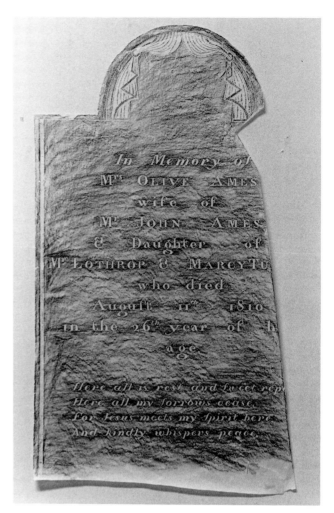

In Memory of Mrs. Olive Ames
wife of Mr. John Ames and
daughter of Mr. Lothrop & Marcy Tupper
who died August 11th, 1810
in the 26th year of her age
Here is all rest and sweet repose
Here all my sorrows cease
For Jesus meets my spirit here
And kindly whispers peace.

G.S.I.

Olive Tupper 1784-1810 married John Ames in 1806. Her sister Eliza was the third wife of Ebenezer Parker.

June 14, 1920

On Monday evening of last week a meeting was held in the vestry of the Baptist church for the organization of an association to improve and care for the cemetery.

Mr. Walter I. Fuller was chairman of the meeting; Mary L. Crocker was appointed clerk; Miss Margerie Leonard, Treasurer.

A motion was made, seconded and carried that the name of the association be called "Hillside Cemetery Association" of Osterville.

Mr. Joseph Tallman was elected president for the next meeting and Mrs. E. M. Crosby, vice president, Mr. Charles Lewis, clerk.

In Memory of Mr. James P. Crocker
He died November 16, 1814
in his 23rd year
Unveil thy bosom sacred tomb
Take this new treasure to your trust
And give these sacred relicts room,
To seek slumber in the dust.

Committee on by-laws: J. Milton Leonard, Charles E. Lewis, Mrs. Ellen Scudder.

Mr. J. W. Tallman was chosen to interview the Selectmen in regard to the fund which they hold in trust, also the appropriation by the town for cemeteries.

Buried in Osterville
Wife of Capt. Ezekiel Sturgess
Behold and see as you pass by
As you are now, so once was I
As I am now, so you will be
Prepare for death and follow me.

G.S.I.

May 7, 1923

The annual meeting of the Hillside Cemetery Asso. was held in the Baptist vestry Monday evening. The association is very fortunate in having Joseph W. Tallman at the helm. Since his election as president, Mr. Tallman has taken a great interest and has done much gratis which the association would have been unable to handle. Mrs. Ellen Scudder is chairman of the soliciting committee, assisted by Mrs. Dora Braley, Mrs. Ellen Spooner, Mrs. Edith Crosby and others.

May 2, 1929

The annual meeting of the Hillside Cemetery Association was held on Monday evening, April 29, at the Public Library. The following officers were elected for the ensuing year: President, Miss Katherine E. Hinckley; Vice President, Miss Sarah H. Boult; Secretary and Treasurer, Mrs. Charlotte L. Parker; Directors, Chas. E. Lewis, S. H. Bates, Mrs. Ellen W. Scudder.

Memorial Day Observances

June 11, 1872

Memorial Day was observed in a fitting manner. A procession of the school children with teachers, and others, singing, and some short speeches by several of our citizens.

June 6, 1876

Quite a number of our citizens met at the Hall Decoration Day. The meeting was called to order by Erastus Scudder, Esq., with some remarks very appropriate to the occasion, after which all proceeded to the soldiers' graves and placed a goodly number of flowers upon them. Remarks were made by Rev. Mr. Cleaves and Capt. Lot Phinney, with some very fine singing by the audience.

June 2, 1885

Memorial Day dawned bright and pleasant. At ten o'clock, a procession formed in front of the Baptist Church led by the Excelsior Band, and proceeded to the Cemetery where, after flowers had been put upon each of the soldiers' graves, select portions of poetry were recited by Rev. E. B. Hinckley, remarks by Rev. Mr. Codding, music by the band and prayer and benediction by Rev. E. B. Hinckley. The services were interesting and the attendance much larger than usual. The band also played a dirge at the grave of one of their former members, Wallace F. Crocker, each member placing a bouquet of flowers upon his grave.

June 13, 1893

Memorial Day was suitably observed on the 30th. A long procession of school children marched to the cemetery, placing beautiful bouquets upon the soldiers' graves. The exercises were in the charge of Miss Lovell, assisted by Mr. Crocker, of the schoolboard. Rev. James R. Goodspeed offered prayer, after which Mr. W. C. Smalley gave a brief address, and the Primary School recited appropriate selections.

June 3, 1895

Memorial Day was observed, according to the usual custom, by the pupils of the public schools in the charge of Miss Lovell. At nine o'clock the procession of young people, bearing bouquets and flags, started from the schoolhouse led by Veteran Josiah A. Ames and David Fuller, with Walter Fuller as drummer and Harold Crosby as color-bearer. At the cemetery our National Hymn was sung, after which Rev. J. R. Goodspeed offered prayer and Rev. G. A. Sisson gave a patriotic address. The children of the Primary School recited some appropriate selections as they placed the flowers upon the soldiers' graves.

June 1, 1896

The graves of the soldiers were appropriately decorated on Saturday morning. A procession was formed at the schoolhouse, led by Master Walter Fuller with a drum and Frederic Scudder in uniform, carrying the flag, and marched to the cemetery, under the direction of Miss Bertha Lovell, assisted by Mr. D. B. Fuller, where exercises were given by the children, prayer was offered by Rev. James R. Goodspeed, remarks by Rev. O. A. Farley, and "America" was sung by all.

June 7, 1897 — Large Memorial Day Service

Our schools held appropriate Memorial Day exercises on Tuesday last. Upon this occasion, Master William P. Hodges of the 7th grade recited an original poem, "The Dying Soldier."

June 7, 1897

Memorial Day services were unusually interesting, both at the Baptist Church and at the cemetery. A large delegation of the G.A.R., W.R.C. and S. of V. were present and listened to an able sermon from Rev. B. McLellan. The Church was handsomely decorated with bunting, flags and flowers and the beautiful day drew a large crowd to listen to the very interesting service. At 2:30 P.M. the children, with Miss Bertha Lovell, assisted by Comrades Baker, Jones and Childs, marched to the cemetery, where the graves were covered with beautiful flowers. Prayer was offered by Rev. J. R. Goodspeed. All joined in singing America.

June 1, 1903

Very interesting Memorial Day exercises were held in the Grammar schoolroom Friday afternoon, all grades uniting in the service. At the close the scholars formed in line and marched to the cemetery, where they were met by Comrade Baker and the graves of the soldiers were appropriately decorated.

June 13, 1904

Unusually interesting Memorial Services were held on Sunday afternoon, May 29th. At an early hour a large crowd gathered in front of the Baptist Church, and led by the Osterville Silver Band, formed in line and marched to Hillside Cemetery where the graves of soldiers were covered with flowers. Prayer was offered by Rev. Charles N. Hinckley. Misses Lillie and Maud Baker sang in their usual charming manner. Very interesting remarks by Rep. Thomas Pattison and Principal Edward Damon, and selections by the band, appropriate to the day and occasion, closed a service interesting beyond other years.

Osterville Honors Her Dead and Living Heroes

June 6, 1929

Never has the village paid tribute to its honored dead and living heroes in its widest scope, as was witnessed the 30th of May when a large gathering of citizens from this and surrounding towns gathered to pay tribute to the boys of the World War, Spanish, and Civil Wars, who went from this village to uphold their nation's honor and the ideals of those who had passed on to the last roll call. The day was all to be desired and nature in her regalia of leaf and blossom supplemented by the colors of our national emblem made a fine setting for the beautiful plot on which rests the handsome boulder and flag which was dedicated at 1:30 with Lauchlan Crocker, president of the Barnstable Memorial Association, in charge. Commander Clarence Brooks, in charge of the American Legion, Barnstable High School Band, and Boy and Girl Scouts did fine work in his arrangement of troops and added much to the interest of the exercises.

At the bugle, sounded by Miss Barbara Sprague, Girl Scout Miss Elaine Tallman raised the beautiful flag to the peak in a very pretty manner. She was supported by four color guards, Miss Emily Crocker, Miss Eileen Duffin, Bradford Tallman, and Irving Fuller. The Star Spangled Banner was led by Arthur Duffin, accompanied by the crowd and band.

Clarence Baker, 86 years of age, the only surviving member of the G.A.R. in this village, with reverent hands unveiled the beautiful tablet, and Lauchlan Crocker read off the names of the 53 boys and girls who offered their lives in the cause of the country and their fellowmen. A remarkable fact is that everyone returned, and but one succumbed to the effects of that terrific struggle, and to the memory of Leo Beaumont, we pay loving tribute.

Mr. Crocker introduced two well-known citizens of the town, J. M. Leonard who, in a few well-chosen words in behalf of the committee, presented the flag and boulder to the citizens of the village, and G. W. Hallett, in a fine patriotic speech, accepted as a sacred trust.

They were followed by Rev. Father Killigrew, pastor of Our Lady of Assumption Church, whose fine address teemed with patriotism and tribute to the living and dead heroes. He said we must not only remember the soldier dead, but to remember to be a soldier of Peace. To let them be an inspiration, not to misjudge, to always look for the good in each individual, no matter what his origin and to work for upbuilding character and the enforcement of law and in the cause of righteousness.

Our own Congressman, Charles L. Gifford, gave much pleasure on his appearance, and his address was, as usual, brimful of enthusiasm and patriotism as he paid highest tribute to those who left home and friends, and fared forth into the arena of the battlefield to help right a great wrong. The cause is very dear to the heart of Mr. Gifford, and his words carried the weight of high ideals and purposes, and a warm regard for the living heroes as well as those who have left us.

A beautiful wreath, made by Robert Cross, was presented by the Association for the occasion and was much admired.

At the close of the exercises at the boulder, an oration was delivered in the Community Church by the Rev. Frank Potter of Dorchester. The auditorium was packed to the doors, many being unable to gain entrance. Rev. Raymond Hibbard offered prayer. Mr. Potter took as his theme, "The Inspiration and Challenge of Heroic Memories," basing his remarks on the heroic ideals of a patriotic people who fought all our bloody wars for a great principle. Memories cluster not only upon our great leaders, but upon our private soldiers who fought the greatest battle of all in conquering self when the time came to leave home and loved ones for the sake of their country, and who never faltered in their high purpose, and who realized that the last look on the face of parents, wife, or children, might be really the last.

Yes, Memorial Day is a day of sad memories, but one fraught with love and tender remembrance for those who sleep in this and other lands, innocent victims of political greed. The little crosses in Flanders Field testify to a great faith and a protest against a great wrong, but even though we pay tribute and erect monuments and line our streets with the national colors, if there is no response in our hearts to the faith of these boys who sacrificed their lives, there is no patriotism. There is a laxity in the observation of law and order which is a real menace to our nation. We need to take unto our individual lives the great motive power of brotherly love and helpfulness, to reconsecrate ourselves to the upbuilding of character, and to walk in the ways of righteousness. Then and only then will wars cease.

Then we will have paid our full tribute to the heroes of the past.

The double quartette rendered "Tenting Tonight," and another selection.

A fine tribute was addressed to the three Grand Army men present by Mr. Potter. Mr. Crocker gave a short account of the first monument erected in Massachusetts in 1865 which is the Soldiers' Monument in Centerville. Mrs. Hallett, secretary of the Barnstable Memorial Association, read the resolutions on the death of past members.

The national hymn was sung and benediction pronounced by Rev. Raymond W. Hibbard.

Dinner was served to 135 members of the association and friends, the Legion, and others, under the management of Mrs. Myrtle Tallman.

The church was prettily draped with the national colors.

The committee, consisting of H. P. Leonard, Mrs. Myrtle Tallman, Robert Cross, Miss Jean Hinkle, and all others who assisted in carrying out the program, wish to express their thanks to the Barnstable Memorial Association and the American Legion and Boys Band for their splendid cooperation. The band, under the fine leadership of Mr. Griffiths, musical supervisor of the Barnstable schools, was most excellent and of much promise.

Mr. Crocker put in some hard work, as well as all the committee.

Independence Day Celebrations

Democratic Celebration at Osterville
July 12, 1837

The citizens of that village celebrated the Fourth in their usual happy way, by orations, and by a social entertainment, of which ladies as well as gentlemen partook in a pleasant grove, all of which was very appropriate to the occasion and seemed to be enjoyed with much zest, not only by those of that village but by a goodly number from other villages of the town.

The services in the meeting house were the same as is usual on these occasions, with the exception that there were two orations instead of one and a song, "The Pilgrim Fathers," was well sung at the close of the exercises by Mr. Stevens, of Hingham. The Orators of the day were Zeno Scudder, and Nathaniel Hinckley, Esqs. of this town. Their orations were truly democratic, and characterized by much good sense and truth, which is more than can be said of all Fourth of July orations, as too many orators make up in noisy declamation what they lack in sense and truth. Both of these gentlemen adverted to the causes which have operated to produce the present commercial paralysis, and dwelt on other important subjects which daily affect our country's welfare.

After the exercises at the meeting house, the citizens and visitors were invited to repair to a pine grove on the banks of a little lakelet (as the English would dignify a pretty pond, and we always love to copy the dear English) a short distance from the village, where there was what is called a "Bake Out" or, as we should term it, a steam out in progress, as the process of cooking was performed by steam, on a new principle to us, but an old and familiar one to Osterville, our Indian aborigines having prepared their food thus, we cannot if we would, tell how many centuries agone. In this delightful grove the ladies of Osterville had prepared with their characteristic industry and liberality a rare treat of the finest scupaugs and quahaugs from their great steamer (which is better deserving a patent than half the cooking apparatus, that do get patented) abundance of nice cake, lemonade and all needful etceteras, of which between seventy and eighty ladies and gentlemen partook with the greatest apparent relish and enjoyment. After the repast, toasts were offered (some at the expense of the bachelors present and some were highly complimentary to the ladies) and songs were sung which prolonged and added much to the festivity of the occasion. The day was closed with music and dancing by the younger members of the party.

Celebration at Osterville 5th of July
July 20, 1858

First regular toast: "The day we celebrate." Henry L. Hallett, Esq., of Boston, being called on by the President, responded to this toast.

Mr. Hallett's speech

I thank you, Sir, for the honor you have done me, in calling upon me, to respond to the sentiment which has just been read. We have done well to assemble here, in this temple of Nature, to do honor to this day, a day that should always be remembered with respect, by every true American.

This is a Nation's Thanksgiving day, and throughout this vast Union in every portion, however remote, people are assembled together as we are here to testify to their love of their country. No other people or kindred have such a holiday as this. It is the anniversary of the birthday of a glorious Republic. Eighty-two years ago we were not a power on Earth, but a mere dependency.

Could the men, the noble men, who braved all, and staked all life, fortune, peace, comfort, everything dear to the heart of man, to gain the Independence we now enjoy, be with us today, and see what a grand, glorious, and proud nation we have become, they would be well repaid for all their sufferings.

They struggled and endured, not for themselves, but for us, their children, and let us today, remember them with gratitude and honor, those true-hearted, unselfish men of the Revolution, who by their valor wrought out for us this free and independent government we now possess.

The story of the revolution is familiar to each of us, and needs no recital by me. All of us have read, and some of the grey-headed men I see around me, have been told by their fathers, of the trials and sufferings of the thirteen little colonies in their struggle for independence.

But remember the History of the Revolution: let us not forget the principles which were contended for, and for which our fathers shed their best blood. Theirs was not a contest for wealth or power. They fought for the right of Self Government. To give each man an equal share in the State.

It is not to be presumed that, in their sober judgment, those strong men of the olden time, could have expected or even hoped that in so short a period we should have attained to such a state of national prosperity. But God has been merciful to us, and History furnishes no instance of success and advancement equal to ours. From three millions of people we have grown to thirty millions — from thirteen small colonies to thirty-two Independent States. Our merchant marine equals that of the proudest nation in the world — our granaries feed the starving millions of Europe — our looms clothe the naked of every land — and from our borders we send out the missionary of God's Holy Word, to enlighten the poor heathen all over the world.

At home, all is prosperity, and our people enjoy more individual blessings and comforts than any other people under the Heavens. Our children are better educated, our poor better fed and clothed, life and prosperity safer from harm, and above all, we are respected by other nations.

And all these blessings, under God, we owe to men of the Revolution, the men of '76 as we love to call them. Ought we not then, at least once a year, to set apart a simple day to do them honor, and pour forth songs of praise and thanksgiving for all the blessings they have bequeathed to us. This, Sir, is I believe the first public observance of this day in this village. I trust this will not be the last. And may our gathering together result in good to all. May the old have their pulses quickened by the joy and mirth they see around them. May those of us who have entered upon our career of life, here renew our love for our Country, and our reverence for the authors of its laws and institutions, and may the youth here participating with us, turn with increased eagerness to the pages of History which record the progress of the Republic, and early in life imbibe deep love and reverence for its laws and form of Government.

All of us, young and old, high and low, rich and poor, all, are equally interested in the success and prosperity of our common country.

Osterville may yet furnish a President for the United States, and the poorest and most unfriended boy, here present, may be the person.

Here then let us promise, each to the other, that by no word of deed of ours, shall this noble

Hurrah For The Fourth Of July

Antiques and Horribles, c. 1890

Left to right — 1. Nelson (Nelly) Bearse, 2. May (Molly) Bearse, 3. Mary (Lovell) Crocker, 4. Isadore (Leonard) Crocker, 5. Frances (Lovell) Fuller, 6. Minnie (Jones) Bates, 7. Sarah H. Boult, 8. Minnie (Cammett) Allen, 9. Elizabeth Small, 10. Addie (Bearse) Nickerson, 11. Velina (Ames) Crosby.

---

heritage of our fathers be weakened or impaired. And pledge ourselves to a perfect and entire devotion to this Union, to love it, and cherish it — and to bring up our children with a holy reverence and awe for it.

And now and at all times let our hearts be filled with gratitude and love to God, that he has given us such a country to live in, and such a wise system of laws to protect and guard us.

In retiring from the happy group assembled beneath the tall and graceful pines, which served as so many Liberty poles — the thought occured, that this and similar unceremonious and social keepings of the national birth day were more likely to leave a happy and perhaps a stronger moral impression on the mind than the formal and pompous pageants which are more frequent on this anniversary; and we wish that such gatherings for the remembrance of the Fourth, of friends and acquaintances were more common in all country towns. The idea is too prevalent that the Fourth of July cannot be duly kept without a great display of military, the roaring of cannon, processions, etc., etc. It is all a mistake. The day may be observed very appropriately and happy too in a less ostentatious way. The people of Osterville are fully aware of this and have for several years celebrated the Fourth in a manner similar to the last.

July 14, 1874

Our citizens held a glorious Fourth of July picnic in "Uncle Sam's Grove." A collation was served up, embracing all the delicacies of the season. Boating on the Pond, singing, croquet and other games entered into the programme. Good music, both vocal and instrumental, added much to the occasion. Miss Jessie Hinckley presided at the organ, and Asa E. Lovell, Esq. was the orator for the day.

Fireworks were set off on the evening of the Fourth from the Cotocheset House, and from the residence of Mrs. George H. Hinckley.

July 10, 1877

The Fourth passed off very quietly in this village, the only notable event being a grand foot race (running and walking) distance one-half mile. In the running match there were two classes. First, those over 15 and under 20 years of age. The entries in this class were Wm. W. Crosby, Frank M. Boult, Wm. H. Linnell of Boston, Frank H. Williams, Charles E. Lewis. The first prize was taken by Wm. W. Crosby, time 2:43; second, Frank H. Williams, time 2:43. (This being a tie lots were drawn for the prize). Third, Frank M. Boult, time 2:47. The entries in this class were Charles F. Whippey, Zenas S. West, Frank E. West, Geo. E. Williams, A. Lincoln Parker, Howard Linnell of Boston. The first prize was taken by Geo. E. Williams, time 2:46, second, Frank E. West, time 2:46. (This was also a tie and lots were drawn for the money). Third, Charles F. Whippey, time 2:56.

In the walking match, first class, the entries were Wm. W. Crosby, F.M. Boult, Charles E. Lewis, Charles F. Whippey. The first prize was taken by Charles E. Lewis, time 4:18; second, F.M. Boult, time 4:55; third, Charles F. Whippey, time 5:15.

The entries in the second class were Bradford L. Ames, Charles A. West, Geo. E. Williams, Zenas S. West, Henry Ells of Washington, D.C., Frank E. West. The first was taken by Geo. E. Williams, time 5 minutes; second, Charles A. West, time 5:20, third, Henry Ells, time 5:35. The prizes were small, ranging from 75 cents downward. About fifty spectators were present, and an interesting time was enjoyed by all.

July 9, 1878

The Fourth passed with ringing bells, firing guns, toy pistols, etc. Crosby and Son sold all out of ice cream.

John W. Lewis put up a rough tent opposite the Post Office where he sold small beer, cakes, torpedoes, toy pistols, caps for the same, etc., but rather a dull day for Osterville.

July 10, 1883

The 4th passed off nicely; besides a boat race at the beach we had a baseball match between Osterville boys and city boys from the beach. The score was, Osterville boys, 15, beach boys, 8. Then there was a family party at Mrs. H. N. Lewis's. They gathered to the number of thirty, had fine music and a good dinner, and a good time generally.

July 10, 1883

The bells were not rung on account of sickness, but we had the usual amount of noise from fire crackers, toy pistols, etc., also the flag staff was decorated with two flags on the 4th.

July 8, 1884

The 4th was a busy day, ushered in by the usual crowd of young America with the ringing of bells, firing of guns and the usual amount of noise.

The annual regatta at the beach attracted a large crowd of spectators to witness this most interesting part of the programme of the day. The wind was steady and favorable to all classes of boats making the contest a close and exciting one. About twenty-five boats started in the race, but, owing to discouraging circumstances, but sixteen continued to the end.

We give below a list of the winning boats and the names of their commanders:

First Class
Pansy, Capt. Daniel Crosby — $25.
Almira, Capt. Wilton Crosby — $15.
Mischief, Capt. N. H. Bearse — $10.
Second Class
Muriel, Capt. Smalley — $15.
Lucille, Capt. Bradford L. Ames — $10.
Lucy, Capt. R. Nickerson — $5.
Third Class
Toad, Capt. C. W. Crosby — $10.
Roy, Capt. D. Nickerson — $7.
Wraith, Capt. E. L. Bearse — $3.

Immediately after the regatta a band concert was given by the Excelsior Brass Band in the vicinity of the Cotocheset House. The 'boys" played finely, notwithstanding a little evident embarassment in performing before a music cultured people.

At the close of the concert the band lunched at the hotel after which they attended the baseball game at the village, between the "Beach Nine" and the "Village Champions." This was a close, exciting game resulting in favor of the "Champions." During the process of the game much speculation was indulged in as to the result of the playing, but the "Beach Nine" (and their friends) were evidently too sure of their game.

In the evening a large crowd assembled in the vicinity of Flag Pole Hill to see the display of fireworks, which were furnished through the liberality of our citizens and friends. The band kindly tendered their services and evening promised to be one of enjoyment to all, but unfortunately the dampness and rain suddenly interfered and broke up, what would otherwise have been a successful display.

A tent near the wharf caught fire during the day from a firecracker and was destroyed.

July 8, 1890

Fourth of July in Osterville was very quiet, even with the large number of guests here that the village entertains. The boys were obliged (in measure) to forego the pleasures of bell ringing (?), but bright and early the Antiques and Horribles began their parade and this procession filled the minds of the young element and attracted the attention of many of the older ones beside. We think antiques and humorous would better describe the pageant, for there was certainly nothing very horrible about it and there was much that would stir up the *"risibilities."* The marshal of the procession was mounted on a white horse but was of the masculine gender and did not have red hair. Following him was an "antique" stagecoach loaded with clowns and other grotesque characters. Then followed vehicles of numerous kinds, including the traditional "one horse shay," although there was no way by which we could determine whether it was the original one built by the 'Deacon" or not. The characters assumed by the occupants of all the carriages were well taken and well costumed and served to put everyone in a better humor to bear what proved to be the most uncomfortable day, as to weather, we have experienced this season.

July 8, 1895

The fourth passed off rather hard for the younger of our village, on account of the storm. Friday night the Antiques and Horribles gave us the parade promised the day before. It was a wonderful display, and much credit is due to the ones who arranged it as well as those who executed it.

July 14, 1902

Fourth of July has come and gone with all its stir, noise and disaster, still it has left in its wake renewed patriotism in the hearts of every lover of liberty. Early on the eve of the Fourth the boys commenced to get in their good work and at 12 o'clock American patriotism had reached its height, which culminated in the ringing of the bells of the Churches and schoolhouse, which they kept up until the nerves of the nearby residents gave promise of a total collapse. We rather think there was a controlling power as they suddenly ceased after an hour or two, until towards morning, when after an uneasy slumber, we were again aroused to the fact that the boys were again on hand. The day was comparatively quiet here — many going to Cotuit, as also did our band. In the evening all repaired to Wianno Beach and witnessed the fireworks displayed from the pier. The Osterville Silver Band, after an arduous day's work in Cotuit, were present and rendered several fine selections to an appreciative audience, if we can judge from expressions on all sides. Speaking of the band, isn't it a precocious youngster for only five months old? It could hardly be otherwise with their manly leader and the enthusiasm which inspires every member. The men with their new uniforms of maroon and black coats and caps, white duck pants and handsome silver instruments, looked trim and natty and were an organization of which any village may well feel pride and interest.

June 29, 1908

There will be a ball to celebrate the glorious 4th in Union Hall Friday evening. Wyman's orchestra of seven pieces will furnish the music.

July 6, 1908

The boys thoroughly enjoyed themselves. The bells were rung between twelve and one o'clock, at four in the morning, and at evening. The Horribles paraded between seven and nine through the main streets of the village, and everywhere were greeted with applause. There were Turks, clowns, Chinamen, Negroes, merry widows, the coming President Taft, antiques and others too numerous to mention. The night before, as well as the night of the 4th, the sky was brilliantly illuminated with fireworks in several places.

July 12, 1910

What? When the 4th of July comes on Monday to see such an orderly community Sunday evening. All was as quiet as on any other Sabbath. To stand in front of one of our hotels as for instance, East Bay Lodge, where of the sixty-five rooms every one but one was occupied, and see the guests seated on the veranda listening to the sweet strains of sacred music, makes one feel not a little proud to live in such a place where the very atmosphere itself, that evening, seemed to say "we live in a Christian land."

July 12, 1910

July 4th celebrated. The boys as usual had their pranks early Monday morning. The bells were rung at midnight, at four, and at six o'clock. A signboard, "Dump no more rubbish here," was found in a vehicle on the hay scales. Tin horns and fire works disturbed the slumbers of the neighborhood.

Revolutionary War

Revolutionary War Records

Below are some records of Osterville men who served in the Revolutionary War. The records of Nymphas Hinckley are believed to be of one individual. Other records of individuals who served in the Revolution are to be found in biographical material to be released in the author's second volume.

Cornelius Lovell, Barnstable, Private; order on David Jeffries, Paymaster, to the Provincial Army, payable to Capt. Micah Hamlen, dated Boston, June 27, 1776, signed by said Lovell and others belonging to Capt. Hamlen's Co., Col. Thomas Marshall's regt., for advance pay for 1 month, etc.; also, Capt. Micah Hamlen's Co., Col. Thomas Marshall's regt. Enlisted June 13, 1776; service to August 1, 1776, 1 mo., 19 days; roll dated Castle Island.

Jacob Lovell, Captain of a company, Col. Freeman's regt., payroll for service on an alarm at Bedford, Dartmouth, and Falmouth in Sept. 1778; also, Captain, 3d (also given 7th) Co., 1st Barnstable Co. regt. of Mass. militia; list of officers; commissioned October 22, 1778.

Joshua Lovell, Capt., Jacob Lovell's Co. Col. Freeman's regt.; service, 10 days, on alarm at Bedford, Dartmouth, and Falmouth in Sept. 1778.

Nymphas Hinckley — Private, Capt. Elisha Nye's Co. enlisted June 1, 1776; service to Sept. 1, 1776, 3 mos.; company stationed at Elizabeth Islands; roll sworn to in Barnstable Co.; also, list dated Naushon, August 10, 1777, of men belonging to a company stationed at Naushon who signed a petition for increase of wages or their discharge in case such request was not complied with.

Nymphas Hinckley, Capt. Jacob Lovell's Co. Col. Freeman's regt.; service, 10 days, on an alarm at Bedford, Dartmouth, and Falmouth, in Sept., 1778.

Nymphas Hinckley — 1753-1832

For Revolutionary War Record, see above. This is the oldest known likeness of an Osterville resident.

Benjamin Hallett — 1760-1849

In the War of Independence, he served three years on board the Frigate "Dean" and in the land forces. His extensive Revolutionary War Record will appear in "OSTERVILLE," Volume II.

Civil War

Flag Raising in Osterville
May 28, 1861

On Saturday week a large and beautiful flag was thrown to the breeze from a staff erected in Osterville. The occasion was made one of much interest to the citizens of this patriotic village, men, women and children being present, and the incidents of that day will not soon be forgotten. The flag hoisted, furled, to the top of the staff, and when the cannon gave the signal, was unfurled in majesty to the winds of heaven. The Rev. Mr. Newell then offered to God an appropriate prayer, which was followed by the song of "The Red, White and Blue." Appropriate and very patriotic speeches were made by the Rev. Mr. Robinson, Rev. Mr. Hooper, A. M. Folger, Sylvanus Jagger, Asa E. Lovell, and last, but not least, by William Blount, one of the old War of 1812 soldiers. Hearty cheers were given for President Lincoln, the faithful Scott, the noble Anderson, the patriotic ladies of Massachusetts, and the flag of our Union!

Civil War News
October 22, 1861

Four transports and two gunboats sailed from New York on Saturday week, with a number of surf boats and surf men. Steamers Atlantic, Baltic, Vanderbilt, Empire City and Ocean Queen have also surf men and surf boats on board. Their destination is not known, but they will soon be heard from doing effective service somewhere. Capt. Samuel S. Baxter of Marstons Mills is master, Mr. Frank Young of Osterville, mate.

July 29, 1862

Henry Goodspeed enlisted in Army.

August 12, 1862

Barnstable Volunteers: Obed A. Cahoon, David J. Coleman, Joseph C. Scudder, Howard M. Lovell, Johnnie A. Fernando, and Josiah A. Ames.

September 23, 1862

Henry Goodspeed was a Corporal.

September 23, 1862

Warren Cammett was in the Tiger Regiment.

July 15, 1863

The names of those drafted for the war in New Bedford, July 15, 1863, and live in Osterville: George W. Weeks, Joseph Alley, William B. Parker, Osmond Ames, Granville Ames, James H. Parker, Henry N. Lovell, David C. Lewis, Reuben H. West, Oak S. Crosby, Edward M. Lovell, Bradford Ames, David J. Coleman, Charles G. Lovell, Herschel Fuller.

Pvt. David Fuller

This letter was written to George Henry Hinckley who kept the store in Osterville during the Civil War. The writer, was Henry Goodspeed, son of Allen Goodspeed, Jr. Henry was an only child. After the Civil War Henry moved his family to the Midwest. At the time the letter was written, Henry Goodspeed was a soldier in the Union Army, and a patient at Carver Hospital at Washington, D.C.

Carver Hospital
August 28th, 1863

Dear George,

I received your letter today with much pleasure and, as my time *now* is of no account (or hardly ever was) I will answer by giving you a short description of our Hospital and arrangements. The grounds are triangular in shape and contain about eight acres surrounded by a high fence with three gates. A guard is at every gate, and it is hard work to get out. There are about eighty wards or buildings for the sick. They are about thirty by one hundred feet, low and white-washed. In each are about twenty beds, cast iron frames. The wards are kept clean and everything is neat as wax. One man does nothing but tend to the sick and keep the ward in order.

The day I got here I was dirty, lousy, had on a ragged shirt and stockings, no handkerchiefs or towel, when along came our state Agent and he furnished I and others with all the things necessary and a bag of sewing materials. You can believe they came extra acceptable. The boys from other states say there is no state Agent like Mass. for looking out for her soldiers, and I think so too. Our Agent comes around once or twice a week and brings to the very sick wine, jellys and anything they may need, and his coming is looked for with interest. I believe Osterville has never sent but little to the Sanitary Commission, but she has enough at home to look to, so many widows and orphans. I trust this war will make no more.

We live quite well here, but not so well but what the boys spend a lot of money with the apple women and suttlers. The suttlers must make a fortune. What would you think to have your counter thronged with men all trading with cash, and you getting double price for everything. So it is. Some boys spend all of their money with the suttler. We are rather lonesome; we have a brass band started, playing one evening in the week, meeting Sundays and quite well attended; the men are away from home, and a meeting is a place that makes a man think of home.

Every night *Pres.* Lincoln goes by with his escort of twenty men. He generally rides a grey horse and is not to me a bad looking man; if Fred Scudder had had dark eyes, he would have looked like him. He looks about used up, but I guess he will see this war through. Not a man but respects him in the army. Not so with the army officers. Hooker was *Drunk* at Fredricksburg. It is a fact. Liquor has killed more men than bullets. The officers get down a dram, then they forget the men, and march the men to death. Our *ry* (regimentary) officer wont run away from whiskey. Uncle Sam tries to do his duty, but he gets dredfully cheated by officers and men. The officers resign when they get tired or sick but the men play off. There are thousands that do it. Some of our men put pepper in their eyes so they need not go into the fight at Gettysburg. Blinkers' division that ran at Fredricksburg here ran in every fight yet. They are Dutchmen, the rowdies of Philadelphia and New York, and they are bounde to rob every defenceless house they come to, Union or reb rebel), but that is only one division. Most of the men I no would make good citizens.

The last men that came out are a better class than the first. I got acquainted with men from every union state, and it is pleasant to talk about the different ways of living we have, but every man thinks his own state is the best, and for farming I guess Osterville is about the poorest place in the Northern States.

I was in hopes to have seen some vol's or drafted men from our town, but it seems all of the *men* are out here. I did not know so many were *feeble* before, or that it was so easy for men to raise three hundred dollars in cash. If I had had a $1000 or, and nothing to do with it, I would cut for $500.00, let a drafted man have a dollar. That is the way I and others feel about it. I feel now just as I did when I enlisted. That it is the duty of every man to do what he can to put this rebellion down. If any man is going to stop at home, it will be some time for it. It is not any man out here that came for money, many of our ry were making money when they left home. I say, if we leave all and come out the folks at home that won't come be made to pay us. I should have liked to have been to that town meeting. I guess all of the *B.*boys will say they have earnt their money and I am afraid the boys are catching it now. Still I should like to be with them. I should hate, if I ever got home, not to say that I was at the fall of Charleston. Many of our ry are in the Hospitals. I think owing a good deal to the officers in not furnishing better food and marching us so hard.

I am better yesterday and today. I have to be careful how much I eat. We all have good appetites and the diarrhea at the same time. My throat troubles me, it is sore inside. I would like to get a furlough as I think, if I was in Osterville, I should now get well, but that is something not easily got.

Now I will write a little about our affairs. Tempy wrote me some time ago how much I owed you. I was sorry to see it was so much, but as you are the only one I do owe, it is not so bad on my account, but I suppose you would like your pay. I hope my expenses will soon be less. Next winter, if I am not at home, I shall not pay so much for hired help and if I can't pay you any other way, there is one more bank at any rate good for me yet, and you shall receive the benefit of that. You must take what you can from the firm (that is, if you can get anything), and sell as cheap as you can, not listen to Mr.

Scudder. I would not trade with either of the S's for anything so you will get my trade, and I hope you nor I either will be the loser for it. Give my children a stick of candy once in a while and charge it to me.

I have written this in a very short time and very poorly (my habit). I hope you will be able to make it out. Give my respects to all Union friends.

Yours with respect,

S/Henry

James Small — served in the U.S. Navy during the Civil War.

October 6, 1863

Men in war sick — Joseph C. Scudder, Obed A. Cahoon, Henry Goodspeed. Have diarrhea and scurvy (from eating salt meat).

May 10, 1864

Funeral of volunteers in Osterville. We learn that funeral services over the remains of the late Joseph C. Scudder, who died in Osterville on Monday of last week, and of Obed A. Cahoon, who died at Folly Island some months since, both members of Co. E, 40th Massachusetts Regiment, were solemnized on the afternoon of Friday last, in the Baptist Church in Osterville. It was one of the largest and most deeply sympathetic gatherings ever held in that place, and the exercises were very impressive and affecting.

May 17, 1864

Two Methodist Ministers — Rev. Mr. Chase of the village, and Rev. Mr. Edson of Osterville, were among the drafted from this town on Saturday.

Pvt. Joseph C. Scudder

May 24, 1864

Cape Men Killed and Wounded — By letters received in this village yesterday, from members of the 40th Mass. Regiment, we learn that that regiment suffered severely in the late conflict.

The following is a partial list of the casualties in Co. E. — Wounded: Sergt. Howard M. Lovell of Osterville, badly.

December 13, 1864

The Treasurer of the Army Committee of the Boston Young Men's Christian Commission acknowledges the following contributions to the funds of the Society — Methodist Church, Osterville $26.25.

Obed A. Cahoon — A member of Co. E 40th Regt. Mass. Vol. Mil. died at Beaufort, S.C., November 21, 1863, age 18 years.

June 3, 1879

Friday quite a number met at Village Hall, and headed by Mr. E. Scudder, marched to the graves of our soldiers where speeches were made by Rev. S. K. Day; Rev. E. B. Hinckley and E. Scudder, Esq. — Prayer by Rev. S. H. Day. Singing by all the singers, and flowers were strewn in abundance on the graves.

August 19, 1890

Dr. T. R. Clement, Watson F. Adams, David B. Fuller, and Clarence L. Baker went to the G.A.R. Encampment in Boston last week.

December 19, 1893

The entertainment given by the Theodore Parkman Post, G.A.R., in Village Hall last week, was a very pleasant affair. The cake and ice cream were very nice, and the music, singing and dancing, by the different members of the very talented Bearse family of Cotuit, pleased everyone. Mrs. Jenner of Osterville very kindly added to the good cause by two of her charming recitations.

October 25, 1909

David B. Fuller and James Small attended the reunion of the Civil War Veterans, held in Hyannis the past week.

Notes on the Civil War

HISTORY OF BARNSTABLE COUNTY, MASSACHUSETTS, Edited by Simeon L. Deyo

Barnstable commenced raising troops early, and held its first special town meeting May 10, 1861. At this meeting liberal bounties were offered, promises were made for the support of soldiers' families, and money was placed at the disposal of the governor for the assistance of the troops of the state. On the 21st of July, 1862, still stronger resolutions of patriotism and aid were passed, and the bounties were increased. The work of the selectmen and clerk was most arduous, but was cheerfully accomplished. The number of men reported as sent was 272 — thirty-five over and above all demands. The acting adjutant general of the state reported that Barnstable had underrated the number sent. Three of these men were commissioned officers. The sum appropriated was $38,574.15, besides $19,652.93 for state aid, which was refunded. The work of the Barnstable ladies was important. Three aid societies were organized — one each in its three largest villages — which contributed the sum of $1,283, and many thousands of articles of clothing, bandages and luxuries.

The Town of Barnstable is having made a careful manuscript record of her soldiers, for preservation in her town archives. The compiling, entrusted to Gustavus A. Hinckley, is to be finished in 1890.

In grateful remembrance of fallen heroes, five towns have erected monuments to their memory, Barnstable having the most elaborate. It was erected at Centreville, dedicated July 4, 1866, being the first in the state in point of time. Its cost was $1,050, the site being donated by F. G. Kelley, and the beautifully proportioned pile of Concord granite bids fair to stand forever. . . The grounds around this monument are beautifully laid out and well kept.

Sword and scabbard belonging to James Jones, a soldier in the Civil War.

Town of Barnstable Records of Osterville Men Who Served In The Civil War

Josiah A. Ames, Private, 40th Reg. Resident of Barnstable. Age 35. Occupation, laborer. Enlisted, August 8, 1862. Mustered, August 31, 1862. Discharged February 23, 1865, for disability, at Chapin's Farm, Virginia. Battles: Fort Sumter, S.C., Siege of Petersburg, Va., Fort Wagner, Mine Explosion, Bermuda Hundred, Va.; was in hospital several times.

Osmond Ames, Private. Resident of Barnstable. Age 21. Occupation: _____ . Enlisted, September 12, 1862. Mustered, September 26, 1862. Discharged October 30, 1862, at Boston, Mass., on surgeon's Certificate of Disability, a rejected recruit.

Clarence L. Baker. Resident of Barnstable. Age 21. Occupation: _____ . Enlisted, September 2, 1864 at New Bedford, for one year, as ordinary seaman. Credit Barnstable. Served on Recg. Ship Ohio, and U.S.S. Rhode Island, from which he was discharged August 9, 1865 as ordinary seaman. Battles: Engagement at Fort Fisher, N.C.

January 21, 1918

Elliott Lewis has gone to Newport and entered the aviation service.

January 21, 1918

Mrs. Thomas A. Whiteley has just had a letter from her son, William T., at Camp Gordon, Atlanta, Georgia, wherein he tells of his first rifle practice.

February 4, 1918

The entertainment for the benefit of the French relief fund, held in Union Hall the 24th, drew out a crowded house. A very fine program was rendered and over $40 was realized.

February 18, 1918

Merton Bates has had a relapse and is again in the hospital at the training camp in Anniston, Alabama.

February 18, 1918

A community flag was dedicated in Union Hall Friday evening to the brave boys of our village who have answered the call of the colors. The people of the village showed their interest by filling the hall to overflowing. The flag is a beautiful one of red and white wool bunting containing twenty-eight stars.

The Crosby orchestra was present and rendered some inspiring music. The school children marched in with banners flying and afterwards sang several selections.

On the platform were the Civil War veterans, the speakers of the evening and Boy Scouts.

March 4, 1918

Mr. Cecil Goodspeed went to Newport last week and entered the Navy.

Service Flag with 28 stars dedicated to the boys serving their country. The flag hung across the street in front of the old Public Library, which is now the site of the Osterville House and Garden Shop. c. 1918.

March 4, 1918

Messrs. Verner Childs of New York and Jesse Murray of Newport were in the village for the day, February 24th. Mr. Childs had just returned from a trip across to France on a large transport ship of which he is an officer and was expecting to sail again for France. Mr. Murray was transferred to Virginia from Newport last week.

March 11, 1918

Red Cross — 199 bath mitts, 341 muslin slings, 414 handkerchiefs, 51 helmets, 59 prs. wristers, 66 mufflers, 45 sweaters, 41 prs. socks, 43 surgical shirts, 30 prs. pajamas, 96 knit sponges, 1 hot water bottle cover, 6 chin bandages, 35 surgical oil cloth rest pillows, 3 abdominal bandages, 1 sleeping cap, 14 patchwork quilts, 778 4" compresses, 517 9" compresses, 24 gauze sponges.

The following have been sent to our boys at camp and in the Navy: 39 sweaters, 31 helmets, 30 mufflers, 30 prs. wristers, 74 prs. socks.

The above, with finished work at the Red Cross rooms, make a total of 3192 articles made since our branch organized June 21st, 1917.

March 25, 1918

Word from Max and Carroll Crosby states that they are near the enemy's lines.

April 8, 1918

Word from Donald Coffin and Stuart Scudder says they have reached Texas and are all right.

April 15, 1918

Since the first of November, there have been 25 comfort bags filled and given to our soldier boys.

April 22, 1918

An entertainment for the benefit of the Osterville branch French Relief was given at Union Hall on Friday evening.

April 22, 1918

At the meeting of the Osterville branch French Relief held at the Baptist vestry on Wednesday evening the following articles were packed for shipment: 49 crash towels, 40 handkerchiefs, 3 games checkers, 2 girls dresses, 3 prs. boys pants, 1 boy's blouse, 6 babies' bibs, 1 pr. socks, 1 helmet, 1 trench cap, 2 sweaters, 1 pr. linen pants.

April 29, 1918

Friends of Cecil Goodspeed will be glad to hear that he has again arrived safely in New York, but sorry to hear he is in the hospital with the mumps.

May 6, 1918

Joseph Gomes was called into the service last week, making thirty-one boys who have thus far gone from our village.

May 20, 1918

Word from Donald Coffin from Florida says that the boys occasionally have a chance to chase a few rattlers.

June 3, 1918

Philip Chadwick is another of our boys to enter the service.

June 17, 1918

Verner Childs spent Monday and Tuesday with his parents, Mr. and Mrs. Everett Childs. He has just returned from another trip across when his boat encountered about seven submarines on the way.

June 17, 1918

Word received this week from Joe Daniel tells of his safe arrival again in France.

July 15, 1918

Robert Bell, who recently enlisted, is in the tank service and is located at present in Pennsylvania.

August 26, 1918

We are sorry to learn that Carroll Crosby has been gassed and is in a hospital in France.

September 9, 1918

Another star will be added to our service flag this week as Frank Allen has been called to service and has gone to Syracuse, N.Y.

September 9, 1918

Word has been received from Miss Marie Hansberry, daughter of Mr. and Mrs. John Hansberry of this village, who is in France, that she is located about 30 miles from her brother, James, who went across some time ago.

September 23, 1918

The Osterville branch of American Red Cross has had a call for 200 lbs. of clothing, shoes, etc., for the Belgium Relief, and the village will be canvassed during the early part of the week for all contributions.

October 7, 1918

Word from Stuart Scudder states that he is to be transferred from Camp Jackson, South Carolina, to Omaha, Nebraska, where he is to enter the Officer's Training Camp.

October 28, 1918

Elliott Lewis has been transferred from Pensacola, Fla., to Hampton Roads, Virginia.

October 28, 1918

Red Cross — The regular business meeting for the month of September of the Osterville branch, American Red Cross, was held on Thursday afternoon at the old schoolhouse. The work committee reported as finished work for the month: 1 helmet, 1 pair wristers, 8 sweaters, 60 pairs socks, 4 pinafores.

Mrs. Lillie S. Parker — Chairman

The shippings committee reported 31 kit bags, 31 needlebooks and 555 pounds of old clothing for Belgium Relief.

Mrs. Mathilde Adams — Chairman

(One hundred and eighty-four pounds of peach stones have been shipped to Brockton headquarters recently. Peach stones are to be again shipped on Friday, November 1st.)

November 11, 1918

Word from Jesse Murray states that he is at present located in England.

Victory Celebration

November 18, 1918

Osterville truly has done its share of celebrating the victory of the great world war the past week. The church bells were rung on Monday, Nov. 11th, from seven o'clock in the morning until seven at night, stopping only long enough for the boys and girls who helped so steadily at the bell ropes to take part in the parade which started at 2 pm from Post Office square. It was led by school children dressed in the national colors of the Allies, members of the Red Cross with the banner and six young ladies in patriotic attire bore our service flag with its 42 stars, followed by a long line of gaily decorated autos.

Marching to the music of horns and drums the procession proceeded through the main streets of the village and when reaching the residence of Mr. J. M. Leonard disbanded, only to join the auto parade of 15 cars which continued on through Marstons Mills and Cotuit and returning through Santuit, meeting occasional cheers from passers-by.

At 7 o'clock in the evening several hundred people assembled in the large field near the post

Flag Raising — World War I. Baptist Church can be seen at the left. — 1918.

Flag Raising — World War I. Daniel Block can be seen in the background. — 1918.

office. As the flames of the huge bonfire burst forth enveloping the form of the Kaiser that was to be no more, the Camp Fire Girls formed a circle and sang "Burn, Fire, Burn".

Then followed music by the Osterville band and a very appropriate and stirring address followed by prayer by Rev. E. F. Newell.

After singing The Star Spangled Banner, the crowd dispersed, some going to Hyannis to continue the celebration there, others assembling in the M.E. Church for a service of praise and prayer to Almighty God for his merciful care for us all and for this peace which we trust may be everlasting.

Postal card bearing 2 cents postage, mailed at Osterville on Nov. 28, 1918 at 7 AM, and addressed to Mr. and Mrs. H. Manley Crosby, Osterville, reads as follows: "As a "Memorial" for our boys in the Army and Navy from Woods Hole to Provincetown, you are asked to place a lighted candle in a window of your home for each enlisted member of your family, Thanksgiving evening at 6 o'clock." Signed: Alice F. Coombs, Sec., W.C.T.U., Osterville, Nov. 27.

Flag Raising

November 18, 1918

It was a happy thought which recently came to the mind of Henry P. Leonard that one of the masts of the unfortunate schooner which went aground a few months ago so near our coast, should be purchased and placed in the center of the village

Flag Raising Ceremonies — World War I. — 1918

as our much longed-for flag pole. After talking the matter over with several of our business men, they all agreed the plan was a wise one and proceeded to make the idea a reality.

The mast was purchased, brought to our shore, repaired and painted and brought to the village in two sections, where it was erected at P.O. square, which was deemed the most central locality. The next question was how best to procure a flag suitable for such a giant pole.

Mr. George S. Baldwin of Wianno very generously settled that query for them by presenting to the village the handsome new flag which was flung to the breeze for the first time on Sunday afternoon, when services appropriate for the occasion were held in the presence of a large majority of the inhabitants of our village as well as some of the neighboring ones.

Mr. J. M. Leonard was master of ceremonies and, after making a few opening remarks, at a

The flag pole raised to fly the flag was one of the masts salvaged from a schooner which went aground off Wianno Beach. The wrecked schooner is shown above, her decks awash, but her masts intact. The pole's original site was the small park next to the Baptist Church; after the armistice was signed, a boulder bearing a plaque with the names of all those who had served Uncle Sam during the war was placed in the triangular park at the intersection of Main and Bay Streets and Parker Road. The flag pole was moved there, too. Over the years, to accommodate vehicular traffic, the triangle has been reduced to its present size and shape.

---

given signal the Boy Scouts, holding the flag in readiness with the assistance of Mr. G. Webster Hallett and Mr. Henry P. Leonard, raised our new Old Glory to the breeze as the Osterville Band struck up the Star Spangled Banner.

The Scouts and school children then gave the flag salute and pledge, after which the band favored us with another selection. Mrs. L. M. Boody of Hyannis very kindly consented to be present and led the singing in two songs rendered by the school children, Speed Our Republic and, The Battle Cry of Freedom. An instrumental duet by Fred and Wilson Scudder was greatly appreciated by the assembly and the two speakers of the occasion were Dr. E. F. Newell of the Methodist church and Mr. Raymond Cooper of the Baptist church, both of whom gave very appropriate and stirring addresses with frequent applause.

At the conclusion of the exercises, Mr. Hallett made a few remarks, after which a collection of over forty-seven dollars was taken toward the expenses of the pole, other contributions having already been received. The band then played Home, Sweet Home and, America. and as the assembly dispersed and Old Glory still waved in the breeze we could truly sing:

"Tis the Star Spangled Banner
Oh long may it wave
O'er the land of the free
And the home of the brave."

December 2, 1918

Osterville observed the request to burn candles in the windows for absent boys on Thanksgiving night.

December 16, 1918

Thornton Adams and Karl Chadwick are enjoying a ten days' leave of absence from their duties at Woods Hole.

January 11, 1919

Leon Hinckley and Jesse Murray have gone to New York to get their discharge from service.

January 13, 1919

The many friends of Carroll Crosby, son of H. Manley Crosby, are glad to welcome him home. We are more than proud of the boy who has made good "over there" and wish his furlough might be prolonged until his health is fully recovered.

January 20, 1919

Among our boys who have recently returned home are Fred Nute, Merton Bates, Philip Chadwick, Burton Chadwick, Rawson Ashley and Elliott Lewis.

February 3, 1919

Hallett Boult has returned from Camp Jackson, South Carolina.

February 10, 1919

Max Crosby, who is still in France, is enjoying music lessons under a French instructor. He was on the front lines from the time he first went across, and has well-earned this rest and enjoyment.

February 17, 1919

Corporal Leo E. Beaumont, who recently arrived home, was formerly of Co. F, 101st Engineers, but later transferred to Co. F, 101st Infantry. He was in active service at Chateau Thierry, Belleau Woods, and at Argonne Forest where he was gassed and later sent to the hospital, where he remained until he was able to return home.

February 24, 1919

William Whiteley, who is still at the U.S.A. general hospital at West Haven, Conn., has decided not to accept his discharge just at present as he is learning the auto business, and expects soon to work for the government along that line.

March 17, 1919

About 300 people assembled at the patriotic meeting held in Union Hall on Friday evening to welcome home those of our boys who have already been honorably discharged from service.

Shortly after 8 o'clock the Crosby orchestra struck up the Star Spangled Banner. At the same time, the curtain was drawn, bringing to view fourteen of our boys in khaki and blue.

April 21, 1919

A public meeting of the citizens of the village was held in the M.E. vestry Monday evening for the purpose of making arrangements for erecting an honor board for the boys and Red Cross nurses who registered from Osterville. Mrs. Edith Crosby presided and called upon Mr. G. W. Hallett to explain what had already been done. A committee of five was appointed to wait upon the trustees of the library and see if permission would be granted to place the board on the library grounds if it was desired, and to consult and look about for other suitable locations. The committee is as follows: Messrs. G. W. Hallett, Azor D. Hall, Thomas Whiteley, A. L. Robbins and W. Scott Scudder. They will report at another public meeting to be held in the M.E. church vestry on Tuesday evening at 8 o'clock.

April 28, 1919

Mrs. E. P. Childs has received word from her daughter, Marion, that she is now located in Lemur, France, and her son, Verner, is on his way to Plymouth, England.

June 16, 1919

We are glad to welcome home this week one of our Red Cross nurses, Marie Hansberry, who has recently returned from her work overseas. Her brother, James Hansberry, and Shirley Evans, two more of our boys, have arrived in New York.

June 30, 1919

Capt. Joseph Daniel sailed from New York for Copenhagen, Denmark, on Friday.

July 14, 1919

Leonard Tallman enlisted in the Navy the past week and is now at Charlestown Navy Yard on a destroyer.

July 14, 1919

We were glad to welcome home another of our boys the past week, as Maurice Allen has returned from service.

General Clarence Edwards, Commanding Officer of the Yankee Division. Max and Carroll Crosby, Ed Daniel, and Leo Beaumont, all from Osterville, served under him during World War I.

August 4, 1919

Ernest Jones, another of our boys, has returned safely from overseas, and we are glad to welcome him home the past week.

October 6, 1919

Verner Childs, U.S. Navy, writes that he has been spending some time at Paris, and expected soon to leave for Turkey and China.

March 29, 1920

We are very glad to report that the pupils of the Osterville School have contributed $12.60 toward "America's Gift to France."

October 22, 1925

A meeting of the citizens of Osterville is called Wednesday evening Oct. 28th at 8 P.M. in the school house, for the purpose of discussing plans for erecting a memorial to the World War Veterans. We would like a full attendance.

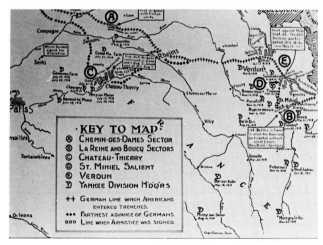

Map of northeast France showing where Osterville men fought in the trenches during World War I.

December 12, 1925

A public meeting will be held at the Grammar School on Friday evening, Dec. 11th at 8 o'clock, to receive the reports of the Boulder Location and Finance Committees, and to take action thereon.

Scenes of Battle — World War I.

The four Osterville men who went to the front in World War I served in the 101st Engineers.

The town of St. Remy, showing the effect of German shell fire, also Company F, 101st Engineers, taking a short rest on their way to the front. St. Remy, Vosges, France, September 26, 1918.

Members of the 101st Engineers, 26th Division, commanded by Captain E. M. Brush, repairing the road by filling in shell hole made by American artillery in the advance of September 13, 1918. Some of these shell holes are twenty feet deep and twenty feet wide. Near St. Remy, Meuse, France, September 16, 1918.

Max Crosby, Carroll Crosby, Ed Daniel, and Leo Beaumont all served in these areas during World War I.

Radio Electrician 2nd Class, Maurice B. Allen: He enlisted in the U.S. Navy on August 21, 1917 for a four year term. After attending radio school at the Brooklyn Naval Yard, he served on the U.S.S. Texas, U.S.S. Pennsylvania, U.S.S. Maine and the U.S.S. Waukashaw. He made one trip to France on the Waukashaw and also served in the West Indies, Rio de Janiero, South America and Panama. Before his discharge in 1919, he served aboard the U.S.S Tern in San Diego.

Radio Electrician 2nd Class Maurice Allen

. . . Letters to home

(Letter written September 1st, 1917, by Maurice Allen to his mother Mrs. Edith Allen. Letter was written from Newport, R.I.)

My Dear Mother:

Just a word to let you know that I am all right and am getting along fine. If you send me any cake or candy be sure and wrap it up good so it won't get broken up. Just wrote a letter to Frank and I was very glad to hear that he was exempted and hope that he will always be as lucky.

I hope you will notice my address is changed because if you send it to my old one I won't get it. Have you heard from Sybil? I wrote to her but haven't got any answer yet. Saw Karl Chadwick and Leon Hinckley yesterday. Some glad to see them two believe me. I suppose you have seen Betty by this time and what does she say. I am going to write to her tonight after I finish this. Hope you are well and strong. Wish I was there to get some of your vegetables. If anybody says anything about sending anything don't stop them — am just dying for something civilized.

Lots of love,
Maurice

Walcott Ames, Chief Pilot U.S.N. He served in the Navy for 22 months as a warrant officer in naval aviation, based in Norfolk, Virginia.

Walcott Ames

145

L. to r., C. Dudley Armstrong, 1st Lieut., U.S. Ordnance Corps., and his brother, Dwight L. Armstrong, Ensign, U.S. Naval Reserves.

During World War I Dwight Ludden Armstrong (1895-1944) trained at Newport, R.I. He was an Ensign in the Navy and was serving aboard the U.S. George Washington when President Woodrow Wilson crossed the Atlantic on that ship to sign the Armistice.

Charles Dudley Armstrong (1888-19) served in World War I as a Captain in Chemical Warfare. He saw no overseas duty.

Rawson H. Ashley

Rawson H. Ashley, United States Navy. Trained at Newport and was stationed there for the duration of the war. He served as a guard.

PFC Merton H. Bates, Amb. Co. 20, 6th Div. Reg., Camp Wadsworth, South Carolina.

Private 1st Class Merton Bates enlisted September, 1917 at New Bedford, Mass. He was stationed at Annistan, Alabama and Camp Wadsworth, South Carolina. Served in Medical Corps. Was discharged at Camp Devens in November, 1918.

. . . Letter to home
from Pvt. 1st Class Merton Bates

May 29, 1918

Dear Mother and Dad:

Got Dad's letter today and was sure glad to hear from you all.

We have been so busy getting the most important part of our training, (the use of the gas mask) that I have had very little time to myself.

This morning we had our final test with the mask — the trenches, with an actual gas attack. It was led by a very smart English captain, who had been in France three years and wears wounded stripes. Yesterday we went through the chlorine gas and tear gas chambers. We wore our masks but took them off as we went out of the door to see what the stuff was like. The chlorine, although one hundred times weaker than the German's, gave me a funny feeling in the stomach.

The tear gas did not feel bad, although I cried with great vim. One of the lieutenants had told me not to rub my eyes, so I got off easier than some of the boys.

We came in at ten o'clock and polished up our quarters. Got through at 10:30 and lay around until 12. Had a good dinner, steak, mashed potatoes, gravy, cake, apple butter bread and lemonade.

At 1:15, twelve of us took picks and shovels and made a road around the officers' quarters. It was 102 degrees where we were working, and big rivers of sweat poured off me as I swung the old pick. At 4:30 we quit and lay around until "chow" call.

In the evening I went to the library and got a few books, came back and tried to read, but couldn't: the flies wouldn't let me. They are the greatest pests of our present life.

Am on guard duty tonight and tomorrow, a very pleasant way to spend the 30th. Have gained 26 lbs. since I came out of the hospital and am still gaining. The life sure does agree with me.

The old southern sun has burned me as black as can be. Never knew what heat was 'til I hit South Carolina. We are only two miles from Spartanburg, a very little city. Have been down two or three times to the Y.M.C.A. there to take a swim in the pool.

Well, it's nearing the time for my relief to go on, so will put on a few clothes to appear dressed.

Love to you all, and best regards to all the folks.

Corporal Leo Beaumont, 101st Engineers, 26th Division, Company F.

Enlisted August 28, 1917, in Boston, Mass. Because of the death of his platoon leader, his records were never completed. The following article appeared in print Feb. 17, 1919: "Corporal Leo E. Beaumont, who recently arrived home, was formerly of Company F, 101st Engineers, but later transferred to Co. F, 101st Infantry. He was in active service at Chateau Thierry and Argonne Forest where he was gassed and later sent to the hospital where he remained until he was able to return home." He was discharged Feb. 3, 1919. His widow of more than 55 years, who lived in Centerville, states that her late husband was gassed

twice and saw front line duty also at Belleau Woods, and maybe Seicheprey. She states that being a widow these many years, it is difficult to remember just where her husband served. It is believed that Beaumont served at the front from the Chemin-des-Dames through the Argonne Forest. In 1925 Beaumont was the first of the WWI veterans to die from lung damage sustained in the great war. Mrs. Leo Beaumont is now deceased.

Sgt. Robert Bell   Pvt. Hallett Boult

Sgt. Robert Bell served in the U.S. Army Tank Corps. A native of Nova Scotia, Bell came to Osterville about 1893-4. He was stationed at Gettysburg, Pennsylvania. He was the oldest Osterville man to serve in WWI.

Pvt. Hallett Boult, French mortar detachment, 20th, F.A. was stationed at Camp Jackson, South Carolina.

Seaman 1st Class Karl W. Chadwick. He served in the U.S. Navy prior to World War I, where he trained at Newport. He served again in the Navy during the War.

Pvt. Burton Chadwick: cited by the late Louis Boody, principal of Barnstable High School, as an outstanding student, Chadwick was attending Harvard when called into service. He was sent by the army to the Aberdeen Ballistics Center in Maryland until the Armistice. He returned to Harvard and was graduated Phi Beta Kappa, class of 1920.

Seaman 1st Class Karl W. Chadwick and Pvt. Burton Chadwick

Marion Childs

Nurse Marion Childs, U.S. Medical Corps. She graduated from nurses' training school at Massachusetts General Hospital and enlisted in the American Red Cross Nurses Corps, which served as a nursing unit for the U.S. Army. She served in France during the war. After the war, her children could remember her using army mess kits in the kitchen. Tin cups, tin forks and an old broken army knife — for opening oysters — were but a few utensils she used frequently after the war.

PFC Donald Coffin

Pvt. 1st Class Donald Coffin enlisted in 1918 and was stationed at Kelly Field, San Antonio, Texas. Then he went to Dorr Field, Arcadia, Florida. He was stationed there until he was discharged in 1919. He was an airplane mechanic.

Letter-To-Home Written By Donald Coffin to Alice Coombs

Dorr Field
Feb. 29, 1919

Dear Alice:

Have got a few minutes before dinner so thought I would scribble you a few lines to let you know I am still alive.

We have been having a warm spell here and are having quite a lot of rain now. It has been so hot that all we wore was overalls. From what mother writes, winter is about over for this year. I was talking with a "Cracker" yesterday and asked him when they had their rainy season. He said it was during last of May and June.

We have to go out and drill an hour every afternoon and we do everything we can to get out of it. They are getting up a baseball team and I get out of drill 3 times a week by being on it. Think I will make the regular team and probably get a few trips to different towns. A good cheap way to see the country.

They are still doing more or less flying here and from the way things look, it will be some time before we get out. A lot of the fellows have got affidavits and put in for a discharge. Have to have dependents or a darn good excuse. I haven't got any dependents (so far as you know) and the only excuse is that Herb wants me. Don't like to stay here but guess I can stand it if the rest can. One fellow put in for a furlough but he was turned down so he went A.W.O.L. for 13 days and all he got was confined to camp for two months and reduced from 1st class private to buck private. Think I would take a few days off if I didn't think I would get more than that.

The mess call just blew so will go over and see what they have got to eat. Well Alice, we had some dinner today. Got some chewing gum they called roast beef, mashed spuds, pear that had worms in them, bread, apricots and ice water. Yesterday we had beef stew and that was full of cockroaches. We sure are getting poor eats now but perhaps they will be better before long.

Have got a few pictures of four of us together and will send one along with this. Took some of myself alone but there was something the matter with the film and they didn't turn out good. Was gong to take some last Sunday but I was on K.P. Don't expect to be on next Sunday and will take some then.

Well Alice, it is time to go to work so will close and mail this so it will go this P.M.

As Ever
Don

PFC Malcolm Crosby and his brother PFC Carroll Parker Crosby

PFC Malcolm Crosby, 101st Engineers, 26th Division, Company F. Enlisted Aug. 25, 1917, at Boston, Mass. Truly an outstanding soldier of World War I, Uncle Max (as he was known to many) served at the front with the YD during their entire involvement at the front, Feb. 10 through Nov. 11, 1918. He participated in the following defensive and offensive battles, sectors and a raid: Battles — Chemin-des-Dames, Champagne-Marne, Aisne-Marne Chateau Thierry, St. Michiel and Meuse-Argonne; Sectors — Toul, Pas Fini, Rupt, Troyon and Definsive: Raid — Marcheville. On Nov. 11, 1918. Uncle Max was at Verdun.

Over a period of years the writer of this series of articles spent many hours in the Crosby home, several times with a tape recorder. The life history of Mr. Crosby and also his war experiences have all been recorded. On one occasion during a battle, the soldier beside Uncle Max was instantly killed. Upon his return to the U.S. in the spring of 1919, Uncle Max participated in the welcome home parade the Yankee Division held in Boston. More than one million New Englanders roared home this great division with a tremendous welcome. He was discharged at Camp Devens, April 28, 1919.

He worked for a short while in the oyster business, then built boats at West Bay until he was nearly 80 years old. Asked if he ever took a coffee break, his answer was "Never." Asked why, his reply was "couldn't waste the time." In April of 1979, Uncle Max died. He was nearly 86 years old.

PFC Carroll Parker Crosby, 101st Engineers, 26th Division, Company F. Enlisted Sept. 18, 1917, at Boston, Mass. Served at the front from February, 1918, until July 26, 1918. He participated in the following battles: Chemin-des-Dames, Feb. 9 through March 21, 1918, and Chateau Thierry, July 9 through July 26, 1918. He also saw front line action at the Toul Sector, March 30 through June 26, 1918. On July 16, 1918, during the battle of Chateau Thierry, Crosby was seriously gassed while 200 yards from the enemy lines. He made several attempts to go back to the front. On July 26, Crosby was removed from the front to the evacuation hospital. He had sustained severe lung damage. He remained in the hospital until Dec. 9, 1918, when he sailed for the U.S. He arrived in the U.S. Dec. 20th and was sent to Camp Mills, N.Y. for further treatment. He was discharged Jan. 16, 1919, at Camp Devens, Mass. A son who resides in Osterville today states that his father never fully recovered from the effects of gas. His diary written while at the front has been very helpful in the writing of these articles. This diary will be featured in future articles.

Excerpts from diary kept by PFC Carroll Crosby during WWI

January 9, 1918

Somewhere in France — "7:00 AM pretty cold, regular blizzard. Am working down at the barracks today. Max had quite a party last night. (12:30 pm). Mail — 5:30 pm. Fine box from Sal & folks. 8:30 pm Have taken down my laundry. Stayed with the old lady for a while. Learned French.

Sarah (Alley) Crosby (Mrs. Carroll P. Crosby)

January 26, 1918

Put one of Sal's pictures in my diary. Got our steel helmet.

January 28, 1918

6:45 am — Heavy mist. On detail to next town. Lots of shooting on the range.

January 29, 1918

We got our gas masks today. Had our drill with them. Have to put them on in 6 seconds.

January 30, 1918

Went on 5 miles hike and took our first gas test with tear gas. We go into closed house and they turn on gas.

February 8, 1918

5:30 up. Fair and warm. 9:30 all packed and ready. 12:00 down to the train and all aboard. Started about 1:30. West to Neuf Chateau. Through Gondrecourt etc. Not much sleep tonight. Slept out on a flat car.

February 11, 1918

9:00 am Nothing much to do today. We are in an underground cave. Our whole Company F and lots of French besides. Walked down to canteen only 1½ miles. Have to be pretty careful. Slept good. Had corned willie and hard tack for dinner. Can hear the guns now and then. We are about 2½ miles from the front. You could see the flash of artillery fire.

February 16, 1918

10:30 am Cold and clear. The Boche are sending over a few shells. Aircraft are very active. The infantry had to vacate town below us. They call it the mound of tombs. Because of so many graves. 1:00 pm out again, cold. Back 9:30 pm. Under fire for first time. The shells went just over our heads. Little excitement.

February 17, 1918

10:30 am up feel good. It is not quite so cold. All details called in. Expect heavy bombardment this after. Out to work at 6:00 pm, Some night, heavy fire by the Allies. Must have had a (stop over). The Boche also sent some shells over. Had to quit work and take to cover. Ran into our first gas, nobody hurt but some got pretty well scared.

February 19, 1918

Fritz has sent over a few more shells. Beautiful day. 1:30 pm movies. Have written Harold. 4:30 pm — got a Saturday Evening Post. Out at 5:45 pm. Back at 10:30 pm. Worst night yet. Under shell fire good and proper. Fritz got the range of the field and he certainly put them in here. We certainly are lucky to be all together. One shell threw a shower of dirt over us, was some scared.

Feb. 20, 1918

7:15 am Ed (believed to be Ed Daniel) brought in my breakfast. Mail — Mother, Uncle Bill and Sal. Out to work at 5:15 pm. Fritz only drove us off the field once tonight. Gave us a little tear gas. Most finished on the barb wire. Back at 12:00. Little bacon, bread and coffee. Am pretty tired.

March 2, 1918

7:00 am Snowing. Didn't sleep very good. Got more cold. Heavy firing at front all night. Lots of rats in the barracks to keep us company.

April 11, 1918

5:30 am fair and warm. Still on latrine detail. Didn't do much in the afternoon. Lots more mail came in but none for me. Heavy artillery duels all day. Wrote mother, Harold and Edith. Feel pretty good. Company goes out to string barb wire.

April 13, 1918

2:00 am back from work. Quite a lot of shooting. One 77 landed in barb wire just before I got there.

April 20, 1918

5:45 clear and cold. Up to the cave with the rest today. 12:00 am helped two French carpenters Fritz sent over a few shells this morning. 3 pm just getting back to work. Fritz sent over lots of heavy shells. One piece of a H.E. shell went right by my head and struck the ground at my feet. Some close.

———————

April 22, 1918

Didn't sleep till 3:30 am. Mice awful thick in the cellar where we sleep. Not much shooting.

———————

April 23, 1918

Fritz shelled us a little when we came home to lunch. Boche planes active. 1:00 pm several shells landed right in the path we use. Gave us some gas about 2:00 pm.

———————

April 26, 1918

6:00 am clear and cool. Slept through a barrage so must have slept sound. Nothing to do this morning. Fritz sent over quite a few shells. The pieces splatted all over the roof of our shack. 5:00 pm our lumber has come. Fritz still shelling.

———————

April 27, 1918

3:00 am guard till 5:00 am. Heavy barrage opened up as I went on guard. Lasted 1 hour and 30 minutes. 7 am on barracks today. Cleaned up and then slept till dinner time. Made a mouse trap in the afternoon.

———————

May 18, 1918

7:30 am beautiful day. The 8″ boys did some tall speaking today. Airplanes very active on both sides. Some pieces of shrapnel dropped pretty near us.

———————

May 20, 1918

5:45 fair and warm. Am working on the old shift now. 8 hrs. per day. One piece of shrapnel hit our elephant dugout this morning.

———————

May 22, 1918

9:00 pm Leo got back to the Co. again. (Leo — believed to be Leo Beaumont.) Guess he has had a pretty hard time and glad to get back.

———————

May 24, 1918

Off to string barbed wire at 8:00 pm. Back at 11:00 pm.

May 28, 1918

Airplanes, Boche & Allied very active. A piece of shrapnel landed in the street about 20 ft. from Max.

———————

June 3, 1918

6:30 up. Fair and warm. Out with the rest of the platoon for barb wiring, camouflage. Back at 11:30 am. Fritz sent over 8 shells at a trench digger. Everybody thought they were shelling the town and scattered. Hear Leo is to leave us again. This is no place for him. Poor Leo, I pity him. (Leo — believed to be Leo Beaumont.)

———————

June 8, 1918

We work within 200 yds. of the front line..

———————

June 16, 1918

7 am (gas) everybody up to put on gas masks. Heavy barrage by Fritz. Our guns answered. Fritz still sending over some big ones. 9:00 pm out to dig trenches just outside the town. Back at 2:30 am.

———————

June 21, 1918

The roof over our shack leaks like a sieve.

———————

July 3, 1918

Up at 2:45 am and hiked 18 kilometers to (blank in diary). Believe me we were sleepy. I have had no sleep to amount for three days. Had 2 meals the last two days. Gee but we certainly got it shoved to us proper. We all thought we were going to a rest camp. Turned in at 8:30 am and slept till 4:00 pm. Had some kind of a mess.

———————

July 4, 1918

7:30 up and breakfast. Fair and warm. Slept pretty good. Big guns going all night. Believe me this is some lively front. Fell in at 11:00 am to see if we each had all of our equipment. Baseball game in the afternoon, between the officers and the boys. Had to make our packs up again but didn't move. Saw a dead French man float down the river. Some fourth of July.

———————

July 5, 1918

Saw an airplane that was forced to land. It was full of bullet holes and tipped upside down when it landed. Had a bath in the Marne river after supper. Fritz shelled the railroad near here about 10:30 pm.

July 8, 1918

Arrived at our camp in the woods at about 2:30 am. Had a hell of a time finding a place to sleep. Max and I dropped some where and were asleep in no time. We hiked about 7½ miles. Was some tired. Slept till about 10 am. Had dinner at 12 am. Slept a little more after dinner. No water all day. Am pretty thirsty.

———————

July 8, 1918

Went out to dig trenches at 9:00 pm. Got to where we dug them at 11:30 pm. Max didn't have to go as he worked all day. They sure do some shelling here. Nobody hurt going out.

———————

July 10, 1918

2:30 am started home. One of our teams and a horse was hit with pieces of shell. Got home at 4 am. Some long walk for 3 hours work. Coffee and bread. At 4:30 am turned in and slept till 11:30 am. Did a little work at Y.M. after dinner. Went out at 9 pm. Got on the job at 11:30. Fritz made it pretty hot for us. D Co. had 3 men wounded. Max went out tonight.

———————

July 11, 1918

Left for home at 1:55 am, got home about 3 am. Had coffee and bread. Slept till 11:30 am. Y.M. opened in the afternoon. It has rained most all day. Ed is with us again. (Ed — believed to be Ed Daniel.) Out at 9 pm. Beautiful night. Fritz put some over tonight good and proper. Yours truly came as near getting it as he ever wants to. Changed our position.

———————

July 12, 1918

Back at about 3:30 am. Had coffee and bread. Slept till 12 am. Rained in the afternoon. Wrote Sal. Out to work at 9 pm. Got as far as the ravine and they started shelling us. One shell hit in the ravine and F Co. got her first casualties. (Killed Corp. St. Lawrence, Private Shaw, Private Shirley.) Wounded Priv. Grocott, Priv. Fry and Sarg. Jenson.

———————

July 14, 1918

12:30 pm dinner time. Raining. Out tent leaks like a sieve. Max and I stayed inside most all the time. Out again at   pm. Raining like the devil. Got up the road a little ways and the Co. turned back. I was on a loading detail and we kept going. Got up to Lucy before midnight. Fritz shelled the town and ravine. We got gas on way home.

July 15, 1918

Home again at 2:30 am. Had quite an exciting time. Fritz planted some pretty near us. Everybody out at 8:30 pm, even the cooks. Stand to tonight. Went up the road and stood ground for two hours. Went down to 3rd line and started digging.

———————

July 16, 1918

Bayonets and mess covers. Some outfit. I got down about a foot and Fritz got a line on us. Some of us got out and some of them stayed. Anyway we got 21 casualties. Fellows got pretty well cut up. The others were gassed. I got a good many whiffs of it too. Everybody had to leave their packs and there was mustard gas. Got home about 4 am. Slept till 12 am. Feel rotten. Went to sick call but they didn't do anything for me. Co. went out at 9 pm as usual.

———————

July 17, 1918

Up early as I wasn't up last night. Didn't sleep hardly any. Max got in about 3:30 am. Had hot coffee and doughnuts for breakfast. Turned in again as I was feeling punk. Guess I got gas all right. Went to sick call and they gave me some pills. Got a letter from Alma. 56 of our Co. go out tonight. Max is going. I am not as I don't feel very good. Good luck to them as I guess it is a dangerous job.

———————

July 18, 1918

Bob wounded today. 4:23 am awoken by the barrage. Slept very poorly all night. Had a tempest during the first part of the night. My mansion leaked pretty badly. Up at 8:30 for a bite to eat. Feel pretty bum. Pains in stomach all night. Max and a few others came back at about 2 pm. Guess they got there just too late to go over the top. Went to sick call.

———————

July 19, 1918

8:30 am on a road-repairing detail today. 12 am hung around all the morning but the truck did not show up. Off at 1 pm. Back at about 5 pm. Filled up lots of ruts, holes, etc. 8 pm Fritz sent over some wash boilers. They go over in the town of Montreal.

———————

July 20, 1918

7 am Breakfast. Same detail today. Worked between Pans Farm and Lucy. Filled some big shell holes. No work in the PM, so layed down and slept. No work at night. Fritz planes came over last night and dropped some bombs.

July 21, 1918

7:30 am fair and warm. Rained during the night. Didn't sleep very good. Awful cramp in my stomach. Road detail again today. Worked in Lucy cleaning up. The whole Co. moves up tonight. Went back to camp after my stuff. Came back in truck, slept out under the stars.

July 22, 1918

6 am breakfast. Slept rotten, some pains in stomach. On a wagon loading detail in the morning. Left Lucy at about 1 pm. March to Torcy — 3 kilos, then to camp 7 kilos more. Got our bunks all made then had to move again. March from 10 pm — till -

---

July 23, 1918

4 pm to the lines. Find then that we were supposed to go over the top, but we didn't go over. Stayed in a little strip of woods till 10 am. Rainy, guess I have a good cold. Marched up to a town where we are to have a little rest. 5 am expect to try and take town near here sometime this after. God be with us.

July 24, 1918

4:30 am everybody up. I am to see the doctor so don't go out. Coughed all night, didn't sleep a wink. 9 am saw the doctor and he gave me some pills, etc. I know what it is all right. Bronchitis. 10 am the boys are back, guess that they dug a line of trenches. Fritz has taken to his heels. Think he must be 8-10 kilo from here now. Yesterday one couldn't cross any of these neighboring fields without being shot at by Fritz. Machine guns.

July 25, 1918

5 am the boys are back. They hiked way up to the front about 7 miles and back. Glad I didn't try and go as I never would have made it. Fritz sent lots of shells during the night. Most of them were duds. None hit the little farm. Went to sick call in the afternoon and am to be sent to the hospital. Saw a swell air fight just as I was getting into the ambulance at 6:30 pm.

July 26, 1918

Arrived at evacuation hospital at about 1 am. A Frenchman who was over me in the ambulance died before they could get him to the hospital. Stayed here all day.

September 2, 1918

7 am fair and warm. Labor Day today. Suppose the summer people will be leaving Osterville

soon. The doctor looked at me about 9 am. Said that a little work would help my lungs. Worked at carpentry in the PM. Went for walk after supper.

PFC Carroll Crosby remained at the hospital until December 9th when he sailed for the United States. Arrived in New York on December 20th, 1918, and was sent to Camp Mills, New York.

PFC Carroll Crosby on his return from the front, World War I

Letter to Home

May 27, 1918

The following letter was received recently from Max Crosby, son of Mr. and Mrs. Manley Crosby.

France, April 16, 1918

My Dear Mother:

I have just received your letter dated March 20th, and was some pleased to get it.

Last night I received Alma's letter with pictures in it and they are fine. The one with father standing beside the new boat is a dandy and also the one of you and Billy. Carroll received the pictures Alma sent this noon, and you can believe me that the old homestead looked good to me. Have shown the pictures of the boats to some of the boys here and by the way some of them talk we might stir up a little business when we get home.

Have a little extra news this time, Carroll and I have been made first class privates and Edward, a corporal. All the boys seem to think that a first class private has the best job in the army and it looks that way to me. Carroll and I have been called to go on another detail and are supposed to have our things ready to jump at any moment, so do not worry if you do not hear from us very soon.

Yes, I would saw wood for a month if this thing would end and I could get home. Am glad to hear the weather is getting warmer at home; as for the weather here, it is cold and rainy. I was out working the other night and got caught in a hard thunder shower, got wet through and had nothing dry to put on, but didn't get cold. Well, mother, will have to close for this time.

Best of love to all the folks.

Your loving son,
Max.

Letter from Max Crosby
December 23, 1918

The following is a letter received by Mrs. H. Manley Crosby of Osterville from her son, Max, who is in the 101st U.S. Engineers. It is the first letter received from him since the war ended:

Meunoreaux, France, November 27, 1918

Dear Mother:

It is the day before Thanksgiving, and I have nothing special to do, so thought as I had not written to you lately that it would be a good time to write you a few lines.

The censorship has been lifted since the close of the war, and now I will be able to tell you a good deal more of what I am seeing and doing.

During the last part of the war, my company was up on the Verdun front where they had the great battles of 1916, and we surely saw some great sights. We had some pretty warm times while we were there, as that front was always very active. One of the worst places I was in was the city of Verdun when they were shelling it with their big guns.

The last day of the fighting, we were fixing a road to get artillery over, and I was working right near a battery of seventy-fives, and the word came to stop all firing at eleven o'clock, and you can just bet we were some happy when they said it was all over.

We stayed on the front two days after the war ended, then started on one long hike back to the town in which we are now settled. The hike lasted eight days and we walked over a hundred miles.

This town is a small place near Chaumont, where we were last winter.

All of the boys are hoping to get home for Christmas, but, of course, we do not know what is going to be done. There is a bunch of us boys got a nice billet with a big fireplace in it, and believe me, we keep it roaring all the time. The weather is beginning to get quite cold and a nice fire feels very good. Have not heard a word from Carroll for

over a month, and I do not know if he will get home with me or not. Would like to hear from him so I could tell how he is getting along. Have not heard from any of the other boys for a long time, so cannot give you any word about them.

Last night I received a letter from Alma, written November 10th. Guess by what she wrote, the people of New England did quite a bit of celebrating when the war ended.

Well, Mother, I could write and tell you my whole story as a soldier over here, but will wait until I get home, as I think I could do a better job talking than by writing.

Tell father to get ready for the big celebration and don't forget to have a full pantry with lots of pies and puddings, Indian pudding especially.

Well, Mother, here's hoping I see you all very soon. Best regards to all, love to the family,

Max

Cpl. Edward C. Daniel

Corporal Edward C. Daniel, 101st Engineers, 26th Division, Company F. Enlisted in August of 1917 at Boston, Mass. We regret his personal records cannot be found. Members of the family recall he saw front line duty at the Argonne Forest where he was gassed. In the personal diary kept by PFC Carroll Crosby, 'Ed' is mentioned during the battle of Chateau-Thierry. This is believed to refer to Edward Daniel. It is believed by the author that Cpl. Daniel served at the front from the Chemin-des-Dames until removed from the front after the battle of the Argonne Forest. As a result of the residual lung damage from gas, Daniel fled to the southwest U.S. after the war, where he lived for many years.

November 11, 1918

Letter from Edward Daniel to his niece Rachel Daniel, now Mrs. Rachel Campana of Bay Street, Osterville.

October 12, 1918

My dear Rachel:

Your letter came last week and it was a good one too, lots of things in it that no one else remembered to tell me. I am living now right next to the school in this town, and there are a lot of children outside now, making just as much noise as American kids, too. They really have two schools, one for boys and one for girls, each having their own room and playground. The boys mostly wear black, so you have to look twice some times to see which are boys and which are girls.

Yesterday was market day and the market place is near, so I saw that too. It is a big square and they put tables all around just like a fair at home. They had most everything to sell. I saw one old lady going home with a live rooster under one arm and a big bottle of wine under the other. Most of the people who were selling things came in from the farms, some of them driving horses, but a good many more driving donkeys. I saw one cart driven by a very good-sized lady and pulled by a donkey not one-third as big as the one Mrs. Sawyer used to have. Do you know what I had for dinner the other day? A piece of apple pie! The first piece we have had since last January, and I wouldn't have taken ten francs for it. I don't know if all my letters get home or not, so if you get this tell Georgie I just had a letter from her dated September 8th, a fine one, too. Your pictures were fine and will you thank Miss Hinckley for the one she sent of the service flag and tell Mrs. Parker at the Post Office that I will try to write to her soon. Remember me to the rest of the family. Tell papa if he is going to fight Germans, he'd better get a move on or there won't be any left for him.

No more now, but lots of love.

From Uncle Edward

Lieut. (S.G.) Joseph Daniel, second from right.

U.S.S. Albert Watts, torpedoed by a German sub on Thanksgiving Day in 1917. Lt. Daniel swam through flames to save his life.

Joseph Daniel, Lieutenant (S.G.) U.S.N., a graduate of U.S. Maritime Academy. During years of World War I served in Merchant Marines.

Was member of crew of the U.S.S. Albert Watts, an oil tanker, which was torpedoed by a German sub on Thanksgiving Day 1917 in the Mediterranean. As the Watts was being towed into the port of Genoa, Italy, severely crippled and leaking oil, it suddenly burst into flames from a match tossed overboard from a small boat nearby. All hands and the cook went overboard without orders. Lieutenant Daniel swam through flames and was one of the crew to reach shore — an experience he never forgot.

After the Armistice he served as first mate on the Leviathan. Was member of the Naval Reserves 1919-1922.

1st Lieut. Stewart Elliott

Stewart Elliott, First Lieutenant, 13th Squadron, 2nd Pursuit Group. Believed to be the only overseas pilot from Osterville to serve in World War I. A graduate of Harvard College, he was a student at M.I.T. when war was declared. Enlisted in the Aviation Signal Corps, U.S. Army in May of 1917. Was admitted to the School of Military Aeronautics. Trained at Mineola, Long Island, N.Y. While on Long Island he spent weekend with ex-

President "Teddy" Roosevelt at his Sagamore Hill home. Elliott's father was own cousin to Roosevelt.

He then trained at Kelly Field, Texas. On October 27, 1917, he sailed from New York to Liverpool, England. Crossed England and landed at Le Havre, France, where he then trained at Issoudun, France.

His first assignment was Orly Field, Paris. Then was sent to the front at Toul, France. Was engaged in aerial combat with enemy aircraft while at the front.

He participated in the following air battles: St. Mihiel and Meuse-Argonne. During the air battle of Meuse-Argonne his plane was hit by enemy fire.

He had a total of 82 hours of flying missions over enemy lines.

Elliott was born in Osterville in 1892 and was the nephew of Mrs. Thomas Gaff.

In 1974 Elliott was the author of a book "Wooden Crates and Gallant Pilots." The book tells of his life and experiences as a pilot during World War I.

PFC Shirley S. Evans   Pvt. Joseph V. Gomes

Pvt. 1st Class Shirley S. Evans. Group A, Section 3, 301st INF. Repair Unit. He enlisted Sept. 20, 1917, and sailed for France in January, 1918, from Hoboken, New Jersey. The troop ship was so crowded with soldiers some had to sleep on deck. There was just enough room to turn over at night. He served in France for eighteen months. He was discharged at Fort Devens in June, 1919.

Private Joseph V. Gomes. Served with the U.S. Army at Camp Upton, N.Y. He was an interpreter for the Portuguese-American men serving in the U.S. Army. Private Gomes travelled from camp to camp performing this duty.

Cecil Goodspeed   PFC James Hansberry

Cecil Goodspeed, U.S. Navy. He enlisted at Boston, January, 1918. He was trained at Newport, R.I., for three weeks and then sent by train to New York City where he picked up the troop carrying ship Northern Pacific, which sailed to Brest, France. The ship brought back 125 French soldiers. He was then stationed at Ellis Island. Then he served on the U.S.S. Vulcan stationed at Norfolk, Virginia. He went to the West Indies and Cuba. He was discharged in July, 1919, at Norfolk, Va.

Private 1st Class James Hansberry. 302nd, INF, Repair Unit. Served in France. Private Hansberry also served in Washington, D.C.

Nurse, U.S. Med. Corps, Marie Hansberry. She served at Base Hospital, Lemur, France. Marie was a graduate of Carney Hospital Training School for Nurses and served overseas with the army. On her return from France, she was in charge of the training program at General Hospital, Port Au Prince, Haiti, in 1920.

(Extracts from a letter written to Margaret Hansberry by her sister Marie, a Red Cross nurse in France)

August 22, 1918

My dear Margaret:

This has surely been sunny France for the past few weeks; such heavenly weather I have never seen. It is very warm but not as uncomfortable as at home in the summer. Another one of Jim's pals is in my ward. I feel quite at home knowing that nearly all my friends are "somewhere in France." Have heard splendid things about Ed Daniel from one of his men. Also about Max Crosby. Did you know Ed had been commissioned?

Nurse, U.S. Med. Corps, Marie Hansberry

Tell some of Max Crosby's people that I have heard splendid things about his soldiering and they have reason to be very proud of Max. Ed is said to be exceptionally clever in his line. This is surely a small world. Send me the addresses of any of the people whom I used to know at home who are out here so that I may write them or inquire about the various "outfits" from my boys.

. . . Contrary to any of our wildest imaginations, last night every one of us had a glorious evening at our first dance — "somewhere in France." Our base hospital gave the dance and invited some of the officers from neighboring camps and also the French people of the village, who have been very kind to all of our men and officers. The party was given in a casino which had been converted into a ward. The men moved all the beds out for the occasion and we volunteered to make them up again after they had moved them back. The hall was decorated in flags and looked so much like one we might find in the states that I am sure all of us forgot we were in France on such a serious mission. The American boys who have been over here for a long time treat us as if we were very wonderful creatures. Life goes on very happily for all of us here. Do write soon and often. A loving good-night and God bless you all.

Affectionately,
Marie

Quartermaster 1st Class Leon G. Hinckley. U.S. Navy. Air Service. He served in the Navy prior to World War I. He enlisted again in April of 1917 and trained at the Naval Air Station, Chicago, Illinois. He served in Eastleigh, England, assembling and repairing Liberty Motors in DeHavilland planes which were Britain's most famed medium bombers. He was discharged in April, 1921, at Pelham Bay, N.Y.

Quartermaster 1st Class Leon G. Hinckley on left. Machinist's Mate 1st Class Jesse Murray on right.

Private Ernest Jones. 2nd Army, A.E.F. He trained at Camp Mills, New York. He served in France at Autun and Toule with the U.S. Army Ordinance Dept. He returned to the Cape in 1919.

Pvt. Ernest Jones   Quartermaster 1st Class Elliott Lewis

Quartermaster 1st Class Elliott Lewis. Elliott served with the U.S. Navy Air Service. He was the youngest man from Osterville to serve in WWI. He enlisted on January 9, 1918 at Newport, Rhode Island, where he first trained. Later he was sent to 3rd Reg. 7th Co. 1st in Charleston, S.C.; then to U.S. Naval Air Station, Pensacola, Florida and later to Hampton Roads Naval Training Station, Norfolk, Virginia. He was discharged in Boston in 1921.

Machinist's Mate 1st Class, USN, Jesse Murray

Machinist's Mate 1st Class, USN, Jesse Murray. He joined the naval reserve in 1917 and transferred to naval aviation in England. Mr. Murray was stationed at Eastleigh Air Base just outside of South Hampton until the end of the war. He was discharged in January, 1919. Mr. Murray lived in Osterville and died in 1984.

Fireman 1st Class, Edward F. Souza

Fireman 1st Class Edward F. Souza. Enlisted in the U.S. Navy September 1917 in New Bedford. His basic training was at Norfolk Naval Station, Virginia. Ed was sent to France in March of 1918. While serving in France, he was sent to England to serve aboard a converted German liner/troop ship that transported American troops to New York. He made several trips back and forth between France and the U.S. bringing troops home at the end of the war. He was discharged in July, 1919.

Pvt. William T. Whiteley

Pvt. William T. Whiteley served in Co. E, 307th Engineers, 82d Division. Enlisted October 4, 1917 at Fort Devens. Trained at Camp Gordon, Georgia. Spent 2½ months in France where he was accidentally gassed (see Recollections of War). Returned to this country and spent eleven months in U.S. Army hospital in New Haven, Conn. Discharged May 16, 1919.

Letter written by Pvt. William T. Whiteley to his sister Mrs. Rose (Whiteley) Crocker.

July 5, 1918

Dear Sister,

Just a few lines hoping you had a good 4th. I had a very good time myself. We had a nice dinner. We had steak and mashed potatoes and peach pie and all the cherries we could eat. You see, they raise a lot of them over here. Everywhere you go, it is cherries they grow, just like our wild cherries do over home. That is the way it looks but I suppose they set them out. They have them all along the road for shade trees and they sure are dandy good big ones.

Well, Rose, we are having very good weather. Once in a while a day that is cloudy and a kind of foggie but not very bad. I suppose it is kind of dull home this summer where all of the fellows are away and I suppose it makes quite a lot of difference to the summer people about coming. I guess that the hotel won't be quite rushed up this summer as they have been.

Well, it will seem good to get some mail. I haven't had any since I have been over here, some difference than in the States where I had mail about every day from someone. I suppose when I do get it I will get five or six. That is the way the fellows have been getting their mail.

I would like to run into Max and Carroll. We sure would have a good time but I can't seem to find out just where their regiment is at, but I suppose they are up quite near the front by this time.

I wrote a letter to Henry yesterday. I suppose it will be a year before he will write by the way he wrote to me at Camp Gordon.

I hope that you have a good garden this summer that will save you quite a lot, also the folk at home.

Well, Rose, as there isn't anything more that I can think to write this time, I will close.

From your loving brother,
Bill

. . . Others who served

Victor F. Adams. Enlisted while attending Brown University on September 15, 1918. He was stationed at Fort Monroe, Virginia, in an officer's training camp — Company F. Was discharged after the Armistice in November. Mr. Adams served in the R.O.T.C. at Brown, as a sergeant, in 1917-18. Graduated from Brown with the class of 1920, he served as selectman for the town of Barnstable for 33 years.

Thornton R. Adams. Chief Machinist's Mate, U.S.N. Thornton was the first man from Osterville to enlist in WWI — April, 1917. He trained at Newport.

Frank D. Allen. Private. Enlisted September 5, 1918 and was sent to Fort Devens. He served in the 2nd Searchlight Division. His duty stations were in New York, Washington and Virginia. He returned to Fort Devens after the Armistice and was discharged Nov. 21, 1918.

Joseph Barry. Private, Co. C, 301st Engineers, 76th Div.

Machinist's Mate Second Class Alphonse J. Beaumont, United States Navy. He enrolled in the service December 13, 1917, and served aboard Sub Chaser No. 62 out of State Pier, New London, Conn. He was assigned to protecting convoys in the area from New York to Liverpool, England to Brest, France "where we would meet the convoys returning with the injured. . . Once we were struck by an English tanker in the fog but were able to limp back to port. No injuries. . . Another time we

lost the convoy in heavy fog. When we came out of the fog, we came upon a German submarine that had just emerged. Our ship had one 3-inch gun and four machine guns. The men wanted to engage her but we were ordered back to port when the submarine submerged." Discharged honorably September 30, 1921.

Philip Chadwick. Corporal, 10th Reg. Field Artillery.

Everett Verner Childs. Enlisted April, 1917 in service of the U.S. Naval Reserve, Osterville, Mass. Called for duty in August, 1917, U.S. Navy, Newport, Rhode Island. I made two trips to Liverpool, England and three trips to Brest, France on troop ship U.S. Levithan. Discharged: August, 1920 in Charlestown, S.C.

On one crossing to Brest, France, as we slipped into the harbor, we saw 5 submarines. On another trip to LeHavre, France in a convoy of 21 freighters, just at sunset, we witnessed a torpedo missing our bow and hitting the Tippecanoe in stern which sank in 27 minutes. The crew abandoned ship and took to life boats; they were picked up by a destroyer the next day. I made several more trips on freighters; these ships did not carry big guns for protection, all we had on board were a few rifles.

James L. Corcoran, Private 1st Class, 335th Reg. Q.M.C.

Harry Drinkwater. Captain, U.S. Merchant Marine. Married Mildred Taylor of Osterville.

Charles A. Hinkle. Seaman 1st Class, USN, RF.

Sgt. James G. Hinkle. James G. Hinkle was a student at St. Mark's School in Southborough, Mass. at the outbreak of World War I. He trained at a camp run by the school, and also at Plattsburg, New York (July 5 to August 8, 1916). In 1917, he enlisted as a soldier, and served during 1917 and 1918 with Hdqtrs. Co., 34d D.B., 76th Division, in France. He did not see action at the front, and was discharged as a Sergeant after the Armistice was signed.

Guy Jones, Private, Vet. Hospital No. 1, 76th Div.

Frederick C. Nute. Second Lieutenant, U.S. Air Service. Did most of his training in Texas where he was stationed. Flew Jennings aircraft.

Frederic Scudder. Quartermaster, U.S. Merchant Marine. Was commissioned quartermaster in 1917 aboard the U.S.S. Dakotan. The Dakotan transported U.S. Army troops, arms and equipment from New York to St. Nazaire, France.

The following is a letter received from PFC Stuart Scudder who was serving in the U.S. Army and stationed at San Antonio, Texas. He was later stationed at Camp Jackson, South Carolina.

April 21, 1918

Dear Mother:

I guess I will drop you a little note just to let you know I am well and enjoying life as much as anyone can in the army. I have been in this camp a week. The food is fine. The fire call just blew and I must get out and get the men out in formation lines.

Well, I have got them started on their way to the fire but I must stay behind as I am in charge of the company tonight, so can't leave headquarters.

I was appointed orderly to the Lieutenant when we first came here. Every morning I call the men out and call the roll and read the notices for the morning. After mess, I make out the sick report and carry it to the Lieutenant to sign and then I march the sick men to the hospital for treatment and get the doctor's report on each man. I get the mail and distribute it and make out details for work on guard duty and anything that comes up. I am supposed to be a bugler, but I haven't had hold of a bugle yet. I suppose I will when I get transferred to a company for duty.

I play in the Post band and in one of the company orchestras. They have a valve trombone just like mine exactly, same make and everything. I was up there one night and the horn was sitting there with no one to play it, so I asked if I couldn't try it on an easy one and he said "Go to it" and I did.

Now they are after me all the time for band practice and the like. I played in the orchestra at the Y.M.C.A. last night and enjoyed it very much. I want you to send me my trombone right away.

Well, the fire is all over and the men are back again. It was only a pile of brush where they had been doing some camouflage work.

Tell Walter I will write him a letter about all the funny animals, etc., we see down here, lizards, horned toads, tarantulas, coons, and all sorts of funny animals, most of them poisonous.

Give my regards to every one. Tell them I will write sometime later.

With lots of love,
Stuart

Winthrop D. Scudder. Cadet, Students Army Training Corps.

Edward J. Sullivan. Private, 103d Infantry, 26th Div. Served in France with the Yankee Division and was gassed. Pvt. Sullivan was first cousin to Mr. John Shields of Osterville.

Recollections of World War I by Mrs. Edith (Alley) Williams

"At nearly 88 years young, there is a lot I could say about World War I and its relationship to Osterville, however much has already been covered. There was the knitting done for the boys at the old Methodist Church on Main Street. What we didn't do there, we would take home and finish.

"Then there was the letter-writing. How the boys enjoyed hearing from home! Letters were their lifeline. Until just recently, I had kept my old address book with all the addresses of the boys in it." (Mrs. Williams is shown above reading a letter she had received in 1918 from Bobbie Cameron. Bobbie was with Max and Carroll Crosby at the front in France. In his letter to Mrs. Williams he describes how he was wounded in the head on July 18th, 1918 during the battle of Chateau-Thierry, and was then dragged into a trench and bandaged. He states in his letter that the shells were coming thick and fast. A German prisoner then took him to an ambulance. His letter was written from Cape May, New Jersey, where he was recovering.) Mrs. Williams says, "We were encouraged to write to different soldiers who had been wounded, even though we never met them."

"Then there was the victory celebration. It was just a joyous time. Everyone gathered in the center of the village on that November 11th, 1918, a day that I will always remember."

Mrs. Williams died in 1984 at age 90.

A patriotic French post card featuring the Statue of Liberty with the words "Pour la droit" and "Pour la Liberte" on its base, the American and French flags, an American and a French soldier standing side-by-side in front of barbed wire, and the caption: FRERES d'ARMES.

IN FLANDERS' FIELDS

In Flanders' fields, the poppies blow
Between the crosses, row on row,
That mark our place; and in the sky
The larks, still bravely singing, fly,
Scarce heard amid the guns below.
We are the dead. Short days ago
We lived, felt dawn, saw sunset glow,
Loved and were loved, and now we lie
In Flanders' fields.

Take up our quarrel with the foe!
To you, from failing hands, we throw
The torch. Be yours to lift it high!
If ye break faith with us who die
We shall not sleep, though poppies blow
In Flanders' fields.
John McCrae.

Nov. 1, 1928. An Armistice Day supper will be extended to the boys and girls and invited guests who served in the World War, Saturday, November 10, 6:30 P.M. at Union Hall, under the auspices of Osterville Community Organizations. An 8 o'clock program of exercises will be held to which the public is cordially invited. A prominent speaker will address the company, and a program of music will be rendered.

Armistice Day Exercises at Union Hall.

November 15, 1928

Armistice Day with its glorious message of Peace was observed in a patriotic manner in Union Hall, Saturday evening, Nov. 10. Its observance created in the hearts of all a renewed spirit of thankfulness for the Blessed Peace that pervades our country and other lands, for the safety of and return of the 52 lads that gladly shouldered the gun and bayonet and went forth into the arena of the battlefield to guard homes and loved ones, to make secure from the hands of the invader the land we love so well, America the Beautiful, and a sense of thankfulness for the peace that reigns in foreign lands that were engaged in the Great World War Conflict.

We need these patriotic meetings to bring to us more forcibly the great privileges we enjoy in this greatest of all nations, to comprehend more fully the sacrifices made by those who left home and friends and fared forth to battle with the evil forces of war.

At 6:30 Saturday evening a fine supper was given to the boys and a few invited guests at Union Hall. Chicken pie, mashed turnip and potato, cranberry sauce, pickles, celery, hot rolls, grapes and apples, mince and squash pies, and hot coffee combined to make the best ever, the boys declared. J. M. Leonard acted as toast master and called upon various members and boys of the party for a speech, among those who responded were Lauchlan Crocker, Rev. J. W. Chesbro, pastor of the Baptist Church, Rev. Father Killigrew of the Catholic Church, Edward Daniel who went across, Clarence Brooks, Commander of the American Legion, and Edward Childs of Centerville, one of the three remaining Civil War Veterans.

Mrs. Dora Braley read greetings from Miss Marie Hansberry, one of the two girls from here who braved the dangers of the war in all its hideous form across the sea and returned home after the war was over. Miss Hansberry is at Sulphur Springs, West Virginia. Her greetings were warmly applauded.

The speakers were all enthusiastically applauded. At the close of the supper all repaired to the upper hall where a patriotic program was presented to a packed house. The visitors were greeted by Nickerson's orchestra who rendered the popular airs and also fine selections throughout the program.

J. M. Leonard acted as chairman and presented Rev. Father Killigrew who gave the invocation. G. W. Hallett delivered the address of welcome in his usual gifted way, a fine tribute to the memory of one of our boys, Leo Beaumont, who passed away not long ago and, while heads were bowed in silent prayer in honor of the dear dead, Taps was sounded by Miss Barbara Sprague.

Mrs. Dora Braley read an original sketch and an address of a patriotic nature followed by Dr. E.

C. Hinckley of Hyannis whose address revealed a depth of deep feeling for the boys and love of country. It was a pleasure to hear Dr. Hinckley, and his friends here were glad to know his health permitted him to be present. W.I. Fuller rendered a very lovely solo in his usual pleasing way. The Cape Cod Male Quartette contributed several selections and led in the Congregational singing of patriotic songs.

Hon. Charles L. Gifford was the last speaker, but not the least. Not a word of his splendid address was lost. It was evident to all that the boys have a staunch friend in Mr. Gifford, for he is the son of a soldier, and is intensely interested in all that pertains to our Civil War veterans and those of the Spanish and World Wars, and we believe that where the need arises, Congressman Charles L. Gifford will be at the front in the legislative battle, fighting for aid in the interest of the men and boys who engaged in mortal combat to right the world's sad plight. His insight into the situation between our republic and foreign nations was replete with statistical facts and was a source of enlightenment to many who have not kept run of the vast sums of money owing us by foreign nations.

Miss Virginia Fuller acted as accompanist in her usual efficient manner.

The committee in charge of the supper, which was given under the auspices of the Osterville Community Organizations, were as follows: Miss Katherine Hinckley, chairman; Mrs. Fred Dill, Mrs. Chessman Crocker, Mrs. Hannah Hinckley, Mrs. Robert Cross, Miss Ellen Hansberry, Mrs. Joseph Swift, Mrs. Robert Daniel, Mrs. Florence Coleman, Mrs. Harding Joy, Mrs. Alcott Hallett, Mrs. Maurice Allen, and Mrs. Alta Crosby. Mrs. Mona Hinckley assisted.

April 18, 1929

The new flag pole was erected Monday on the site of the old hay scales, back of the boulder that has been erected for our boys who served in the World War. The pole was secured through the efforts of H. P. Leonard and was given by Manley Crosby, boat builder at West Bay. For some time it has been on the premises of Azor D. Hall who, with the following, have put it in shape: Wilbur Crosby Lester Lovell, Fred Williams, Mr. Washburn, Charles Hall. S. H. Bates gave it three coats of glistening white paint. The golden ball which surmounts it was the gift of Cornelius Driscoll, and the fine gilding was done by John Carlson, one of our best sign painters. It is sixty feet in height and most imposing.

Even in the summer, parking was no problem when this Main Street view of the Fruit Store, at left, and the Osterville Free Public Library, at right, was taken in the early 1930s. Note the boulder at the foot of the flag pole on the green, placed there in 1929 to honor local men and women who served in WWI.

World War II

Camp Have-Dun-It. Fairway of second hole of Wianno Golf Course is visible behind the tents pitched on land where West Bay Inn had burned some years before. The property had stood vacant ever since. Off-shoots from Camp Edwards, Camps Can-do-it at Cotuit and Have-done-it in Osterville were training camps for the men who would ride the amphibious landing craft to the beaches at Normandy, France, in Italy, and in the Solomon Islands, the Gilberts, the Philippines, the Marshalls, the Marianas, and at Iwo Jima and Okinawa.

Soldiers marching down West Bay Road from Eel River Road toward the bay.

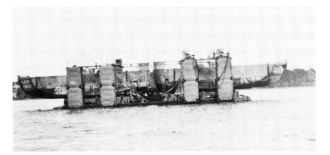

Amphibious Landing Craft moored in North Bay, World War II, 1944.

It was the author's wish to write a similar history of World War II in regards to Osterville as was written about World War I. However, because there were so many who served, their whereabouts today would be just about impossible for the author to trace down. So he has left this for someone else to do.

163

The 1944 Hurricane

The Hurricane . . . September 14, 1944
By Grace and Ronald Chesbro

All day long the radio has been sending out warnings of a hurricane that is coming up from the Caribbean and is expected to hit the Atlantic seaboard during the day.

Thursday morning, September 14, at 7:30 A.M. received warning of hurricane. The sky is overcast, but the weather is very mild. About 5 P.M. we took in our garden furniture and picked as many grapes as possible before dark. Everything has a very peculiar, grayish look.

7:30 P.M. The wind has begun to freshen. About 8 P.M. I walked up town to the church; no one was out and the streets were barren. The manager of the theatre was taking down his sign. The wind was blowing a little harder. I'll admit I hastened back very soon. Soon after, it started to rain and lighten. Our tenants wanted company, so I went over to stay in the big house; Major Moriarty was on duty at Camp Edwards. The rest of the family and I stayed in the living room. Ronald stayed in the camp with David and Paul. The boys went to sleep around 8 P.M.

9:30 P.M. The wind has reached gale force.

10:40 P.M. The electric lights have just failed. The wind is at hurricane strength and the barometer is still falling. We have lit candles and Ronald has the lantern lit, and we feel we are good for the night. We are all wide awake, somewhat apprehensive as to what is in store for us.

12:00 Midnight. The storm is getting worse. We have lost some of the trees as near as we can see in the dark. Ronald came to the big house at this time to see how we were doing. The wind is blowing down the chimney in the fireplace, and we are unable to keep the draft closed. The noise is deafening, and each gust of wind makes us jump. Ronald has fastened the garage doors with ropes inside. The strong smell of fresh cut pine prevails both inside and outside the house. It seems as though we are closed up in a mothproof closet, the pine smell is so pronounced. Ronald says he could hear the tops of the trees snap off as he came to the house from the camp. His glasses were covered with a film of salt spray so he had to clean them. He could also taste the salt spray and hear the roar of the sea, almost a mile away.

1:00 A.M. The storm is as bad now as it has been. Ronald has come over to the big house again, still warning us of the fierceness of the storm, each time his glasses covered with salt film.

2:00 A.M. The barometer is starting to rise and the storm to let up a bit. I came over to the camp soon after and the impression of the trees gone and the old telephone pole standing in the yard, I'll never forget. It was a shock of surprise and disappointment. The big space made by the loss of trees was indescribable. I went to bed about 2:45 and fell asleep about 3:30 A.M. with lots on my mind and really dreading to face morning.

The next morning we were all up early to take a survey of damage. The boys asked if there had been a hurricane. Later that morning we learned the wind was blowing at 110 miles an hour at Camp Edwards when their instrument broke. Someone said the wind reached 125 miles per hour along the waterfront. When we went outdoors about 6:30, Aunt Ada was out in our yard, headed for Marie Whiteley's. Ethel Riedell soon came down the street and told us her yard was full of trees. She and the children were alone all night as Carl was on vacation. I ran out in my pajamas, I was so excited, and folks were gathering so early here. Mrs. Moriarty had been up all night and outdoors earlier. A lot of trees have been blown down here. The leaves of the trees have all turned brown from the salt spray and wind. There is a mat of pine needles, leaves, etc., about one-quarter inch thick on the ground. The tree that had the sign (Ronald A. Chesbro) was lying across the electric light cable. Fortunately the cable was not torn down. Looking up the street, we noticed the steeple had been blown from the church. Many, many trees are down all over the place in every direction we look. No telephone, water, lights, etc., and we soon learn that there is no communication whatsoever on the Cape. It certainly gives us a very funny feeling. The place looks a sight.

Ronald and the boys went upstreet to survey the damage there about 7 o'clock. I remained at the camp. Soon some soldiers' wives walked over to see Mrs. Moriarty. The only way to find out anything that morning about your friends was to walk or crawl. Eileen Elliott soon called on me. Eileen has lost a garage door and a tree has fallen on her garage roof — a common site to see this morning. Most everyone had a tree hit their house or garage. We were very fortunate none hit our buildings. The wind blew from the southeast. The boys lost their swing, and one tree in the grove.

The first thing Ronald saw was a number of pieces of slate blown from the roof of the telephone exchange. Some of the big maple trees in front had knocked the wires from the telephone poles. No one could get down Parker Road or West Bay Road as many trees were across the streets. They went to the church and found the church steeple had landed right next to Lagergren's Garage, doing no damage to either building. Then they went down by the Post Office where the two maple trees in front were uprooted. One of the big spruce trees in front of Bob Daniel's was blown over and resting on the electric light wires. The house of G. W. Hallett lost three of the big spruce trees. Milton Crocker lost five big trees, as did Dr. Kinney, John Shields, and Mrs. Ralph Crosby.

Major Moriarty came in from Camp Edwards to find out about his family. He volunteered to drive Ronald to the railroad station at West Barnstable (his place of work). I went along for the ride. We had an awful time getting as far as the road that goes into the Town Dump. On our way we noticed Tom Milne's yard was one awful mess. Trees were down everywhere. Cecil Coleman had a roof blown from his car stand. Maurice Allen lost three of his large elms, and we noticed many others were down as we drove along. When Major Moriarty reached the road to the dump, he gave up as he could not swing into the woods on account of a ditch. Ronald got out and started to walk; he was soon picked up and arrived at work only two minutes late, at 10:02 A.M.

Friday afternoon the boys and I walked to Wianno. Men were clearing the road in front of the Wianno Club on Sea View Avenue with bulldozers and cranes. The avenue looked like pictures I have seen of jungles and war pictures of the islands in the Pacific. Telephone poles all down, wires everywhere. Going up the avenue, all pine trees are either uprooted or snapped off about 15 feet up; a very devastating sight. The homes of Dr. Niles (W. I. Fuller's house), Roscoe Hinckley, H. P. Leonard, B. T. Livingston, and all those on the way to the beach were one awful sight.

Fifty feet of the bank at Mrs. Blodgett's had been washed away, leaving one tree standing. The roof was blown in, the chimney gone, and the garage down into kindling wood. Not a sign of a bathhouse left on the beach. The beach itself looked

wonderful, and the water was then as calm as a lily pond. As the boys and I walked along the shore, we saw tumbled-down chimneys, water towers, furniture, wood, everything you could think of, and trees too many to mention. Almost all of the homes along the waterfront were left without a bit of yard. In some places the bank had washed out from under the summer homes along Wianno. Our famous Wianno Club itself looked as though it was all ready to tumble. We walked as far as Minerath's and then climbed a ladder someone had put there to reach their yard. From then on, we crawled over and under downed trees, telephone poles, and wires until we got back to Blodgetts.

Sunday: Three days later. Ronald, David, Paul and myself took practically the same walk to Wianno. The clean-up crews had made some wonderful headway clearing the road and were as far as Mrs. W. E. Jones' near Crossett's. Men were still working with the bulldozers, etc. Mrs. Frank Day's pretty green lawn was all brown. Many trees were down and the street looked like a dirt one where the sand had blown up onto it from the beach. Her place looked a sight. It looked as though a bunch of Japs had been firing at it for weeks. From there, we walked down Eel River Road. The road to Mrs. Briggs', where Eel River comes up almost to the beach, was all washed out. Only a dirt road was left there. All those places — Mrs. Briggs', Carter's, Dr. Talbot's — looked terrible. At Eel River Road, the Graves' Estate was by far the worst with many trees blown down and piled on the beautiful azaleas and rhododendron.

We went along to Crosbytown where the water had come up into Con Driscoll's cellar and all the end there had been under water. Parts of the houses were knocked off, seaweed hung on the fences, and there was a diving float in Harvey Hallett's yard. Scott's place across the street was a mess. We could see the roof of du Pont's hangar out in the bay. Johnny Crosby's oyster house was gone, and the remains were blown into the woods. The bridge was washed out at both ends. Piles of lumber and broken piers, boats, and other debris were heaped along the bridge approaches and the shores of the bays. Motors at Chester Crosby's had taken a licking. You could hardly see Johnny Crosby's house for downed trees and other wreckage.

The water had nearly covered Little Island. As we approached the Gate Lodge, the telephone cable on the right was draped with marshgrass and seaweed. The cable was about 15 feet above the road. The Oyster Harbor's Club's stables had had about six feet of water inside, and the horses were swimming. At K. T. Phillip's beautiful home, the first floor was flooded with salt water. From the Gate Lodge to the Oyster Harbors Club, trees were down everywhere. Believe me, there will have to be some swinging of axes this winter. We hear the sounds of axe and hammer quite often, these days.

We are still without telephone, lights, and, worst of all, water. My tenant, Mrs. Moriarty, and I are cooking in the camp. The big house has an electric stove. We are lugging our water from Mr. Burlingame's. It takes two buckets of water to flush the toilet and we have to get it from about 100 yards away. A week later, we extended a hose from Mr. Burlingame's house to our yard, and soon after that we ran it into the house. We were two weeks and two days without water or lights. Some got theirs sooner; many others waited even longer. Big contracting concerns set up offices in the villages to clear the trees, although their prices were too high for poor folks to pay. At Wianno a good job of clearing was done, and of course, people there can afford it. Fees ranged from about $50 to $100 a tree.

East Bay suffered damage as well as other parts of the village. Mrs. F. Delano Putnam's house was washed off Dowse's Point and driven across the bay where it landed on the beach in front of Broome's. Frances Jennings and her aged father were in the garage apartment. Another family were living in a cottage on the causeway at Phinney's Bay. The occupants of both garage and cottage crossed the bay in those buildings when they floated from their foundations.

On the way to Centerville, at Mrs. Hinkle's and the Gaff's, trees and wires and poles were down everywhere. What a mess! The bridge at Bumps River was partly washed out so that no traffic could pass for a time. Part of a house was perched on the bridge. All the poplars along the bank of the river were down. A channel had broken through Long Beach at the mouth of Bumps River and piles of splintered wood and debris had washed up on the marsh to a depth level with the road. Water from Centerville River had flooded Centerville's West Main Street. Rev. George's place was partly ruined and the high-water marks left after the flood receded were almost unbelievable.

As soon as the road was passable, Mildred came over to see how we were. There was still no other way to communicate. I think, at this time, a few telephones in Osterville were back in service.

October 1. We rode over to Craigville Beach. We almost did not know the place. The water had come up almost to Mr. Henry Bearse's house. The cute houses on the left, built a few years ago and known as Craig Village, were all blown off their foundations. Some had been carried as far as a hundred yards. The lovely homes at Long Beach were a sorry sight. As far as we could see, buildings were in ruins. All sorts of furniture could be seen in the river, and the houses were tipped at odd angles, some broken apart. We have heard

that the waves coming ashore there were fifty feet high. I can believe it. The well-built band stand on Craigville Beach is gone. The Brogan's eating place was in the street and most of the street was washed out. Bath houses, or what was left of them, were in heaps of broken lumber, some as far back from the street as 200 yards, and no usable ones were left on the beach. We hardly recognized the place and find it difficult to describe the damage suffered by the valuable properties at Long Beach and Craigville. I can't see what they can do with these homes except declare them a total loss. To appreciate the awfulness of the hurricane's power, this destruction must be witnessed.

All along the Cape's south shore, similar damage was left by the storm. In Hyannis, homes on Estey Avenue were badly battered. Residences on Bass River took a beating, and most of the small summer cottages on properties at Parker's River in South Yarmouth were washed completely away. Destruction at Falmouth, Woods Hole, Maravista, and Cotuit amounted to millions of dollars. Congressman Gifford lost over 1,000 valuable law books in his library as the result of the storm. His piano and his violin were also destroyed.

It is now October 8 and we are just beginning to get our bearings. Ask anyone on Cape Cod, especially anyone who was living on the south shore during the hurricane of 1944 — anyone who went through that storm had a never-to-be-forgotten experience. And the folks that visit in years to come may say, "Oh, you have trees!" but we look at them and feel they are very small. The largest and most beautiful trees that grew in this section of the Cape are gone. When we awaken in the morning, now, we can still see many uprooted and broken-off trees. One positive result of the hurricane, however, is that we feel closer to those families who live near us. I can see the water tower, now, from my yard, and I can see my neighbors' homes.

We should also mention the trees that blew down around Dr. MacDonald's camp (Myrtle Black's). They are many; yes, I should say so; and also around Mrs. Henry Leonard's camp and all through the woods. No longer is it possible to walk the paths through the woods; they are blocked by fallen trees and limbs.

On Pond Street, my grandfather's old place lost lots of trees. Telephone poles were down there, too. On my father's place, a shed or two and one apple tree were blown down. Men were chopping their way to work on the morning of September 15, 1944.

The hurricane gave our sons a few extra days of vacation. Roads were entirely blocked, no communication was possible, no one had any electricity. People brought out a lot of old things like lamps, lanterns, and flat irons. I did my washing at my mother's as she had town water, but I ironed my clothes at home with two old flat irons. We took baths in the pond or went without bathing. The night the electricity came on, we were all some happy, most especially to see and hear the water run. The crew working down here on my telephone had come from Bangor, Maine, and they told me they had a winter's work here. There are many companies helping out. We are trying to clean up our trees ourselves. We lost 14 pines and one oak. There is plenty of wood for everyone who wants any, and every day truckload after truckload of wood is carted to the dump.

We will certainly miss the beautiful autumn foliage this year; instead we see salt-burned leaves and broken twisted trees left as a reminder of that frightful night of September 14th, 1944.

Author unknown, but obviously this report was written by someone living on or near Wianno Beach during the 1944 hurricane.

September 14, 1944

12:30 P.M. Have just returned from working at Rummage Sale. Hot and muggy. The sea calm and beautiful, blue sky and sunshine. Storm warnings on radio very insistent. Can it be possible that the hurricane is coming our way?

4:00 P.M. The sky is overcast, sea gray with white caps and strong breeze. We are in for a storm.

5:30 P.M. Breeze approaching with force. Have brought in everything movable from both porches. Miss Noyes and I hoisted hammock to ceiling, turned all porch furniture upside down in most sheltered spot. Barricaded doors to sun porch. Papers and radio warn us that hurricane will follow coast line and hit the Cape between 10:30 and midnight.

7:00 P.M. Have been to Post Office where I learned that the Governor had ordered all cars off roads by 9 P.M. Thank God, for many tragedies of 1938 will not be repeated. Mina and I went across to Blodgetts to gather flowers. Hurricane or no hurricane, we must "say it with flowers" on dining room table. Wind is getting very strong and spray coming twenty feet high. Sea very angry.

8:30 P.M. Mrs. Morrison called on phone to say they were leaving house and going to the village for night. I am thankful for they are on the most exposed part of point. Four women, two small children and Mary Phillips expecting her third baby next month! What a fool I was not to think of moving earlier in the day. We are spending a peaceful evening and knitting, but I anticipate a night of horror and can imagine what is in the hearts of Mrs. Osborn and Miss Noyes.

9:00 P.M. Mina has just called me in the kitchen to give me latest radio report which says storm will reach peak at midnight with wind a hundred M.P.H. Rain, thunder, and lightning. Lights still on.

9:15 P.M. Mrs. Osborn has gone upstairs. Miss Noyes and I just going when I find a large pool of water on living room floor coming in underneath the door to porch. Rain, not sea. After mopping up, turned back rug, and blocked crack under door with small rug and barricaded door with step ladder. Water and soot coming down chimney. Barricaded in front of fire place.

10:00 P.M. Miss Noyes says she won't undress as we may have to leave house at any minute. We CAN'T leave. Mrs. Osborn looks like an exquisite French marquise in her very best nightie and bed jacket. Whatever happens, she will be a cheering sight. Lights have gone now and house is shaking.

10:30 P.M. Just went down to see if doors are holding. They are. Many peculiar noises which I can't account for since everything on front porch seems okay.

10:45 P.M. Doors holding. Have located one weird bang. The trap door leading to attic is loose, and something in attic has given way. Mina and I have tried to shut the trap tight and secure it, but I can't find hook and eye large enough, and with only a candle and flashlight, we can't be very efficient. Would like to go up into attic but Mrs. Osborn won't let me. Now she and Miss Noyes have shooed me off stepladder and say they don't mind the noise. I hope the darn door won't fall on anyone.

11:00 P.M. Have found that we can let trap down a little and secure it open part way which stops banging and also gives us ventilation which is badly needed as it is a hot night. Mina and I have been conferring as to places of safety in case we need to leave our rooms. If the water rises, we should go to attic. If wind breaks roof we should go to cellar, but we don't know which it will be, so for the present, we will stay on second floor. Everyone outwardly calm.

11:15 P.M. Doors are holding. Most violent shaking against my west window. Find that tree is fallen on roof outside and become wedged against window. Scraping caused by branches. Groans and creaks are like those of a sailing vessel in a storm. Rather a pleasant sound. Another tree has fallen against Mina's window but is too dark to distinguish much. Doors still hold. Mrs. Osborn calm and charming. Miss Noyes and the maids very brave.

11:30 P.M. I think we are nearing apex of storm. The house is rocking violently. Screens on Mrs. Osborn's balcony banging half on and half off. (Would like to go out and pull them entirely off but Mina won't let me.) Railing on front porch creaking. Other noises probably caused by falling trees, but with wind howling and seas pounding, it is hard to know. Thank heaven it's dark and we don't have to see the destruction that is going on.

11:45 P.M. No change. Doors holding.

12:00 midnight. No change.

12:15 A.M. Mrs. Osborn has gone to downstairs bedroom.

12:30 A.M. Doors holding. Mrs. Osborn is asleep. No change outside.

12:45 A.M. Now — I'm sure this is the peak. It's here. Wow!

1:00 A.M. No change.

1:30 A.M. No change.

1:45 A.M. Occasional lull. Lasts long enough for me to count five.

2:00 A.M. I can count ten in occasional lulls.

2:30 A.M. The hurricane is reluctantly leaving us. The house not shaking so violently.

2:45 A.M. It is gone, leaving only normal high winds. "After the storm and raging of the elements, still small voice." How heavenly the quiet is, but what we shall see when daylight comes is heartbreaking to think of, but we are all alive and unharmed. I always knew I was born to be hung. Hope the garage stood.

September 15th

6:45 A.M. Woke and looked on devastation. The face of our little world of Wianno is changed beyond recognition. The road blocked up by fallen trees, the Blodgett house across the street has a hole in roof, our front yard is a mass of fallen trees, broken branches, telephone and electric wires, the driveway is entirely obliterated, one tree is on the roof outside my west window with large branches right against the window. From the bathroom I notice that the beautiful twisted pine that was so full of birds and that I loved to look at every morning is torn up by the roots. The balcony screens are caught on edge of roof. Ironically, the sea is in one of her loveliest sparkling smiling moods. The sky cloudless. Sun shining brilliantly. One of our best mornings. It is hard to believe that such a day could follow the demonic tantrum of last night.

7:15 A.M. Downstairs to further heartbreaks. The porch is covered with sand, pine needles and sticks. Porch railing down, two screens from porch hanging, one tree filling west corner of porch, another against window in butler's pantry. The noise that woke Miss Noyes at 1:30 was the tree falling on the roof of her room, twining itself around the chimney. All vegetation still standing — trees, shrubs, flowers, and vines — seared and dessicated (that is, from salt spray). Made my way by climbing over and under debris to garage which miraculously still stands, apparently intact, but the doors are blocked by three large pines and an oak is on the roof. But we are alive and unhurt.

8:15 A.M. Mina and I have swept porch as far as we can. We must have breakfast.

8:30 A.M. We sit down at the usual time to the usual breakfast served as usual. We try to keep our minds on our blessings; namely,

1. We are alive and unharmed.
2. We have food.
3. We have water.
4. Gas stove to cook on.
5. A sound tight house.

Miss Osborn, maids, and Miss Noyes, cool and cheerful. I am dazedly wondering:

1. If I'll be able to get to the village to buy food for the weekend.
2. Will stores be in existence?
3. If so, will there be any food to buy?
4. Can we get garage freed?
5. Can we keep well with no refrigeration?
6. Can I pull myself together and be somewhat efficient?

9:00 A.M. Got to Post Office. Of course, there is no mail, but by superhuman effort the postmistress and her sister were there. "We are here," they say, "but we don't know why or what good we can do." Bridge is out at Buzzards Bay but men already at work. Men are on roads moving trees so that cars and pedestrians can get through.

9:30 to 10:00 A.M. Made beds, cleaned room, and just to show our nonchalant attitude to a little thing like a hurricane, arranged flowers we gathered last night. Neighbors and friends drop in to see if we are all right. And we are glad to find that they are. All very chatty and cheerful, but everyone shows signs of fatigue, strain, and anxiety. It seems that we were the only family who stayed on the street last night. But, those who left fared no better than we did. Doors flew open in the Bird house

Hurricane damage at bridge to Little Island, looking west, September 1944.

Aftermath of 1944 Hurricane, Grand Island Bridge, looking southwest.

after they left, and practically ruined the billiard room. Every bath house on the beach is wrecked, some piled up on the bank, others a half-mile or more away. Mrs. Putnam's little beautiful cottage on end of point has disappeared and no one knows where. Not a stick or a stone to show where it stood. Mrs. Dowse's butler and his daughter, his chauffer and his wife, found the garage, over which they lived, was beginning to move. They went down into the garage, found water up to their knees. There was a boat in garage containing life preservers. They put these on and clung to the boat for four hours with garage drifting they knew not where. Finally stopped in front of Broome's and signalled with flashlight until they were rescued. I saw the butler's daughter this morning and she was chipper and smiling, in borrowed clothes and her hair still in curlers. How wonderful people can be!

12: noon. Found several oil lamps in good condition and five gallons of kerosene in cellar so we won't have to be in bed by dark.

1:00 P.M. Mrs. MacColl stopped by to say she had her car outside and could take me to village if I could go immediately. I could and did and was fortunate to bring back a huge basket of supplies which would see us over weekend. Hurrah!

2 to 4 P.M. Slept.

4:00 P.M. Got to post office again and asked postmistress and her sister to come over at 5:30 and have a hot supper. Repairs to bridge are getting under way and mail and papers will probably come through tomorrow.

6:00 P.M. Had supper which we all enjoyed. Went to bed at 8:15. Slept like the dead.

September 16th

6:15 A.M. Woke to another beautiful day. Dressed in working blues and raked debris, rolled up telephone wires and piled all branches which were not too heavy, for an hour. Windows are covered with "goo." Must take hose to them.

8:30 A.M. Everyone calm and collected and helpful but me. As usual in an emergency my temper is badly frayed around the edges. I preserve a glum and forbidding silence while trying to think of some way of keeping food from spoiling, how to get car out of garage, get packed, and up to town as soon as possible so that Mrs. Osborn can get away from this desolation which must depress her beyond measure though she shows no signs. She is marvelous and everyone very forebearing with me. We are all feeling the strain and exhaustion of nervous shock, heart-breaking scenes all along the avenue, every home we know is so much worse off than we. Oyster Harbors has reached the ultimate in its exclusiveness. The bridge to Grand Island is gone and Oysters Harbors is isolated.

9 to 10 A.M. Planned meals for next two days. Made beds, cleaned lamps, etc.

10 to 12 noon. Raked, picked up sticks and with Mina's help moved broken screens (very heavy and unyielding) back of house. Got on the roof and pushed balcony screens off onto ground as they are likely to fall and hurt someone. Swept balcony and am having a wonderful time picking other debris off roof and Mrs. Osborn sees me and makes me come in off roof. Milkman came.

1:00 P.M. Dinner.

2:00 P.M. Mail and papers came through by train to Buzzards Bay, from there by truck. Bridge almost ready. Also vegetable and fruit man came.

2:30 to 4:00 P.M. Slept. Wrote letters and went to Post Office to mail them. Mina, bless her heart, raked side yard while I slept. After supper lit our gorgeous center lamp, read aloud and knitted until 9:30. "And so to bed." No sleep for me. Spent the night in mental cantillation wondering if I was a man or mouse, wishing I could be more efficient and praying for strength of mind and temper.

September 17th

7:00 A.M. Got up, dressed, and hosed off windows on one side of house. Raked and picked up more sticks.

8:30 A.M. Everyone still cheerful. Mina and I dug hole in garden for milk, cream, and butter to keep them cool. Raked some more. Got out of

1944 Hurricane — After the storm — Centerville-Osterville Bridge.

Main Street and Blossom Avenue — The morning after the 1944 Hurricane.

working blue, took bath, and got into a dress!!

1:00 P.M. Dinner. Very good.

2:30 P.M. Trains will be running tomorrow. Mr. Daniel came. I had just decided that by borrowing a double-ended saw, Mina and I could saw trees blocking garage into sections possible for us to move and free the car. I asked Mr. Daniel if he would lend me the saw. He said, "I'll get the tractor here just as soon as possible and have the trees away in half an hour." Bless him! I hate to put an ounce of extra burden on his shoulders, but on the other hand, feel that Mrs. Osborn must be gotten away from all the strain and inconvenience. Also, found I can get ice tomorrow. When I think of the hardships and horrors the boys overseas are undergoing, the problems that confront everyone in Wianno, especially the year-rounders, we can't hope to get away from it all, and I am deeply ashamed of the pessimism and anxiety I have indulged in. The heroism and uncomplaining cooperation of Mrs. Osborn, Miss Noyes, and the girl have been incredible. The worst is over and I'm still marvelling over our miraculous escape. If any one of the trees resting on the roof had come through the windows, we would have been killed, or worse still, incapacitated. If the water had risen a foot higher, we would have been washed away. "Wonderful are thy works, O Lord."

Osterville Baptist Church lost its steeple in the 1944 Hurricane.

The pine grove west of the Wianno Club after the 1944 Hurricane. Overnight, forty feet of the waterfront at the Wianno Club disappeared, ravaged by the 1944 Hurricane.

Looking west from in front of the Wianno Club on Sea View Avenue the morning after the 1944 Hurricane.

Remains of the pine grove at the Wianno Club on Sea View Avenue looking east the morning after the September 1944 Hurricane.

From the beach, looking east, from in front of the Wianno Club. Green Lodge is the first building to right of the shattered remains of bathhouses and boardwalk that had lined the beach prior to the 1944 Hurricane.

The morning after at the Wianno Club, 1944 Hurricane.

Baseball

July 26, 1887

The baseball game played week before last between the Ostervilles and Wiannos resulted in favor of the Ostervilles — 17 to 9.

July 31, 1888

On Monday the game of baseball between Craigvilles and Cotochesets resulted in a score of 21 to 14 in favor of Cotochesets. The game was very exciting and largely attended.

July 25, 1893

A baseball game on Lovell's diamond on Saturday was played between Sandwich and Osterville nines, in favor of Sandwich; score 16 to 7.

August 1, 1893

The Osterville Baseball Club went to Hyannis and were defeated in one of the most hotly contested games of the year. The score being at the end of the eighth inning 0 to 0. In the Osterville first half of the ninth they did not score, and in the last half of the Hyannis inning, they made one run, therefore beating by a score of 1 to 0. Eddie Crocker of Osterville pitched for the Ostervilles and pitched a remarkably fine game, retiring thirteen men on strikes, a wonderful record especially against such a crowd of "sluggers." Eddie Crocker familiarly known as (Better) is a coming pitcher, one of whom Osterville may well feel proud, being cool-headed at critical times, and always displaying excellent judgment; of course he was admirably supported by Frank Hallowell of Harvard College fame who always plays an errorless game. The batting of the Ostervilles was heavy but they were unfortunate in placing their hits. Those who missed the game lost a fine opportunity to witness an excellent game of ball.

Osterville Baseball Team

Members: five in back row: J. Mott Hallowell, W. Austin, Bradford Ames, J. P. Loud, Fred Mead; Four in middle row: ?, Rivers in straw hat, Holland, C. E. Loud; Front row: Chapman leaning on railing, J. Austin, F. W. Hallowell holding sign, McPherson, A. Merrill.

The nine that never lost a game; "You have done noble."

Taken on steps of "Hallowell" cottage — 1886. Mrs. Richard Hallowell, mother of the Hallowell boys, sitting in chair.

August 15, 1893

The Craigvilles came to Osterville Friday and completely demoralized the Ostervilles in a well played and interesting game. The Craigville pitcher, Barney, had the Ostervilles entirely at his mercy and retired the heavy hitters of the "college boys" without a run. Eddie Crocker for the Ostervilles also twirled well, and had he been properly supported, the result would have been very different. In their first inning, the Craigvilles made three runs and after, they could do nothing with the swift shooting curves of Crocker. The Ostervilles were retired without a run, second time they have been whitewashed this season. Batteries Crocker and Winslow, Barney and Chamberlain.

July 27, 1908

C. Wesson Fuller of Osterville has received an offer from the West Newton Junior Baseball Club of $50.00 to pay ball for the remainder of the season at that city. The writer witnessed the game with Wianno and Ostervile at West Bay Inn, and saw young Fuller perform in the field and on the diamond. When he is in the game for his school, he always hit the ball for a homer or anything from second to home. Norman Williams has also an offer from West Newton. Fuller and Williams are the two best hitters on the Grammar School team of Osterville.

March 22, 1909

Ball team positions: Catcher, Harry Bell; Pitcher, Norman Williams, 1st Base, James McCabe; 2nd Base, H. Hinckley; 3rd Base, Wesson Fuller; S.S., Malcolm Crosby.

May 10, 1909

The Osterville Junior baseball team is keeping up its winning streak by defeating the Wareham Juniors by a score of 12 to 5. Fuller did some fine catching for the victors, not making an error. Williams pitched an extra-fine game, striking out fifteen batsmen. That's going some for Osterville, by gum! McCabe did the base running for the home team, stealing four bases. Hinckley and Crosby did some fine batting.

June 7, 1909

The Osterville single men won an interesting game of ball from the married men, Monday. Score 10 to 5. Line-up as follows:

Single Men	Married Men
W. Fuller, catcher	L. Lovell, catcher
N. Williams, pitcher	D. Lewis, pitcher
H. Hinckley, 1st base	E. Fuller, 1st base
A. Crosby, 2nd base	O. Coleman, 2nd base
J. Dixon, 3rd base	F. Adams, 3rd base
E. Jones, S.S.	V. Cross, S.S.
D. Pattison, R.F.	J. Swift, R.F.
J. McCabe, C.F.	H. Whiteley, C.F.
M. Crosby, L.F.	W. Crocker, L.F.

Just who J. Dixon is, is unknown.

D. Lewis — The D. could be a misprint.

Neither Owen Coleman nor Henry Whiteley was married at that time although they are listed under the married men.

September 3, 1925

The pennant will fly over the Osterville baseball field another year. The local fans are very glad, and hope to see the same team here another year.

Twilight League Champions — 1934

Defeated Chatham two out of three games for Cape Cod Title. Top Row, left to right: Edward Tevyaw, Tom Clark, Graham ("Gummy") Scudder, Leo Shields, Howard ("Pop") Sears, Arnold ("Red") Lane. Bottom Row, left to right: Alcott ("Bucky") Hallett, Jr., Henry ("Hank") Small, Perkins ("Perk") Evans, Cecil Coleman, Irving Coleman, George ("Mutt") McGoff, and bat boy William ("Billy") Mott.

Osterville
Athletic Association

May 2, 1921

The Osterville Athletic Association was organized on Wednesday evening at the Beacon Club rooms. The following officers were elected:
President and Business Manager — Everett Fuller
Vice President — Freeman Adams
Treasurer — Charles F. Marr
Secretary — Ralph Williams
Executive Committee — G. W. Hallett, J. M. Leonard
Team Manager — Lester Lovell

April 30, 1923

A meeting of the Osterville Athletic Association was held Apr. 18th and officers elected as follows:
President — Ralph W. Crosby
Vice President — Freeman Adams
Secretary — W. Ernest Jones
Treasurer — Henry Whiteley
Entertainment Committee — Forrest Burlingame

MUSICAL ENTERTAINMENT

UNION HALL, OSTERVILLE

Benefit Osterville Athletic

Association

FRIDAY, AUGUST 25, 1922

Admission 75 Cents, Including War Tax

Poster advertising entertainment.
(Note that admission includes a War Tax)

January 21, 1924

Officers of the Osterville Athletic Association for the ensuing year are: President, Arthur Duffin; Secretary, W. Ernest Jones; Treasurer, Charles Lewis.

September 9, 1926

A dance for the benefit of the O.A.A. was held in Union Hall Tuesday, and was quite largely attended. Music was furnished by Wyman's Orchestra.

MINSTREL SHOW

For the Benefit of the Osterville Athletic Association
Tuesday, March 17, 1925

IDLEHOUR THEATRE   HYANNIS, MASS.

PROGRAM

Curtain at 8.00

PART I

Selections by Crosby Orchestra

Opening Chorus,	Circle
How Do You Do,	Ed. S. Crocker
All Alone,	Walter I. Fuller
Oh, Eva,	Stuart Scudder
I Wonder What's Become of Sally,	Ralph Williams
Cover Me up with the Sunshine of Virginia,	Louis Thacher
In the Heart of a Rose,	Norman Williams
Struttin' 'Round,	Wilson Scudder
Blue Eyed Sally,	Maurice Johnson
Doodle-de-doo,	George W. Silva

PART II

Motion Pictures

Æsops Fables   Pathe News

Topics of the Day

WHO'S WHO

Left to right—Walter Fuller, Maurice Johnson, George Silva, Stuart Scudder, Delton Hall, Everett Small, Ralph Williams, Wilson Scudder, Interlocutor, Roscoe Hinckley, Lester Lovell, Willis Crocker, Ernest Jones, Norman Williams, Vernon Childs, Louis Thacher, Lauchlan Crocker, Edward S. Crocker.

Minstrel shows always drew a good crowd.

Osterville Bands

May 29, 1883

The young men of Osterville are forming a brass band.

December 18, 1883

One of the principal places of attraction just now is the "Band Meeting" and judging from the crowds of listeners which congregate in the vicinity of the "band room" the efforts of the amateurs are highly appreciated. The brass band was organized about six weeks ago and now numbers twenty pieces and, under the efficient instruction of Mr. Hiram Weeks, is making rapid progress and we think is destined to become one of the most popular bands of the County. The following is a list of the members and the instrumentation of the band:

Hiram Weeks (Leader and Teacher) 1st E flat Cornet; H. Manley Crosby, 2d E flat Cornet; Geo. Williams, 1st B flat Cornet; Frank Williams, 2d B flat Cornet; Thomas J. Maw, 3rd B flat Cornet; Maurice G. Crocker, E flat Clarinet; Edwin H. Coffin, B flat Clarinet; Azor D. Hall, 1st B flat Tenor; James A. Lovell, W. Scott Scudder, 2d B flat Tenor; Howard L. Rich, 3rd B flat Tenor; Wilton Crosby, 1st E flat Alto; Abbott L. Robbins, Nathan E. West, Jr. 2d E flat Alto; Henry V. Cowell, 3rd E flat Alto; Joseph C. Crosby, Baritone; W. F. Crocker, Charles F. Parker, E flat Bass or Tuba; Wm. H. Bearse, Bass Drum; Frank M. Boult, Side Drum. The officers of the band are: A. L. Robbins, Manager; W. F. Crocker, Secretary and Treasurer.

February 5, 1884

The dramatic entertainment given at Village Hall Wednesday and Thursday evening last for the benefit of the Brass Band was a most enjoyable affair, and all got their full money's worth.

May 20, 1884

The Excelsior Brass Band had a torchlight procession one night last week. They started from the schoolhouse and marched to the front of Mrs. Adeline Lovell's, where they played several pieces, then to Mrs. Augusta Scudder's where they played again, then returning to the schoolhouse. They all did well and presented a fine appearance.

July 1, 1884

The Excelsior Brass Band celebrated the holiday now, unfortunately, too much neglected — Bunker Hill Day — with a parade, supper, and informal hop at Village Hall. The marching and playing of the band showed continued progress and the supper, by caterers Hall and Crosby, was a perfect success. Much and valuable aid was given by the lady friends of the organization. The concert, given in front of the Hall, was very pleasant and a treat to the many friends.

August 5, 1884

The members of the band have nearly completed a bandstand from which they will give occasional open air concerts. It is situated on an elevated lot near the schoolhouse. A short concert was given from the stand on Saturday evening.

February 14, 1888

The Osterville Brass Band gave an entertainment to a full house in Village Hall on Thursday evening, assisted by local vocalists and readers, also by the Crosby Orchestra.

January 27, 1902

Since the new year dawned, our village has contained several men of one idea. This idea has grown gradually, being strengthened by new forces, until it has finally developed into the organization of a band. This organized body, as yet without a name, is composed of eighteen members with new silver instruments direct from the manufacturers, C. G. Conn, Elkhart, Ind. Many of the members were members of Excelsior Band of former years, and with Mr. H. Manley Crosby as leader we prophesy success.

March 10, 1902

The entertainment given by the band Friday evening was fine, the music by the orchestra being well worth the price of admission, aside from the other good things on the program. The hall was well filled and no doubt a neat sum was realized that will be of timely assistance to the organization.

May 12, 1902

The newly organized Osterville Silver Band have accepted an invitation to play in Falmouth, Memorial Day.

May 19, 1902

Our band made its first appearance on the street Thursday evening. They made a fine showing with their lights and brilliant music. Much praise is due them for the progress they have made in the few months since the organization was formed.

June 2, 1902

In response to an invitation from the B. F. Jones Post, the Osterville Silver Band, 21 pieces, spent the 30th in Falmouth, where they received a royal welcome from the townspeople. By special request of a comrade, on their return they gave an open air concert, vocal and instrumental, in front of the Tobey House, Waquoit. After partaking of light refreshments they proceeded on their homeward journey, feeling that this day had marked a step upward to a more successful future.

July 7, 1902

The Silver Band of Osterville gave the cottages and guests at the Cotocheset a serenade on Tuesday evening. The work of the band was very creditable and reflects much honor upon the leader and the village which has public spirit enough to support such an organization. The Wianno Colony will hope to hear from it often this summer.

October 20, 1902

The Osterville Silver Band are to have new rooms. The upper part of the barber shop is being enlarged and fitted for their use.

January 5, 1903

The Osterville Silver Band gave a concert in Union Hall Thursday night, Jan. 1st. They were assisted by Miss Alice Savery of Cotuit and Mr. Walter Fuller of this village who rendered several solos, Miss Jennie Baker, accompanist. A social dance was given at the close, the band furnishing the music. The receipts were about $33. We understand they are to give a musical and dramatic entertainment in the near future.

May 30, 1904

The Silver Band are putting in good work, getting ready their engagement at Falmouth Decoration Day.

The Osterville Silver Band on parade in Falmouth c. 1904.

July 4, 1904

The Osterville Silver Band are engaged to play in Hyannis, Monday forenoon and at South Yarmouth in the afternoon, July 4th.

June 5, 1905

The Osterville Silver Band played in Falmouth, Memorial Day. A large party of young people attended the services there. We understand the Band is engaged to play there next year. Mr. H. Manley Crosby took most of the members up in his large steam launch. Capt. Bursley's coaches carried the others over the road in fine style.

February 26, 1907

A box party, for the benefit of the Silver Band, will be given in Union Hall on Friday evening.

March 5, 1907

The dance and box party, held under the auspices of the Osterville Silver Band on Friday evening, proved one of the most pleasant social affairs of the season. Bunker's Orchestra furnished the music, and like good wine it got into the blood, and if it didn't go to the head, it got into the feet, if an onlooker could judge. Mr. Edward Crocker was an able floor manager and the pleasure of the guests was largely due to his vigilant oversight in providing all those who cared to dance with partners. He was ably assisted by Mr. Willis Crocker and Mr. G. Webster Hallett. The boxes were auctioned off and the prize to the lady, whose box commanded the highest price, was awarded to Miss Mamie Norton. The bidding on this box was of a very spirited nature, between one of our young men and a gentleman from Fall River, and caused much merriment. Amid the cheers of the spectators the blue-eyed stranger won out. What's $3.45 for a supper, if you can share it with a charming companion?

Osterville Silver Band about 1905. Left to right, top row: Edward Crocker, G. Webster Hallett, Stephen Bates, Joseph C. Crosby; 2nd row, H. Manley Crosby, Carl Lagergren, Owen Lewis, Everett Small, Nathan West, Jr., J. Milton Leonard; 3rd row: Willis Crocker, Edmund Lewis, Walter Fuller, Frank Williams, Abbott Robbins, George Williams, Harold Crosby; front row: Ariel Tallman, Helge Lagergren.

February 24, 1908

Osterville Silver Band to entertain. Tickets at Israel Crocker's Store: 25¢ and 35¢ each.

February 22, 1909

The Osterville Silver Band will give a grand minstrel show in Union Hall on Friday evening, which promises to be the event of the season. The affair is under the management of Messrs. George Williams and Edward S. Crocker.

November 20, 1930

The Osterville Band, under the leadership of H. Manley Crosby, is coming along finely, if reports are true. The band now numbers about 55, and if all hands stick to it, in time Osterville will surely have a band to be proud of. The boys are certainly interested. Rehearsals are held twice a week in Union Hall and there are seldom any absent. An instructor from Boston comes once a week to give special training. Anyone entering the village late at night will be apt to hear the wail of the saxophone, the silver note of the flute, the penetrating tones of the cornet and the blare of the horns, as the boys endeavor to reach the high notes, so difficult for beginners. We are glad to see so much interest manifested, and we hope that those who feel discouraged will realize that Rome wasn't built in a day, and a musician isn't made in a few weeks. Music means so much in the life of an individual. One cannot overestimate its power, and we are glad that so many have taken up the study. By next Memorial Day, we ought to see our boys in line doing their part toward honoring our dead and living heroes. Let everybody co-operate and show what they can do. The following are names of those who joined, and there are several more the writer was unable to secure: H. Manley Crosby, director, Malcolm Crosby, Wilton Crosby, Carroll Crosby, Horace Crosby, Chester Crosby, Harold Crosby, Carl Lagergren, Alfred Lagergren, Edwin Lagergren, Ralph Williams, Ernest Jones, John Donnelly, Edward S. Crocker, Lauchlan Crocker, Bert Thomas, Elno Mott, Willis Crocker and son Willis, Harvey Lewis and son, Robert W. Lovell, Cyril Hall, Burleigh Leonard, Stuart Scudder, Walter I. Fuller, Irving Fuller, Christopher Bolekas, S. H. Bates, Merton Bates, Maurice Allen, Bradford Tallman, Leonard Tallman, Fred Washburn, George Burlingame, Anthony Souza, Francis Wyman, Howard Lewis, Jack Carlson, Guy Jones.

Music on the Cape
From Reminiscences of Burleigh D. Leonard

March, 1937

Burleigh Leonard of Osterville, talented trumpet player, started his musical career with that instrument in the old Osterville Band about 30 years ago, under the direction of Manley Crosby. Most of the work of learning to play he accomplished himself, taking only about four or five lessons on the trumpet with George Williams of Osterville, at that time playing clarinet in the Osterville Band.

Mr. Leonard played for a number of years with this organization, in Falmouth at the Orpheus Theatre, and for the G.A.R. in Centerville.

Under the direction of Arthur Wyman, he played in a dance orchestra for a number of years. He has some amusing reminiscences of things during his early musical activities. When playing for Arthur Wyman, during one of the numbers given, he forget to respect a certain passage. Mr. Wyman, who was directing and playing violin, lost his temper over the mistake, and with his violin bow swept all the music from the various racks onto the floor, bringing the piece they were playing to an untimely end and startling the dancers.

Mr. Leonard remembers that at that time the people of Marstons Mills were staging a play, "Farmer Hawkins." Mr. Leonard, together with

Chester A. Crosby, Sr., conducting Osterville Band, c. 1940 inside Crocker's Store. In the background, left to right: Mrs. Lester (Minnie) Lovell, Mrs. Chester (Gertrude) Cammett, in doorway, ?, ?, ?, ?, Elizabeth Lovell, Warren Clarke, Harris Lovell (outside window, left of Mr. Crosby), Henry Small (outside, right of Mr. Crosby), Willie Hodges, Harvey Williams (outside window in corner), Bobby Williams, George Tibbetts (?), John Hanlon, Mrs. Sverre (Agnes) Bjerke, Mrs. Karl (Grace) Chadwick (?), Mrs. Alfred (Marie Carlin) Whiteley, Mrs. Mary Souza (?), or Miss Helen MacLellan (?), and Florence Hodges. Band members: Far left, Jimmy Lewis, Lawrence Brooks from Hyannis, Burleigh Leonard, Chester (Chunky) Wyman, all on trumpets; Jimmy Hallett, Cyril Hall, Rodney ?, and Fred Sherman, all on trombones, Gilbert ? with cymbal on bass drum; Sverre Bjerke on alto horn, and two clarinetists from Sagamore.

Frederic Scudder as violinist; Christie Ames, pianist; Herman Williams, clarinetist; Harvey Hallett on the trombone, and John Horne playing bass viol, formed a concert orchestra to furnish music for the play which was presented in every village in the Town of Barnstable, except Barnstable Village. The musicians gave their services, free of charge.

They were sometimes in difficulties as to transportation. A horse and barge were hired, the barge having two seats running lengthwise, for the musicians, and the bass viol was laid between the seats. Often, when traveling over a very sandy road, especially over a hilly section, it was necessary for the company to get out and push or pull, as the case might be.

The old Osterville Band presented minstrel shows to help its support, using various members for participants. This was an annual winter event.

For nine years, the Osterville Band furnished the music for the G.A.R. in Falmouth. Mr. Leonard remembers the trouble they had in getting transportation to and fro. It was necessary to travel by a four-horse bus to West Barnstable, and from there to Buzzards Bay by train. There they boarded the train which ran from Boston to Woods Hole, and so, after a decidedly round-about way, they would reach Falmouth. This method of travel proved rather unsatisfactory, so it was decided to hire two four-horse buses to take them the entire route, 19 miles. At one time they hired a trip by boat, taking a gasoline launch from Crosby's Boat Shop. They started out for Succonesset Point, but the engine went dead, and they began to drift. They finally

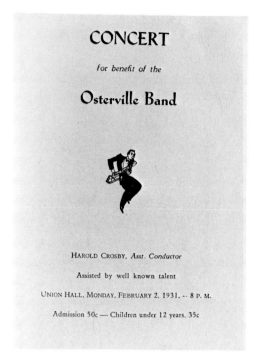

Concert poster.

drifted into a breakwater at Falmouth. From there, carrying their instruments, after a mile-and-a-half walk, they eventually reached their destination.

On Memorial Day in Falmouth, the band would march to the cemetery, and afterwards would play some of their better numbers in the Town Hall. Walter Fuller, vocalist with the band, would sing, "The Old Flag Never Touched The Ground," a great old song of those times. The last time they played in Falmouth, Mr. Leonard rode there in his father's one-cylinder Oldsmobile car, the only car owned by a band member. The car's top speed was the dangerous one of 18 miles an hour! On their way they ran over and killed a sparrow.

Osterville Band playing inside Crocker's Store c. 1940. Band members: at rear: Philip Leonard on double B flat Sousaphone, Ed Crocker on E flat bass horn, Fred Sherman from Hyannis on trombone, Henry Fellows on snare drums, Rodney ? on trombone, Gilbert ? on bass drum, Cyril Hall on trombone, Jimmy Hallett on trombone, Chester A. Crosby, Sr., conductor, Burleigh Leonard on trumpet; Lawrence Brooks of Hyannis on trumpet, and Jimmy Lewis on trumpet; at Mr. Crosby's left: Bernard Horne on alto saxophone, and Sverre Bjerke on alto horn.

Girl Scouts of America and Camp Fire Girls

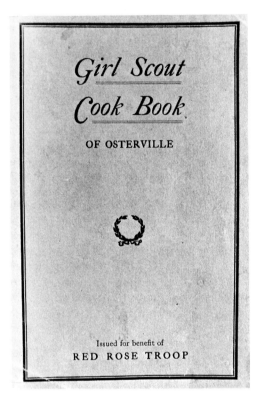

Copies of the Girl Scout Cook Book, issued for the benefit of Osterville's Red Rose Troop of Girl Scouts, are rare, indeed.

Recipes from the Girl Scout Cook Book

SOUPS
Corn Soup

1 can corn	1½ tsps. salt
2 cups cold water	2 tbsp. flour
1 tbsp. chopped onion	3 C hot milk
2 tbsp. butter	1/8 tsp. white pepper

Chop the corn and cook it with the onion and cold water until the corn is soft, or about ½ hour. Scald the milk. Make a medium white sauce. Add this to the milk and cook it 3 minutes, stirring constantly. Rub the corn through a strainer, add it to the milk mixture, boil it 3 minutes longer, and serve it with toasted crackers. **Winnifred Cross**

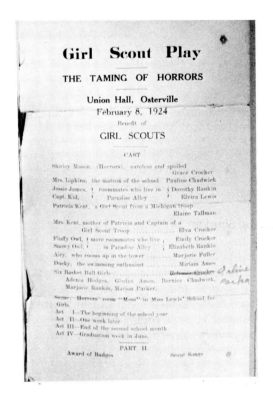

Girl Scouts turned to dramatics to earn necessary funds.

FISH SAUCE
Lemon Cream Sauce (Serve with Boiled Salmon)

Melt 2 Tablespoons butter; add 2 Tablespoons flour, and gradually add 1¼ Cups rich milk (some cream); add the yolks of 2 raw eggs or 1 whole egg. Cook until the mixture thickens, and season with salt, paprika, and lemon juice. **M. Genieve Leonard**

SALADS AND DRESSINGS
Boiled Salad Dressing

1 can condensed milk	4 eggs
1 can vinegar	2 heaping tsp. mustard
2 rounding tsp. salt	

Beat all together in upper part of double boiler and cook until thick. **Marion A. Daniel**

LUNCHEON DISHES
Escalloped Corn

2 C. canned corn	2 tbsp. butter
1 C. fine cracker	¼ tsp. pepper
crumbs	1 tsp. salt
1 beaten egg	1¼ C. milk

Mix the corn, cracker crumbs, salt, pepper, egg, and milk. Pour into a buttered baking dish and dot the top with little bits of the butter. Bake 25 minutes in a moderate oven.   Dorothy Rankin

---

QUICK BREAD AND MUFFINS
Blueberry Muffins

2 C. flour	1 egg
4 tsp. Royal Baking	1 C. milk
Powder	1 tbsp. shortening
1 tsp. salt	1 C. blueberries
1 tbsp. sugar	

Sift flour, baking powder, salt and sugar together. Add well-beaten egg and milk. Add melted shortening, the blueberries (floured). Grease muffin pans and drop a spoonful of batter in each one. Bake in moderate oven. About 18 muffins.

Carrie M. Lewis

PRESERVES AND PICKLES
Mustard Pickles

One quart each of small whole cucumbers; large cucumbers, sliced; green tomatoes, sliced; small button onions; 1 large cauliflower divided into flowerets, and 4 green peppers, cut fine.

Make a brine of 4 quarts of water and 1 pint of salt. Pour it over the mixture of vegetables, and let it soak 24 hours. Heat just enough to scald it and turn into a colander to drain. Mix 1 Cup flour, 6 tablespoons ground mustard, and 1 tablespoon tumeric with enough cold vinegar to make a smooth paste, then add 1 cup sugar and sufficient vinegar to make 2 quarts in all. Boil this mixture until it thickens and is smooth, stirring all the time. Then add vegetables and cook until well heated through. Very good.   Rose Crocker

---

COOKIES
Molasses Cookies

1 C. molasses	½ C. lard

½ C. boiling water with 1 tsp. soda dissolved in it

salt	ginger

Flour to roll.   Mrs. Jennie H. Boult

180

DOUGHNUTS
Sour Milk Doughnuts

1 C. sugar	1 tbsp. soda dissolved
1 C. sour milk	in sour milk
2 eggs	1 tsp. Royal Baking
1 tbsp. butter	Powder
nutmeg and lemon	1 qt. bread flour

Mrs. Chessman Crocker

CAKE
Sponge Cake

4 eggs	3 tbsp. water
1 C. sugar	1 tbsp. cornstarch
Flour	1 tsp. Royal Baking
	Powder

Beat the yolks of the eggs with the water until thoroughly mixed; then beat 5 minutes; add sugar and beat 5 minutes more; then put cornstarch in cup and fill cup with flour and 1 teaspoon baking powder; lastly, fold in the beaten whites of the eggs. Bake about forty minutes.   Mrs. T. A. Whiteley

---

FROSTINGS, FILLINGS AND SAUCES
Chocolate Sauce

½ C. sugar	1 square chocolate
1 tbsp. cornstarch	½ C. cold water

Stir all together and cook until thickened, stirring occasionally to keep from burning. After taking from stove, add small piece of butter and ½ tsp. of vanilla.   Myrtle I. Tallman

---

GINGERBREAD
My Mother's Gingerbread
Measure into the mixing bowl:
½ C. shortening (drippings, lard or butter), 1 C. molasses, ¾ C. boiling water and sift into them:

2½ C. bread flour	½ tsp. cinnamon
1 tsp. soda	½ tsp. salt
1 tsp. ginger	1 tbsp. sugar

Stir all together well, but do not beat. Bake in a moderate oven about 30 or 35 minutes.

Mrs. Norman Williams

PUDDINGS AND DESSERTS
Indian Pudding
(Given by an Indian Guide)

1 qt. milk	1 pinch salt
3 tbsp. Indian cornmeal	⅔ C. molasses
⅓ C. brown sugar	1 pinch cinnamon
1 tsp. butter	1 egg (if desired)

Heat ½ of milk. Stir dry ingredients together until smooth and add milk. Let cook until it becomes thick; then add remainder of milk just before putting in oven. Bake 3 hours in slow oven.

Mrs. Frederick Schaefer

PIES
Cocoanut Custard Pie

2 eggs   1½ C. hot milk
3 tbsp. sugar   ¾ C. Dromedary
1/8 tsp. salt   Cocoanut
Nutmeg

Beat eggs slightly. Add sugar, salt, hot milk and cocoanut. Pour into pastry lined pie pan and sprinkle nutmeg over top. Put into hot oven. After 10 minutes reduce heat and bake about 30 minutes longer or until custard is firm.   Elva Crocker

CANDIES
Soft Caramels

1 qt. of brown sugar   ⅓ C. butter
½ pt. of milk   ½ cake of chocolate

Boil 9 minutes, then remove from fire and stir steadily for 5 minutes. Pour into pan and mark in squares.   Mrs. Ralph Crosby

Camp Fire Girls

Seated in the stern, l. to r., Mildred Lewis, Helen Whiteley, Louise Adams, and Agatha Crocker; on middle seat: Elsie Chadwick, Jessie Lewis, Genieve Leonard; in the bow: Edna Suthergreen and Oliver Scudder. c. 1916.

Front Row, l. to r., ?, Imogene Leonard, Mildred Lewis, ?, Edna Suthergreen, and Olive Scudder; rear, l. to r., Margerie Leonard, Agatha Crocker, Helen Whiteley, Elsie Chadwick, Genieve Leonard, and Annie Nute. c. 1916.

Osterville Dramatic Club

April 1, 1890

The Osterville Dramatic Club will present the comedy "Married Life" in Village Hall on Tuesday and Wednesday evenings. The proceeds are to be devoted to the purchasing of a piano for the hall.

"The Country Doctor"

May 1, 1922

All that needs to be known is that the Osterville Dramatic Club is to present a drama to draw a full house, and that indeed for two evenings.

"The Country Doctor" proved a happy choice for the season's presentation and the cast of characters given below but inadequately conveys the real merit that was shown upon the stage.

Frederick Nute, as the Country Doctor, was par excellence and was ably supported throughout the play, as really all those taking parts are artists.

Mr. Leonard is always to be depended upon, and once more he has demonstrated his ability to make his part real.

William P. Hodges, as Zebediah Bunn, was wonderfully true to his part and his portrayal was followed with utmost interest by the audience for, as a laugh producer, he took the cake.

Myrtle Black, as the leading lady wooed and won by the Country Doctor, sustained a part calling for the most versatile portrayal and on no occasion was Mrs. Black found wanting.

Myrtle Tallman, as the moving spirit in the hotel life of the play, well-performed her part, putting not a little zest into all her acting. She was an able helpmeet to her husband-proprietor, Burton Chadwick, who well-represented the typical genial country hotel keeper.

Beatrice Tallman as the doctor's sister, and Roscoe Hinckley as her sweetheart, did many fine bits of acting and well-depicted the characters they represented.

The part of the doctor's housekeeper was to have been taken by Mrs. Minnie Allen, but owing to an accident she was unable to do so. Genieve Leonard, on two days' notice, took the part and so proficient was she in it that it was hard to realize that she had been called upon at the eleventh hour.

Buddie Wyman, on account of illness, was unable to take his part, and his place was ably filled by Ralph Crosby.

The part taken by Lillian Parker, as the maid with aspirations, gave considerable latitude for Mrs. Parker who was most original in her interpretation, both to the delight of Zebediah and of the audience.

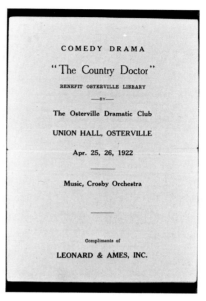

Program for entertainment to benefit the Osterville Library

Indeed, all those upon the stage proved themselves artists of no mean order, and it is hoped another drama will be presented at an early date.

Adding greatly to the pleasure of the evening were the fine selections of the Crosby orchestra. Few villages are so fortunate as is Osterville in having this well-trained and proficient orchestra within is borders. That the treasury of the Osterville public library is greatly enriched by the united efforts of the Osterville Dramatic Club goes without saying.

The cast follows:

Thomas Britton, M.D., the village doctor
— Frederick Nute
Howard Wayne, in love with Dolly
— Roscoe Hinckley
Squire Ferguson, the sheriff
— J. M. Leonard
Sam Birch, proprietor of the hotel
— Burton Chadwick
Zebediah Bunn, who hangs around
— William P. Hodges
Eri, that's all — Ralph Crosby
Ben Shaw, the stage-driver — Unknown
Agnes Gilbert, shadowed by fate
— Myrtle Black
Dolly Britton, the doctor's sister
— Beatrice Tallman
Susan Pinner, the doctor's housekeeper
— Genieve Leonard
Mrs. Birch, Sam's wife — Myrtle Tallman
Anna Belle Umstead, with aspirations
— Lillian Parker

The Factory

The factory site was at the northeast corner of Joshua's Pond

March 14, 1882

There is talk of having a factory built here this spring.

March 28, 1882

Agents of the U.S. Albumen Co., are negotiating for land upon which to build a factory.

April 11, 1882

The agents of the United States Albumen Manufacturing Company have bought land of James West on which to set their factory, and have engaged lumber of J. H. Sears of Hyannis to build.

April 18, 1882

Capt. James West has sold his house and place to a Mr. Hillman, from New York, who is to be foreman in the United States Albumen Manufacturing Co., and Capt. West is negotiating for the house of Mrs. H. S. Linnell.

May 3, 1882

Work has commenced on our factory.

May 23, 1882

The factory lumber is being carted for the factory.

August 15, 1882

"Our Factory" is already bringing its good results — giving home employment to our citizens. Among our coasters now employed here are: Capt. Cyrenus Small, Capt. Austin Lovell, Mr. Isaac Lovell, Capt. Joseph H. Chadwick, Mr. James G. Small and Mr. Warren Lovell.

September 12, 1882

The main building of the Albumen Company's works is nearly completed. It is 100 x 75 feet, two stories high.

October 10, 1882

The buildings of the "United States Albumen Manufacturing Company" now being ready for the reception of the machinery, and the company being desirous of showing its satisfaction with the faithful manner in which their employees have discharged their duties, an entertainment was given in honor of said laborers, Monday evening, 9th inst., in the main building of the Company.

October 17, 1882

About two hundred and fifty of the citizens of Osterville and neighboring villages met by invitation at the newly completed building of the U.S. Albumen Manufacturing Co., Monday evening of last week to inspect the same and otherwise enjoy themselves. The affair was under the management of Mr. Uno H. Hillman, the superintendent of the company, who, wishing to show his appreciation of the manner in which the carpenters and others had done their work, took upon himself to give a "warming" and with a very successful result. There was no speechmaking, but a season was spent in general conversation; an oyster supper was served, a ball was given, and about fifty couples danced to the inspiring music of a local orchestra until the small hours of the morning. The building that was dedicated is the Company's main manufacturing building and is now completed and ready to receive the machinery. It is a very substantial structure, 100 x 75 feet, two stories high, and was built by the day's work under the general supervision of Mr. Hillman. There are several other buildings on the premises that are to be used as storehouses, etc. The plant is situated on the top of a hill in the midst of a fine grove of oak and pine and overlooks a beautiful pond, the purity of the water of which induced the company to locate in this town.

Mr. Edward E. Waters, the President of the Company, and Mr. Hillman are both gentlemen of fine conversational powers, and soon succeed in making their friends as interested in their enterprise as they themselves are. It is said that this is the first exclusively albumen factory in the world.

October 24, 1882

Carpenters are very busy in this place; besides the building by the Albumen Co., there are several cottages being erected.

October 24, 1882

Messrs. Hillman and Maw, the superintendent and engineer of the Albumen Works, are in New York looking after the shipping of the machinery that is being built for them for the new works in this village.

December 19, 1882

Capt. Daniel P. Bursley & Co. have finished carting spawn to the factory here. The first lot consisted of 90 tons.

January 16, 1883

An ice house is being built at the factory.

January 16, 1883

The whistle on our factory was heard for the first time on Thursday.

February 13, 1883

The Factory has commenced making albumen.

August 7, 1883

The factory is enlarging and putting in more machinery.

February 26, 1884

Mr. Thomas Maw is seeking employment in Boston, our factory being closed.

June 24, 1884

We have the cheerful news this week to communicate — and we hope it will prove authentic — that the Albumen Works are soon to be in operation again. The Co. has paid 25 per cent of the claims against them, and made arrangements to meet the remainder. In consequence of which, consent has been given the Co. to resume business in charge of a keeper.

December 16, 1884

The United States Albumen Factory at Osterville has been closed up by mortgage sale. It started out under favorable auspices and we supposed that Osterville would soon become a large and prosperous village, but such is not the case. At the sale, the building and machinery were bought by A. J. Wilkinson & Co., of Boston, for about $3,700. The property cost about $20,000. There has been heretofore 25 percent of claims against the estate paid and from this $3,700 there will soon be

another dividend paid in order of priority of attachment. Those who put on an attachment last will fare worst — some getting nothing. It is said that there will be a new company to take the plant and again begin the manufacture of albumen on a new plan. What albumen there was made only brought a few cents a pound — it having been found impossible under Mr. Hillman's management to economically make a commercial article of equal value with what is now used by cotton printers. But Mr. Waters says that Prof. John M. Ordway of the Institute of Technology of Boston says it can profitably be made there at Osterville, and if satisfactory, arrangements can be made with the present owner. The manufactory will soon be in working order. We hope it will prove a success this time. It is claimed by Mr. E. E. Waters that as foreign corporations have no legal right to hold real estate in this state the sale to Wilkinson will not hold valid and that he will come in possession by some legal means thereby. The sale of the right to redeem is advertised for early next month and we think the whole matter will soon be amicably settled and business resumed on a new and profitable basis. We pity those who have suffered on this enterprise so far, but it is one of those things which cannot be cured and so must be endured, and hope for better luck next time. Mr. Wilkinson is to pay several claims himself, the largest being E. P. Allis's for about $1,400, we presume these being those who attached first. We understand Mr. Hillman, the former superintendent, and a very intelligent gentleman by the way, has sold all his patents to new parties and he is to engage in farming on a large scale at the "sheep ranch" at Greenville in Sandwich.

April 7, 1885

The sound of the factory whistle is again heard.

September 4, 1888

The Atlantic Chemical Co. factory has started up again after a shut down of a few weeks.

January 22, 1889

Mr. M. M. Haskell and family are about removing to Everett, their former home, after a residence here of four years, Mr. Haskell having been employed as engineer for the Atlantic Chemical Co. during that time.

April 1, 1890

E. E. Waters, Esq., is in town, has had a new smoke stack put to the factory the past week.

November 25, 1890

Conductor Messer of the Old Colony "dude train" won a case in the U.S. Circuit Court Friday which gives him $4000. The conductor in 1882 was induced by E. E. Waters of New York, who was a member of the U.S. Albumen Company, which maintained a factory in Osterville, to invest $4000 in the corporation. He came to believe that Water's representations were false, and that the Company could not manufacture the article Waters said it could. Then he brought the suit and the jury, Friday, gave him his $4000 by their verdict. H. P. Harriman of Wellfleet and C. F. Chamberlayne of Boston conducted Messer's case, and F. H. Hall defended Waters.

August 2, 1892

Mr. E. E. Waters was arrested and taken to Boston.

June 15, 1896

The Albumen Factory is being torn down and shipped to Boston.

Entrepreneurs of Osterville

JOSEPH W. TALLMAN
Mason Contractor   **Osterville, Mass.**

During the 40 years that Mr. Tallman has been a mason contractor here he has done most of the mason work on the cottages from Osterville to the extreme end of Wianno Beach, and among his recent work we would mention the handsome cottage of Mr. R. E. Paine (of Boston) at Wianno. He also did mason work on cottages of Andrew Adie, C. D. Barker, Dr. Talbot, and many others. Mr. Tallman makes a specialty of alteration, on a percentage basis. He manufactures colored cement, flagging for walks, builds stone walls, and brick or stone steps, and everything in the mason line, promptly, at reasonable prices. He employs a force of experienced men and can guarantee satisfactory work.

DANIEL BROS.   Osterville, Mass.
Contractors and Builders
Care of Cottages of Non-Residents a Specialty
Hardware and Builders' Supplies   **Shop at Wianno**

This firm has become identified with the building interests of this section from the fact that they have erected a majority of the finest cottages, and gives special attention to all orders, large or small, giving to each that careful oversight so essential to the best results. They employ only careful, experienced men, and follow the architect's plans and specifications on every job undertaken; but they will make alterations and repairs without the aid of an architect and erect an ordinary-sized cottage. This progressive firm has handled many out-of-town contracts, and their work and prices have given general satisfaction. The handsome residence of R. E. Paine at Wianno (illustrated), which is one of the finest in this section of New England, was recently erected by Daniel Bros., and it is one of the "show places" of the New England coast. Daniel Bros. also handle real estate.

"HOMEWOOD," RESIDENCE OF H. P. LEONARD

H. P. LEONARD
Real Estate, Cottages For Sale or To Let for 1920
Wianno Avenue   **Osterville, Mass.**

There is no more attractive section of Cape Cod than Osterville and vicinity, and as property is advancing rapidly each season, it is well for intending purchasers to select their lot this season to secure a good choice. Mr. Leonard is an authority on the present and prospective values of real estate in this section of Massachusetts, and has made many large sales to those who came here first as hotel guests or cottagers, and who have later bought land to erect their own homes, finding no more attractive spot to come to early in the season and remain in for several months. Attention is called to the opposite page on which are shown six cottages owned by Mr. Leonard.

Pine Cottage, above, was located on the east side of Wianno Avenue just beyond Bates Street on land where Henry P. Leonard was to build his own residence, at a later date. Pine Cottage proprietor, Edward S. Crocker, after acquiring property overlooking West Bay where Winfield Lane is now, moved Pine Cottage across the fields to the waterfront site to form a portion of West Bay Inn.

Pine Cottage is located on Wianno Avenue, ten minutes' walk from Wianno Beach, making it a pleasant and desirable place for those wishing a quiet home and to be within easy access of Cape Cod's most popular summer resort.

Pine Cottage will accommodate about thirty-

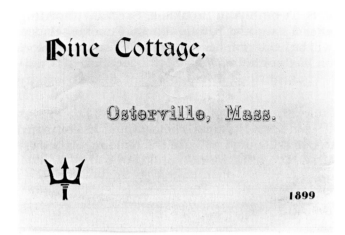

five guests.

The drives about Osterville and vicinity are numerous, with good roads and attractive scenery.

There have been new Golf Links laid out the past winter, known as the "Osterville Golf Links" (Seapuit), which are located conveniently near Pine Cottage.

Boating and fishing facilities are good and boats can be hired for all occasions.

Rates for table board, $8.00 per week. Rooms, $3.00 to $8.00 per week. Special rates for June and September may be had on application.

Trains leave Boston for West Barnstable station, daily, 7:38 A.M.; 1:08, 3:38 P.M.; extra train at 1:38 Saturday only. Stages connect for Osterville, six miles, for these trains only. Stages have to be ordered at an extra charge for any other train.

E. S. Crocker, Proprietor
Osterville, Mass.

Dr. Thomas R. Clement

October 24, 1882

Dr. Clement has purchased the dwelling owned by Mrs. Simonet and will take up his residence here. Osterville being nearer the centre of his practice led him to move from his pleasant location in Centerville.

November 14, 1882

Dr. Clement has at last bought the Simonet place, paid his money and got a deed, after she backed out twice and paid him $100. — to give up his trade once.

The dwelling purchased of Mrs. Simonet by Dr. Thomas R. Clement is that located on the southwest corner of Main Street and East Bay Road. His daughter, Mrs. J. S. Twombly of Brookline, inherited the place from her parents, and the intersection was known for generations as Twombly's Corner.

Death of Dr. Thomas R. Clement

September 19, 1898

Our community was shocked Sunday morning upon learning of the death of Dr. Clement, he having passed away during the night. Cause, probably heart failure.

Dr. Clement was born March 19, 1823, in Landaff, Grafton County, N.H. He received his early education in the public schools of his native town and at Tyler's Academy, in Franklin, N.H. He studied medicine with Dr. Mark R. Woodbury, finishing with Dr. S. G. Dearborn of Nashua, N.H. Graduating from the medical department of Burlington University (Vermont) in 1863, he began his medical practice in Mason, N.H. He was Assistant Surgeon in the Tenth New Hampshire Regiment and held other government appointments until 1868. He practiced at Enfield, N.H., and in 1872 came to Centerville, two years later removing to Osterville. He was a member of Charles Chipman Post, G.A.R., and also a member of the Barnstable Board of Health, and was a gentleman highly esteemed by all in our community.

September 26, 1898

Seldom, if ever, has this neighborhood been thrown into such universal mourning as that caused by the death of Dr. Clement on Sunday, September 18th. Although seventy-six years of age, the Doctor was able to attend to his practice, and was so engaged the day preceding his death, so that when the news spread Sunday morning that he had passed away during the night, it came as a shock to the entire community. It seemed

lost was a brother of the Captain. I think Capt. Frank died at his home.

I have heard it said that at one time, when Capt. Ferdinand was master of Sch. Montana, Capt. Prince Bearse being at home in the winter months, he was bound from Baltimore to Portland, and when off Cape Cod at dark, the weather threatening, the mate spoke to the captain and made the remark that there was a good harbor to the leeward, Provincetown. Capt. Parker, who had a way of holding his head one side, said, "We are bound to Portland." The Montana was a staunch built vessel, built at Quincy by Deacon Thomas, the famous builder. At that time the vessel got a shaking up, loss of boat from davits, etc., but arrived at Portland safely.   A.B.C.

We, the undersigned, do hereby agree to take the portion set against our several names of the schooner called the Balsora L. Sherman to be commanded and sailed by Capt. Joseph H. Alley, he to receive one half the net stock as his compensation for victualing or victualing, manning, and commanding said vessel. The price to be paid to be at the rate of eight thousand and five hundred dollars for the whole vessel.

Owners of the Schooner Spy: Isaac Scudder, Philander Scudder, Josiah Scudder, Sr., Oliver Hinckley, George Lovell, Joseph W. Scudder.

Richard E. Baxter was Captain of the bark Elizabeth S. of Philadelphia in 1856.

Schooner Daniel Webster, built in 1838 in Coxsackie, N.Y., in 1838. Capt. Warren Cammett was captain of her for 35 years. Samuel Lovell of Osterville was ship keeper. Was 122 tons burthen. Had for a figurehead a portrait of the great statesman.

Schooner Tigress, built by Jonathan Kelley of Centerville, in the 1830's, for Captain Philander Scudder, was 74 tons burthen.

Schooner Edwin A. Stevens, built in 1838 in New Brunswick, N.J., captained by Daniel Bacon and Henry Goodspeed of Osterville.

January, 1882

Received of Capt. H. P. Crocker, $109.37, (One Hundred and nine dollars, and thirty-seven cents), in payment for 1/32 part of Sch. B. L. Sherman, and I am to give a bill of sale for same as soon as practicable.

B. C. West

Osterville-built Vessels

December 10, 1900

As correspondents have referred to some of the vessels built by the late Mr. Oliver Hinckley of Osterville, it may interest some of your readers to see a full list of the vessels launched from his yard. The following items are taken from a book in Mr.

Hinckley's handwriting and may be regarded as correct:

1817 . . Sch. Hallett, 69 tons.
1818 . . Sch. Glide, 75 tons.
1819 . . Sch. Louisa, 80 tons.
1821 . . Sloop Echo,
              100 tons . . . . for Capt. George Lovell
1822   Brig Ranger,
              160 tons . . for Capt. Joseph Eldredge
   . . Sch. Mirror,
              110 tons . . . . for Capt. Z. D. Bassett
   . . Brig Calo,
              160 tons . . for Capt. Thomas Percival
   . . Sloop George Henry,
              53 tons . . . . for Capt. James Parker
1827 . . Sch. Alphim,
              55 tons . . . . . for Capt. Isaac Hodges
1828 . . Sch. Talent,
              80 tons . . . . for Capt. John Cammett
1829 . . Sch. Balance,
              70 tons . . . for Z. D. Bassett, Matthew
                          Cobb, and George Lovell;
                          Isaac Hodges, Captain
1831 . . Sch. Page,
              150 tons . . . . for Z. D. Bassett
1833 . . Sch. Frank,
              68 tons . . . . . for Capt. Samuel Wiley
1833 . . Sch. Oranament,
              78 tons . . . for Capt. Harvey Scudder
1834 . . Brig Corina,
              200 tons . . for Z. D. Bassett, Matthew
                          Cobb, and George Lovell
1835 . . Sch. Oliver,
              106 tons . . . . . for Capt. David Fuller
1836 . . Sch. Mariner,
              92 tons . . . for Capt. Freeman Adams
1837 . . Sch. Louisa,
              101 tons . . . . . for Capt. Lot Hinckley
1839 . . Sch. Augusta,
              87 tons . for Capt. Leander Nickerson
1839 . . Sch. Spy,
              69 tons . . . for Capt. Jonathan Parker
1840 . . Sch. Utica,
              89 tons . . . . . for Capt. Andros Bearse
1842 . . Sch. Cotuit,
              92 tons . . . for Capt. David Nickerson
1845 . . Sch. Earl, . . for Capt. Benjamin Hinckley
   A total of 23 vessels in 28 years.

Charles Noble Hinckley
Osterville, Dec. 5, 1900

Reminiscences of the Coasting Trade
by J. Milton Leonard — 1863-1945

From its earliest history Cape Cod has been noted for its activities on the waters of the world. These activities took various forms from fishing in small craft near shore, off-shore fishing in small vessels on the wind-swept and often fog-bound

Grand Banks off the New England coast, and carrying cargo between ports on the Atlantic Coast, to extended whaling voyages lasting several years.

While a few men from Osterville engaged in the whaling business it never was an industry of great importance to our village. The same may be said of what was known as "off-shore fishing." However, small boat fishing by boats that returned every evening has always been popular and, in times past, has been of considerable importance as an industry. While many kinds of fish have been found off our shore and in our bays, the blue-fish was always the most popular and the largest source of income. The importance of the fishing industry to Osterville can be gauged by the almost complete disappearance and return of the bluefish, which is much desired as a food as well as being noted for its sporting qualities. So far as is known to the writer, bluefish was always very plentiful along our shore up to about 1840 or 1845, when the fish strangely disappeared.

The fishing vessel usually was a small two-masted schooner of sixty to one hundred tons burden, staunchly built, and with large sails to carry it swiftly to port when the cargo space was filled. Probably no greater example of skillful seamanship is known than when three or four of these small American fishing vessels raced to port to be the first at the market to obtain the best price for the catch.

Vessels engaged in the coastwise trade, that is trading between all ports along the Atlantic seaboard from as far north as Canada and south to South America, comprised vessels ranging from two hundred to eight hundred tons, schooner rigged, and with two, three, and sometimes even four or five masts. I know more about these vessels because nearly all Osterville men, in my younger days, manned this type. At the age of thirteen I shipped as cook on the Coaster, ANN T. SIPPLES, Capt. Alex. Bacon. Captain Bacon was one of those kind-hearted, jolly skippers, and nothing like the hard-boiled deep-water captains who gave Cape Cod Skippers such an unenviable reputation in those days.

Large and two-masted, the schooner ABBIE BURSLEY was commanded by several different captains of Osterville. The first one whom I remember was Captain James Parker, the eldest son of Temperance Parker, known to all the village as Aunt Tempy, and from whom Mrs. Sprague got the name of her Tea House when she first established it in Aunt Tempy's old home on the Wianno Golf Links some years ago. Captain Parker was lost from the ABBIE BURSLEY, off the cost of Block Island. For a time the Bursley was in command of Captain Bradford Ames who married a daughter of Aunt Tempy. Their daughter is the wife of H. Manley Crosby, one of the well-known Crosby Boat Builders of Osterville. On one passage from a southern port, in a terrific storm off Cape Hatteras, the vessel grounded on Frying Pan Shoal and Captain Ames was washed overboard and lost. Strangely enough the vessel withstood the force of the storm and was finally towed into port and repaired. This vessel had the reputation of getting into more scrapes, without becoming a total loss, and making more money, but paying less to her owners (because of repair bills) than any other coaster sailing out of Boston. However, the ABBIE BURSLEY was staunchly built and was a very able sea boat. While it was common practice for most coasters to go out of commission for about four months in winter, we next find this vessel in commission twelve months each year.

One half of the time she was in command of Captain Cyrenius Lovell and the other half under Captain William B. Parker, both of Osterville. During the winter months voyages were made to the West Indies and South America. After a number of years in the severe and tempestuous service under Osterville captains, she was finally sold to Eastern parties and her final end I do not know. Both her masters, Captains Parker and Lovell, were very able seamen. I know from sailing under them that they were worthy representatives of the best of Cape Cod Captains.

Captain Parker was once sent to Bermuda to bring home the three-masted schooner Marcia Lewis. While on a trading voyage to the west coast of Africa, her master, Captain Joseph Lewis of Centerville, died of African fever. While on the voyage home, in charge of the first mate, she was practically dismantled in a squall, but succeeded in reaching Bermuda. This mate contracted at once for new masts and very extensive repairs to the vessel. In those days this was a somewhat common trick, especially in square-rigged ships, having them repaired in foreign ports a long way from home.

In this case Bermuda was not a long way from Boston. The second mate was a close friend of Captain Lewis and a very fine seaman. (He was second mate, by the way, because he could neither write nor figure out navigation and therefore could not qualify as a first officer.) However, he did go to the American Consul in Bermuda and get him to cable the agent of the vessel in Boston. The Consul took steps to hold up all contracts until instructions came from the Agent.

In consequence of this action by the consul, Captain Parker was sent to take charge, arriving by the next steamer. He immediately cancelled all work planned, and with his own men and very little help from the shipyard, cut down the mizzen mast so that he could set the sail, reefed, not bothering about a fore topmast. Then he brought the vessel home with that rig, saving the owners thousands of dollars. Moreover, I doubt if it took half as long to get to Boston as it would have taken to make the extensive repairs. I saw the vessel as she came into Boston Harbor and she did look strange, but she made port safely. Captain Parker soon retired and went into the grocery business with his son, Horace S. Parker, who still carries on the business in the same store.

About the same time Captain Lovell retired, and he soon after was elected a Selectman for the Town. He also served as Surveyor of Highways. Both Captain Lovell and Captain Parker commanded other vessels before my days of going to sea.

I sailed one season in the small two hundred fifty ton schooner, Josephine G. Collier, Captain John Knox. Captain Knox was not a native of the Cape. He came here in one of the many vessels sailing from here and finally rose to be Captain. He married a girl from Santuit and lived in Osterville.

One other vessel which I sailed in, from Osterville, was the schooner Hannah Willets, Captain Benajah West. He was a very fine man and a very able pilot. I started with him in the early spring as able seaman. During the summer the mate, Asa Ames, was taken sick and was obliged to go ashore. I was appointed to his position as mate. The last trip in the fall, after loading with coal for New Bedford, and on our way east before daylight one morning, we had just cast off from the tugboat that towed us through East River. Before we could get our sails up we were run down by a large three-masted schooner bound in the opposite direction, and the Hannah Willets ended her career off Whitestone. She sank to the bottom in less than ten minutes after the collision, She was soon after blown up by the Government as an obstruction to navigation. Captain West later commanded the three-master, B. L. Sherman. About two years after our shipwreck, when his mate was taken ill, he sent for me and I again sailed with him for several trips.

I also sailed with Captain Joseph Chadwick in the Ira Laffrinier, a vessel built up on the Great Lakes. Captain Chadwick later commanded the G. W. Cummings.

The above named vessels and captains include all those with whom I sailed from Osterville, but I well remember many other vessels and their Osterville captains, often meeting them in various ports along the coast. I remember Captain Nathan West of the Francis Edwards and his son Charles, Master of the W. L. Burroughs. Captain Francis Parker, another son of Aunt Tempy Parker, was master of the schooner Mary Wilson, which was lost on the outside of Long Island in a terrible gale of wind, and was a total loss. The captain's younger brother was lost. One other son of their famous family of seafaring men, Captain Ferdinand, died of fever aboard his vessel, the Ida L.

The R. H. Huntly was for many years commanded by Captain Jehiel P. Hodges and, after he retired, by his son, Captain Freeman Hodges. The Huntly had a very peaceful end. Being laid up for the winter along side of a wharf in New Bedford, she quietly sank to the bottom and never sailed the seas again.

The Virginia, commanded by Captain Nelson H. Bearse, was a fine schooner, heavily rigged with large sails, and was a very fast sailer. Captain Bearse was a driver and noted for many fast voyages. When he retired he engaged in the hotel business and will be remembered by many as the genial proprietor of East Bay Lodge.

The Bay State, a famous packet, long on the regular run between Boston and Albany, was for some years under the command of Captain Henry P. Crocker who later succeeded to the command of the large and famous schooner, Skylark. He was one of our most popular captains and retired to buy out a grocery business at the location now occupied by the E. E. C. Swift Co. on lower Main Street.

Entries in ship's log by Osterville men who sailed aboard the Schooner George W. Cummings:

Samuel N. Ames commenced duty on board Sch. Geo. W. Cummings: April 2nd, 1879, at $20.00 per month. Settled April 21st, am't wages, $13.26. Hospital money, 20 days, 26 cents. Due on settlement, $13.00 Received of J. H. Chadwick in full to date for services on board Sch. Geo. W. Cummings. New Bedford, April 21, 1879.

Isaac Lovell commenced duty on board Sch. Geo. W. Cummings, June 19th, 1879, at $20.00 per month. Settled July 12th, 1879, time, 23 days. Amt. wages, $15.38. Hospital money, 23 days, 28 cents. Wages due on settlement, $15.10. Received of J. H. Chadwick in full for services on board Sch. Geo. W. Cummings. Boston, July 12, 1879.

Frank E. West, commenced duty on board Sch. G. W. Cummings at $16 dollars per month. Settled May 31st, time of service 23 days. Amount wages, $12.19. Hospital money, 23 days, 33 cents. Received of J. H. Chadwick for services on board Sch. G. W. Cummings. Beverly, May 31st, 1880.

John Williams commenced duty on board Sch. G. W. Cummings at $20.00 per month. Settled Sept. 29th, time 25 days. Amt. wages $16.66. Hospital money, 25 days, 32 cts. Wages due on settlement, $16.34. Rec'd of J. H. Chadwick in full for services on board Sch. G. W. Cummings. Boston, Sept. 29, 1879.

Joseph C. Crosby commenced duty on board Sch. Geo. W. Cummings at $15.00 per month. Settled April 21st, 1879, time 20 days. Amt. wages $10.00. Hospital money, 20 days, 26 cents. Due on settlement, $9.74. Rec'd of J. H. Chadwick in full for services on board Sch. George W. Cummings, New Bedford, April 21, 1879.

The Crosby Boat Yards

January 3, 1871

The Messrs. Crosby are very busy in their new and capacious boat shop, having contracted to build all the boats they can for a number of months to come. They have now about completed an "eighteen foot" sailboat for Capt. John Bates of this village, which we don't believe can be easily excelled — especially in the beauty of her model. They are having fine success and deserve it.

June 11, 1872

The Crosby Brothers are fully employed now at making large boats for Waquoit parties; the boats are to be used to carry out pleasure parties from the Vineyard Campgrounds.

August 12, 1873

This place known for its well built and fast sailing boats has now become famous. The last boat launched by the Messrs. Crosby surpasses in model and speed any former one built by them, or owned in this vicinity. This boat, the Vixen, has been purchased by our esteemed citizen, Capt. O. D. Lovell, firm F. H. Lovell & Co., of New York, whose attachment and love for his native village brings him among us often, where he is always welcomed by a host of friends. He, with his nephew, Mr. G. F. Lovell, formerly of New Orleans, are now rusticating at the Parker House where are also quite a number of guests, who find a pleasant home.

Paperweight featuring Crosby Boat Shops. This paperweight is a gift to the Osterville Historical Society from Frank Hodges of Providence, Rhode Island, who is the son of Warren Hodges of Osterville, Mass. Mr. Frank Hodges is the great-grandson of Captain Nathan E. West, Sr.

Crosby Boat Yard, c. 1884. This is the earliest known photograph of the boat yard. House in center of picture was the home of Samuel Wiley. It was later moved to Bay Street when the Wianno Golf Course was constructed.

November 23, 1875

The Crosby Brothers have launched another of their beautiful boats for Chatham parties. They also have five more engaged to build to go to Chatham.

December 28, 1875

The Crosby Brothers have launched another of their beautiful boats for Chatham parties. They also have five more engaged to build to go to Chatham.

February 1, 1876

Crosby Brothers have launched another of their beautiful boats, and still they build.

June 17, 1879

We are glad to see the handsome yacht "Echo" once more at her stake in our bay. She was built and is owned by Mr. Daniel Crosby, of the famous Crosby Bros. boat-builders, and is by all odds the handsomest and fastest sailing craft we have among us. It will be remembered she took the first prize in the "Beverly yacht race" last summer and we have no doubt will do the same this season. Success to you, friend Dan.

July 20, 1880

Crosby Bros. have a nice new wharf to accommodate their own and other boats.

March 21, 1882

Crosby Brothers have launched two new boats the past week and sold one and have two more building.

March 11, 1884

We saw at Crosby's Boat House 8 new boats and 4 more under way, building to go away when spring opens. Busy times there.

March 17, 1885

The Crosby Brothers and Sons have built some seventeen boats since last fall, with several more engaged to build. Business has been good at their boat houses.

May 11, 1886

The Crosby Bros. have sent two new boats round to Boston the past week, Charles F. Whippey sailing one and James G. Small the other. They made the passage in about 24 hours.

March 13, 1888

The Crosby Brothers are having quite a demand for their boats, building for Boston, New York, as well as Cape Cod parties: sold one the last week to Cuttyhunk party, also a call on Saturday from a Nantucket party.

September 18, 1888

Mr. Wilton Crosby is building a new and commodious boat shop.

October 30, 1888

Wilton Crosby's new and large boat building establishment is about ready for occupancy.

February 26, 1889

Mr. Wilton Crosby, one of our popular boat builders, has recently completed a beautifully modeled cat-boat for New York parties.

April 2, 1889

The Crosbys are doing a rushing business this winter, having had at times as many as six boats in process of construction at once. They have now five shops down there and in some have room enough to set up two 28 or 30 foot boats at the same time. Still as fast as they increase their capacity their orders seem to multiply and they have all they want to do to supply the demand.

May 7, 1889

Mr. Wilton Crosby has launched the finest boat ever yet built by the famous Crosby boys. It is for a gentleman in New York City and leaves here this week.

Watercolor painting of the C. Worthington Crosby boat shop, c. 1880s. The building was located at the foot of West Bay Road.

Watercolor painting of the interior of the C. Worthington Crosby boat shop, c. 1880s.

Osterville and Cotuit

June 18, 1889

These two little villages are well represented in the aquatic world, and the former especially, is the birthplace of many smart yachts. Whenever a boat puts out from this little "West Bay" you may be sure she will make a brilliant career, whether at home or abroad, in the races. Among the notables that hail from here are:

Lottie (sloop) . . . . H. F. Crosby
Belvidere . . . . H. F. Crosby
A. P. E. . . . . Daniel Crosby
Florence . . . . Capt. Adams

The Florence is used for pleasure excursions and takes out the summer guests from the Cotocheset House.

The A.P.E. is an able boat, and won first prizes in the Beverly Club races last year; also in races at Osterville and Onset.

Capt. Hodges has built a 20 ft. catboat, after a model of the Crosby crafts, but she has not been "dipped" as yet.

The G. M. C. that took first prize in the Great Head race this season is owned by Mr. George Wooster of Boston, and was formerly an Osterville boat.

The Crosby Brothers whose boat yards (three in number) are strung along the West Bay in Osterville, have built 25 boats this season, and have had orders for many more.

Mr. Herbert F. Crosby has in process of construction a 25-ft., cat-boat for Mr. Marshall of Brockton, who will use her in Onset Bay this summer. She is as convenient and shapely a craft of the kind as the writer has ever seen, being finished in hard wood and having all the appliances for pleasure and speed and seaworthiness. The workmanship is as fine and neat as on a canoe or shell boat, every part being perfectly well fitted.

Messrs. Daniel and Charles Crosby are building a 26 ft. cat-boat for New York parties.

June 25, 1889

Mr. Wilton Crosby is building a 24 ft. boat for Capt. Besse of Bourne.

March 11, 1890

The steam Island Belle of Nantucket was towed to this place on Wednesday by Capt. Cannon of catboat Margie. The Island Belle is to be lengthened ten feet by Mr. Wilton Crosby, one of our noted boat builders.

September 2, 1890

The catboat A.P.E., owned by Mr. Daniel Crosby of this village, took the first prize at the recent Rhode Island regatta at Providence.

January 20, 1891

Messrs. D. and C. H. Crosby are to build a boat for Mr. Geo. A. Greene 26 ft. in length, 12 ft. beam, with a large well, to be launched about April 1st.

July 18, 1893

Wilton, Joe, and Manley Crosby, each in their own boats, have gone westward for a pleasure trip.

February 27, 1894

One of the largest catboats ever built here is now being built by Wilton Crosby. She is about 35 feet over-all, and is to be used for fishing and partying by Mr. James Cannon of Nantucket.

November 13, 1894

Two schooner loads of lumber arrived at the Crosby boathouses last week.

October 28, 1895

Joseph C. Crosby, Manley Crosby, wife and son Malcolm and Frank Williams left on Thursday for New York, where we hope they will be as successful as they have been here. The fame of the "Crosby boats" is wide spread, and our friends are just the right ones to keep up the standard quality of their work.

Crosby Boat Yard — c. 1910.
Oyster Harbors Bridge at right center.

March 29, 1897

The Boston Globe says: "W. F. Scott, who has had a new boat in mind since the sale of the Arab, has placed an order with D. & C. H. Crosby of Osterville for a racer in the third class. She will be an improved Arab in model, and will be a little larger than that boat, since she will be built to the 20 foot limit. She will be 29 feet over all, 9 feet 6 inches beam and 18 inches draft. She will have a wooden board, a water tight cockpit and a good cabin, but will be as lightly built as a good regard for an occasional cruise will allow. She will be a powerful boat and will be given a large sail plan. She will be rigged first as a catboat with jib, but will be given a jib and mainsail rig later if it is believed that she will do better under it.

Veteran Boat Building Firm — How the Construction of the Famous Cape Catboats Originated.

April 17, 1899

Summer visitors and all yachtsmen know well the village of Osterville as the home of the Cape catboat, and as well known as Osterville is the family name of Crosby, builders of this type of craft through two generations. The story of how the

Crosbys came to be boat builders is a remarkable one, well worth the telling.

Worthington Crosby, whose death was announced a short time ago, was the son of a ship carpenter who died when Worthington was 9 years old, leaving a widow and four children, two sons and two daughters. Worthington was the oldest boy and for three years he worked on the home farm in summer and went to school during the winter months. As was usual with the Cape Cod boys, he went to sea as soon as he was old enough and was in a New York packet until he neared his 20th year.

About this time his mother became a convert to spiritualism. She claimed that the spirit of her husband advised that his sons start up a boat-building business, and in 1850 they followed this guidance and formed a partnership as the Crosby Bros. Their first work was on rather a small scale, as they only turned out one boat a year. They cut their own timber and sawed out the planks by hand from cedar logs.

Their business steadily increased until about 15 years ago, when they dissolved partnership. Worthington's two sons, Daniel and Charles, took up their business, and their father worked with them for many years. Of late it had been his practice to build two or three 16-foot catboats every winter to let to the summer folks. Last winter he built two of these handy craft. Daniel and Charles still carry on the boat building trade under the firm name of D. and C. H. Crosby, the best known boat builders on the Cape. A grandson of Worthington Crosby was an honor graduate of the class of '96, M. I. T., having taken the course in naval architecture.

October 23, 1899

Messrs. D. and C. H. Crosby have shipped cat-boat "Guess" to Norfolk, Va.

October 29, 1900

Messrs. Wilton and H. Manley Crosby have enlarged their boat shops to better accommodate the large boats they are to build this winter. They have added electric lights to the shop also. These are the first to appear in this part of the country.

November 26, 1900

Last Saturday, 17th, the oak keel, for the large boat to be built for Chatham parties by Mr. Wilton Crosby, was brought over the road in teams from Plymouth. The keel was purchased of Mr. Ira Ward and had to be brought in two sections. This will be the largest boat ever launched from the Crosby boat houses. Mr. Ward and men returned to Plymouth Sunday morning.

March 4, 1901

The largest boat ever built by the Crosbys was successfully launched from the shop of Wilton Crosby on the evening of Feb. 26, 1901. She is owned by Capt. George F. and R. A. Nickerson of Chatham, Mass. Her dimensions are large, length over all 40 ft., beam 15 ft., draft 3 ft., lease free-board 3½ ft. She will be sloop rigged, and will also have a 16 horse power gasoline engine, made by the Murray & Tregurtha Co., of South Boston, Mass. She will be used in the fishing business.

September 23, 1901

Mr. Daniel Crosby and son are erecting a large shop on Grand Island, at West Bay, where they will carry on the boat building. Mr. Charles Crosby, who has been in company with his brother for many years, will continue business at the old stand on the main land.

January 18, 1904

Daniel Crosby & Son received an order last week for five or more knockabouts to be used in the Wianno Yacht Club races next summer.

January 30, 1906

Daniel Crosby and son are building a 75 footer, the largest and most expensive boat ever built in this vicinity. This firm has an immense shop and every facility for constructng such large and valuable craft. Ralph Crosby, the son of Daniel Crosby, who has lately been admitted to the firm, is a graduate of "Tech" class '96, and a young man of fine ability, having received high honors in his course, that of "naval architecture."

The Coal Dock at the foot of Bay Street, Osterville. Looking across the bay toward Little Island at the shops of Daniel and Charles Crosby. c. 1910.

Aerial view of West Bay and the Boat Yard in 1938.

March 8, 1909

All the boat shops are working overtime in order to get orders out in time for the coming season.

June 28, 1910

Daniel Crosby and Son have recently built and launched a 26-foot cat boat for F. P. Larkin of Philadelphia.

The Crosby House

April 20, 1880

The Crosby House is having another addition to accommodate more boarders.

March 7, 1888

The "Crosby House" is to be enlarged by the addition of another story to a part of the same.

July 8, 1890

We learn that the Crosby House is about filled and the Cotocheset overflowing with guests.

August 5, 1890

The "Crosby House" was struck by lightning during the heavy tempest Friday morning, but providentially none of the inmates were injured. Several of the rooms showed the result of the presence of the fluid as well as the outside of the building, but comparatively small damage was done to the house.

August 18, 1891

The boarders at the Crosby House had a hop in one of the boat shops Saturday night.

May 28, 1892

We hear that all the rooms at the Crosby House are engaged for the coming summer and everything seems to point to a busy, and we hope, a prosperous summer.

August 31, 1896

The past season has been one of the most successful in the history of the Crosby House. The highest number registered at one time was seventy, and at present the House has thirty-five guests, many of whom will remain in September. Some of the guests have been annual visitors for years, and nearly all of the rooms are engaged for the season of '97.

August 22, 1898

Messrs. Ernest and Clarence Briggs, with their friend, Mr. Wheeler of Cambridge, are at the Crosby House for a few weeks. Mr. Ernest Briggs obtained his early education at "Dry Swamp Academy" under Mrs. Hannah M. Whippey some twenty years ago, his father, Rev. Thomas P. Briggs, being pastor of the Baptist Church in this village at that time.

March 29, 1910

The Crosby House has a new horse.

Crosby House Masquerade

July 26, 1920

One of the Crosby House guests reports the following: heralded by secret hall conferences, hushed giggles and a great deal of borrowing from the kindhearted members of our village, a masquerade was staged at the Crosby House on Saturday night, July 17th.

Fifty-two gayly and cleverly attired guests were ushered into the attractively decorated dining room by Harold Crosby, the Twice Crowned King of the Cannibal Islands, whose gruesome black face and grass skirt totally deceived the guests.

The dinner proved an added feature, for it was "tool-less." The soup was drained through straws and the rest of the meal was handled easily with nothing but the hands.

Games and dancing rounded out the evening.

Crosby House — c. 1910.

April 7, 1927

The Crosby House has been sold to Leonard T. Bliss of Pinehurst, N.C. who will take possession of it in April. The building was opened to the public in 1860 by Mr. and Mrs. Horace Crosby, who took a few summer boarders. As their popularity increased, he buildings were enlarged from year to year, until now it accommodates 40 or 50 guests. With all modern improvements, ideally located near the water, and with its spacious grounds, patrons return year after year to enjoy its delightful surroundings. It was run a number of years by Mrs. Crosby after her husband's death. It came into posession of Harold Crosby, a grandson, who has given his undivided attention to improving and making it attractive for summer guests. Mr. Crosby has made many friends who can testify to his splendid management.

A popular summer hotel during the first half of the century, this view was recorded prior to 1910. West Bay Road is not yet paved. Houses on Manor Way now occupy this site.

West Bay Inn

West Bay Inn is situated close to the shore of West Bay, at Osterville, Mass. The Inn is six miles from West Barnstable on the Cape Cod Division of the N.Y., N.H., & H. Railroad, and is reached by Childs' line of stages connecting with frequent trains to and from Boston daily. The service is excellent and the drive forms a pleasant feature of the trip. Mr. Childs will furnish private carriages on request to the hotel. The view is as beautiful as any to be found on Cape Cod, including both water and landscape. The hotel faces the southwest, from which point comes the prevailing breeze. The location is the coolest in Osterville.

January 30, 1906

At West Bay, Edward S. Crocker's Hotel is all closed in and shingled ready for the plasterers, and Mr. Herbert Crosby, Jr.'s, house awaits the finish. These wholly village improvements, we think, show enterprise as well as prosperity.

November 26, 1907

There will be a clay pigeon shoot on the grounds at West Bay Inn Thanksgiving Day at 2 P.M.

August 18, 1919

There will be held at West Bay Inn, Osterville, on Wednesday at 8:00 P.M., a community sing. In case of rain, the sing will be postponed until Friday. Special music will be rendered. Everyone is invited to come.

July 12, 1920

West Bay Inn opened to the public June 28th. A number of improvements have been made and electric lights have been installed which will add much to this popular resort.

Dining room of West Bay Inn — c. 1905.

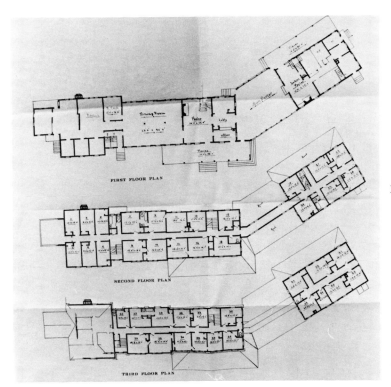

Floor plans of West Bay Inn.

November 6, 1924

West Bay Inn is undergoing extensive repairs.

October 17, 1935

Fire tonight razes West Bay Inn at Osterville

Highly Spectacular Fire Causes Loss of $50,000
Origin Undetermined

Fire of undetermined origin wiped out the West Bay Inn at Osterville tonight, causing a loss of $50,000, so E. S. Crocker, longtime owner of the property, estimated, only partially covered by insurance.

The fire broke out about 9 o'clock in the rear of the building and assumed great headway at once. When the Osterville-Centerville fire departments arrived, its seriousness was so apparent that Centerville, Hyannis, and Cotuit were called on for aid.

But the headway gained was too great to be overcome, and the building burned flat in spite of all the firemen could do.

Mr. Crocker says that the Inn had been unoccupied for two weeks, and he cannot account for the origin of the fire.

The Inn was a large structure containing 65 rooms and was a summer hotel entirely. It has been standing for a number of years and has been one of the best known hotels on the Cape.

Fortunately there was but little wind, and what there was shifted, so that the adjoining property was not endangered, the showers of sparks falling on the golf grounds.

The property was advertised to be sold last Friday.

The blaze was one of the most spectacular on the Cape for years and attracted several thousand people, the traffic jamming all the roads leading to it. It also was visible for a long distance and burned so brightly as to make a most brilliant illumination.

West Bay Inn — c. 1910.

West Bay Cut

March 15, 1897

Friday of last week might well be recorded as a "red letter" day in the history of our village, for we were visited by the Legislative Committee on Harbors and Public Lands and the Committee on Prisons, constituting a delegation of twenty-four as bright, energetic men as was ever our privilege to meet, and by whom their several districts in our Commonwealth are certainly ably represented.

In the evening they gave a hearing in Village Hall to all interested in the proposed "cut" at Dead Neck, connecting the waters of Osterville Bay and Vineyard Sound. The audience was large and evidently interested. A large delegation of remonstrants from Cotuit was present, and testified to the probabilities and possibilities in the case. After discussing the bill at some length it was agreed by both petitioners and remonstrants to amend the bill so as to include Cotuit Harbor, thereby disposing of the remonstrance. The hearing was then declared closed.

Public spirited men both here and in other localities are making every effort to secure this much-needed legislation. After the hearing the Beacon Club kindly proffered the use of their rooms, where a reception was given the Legislative Committee and a collation served by Caterer Ames. The entire Committee left here Saturday A.M. for Boston.

Osterville vs. Cotuit

March 29, 1897

In an article published in your last issue, under the heading "Osterville Vs. Cotuit," certain statements were made which conveyed the idea that Osterville and Cotuit were at variance, brought about by the action of the former village in seeking the legislation of a bill for a cut or channel between the Neck, so called.

In regard to the hearing given by the Committee on Harbors and Public Lands, as before reported, we would state that the testimony rendered at that hearing was in no wise antagonistic to Cotuit; neither did either party get mixed up in the sifting sand as set forth in that communication; neither has it ever appeared that there is any rivalry between the two villages, but simply a difference of opinion as to the effect of the proposed cut, which both sides at this hearing agreed to leave to competent engineers to decide.

The Committee who came down here to this hearing were a party of intelligent, fair-minded men, who gave an impartial hearing and did not in any way get tangled in the subject in hand, and never for a moment considered the idea of referring the matter to the next General Court, as set forth in the article of last week. The Committee will undoubtedly soon report upon the petition.

The only compromise was an agreement made to include Cotuit Harbor in the survey, which was not objected to in the least.

Evidently that article was written by some one who had but very crude knowledge of the subject in hand, or of what transpired at the hearing. He certainly could not have been there and written as he did conscientiously.

Our claim is that we are perfectly justified in seeking the legislation of this bill, which must appear to all fair-minded men to be both a necessity and great benefit, as evidenced by the petitions from the different towns all along the Cape, praying for the enactment of this legislation, which goes to show that not only our citizens, but the citizens of towns all along the Cape, realize the importance of the measure, and the security it would afford them in their vocation, viz., fishing.

The only fact referred to by the writer of that article was in regard to the present entrance to the Harbor, which it is claimed has been steadily growing shallower and narrower for the past twenty-five years, when now, it is, to say the least, very difficult to enter the Harbor, and practically impossible to get through at night; nor is it fair to presume, as claimed by our Cotuit friends, that if we succeed in obtaining this act it must necessarily close up the present entrance, when the new channel will be some three miles distant.

We never, as yet, have heard any good theory advanced to show how it would be a detriment to Cotuit channel, and certainly do not desire to injure

Watching Crosby catboat no. 32 sail into West Bay through the Cut — early 1900s.

Catboat sailing out into Vineyard Sound through West Bay Cut — early 1900s.

a channel which is of as much importance to us as to Cotuit.

It may not be generally known that should we succeed in obtaining this cut from the State that its future maintenance evolves upon the Federal Government, thereby releasing the State from further expense.

At all events, whatever may be the outcome of this effort, we sincerely hope that no one will have cause to regret the stand they have taken in this matter, which must certainly prove of great benefit to craft navigating Vineyard Sound, and in all probability no detriment or injury to anyone.

March 14, 1898

The Committee on Harbors and Public Lands gave a hearing last Tuesday on an act authorizing the construction of a channel between South Bay in Osterville and Vineyard Sound at such a point as competent engineers shall decide would best improve the harbor afforded by said Bay, and of such dimensions as the Board of Harbor and Land Commissioners deem necessary for the passage of vessels to and from South Bay. To defray the expense of the same a sum not exceeding $10,000 is to be appropriated.

Several petitioners were heard and no remonstrants appeared. The Committee reported favorably on this bill.

October 3, 1898

The dredging plant that is to be employed in making the Osterville Channel arrived at Hyannis yesterday from Boston.

October 13, 1898

The work at the "cut through" at Dead Neck is progressing. Several of our village men are employed, making in all quite a large force.

October 31, 1898

The lumber for the construction of the "Cut" has arrived by schooner and is now being rafted ashore at Deep Hole.

February 6, 1899

Owing to a break in the machinery, work at the "cut" is suspended for a short time.

March 13, 1899

The gang of men employed in making the South Bay Cut returned during the past week, having suspended operations for several weeks on account of the severe weather. Work has been resumed and more rapid progress will probably now be made.

August 17, 1908

Work has commenced on the new cut at West Bay.

November 23, 1908

Work is almost completed on the new cut at West Bay, and now the boatmen of Osterville will have one of the finest boat harbors on the south side of the Cape. In years gone by, all the boating from this place had to go by Cotuit.

West Bay Cut

Note: the author believes that the work done on West Bay Cut in the year 1908 was either to enlarge or to repair the Cut, since original construction was completed before 1902.

The Lincoln Club

June 24, 1895

Mr. Josiah A. Ames' house at Breezy Bluff is occupied by a number of "fresh air" boys, with a superintendent, matron, etc.

June 29, 1896

"Breezy Bluffs" is occupied by the same parties as last year. During the past week children from the Lincoln Club Kindergarten, Boston, with mothers and teachers have spent their vacation here. They have returned and we understand others, boys and girls, are to spend short vacations here during the summer.

June 19, 1899

The building at Breezy Bluff which has been in process of erection for the past two months, is now completed. It is a large and roomy structure, built after a Swiss model, and will afford greater convenience to the management in entertaining the many who visit at Breezy Bluff during the summer. Mr. J. P. Margeson, who has had the work in his charge, has returned to his home in Winthrop.

August 13, 1900

About forty-eight young men from Boston are enjoying a vacation at "Breezy Bluff." This is the good work of the Lincoln Club, Boston, who for several years have given the young men, boys, girls and mothers with the babies, a chance to breathe the fresh, country air, and return to their work refreshed and strengthened.

June 22, 1908

The sea bathing is reported to be excellent at the Lincoln Club at Breezy Bluff.

Lincoln Vacation Association House of Mr. Adams, West Bay, Osterville, Mass. c. 1910.

The Lincoln Club House — c. 1910. Home on left was built by Josiah A. Ames in 1887. Homes located just before the bridge to Oyster Harbors.

Bridge to Little Island and Oyster Harbors

November 7, 1853

To the Honorable Selectmen of the
Town of Barnstable

Your petitioners, inhabitants of said town, would respectfully represent that the public convenience and wants requires that a road and bridge should be laid out and constructed beginning at the terminus of the town road near the house of Benjamin F. Crocker in said town, and leading in the most convenient direction through land of the heirs of Andrew Crosby, B. F. Crocker, and James Lovell, to the narrows, so called, thence across sd. narrows, by a Bridge sufficient for teams to cross to land of Lot Hinckley, and thence across sd. land in the direction your judgments may dictate for the convenience of the numerous owners of woodland and marsh on Little and Great Oyster Islands. As in duty bound we pray.

George Lovell
David Cammett

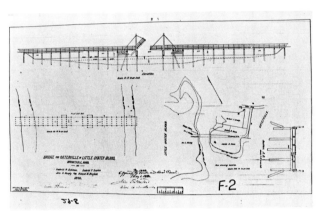

Engineering plans for first wood draw bridge to Little Island.

March 10, 1891

Messrs. Winfield, Dickerson, Murphy and others of the Oyster Island Land Co. arrived at the Crosby House Saturday. Their improvements on Oyster Island are progressing rapidly under the direction of Mr. J. C. Crosby, assisted by quite a gang of workmen. We understand that work on the bridge connecting the island with the mainland will soon be begun, and hope in the near future to see a good hotel in process of construction. The company have one of the finest sites for summer residences on Vineyard Sound, and with energy and capital will soon develop the property.

May 5, 1891

On Great Island the workmen are cutting piles and getting ready for the bridge, which will soon connect it with the mainland. We hear that some of the heads of this new company predict a railroad for the south shore in the "near future."

May 12, 1891

Mr. F. W. Dickinson of Boston came Saturday, and the work on the Grand Island Co.'s bridge began Monday.

May 26, 1891

The piles are all driven for Grand Island Co.'s bridge and work is going on rapidly.

June 16, 1891

The Sch. Luella Nickerson was here Tuesday with lumber for the Island Bridge.

July 21, 1891

The bridge over the "Narrows" connecting "Cockachoise" Point and "Little Island" is completed, and teams are driving over it now. The Grand Island Co. are having a fine wide avenue laid out all around their property, and it bids fair to become a very pleasant resort. They have a very fine location, and we hope to see building begun there soon. Perhaps some moonlight night we may see "Hannah Screecher" making use of the new bridge and coming to visit the mainland for a while. Hope she will bring the "pot of money" with her.

The wooden bridge from Osterville to Oyster Harbors, looking west. 1. Frederick E. Parker's Shanty. 2. Clarence Baker and "Nate" West's Shanty. 3. Looks like Herbert (Doc) Crosby's sailboat, "Lincoln," named for the Lincoln Club.

Open Draw Bridge to Oyster Harbors, looking east — c. 1910.

Grand Island Bridge — c. 1920.

July 4, 1911

Work on Grand Island bridge will begin this week.

Commemorative tea cup featuring the old wood bridge to Grand Island — c. 1900.

Commemorative saucer featuring Grand Island Bridge — c. 1900.

Bridge to Little Island and Oyster Harbors — 1986.

Commemorative demitasse cup featuring Grand Island Bridge — c. 1900.

Little Island

Picture taken just over the bridge — c. 1920s.

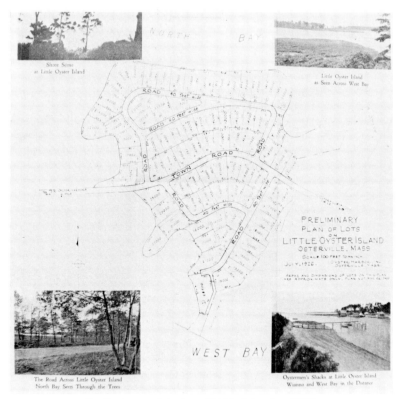

Preliminary plot plan of Little Island — 1926.

Oyster Harbors

January 16, 1850

I hereby certify that I with the parties, viz., Oliver Hinckley, Timothy Parker, Ira Hinckley, Asa Crosby, and others, went on Oyster Island, and ran out their bounds in the Seapuit Cedar Swamp. We commenced sixteen rods north of James N. Lovell's line or bounds through the swamp, thence west through the swamp as stakes are set and trees are marked, which line is the north bounds of Timothy Parker and Oliver Hinckley, and the southerly bound of Ira Hinckley's piece of swamp. We then commenced at the northwest corner of Oliver Hinckley's swamp to a stake set, thence north four rods to a stake set with stones about it, thence east on a parallel line with the other, through the swamp as stakes are set and trees are marked, to a stake set by the upland, which line is Ira Hinckley's north bound and the south bound of Asa, Cornelius W., and Horace Crosby's, and I certify that the parties agreed to the same.

Attest: James N. Lovell

Settlement of Bounds — Oyster Harbors

Settlement of Bounds,
Samuel A. Wiley and Isaac Ewer — 1851

I, James N. Lovell, in the spring of 1851, went to Mr. Isaac Ewer to know if he was willing for Mr. Freeman Crosby to go on Oyster Island with me and renew the bounds between our woodlots. I understood him to consent. Accordingly, Freeman Crosby, with Mr. Ewer's consent, went on with me, July 1, 1851.

We commenced to the West end: to the Southeast end of the North Cedar Swamp, and set a stake; and marked trees and set stakes all through the lot on a straight line to the East and to a heap of stones, and both parties agreed to the same as their bounds October 22, 1851. I put stones and cedar stakes on the bounds.

Attest: James N. Lovell

Settlement of Bounds — Oyster Harbors

April 10, 1851

We, the parties Samuel A. Wiley and James N. Lovell, went on Oyster Island to our wood lots and run out our bounds between our lots, and both agreed to the same, and marked trees, set stakes, and put stones. We commenced at James N. Lovell's Northeast corner, thence ran about South on a straight line, toward the South East corner of the lot that was formerly Benjamin Hallett's, until it come to the cove of marsh, to a stake set thereby which was as far as said S. A. Wiley owned.

And I, James N. Lovell, set stakes, April 15, 1851, straight through from said Wiley's range to the corner of the lot I bought of James Lovell, adjoining Benjamin F. Crocker's woodland, and I named to Oliver H. Crocker, and wanted he should examine them and see if they were right. The summer following, I saw Mr. O. H. Crocker, and he thought they were right. Accordingly, in October, 1851, I carried a load of stones and stakes, and made the bounds plane and good.

New England Superstitions
Written by Adeline Lovell about 1878

We find the following in a late number of the Boston Journal. We recognize the writer, Mrs. Adeline Lovell, of Osterville.

A river and a bay encircles an Island opposite the villages of Osterville and Cotuit, Cape Cod.

This island has a legend almost fading out of the memory of the oldest inhabitant, and as one of that number, my recollections have been revived by the perusal of "New England Superstitions" in the Journal supplement of June 2.

A narrow strip of land divided this Island from the Atlantic Ocean. Many years ago, a black, rakish vessel cast anchor a few hours before sunset in its offing, and a boat was lowered, loaded and manned. Heavy rich robes were placed upon its transom and a lovely woman, escorted by the Commander of the ship, was carefully seated upon its cushions. Her pale face glowed and her eyes beamed with joy as she looked at the green earth and trees before her.

"How well you look, Hannah. I think you have become tired of me and your cabin palace," exclaimed her companion.

"Oh, no," she replied with averted face, "but I do so long for the solid earth, its flowers and birds. The sea and storms and guns have unnerved me."

"You shall have all you desire," he replied as he moved away from her side. The boat stranded, and Hannah, in the arms of the boatman, was carried to the Island. The rugs were spread for her rest, and a sweet langour crept over her. Workmen with their implements were directed to a certain spot and commenced excavating the earth.

"Dig deep and wide," said the Captain as he looked anxiously around, marking the trees and stones carefully. "Now, Hannah, I want you to see us bury our treasure. Come with me." The heavy iron chest of gold and silver rested upon the edge of the vault. Hannah saw it lowered, then upon its top the robes were laid, and she saw no more, knew no more. The earth was placed above her; all seemed hurried and confused.

The Captain and his crew hastened in the twilight to the vessel, sailed away, and soon a lady's wardrobe was thrown from the cabin window, and every vestige destroyed of poor Hannah's presence and captivity.

Captain Kidd never returned for his treasure. To this day, the faithful Hannah guards it, and moans and shrieks have been heard from that Island which, in time, was called "Hannah Screecher's Island." Men, boys and women have attested to seeing her ghost when they have approached a certain spot in pursuit of berries or wood cutting. Money diggers have left their excavations, which may yet be seen, and a word spoken has proved fatal to securing the treasure.

I have conversed with those dwelling opposite the Island who believe in Hannah Screecher's murder, and her guarding the treasure, and who have listened to her plaintive moans in moonlight nights with tender sympathy instead of dread.

A.L., aged 78
"An Old Woman's Gossip"

April 17, 1877

On Friday, about 11 a.m., a fire was discovered on Great Oyster Island, but it being supposed some one was clearing up land, no uneasiness was felt. Toward night, however, it was learned that the fire was among the standing wood, when a goodly number of men turned out and succeeded near midnight in subduing it. The amount of damage cannot be estimated. Among the losers are the Crosby Bros., George Fisher, S. A. Wiley, and Alex Bacon of Osterville.

May 20, 1890

Parties were in town last week negotiating for the purchase of Great Oyster Island (so called).

October 7, 1890

A company of surveyors are engaged on Great Island.

January 6, 1891

Work has commenced on the island recently purchased by Boston and New York parties.

March 24, 1891

Oyster Island between Cotuit and Osterville has lately been sold to New York parties at a good price and they have now a gang of some thirty men clearing out the underbrush and building a road around the island, which is at least five miles around and full of sea indentations and fine bluffs, one of the most charming spots on the Cape shore. The island is well wooded and has good soil.

April 7, 1891

The work on the Island is progressing. The avenue across the two islands is being turfed and the road bed across the marshes built. The bridge is next in order, and a short time will see Osterville connected with the new summer resort.

September 21, 1903

The lodging house and cook room on Grand Island, occupied by the workmen of the Eastern Dredging Co., was totally destroyed by fire Tuesday afternoon, September 15th. All the clothing and considerable money was lost as the cook was alone, the night gang having gone to relieve the day gang.

March 11, 1913

Several telephone men from New Bedford are in town putting a long distance telephone across Grand Island. They have extended it down to the residence of the late Charles Daniel Sr.

July 14, 1927

Daniel Bros., of Wianno, have constructed a large garage addition for A. Felix duPont. An airplane hanger was recently completed for use of the duPont family.

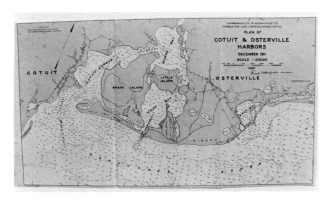

1911 Map.

Aerial view — Oyster Harbors — c. 1925.

The Story of Oyster Harbors

Oyster Harbors today is the fulfillment of a long-cherished dream, the dream of creating a setting of dignity and beauty for the ever-increasing number of Americans who are establishing permanent summer homes.

This return to the countryside has come about largely because parents realize that the summer environment of their children is as important as the educational advantages which they provide. And so instead of going one year to one place, and another year somewhere else, they are selecting permanent locations where their children can have healthful outdoor life and where they can grow up in a congenial social atmosphere.

Before this distinctive summer colony was located off the shores of Osterville, the developers made an exhaustive study of the entire Massachusetts coast, and finally selected Oyster Harbors because it offered more of the advantages which were sought than any other location. Here they found a beautifully wooded tract, surrounded by water, but connected with the mainland by a highway. The tract was large enough to become a self-contained community, and yet near enough to the other established summer colonies on Cape Cod to provide variety and interest.

On the south shore of Cape Cod, sea-bathing is at its best, and the many bays and inlets that surround Oyster Harbors make boating a safe delight. Here, too, the breezes which sweep over Nantucket Sound temper the summer air.

To these natural advantages, the developers have added a landscape design of true beauty, excellent roads, a golf course, tennis courts, and a Club House which has become the center of social life.

Development of Oyster Harbors was commenced late in 1925. Throughout 1926, the work continued. Dense underbrush, accumulated through the centuries, was cleared away over the entire tract, superfluous trees were felled, great clearings were made. And while the work on land progressed, huge dredges and suction pumps made navigable the harbor waters for yachts and sailing boats.

September 1, 1927

The Clubhouse being constructed at Oyster Harbors is not only the largest but the most expensive in this part of the country. It will make a true companion piece for the great golf course. To cost approximately $300,000, with a frontage of 320 feet and covering 15,000 square feet, the two and a half story frame building will embody, in architecture and furnishings, all that is typical of colonial Cape Cod. Sixty private rooms and suites on the upper floor will be available to members and guests for overnight or summer-long occupancy. To the golf lover and sportsman, the appeal of Oyster Harbors is irresistible. At a cost of nearly $250,000, an eighteen-hole course, capable of challenging the skill of the greatest, has been built over the island. Conceived and planned by Donald Ross, its construction to the last detail was supervised by this renowned golf architect. Over 6,500 yards and with abundant natural hazards and long fairways, it is inevitable that the fame of the Oyster Harbors course will extend to wherever golf is played. So perfect are the bathing facilities on Cape Cod, it is difficult to accord full justice to those at Oyster Harbors. On the Sound side of the Cape, the variation between high and low tides is about thirty inches. The average summer-long temperature of the water is 72 degrees. The great, long beaches of smooth, golden sand at Oyster Harbors are numbered among the finest. Throughout the warm summer days even the youngest may bathe with safety, for undertows and back currents are unknown. All sports will receive true recognition there. Adjoining the golf course are tennis courts, with more to be installed in another section of the island, given entirely to recreational purposes. Bowling greens are to be installed, also a baseball diamond and promenade. The code of only creating the finest has applied to the installation of sport facilities, as well as to all things else at Oyster Harbors.

August 16, 1928

At Oysters Harbors Tuesday a boy was killed who attempted to board a heavy truck.

March 13, 1930

A charming house is now under construction at Oyster Harbors for A. Oram Fulton of Newton Center and will be ready for occupancy in July. It is located on high ground amid splendid pines, oaks and cedars, and has a commanding view of Nantucket Sound. The house consists of a large beamed living and dining room with fireplaces at either end, and opening onto a piazza extending across the entire water front. Two guest rooms with bath are located on the first floor together with pantries, kitchen, chauffeur's quarters and bath. On the second floor are large owner's room and bath and fireplace, two chambers, each with bath, and servants' rooms and bath. There is a two-car garage.

Old hand-drawn map of Oyster Island — c. 1850. The following information is written in the upper right hand corner:

Oyster Island	650	Acres
Little Island	175	"
James Lovell, Ded Nake	127	"
George Lovell	12	"
Tirzah Crosby	36	"
Oliver H. Crocker	10	"
Ira Hinckley	10	"
David Fuller, marsh	3	"
Content Scudder, marsh	8	"
	1,031	Acres

Hannah Screecher Haunts Island Now Oyster Harbors

Village Maiden, Slain by Pirates, Watches Over Treasure Buried by Captain Kidd's Bloodthirsty Pirates, According to Tradition (1939)

If this sounds like a fairy tale, remember it is really tradition, deeply rooted in the minds of older residents of Osterville, one of Barnstable's most thriving little villages. Once, long, long ago on a beautiful island near here, densely wooded and most impenetrable, bold Captain Kidd his pirate loot buried. A village maiden, Hannah by name, hidden in the tangled wood, watched the pirates

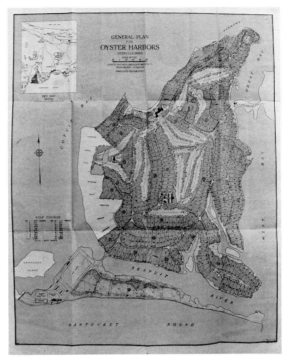

Olmsted Bros. plan of land for Oyster Harbors — 1925.

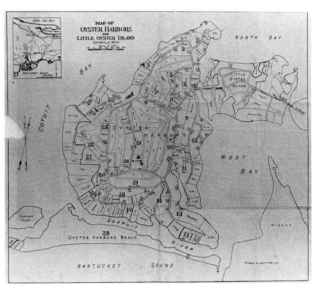

Map of Oyster Harbors and Little Island — c. 1940.

---

bury their golden treasure, was surprised, slain, and her body buried in the very pit in which the pirate chest reposed. Vengeance, and her desire to prevent anyone from ever profiting by finding the hidden gold, caused the spirit of Hannah to forever watch over the chest.

Defying this tradition, many people have dug for the golden treasure, but when they approached near to its exact location, Hannah screeched, an awful, unearthly screech, fearful enough to frighten away any human being. So strongly did older residents believe the tradition that few would even venture to set foot on the island, and those few

221

Ariel view — Cotuit, Oyster Harbors, Little Island, Osterville, and Wianno — 1928.

Aerial view — Oyster Harbors — 1935.

daring men brought back tales of the ghostly guard which Hannah always kept.

As for the truth of tradition, some evidence still remains. For years the island was known as Screecher's Island, and as Hannah's Island. Many older residents of Osterville remember the tradition well today, and even a few refused to set foot on the island. J. Milton Leonard of Osterville remembers the tale well.

"I have many times heard my elders tell the story," said Mr. Leonard. "In the days before my time, people believed it strongly, and I knew many men who always swore the treasure was buried there. There was one story that a man was very badly frightened by Hannah's screech. Perhaps it was an owl. I don't know. But the tradition always clung to the island until the summer people came."

Today there are a few Osterville natives who still remember the tradition, and actually one or two who will not visit the place. But times and men's minds have changed.

It is a long step, a step across a century of time and tradition, to visit Hannah Screecher's Island today. Its name has been changed from time to time, from Screecher's to Oyster Island, to Grand Island, to Oyster Harbors.

For many years, the only way to reach this beautiful island was over a ford at Wianno Head. At low tide men could wade or drive a team over a little river. Mr. Leonard remembers when he crossed in a wagon when the water reached above the box. Men visited the island occasionally to cut wood. He recalls that it was very heavily wooded with thick underbrush.

Until summer people came, the island was never tenanted. The late Professor Edward Channing of Harvard College was its first resident. He built a fine summer residence on the bluff overlooking Cotuit bay. There followed many prominent and wealthy people. Among those owning a large strip across the island was President A. Lawrence Lowell of Harvard University. His holdings, which

have been in his family for many years, stretch right across the golf course where the best of Bay State golfers do play.

Oyster Harbors is an island about 300 acres in area. When Richard Winfield of New Jersey purchased a large part of the island about twenty-five years ago, the name was changed from Oyster Island to Grand Island, and when Forris W. Norris and others purchased the Winfield holdings in 1925, they further changed the name to Oyster Harbors. It may still be remarked here, however, that to many Osterville people, it is still Screecher's Island.

The Gate Lodge — entrance to Oyster Harbors — late 1930s.

Mr. Norris and his associates turned Oyster Harbors into Cape Cod's most exclusive summer colony. They build roads, bridal paths, a fine golf course, tennis courts, bathing beaches, a large clubhouse, a water system, and stables on the island, and a causeway by which it may be reached by auto. They spent, according to Mr. Norris, approximately $1,900,000 in its development.

When the A. Felix duPont residence was begun some years ago, the skeletons of three men were dug up. They appeared to be Indians, and one skeleton was sent to an institution for study. Strangely enough, the two others were stolen from the workmen's camp. No scientist ever had the opportunity to check whether they might have been Captain Kidd's pirates.

The Gate Lodge — entrance to Oyster Harbors — 1986.

Left to right, 8-Connie Ann MacBride, 9-Leah Eddy, 10-Ann Pearmain, 11- Beverly Winslow, 16-Zelda Crocker, 18-Carol Crocker, 20-Pierce Pearmain — c. early 1930's.

A morning ride — at The Gate Lodge — 1940s.

On the trail at Oyster Harbors.

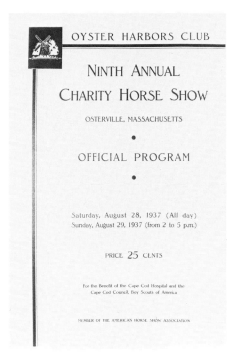

Judging riders and mounts at the Oyster Harbors Horse Show, an annual event — c. 1935.

Oyster Harbors Stables — c. 1935.
Oyster Harbors Horse Stables, formerly located on Little Island, were moved by Chester Crosby, Sr., and are still in use (in 1987) for boat storage.

223

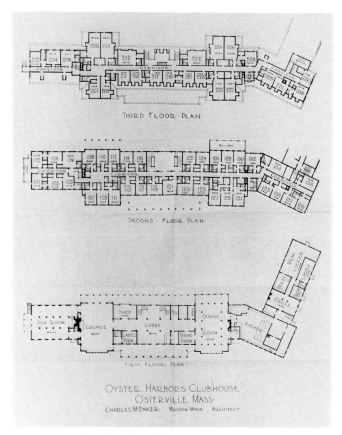

Floor plans for the Oyster Harbors Club.

Interior of the Oyster Harbors Club — c. 1940.

The Oyster Harbors Club — c. 1940.

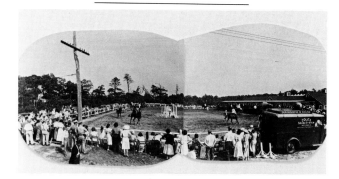

Annual Horse Show at Oyster Harbors.

Interior of the Oyster Harbors Club — c. 1940.

Early 1930s. Left to right, top row: Zenas Crocker, 3rd, Shirley Ellis, Hugh Dangler, Niles Tabor, Nancy Kneale, Frances Walker, June Rockwood, David Bidwell; bottom row: ?, Mary Dangler, ?, Harriet Walker, Jane Bidwell, Sally Stires, ?.

Tennis Anyone? — 1930s. Top row, l. to r.: ?, David Bidwell, David Rockwood, Niles Tabor, Zenas Crocker, III, Hugh Dangler, Eugene Lyne, Dick O'Keefe, Bardy Tabor, Austin Lyne; Bottom row: Kerry Lyne, Louise Rockwood, Carol Crocker, Beverly Winslow, Jane Bidwell, Susan Lyne, June Rockwood, Ann Shedden, and Shirley Ellis.

Charming Lounge with splendid reproductions of early American furniture. One has a delightful view of the water as well as of the golf course.

A bit of detail of main dining room with a glimpse of a private dining room.

Harold Green's orchestra . . . Concert and dancing . . . at the Pinehurst Country Club in winter and Oyster Harbors Club in summer.

Colonial Dining room . . . cool, airy and attractive.

Overlooks the water and the golf course.

Interior views of the Oyster Harbors Club — 1930s.

Tennis courts, yacht pier and boat landing, and part of the gardens at Oyster Harbors.

Oyster Harbors — The Club — The Fairway

Clearly distinguishable are: 8 miles of shore front, sandy beaches, winding private roads, fine harbors, causeway and only approach to Oyster Harbors Colony, as well as 18-hole Donald Ross golf course.

Spacious Colonial Clubhouse facing both the 1st and 18th fairways of the golf course and the waters of Cotuit Bay. Sixty guest rooms with private baths.

First of thousands to appreciate the beauties of summer on Oyster Harbors (then called Grand Island by Osterville residents) was Edward Channing (1856-1932), who in winter months made his home at 5 Craigie Circle, Cambridge, Mass. Channing — author, Pulitzer Prize winner (1925), and holder, until his death in 1931, of the oldest chair of history in the United States, the McLean Professorship of Ancient and Modern History at Harvard University, founded by John McLean in 1823 — was an illustrious member of an illustrious family.

His grandfather, Walter Channing, M.D., (1786-1876), an obstetrician, introduced the use of ether to ease the pains of labor. His father, William Ellery Channing (1818-1901), was a poet and an associate of Emerson, Hawthorne, and Thoreau. His mother was Ellen Kilshaw (Fuller) Channing. His great uncle, William Ellery Channing (1780-1842), a clergyman and leader of the Unitarian church in the early 1800s, was an organizer of the American Unitarian Association in 1825.

Edward Channing was born in Dorchester, Mass., earned his A.B. from Harvard College in 1878, and his A.M. and Ph.D. in 1880 from Harvard University. He built his summer home on Oyster Harbors in the early 1900s; at that time, (1909-1933) president of Harvard University, Abbott Lawrence Lowell (1856-1943), summered at Cotuit,

Edward Channing — first resident of Oyster Harbors. Built his home there in the early 1900s. Picture used by permission of the Harvard University Archives.

and the two educators maintained their friendship across Cotuit Harbor, occasionally calling for a car and driver to transport one of them around the head of North Bay to pay a formal visit on the other.

Show Places of Cape Cod — 1927

Some of the finest "show places" of the Cape are at Oyster Harbors. Twenty-two residences already have been built there, and others are contemplated for the near future.

duPont residence — Oyster Harbors.

Residence of Mr. William A. Kimbel of Ardsley-on-Hudson, New York.

When the duPonts decided to build a summer home at Oyster Harbors, Cape Cod pinned another feather in its cap. The setting of the duPont place is truly "Capey" — green strip of pine trees dividing blue expanse of sea and sky. The Cape is proud to count the A. Felix duPonts of Wilmington, Delaware, among its permanent Summer residents.

Residence of Mrs. Eleanor Phelps Wilds of Aiken, South Carolina.

Walter Hagen putting on the 3rd green of the Oyster Harbors golf course. Horton Smith in the foreground. c. 1930s.

Walter Hagen, Horton Smith, and others on the sporty 17th green of the Donald Ross golf course at Oyster Harbors. c. 1930s.

East Bay

February 17, 1874

The greatest enterprise that has been under-taken this winter is the building of a wharf about 200 feet in length into the East Bay. A grant has been obtained from the Legislature and the work is nearly completed. A wharf has long been needed here, as heretofore vessels wishing to land any thing at this place had to do so over the beach.

October 2, 1899

The "East Bay" is now being surveyed by Messrs. L. H. Bateman, Gery H. Chase and C. F. Powers, assisted by Mr. L. B. Ellis of Harwich. The surveyors are doing the work in a thorough man-ner, and we believe the completed chart will demonstrate to all the great necessity of an inlet being made navigable to and from Vineyard Sound. The need of an inlet, and for a harbor of refuge, has lately been demonstrated in a very forcible manner: a few days since Messrs. Bateman and Chase, in the yacht "Echo," coming from the "West Bay" could not get into the "East Bay" at half tide and were obliged to anchor off the beach. A southeaster blew in the night, and in the morn-ing the boat was ashore, but by hard work was saved. Mr. H. B. Day's boat came ashore, and was almost destroyed; also the yacht "Mighty." This only illustrates the great need of a harbor being provided for the thirty or more boats that use "East Bay" as a harbor, and who are shut out save at high water. It is earnestly hoped that we may be able to have the bill passed at the coming Legisla-ture for this much needed channel to "East Bay." The big fleet of boats are now gone from our Bay, but we hear of a steam launch and four knock-abouts being ordered from the Crosby's provided our channel is improved, and, if so improved, the "East Bay" will not only be a harbor of refuge, but a port for commercial purposes as well; all this we hope for from the coming Legislature.

December 24, 1900

The Harbor and Land Commissioners were in the village Thursday, viewing East Bay Channel.

February 1, 1904

Messrs. Hodgdon and Burke, engineers, have been down viewing East Bay. Large quantities of stone are being carted over the ice to the point of land near the channel, where they will be used. East Bay is frozen so that a pair of horses can carry over 3 tons to the channel.

East Bay, looking northeast. In boat in front, left to right: Rev. J. C. Robbins, Rev. Miner, Rev. B. T. Livingston. c. 1901.

East Bay — 1884. East view of Orville D. Lovell's Boat House. Left to right: Mr. William H. Bearse, Chester Bearse (the architect), Andrus Bearse, Mrs. Orville D. Lovell, Miss Laura M. Bearse, Mrs. A. S. Cornish, Mr. George F. Lovell.

March 7, 1904

March 1st came in with a snow storm. We hope it is not to continue throughout the month. No doubt the three contractors for East Bay cut have been well pleased, for the severe winter, as we understand it has swelled their "pocketbooks," to some extent, the bay being frozen over, enabling them to cart their stone over ice, rather than in a scow, which was first proposed.

East Bay — 1884. South view of Orville D. Lovell's Boat House which was situated on the northeast side of East Bay. Persons in picture: Mr. George F. Lovell on balcony, Capt. Owen Crosby in doorway, Mr. Howard Marston on wharf. In the foreground is the yacht, Dipper.

East Bay Yacht "Bubble" — Ready for the Regatta. This picture was taken at O. D. Lovell's Boat House wharf in 1886.

April 9, 1889

Mr. Dexter was down to see his house in its new completed state. The beach can hardly claim this fine residence as it is and has been for years one of our village residences, and although Mr. Dexter has turned it around and so enlarged and improved the place as to make it almost unrecognizable, still it stands on the same spot and we can claim it as a village improvement.

April 22, 1890

Mr. Dexter is having a windmill for pumping water erected on his place.

Death of Mr. George S. Dexter

December 30, 1901

Mr. George S. Dexter, who for fifteen years or more has been a summer resident of Osterville, died at his home, 660 Tremont St., Boston, on Friday, Dec. 27th. Mr. Dexter's many friends here will miss him when summer comes, especially those who live near his cottage at East Bay. He was 77 years old.

Residence of George S. Dexter, Osterville. Formerly the home of Henry Linnell. c. 1900.

The Armstrong family first came to Osterville in 1905 and stayed at the William Scudder home. There were three Armstrong children. Sometime between 1916 and 1918 they purchased from Barney Goodspeed the home south of East Bay Lodge. Mr. Armstrong was president of Armstrong Cork Co., Pittsburg, which later moved its headquarters to Lancaster, Pennsylvania. He spent summers here from 1905 until the mid-30s.

Mr. and Mrs. Charles D. Armstrong

February 14, 1921

Miss Mary Martha Armstrong, daughter of Mr. and Mrs. Charles D. Armstrong of Pittsburg, Pa., whose summer home is Indian Knoll in this place, sailed for Europe Jan. 8th.

July 9, 1923

Mrs. C. D. Armstrong of "Indian Knoll" went to New York to meet Mr. and Mrs. C. Dudley Armstrong, Miss Mary Martha Armstrong and Miss Laura Hilliard, who sailed from Cherbourg, France, June 28, on the "Bergenland" of the Red Star line.

At the Hay Scales — c. 1910. Mary Martha Armstrong on Taffy and Anne Pillow Halliday on Neddie. The old Freeman Scudder barn can be seen in the background.

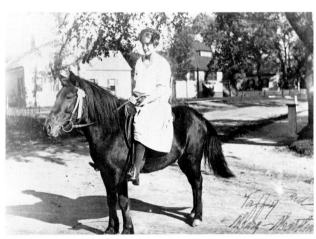

At the Hay Scales, intersection of Main Street and Parker Road — c. 1915. Mary Martha Armstrong on Neddie — Library in background.

April 21, 1927

Mr. and Mrs. Charles D. Armstrong of Pittsburg, Pa., and Osterville, Mass., announce the engagement of their daughter Miss Mary Martha Armstrong to Mr. Andrew McClary of Windsor, Vermont. Miss Armstrong is a graduate of Smith College, Mr. McClary a graduate of Dartmouth.

June 16, 1927

A large number of guests are registered at the East Bay Lodge from all parts of the country to attend the Armstrong wedding on Wednesday.

Mary Martha Armstrong and Anne Pillow Halliday entering Armstrong estate on East Bay Road. c. 1915.

Gardens at "Indian Knoll," residence of the Charles D. Armstrong Family, East Bay Road, Osterville — c. 1937.

Mrs. Charles D. Armstrong died in 1945. The Armstrong Gardens were designed and planted in 1908.

East Bay Lodge

August 26, 1895

Osterville is one of the choicest resorts on the New England shore and the East Bay Lodge one of the best managed houses. A correspondent writes enthusiastically of the place: "This is such a charming spot and such a perfectly kept little inn that I want to speak a good word for it. The situation is lovely. We have all the gaieties of the place and still are just out of the bustle. To be here is like visiting, it is so homelike."

June 13, 1904

Sunday dinners from 1:30 to 2:30 a specialty, East Bay Lodge, Osterville, .75 cts.

January 30, 1906

The many new buildings are rapidly approaching completion. Messrs. Savery and Fish have completed the Lewis House, which is in the hands of the painters and paper hangers. This firm have also ready for finishing the large annex at East Bay Lodge.

February 20, 1906

The East Bay Lodge ice house is being filled with ice from Wequaquet Lake, Centerville.

July 4, 1911

A tower about 50 feet high has been built on the premises at East Bay Lodge and will be used as lodging rooms for the help.

May 28, 1923

East Bay Lodge caught fire Friday morning week, but prompt measures and the quick arrival of the fire engine put a stop to what might have spoiled one of the loveliest hotels on the Cape.

EAST BAY LODGE and HOMESTEAD
are situated very near to the shore of East Bay, a beautiful sheet of water, flowing in from Vineyard Sound, giving to the guests of either house a view rarely surpassed, and making it particularly convenient and attractive for boating. The Lodge has recently been awarded the first prize as the most attractive and best-kept place in Osterville.

For All Information Apply to

N. H. BEARSE, Prop.   **OSTERVILLE, MASS.**

Tel. call 8004 Osterville, Mass.

East Bay Lodge — c. 1910.

Wianno

A New Summer Resort

February 11, 1873

A bluff covered with forest trees and extending for miles along the shores of Vineyard Sound, and embracing within its limits three beautiful lakes of fresh water framed in by trees of Oak and Pine, with shady woodland drives and rambles, and an avenue broad and level skirting the shore forming a magnificent ocean Boulevard, all makes up a picture of Forest, Lake and Sea combined, which is rarely met with, and which combines ample attractions to lure the denizen of the city to its haunts when the hot days of Summer makes him sigh for some cool retreat in the Country. Such a place as described is located at Osterville on the South side of Cape Cod. The poet has said,

> Full many a Gem of purest ray serene,
> The dark unfathomed Caves of Ocean bear,
> Full many a flower is born to blush unseen,
> And waste its sweetness on the desert air.

And so this locality has for generations been left in all its beauty unappreciated and unimproved, till at length a party of gentlemen in Boston and New York, satisfied of its unrivaled attractions for a country home, have purchased this large tract of land and are now laying it out in Drives, Avenues, and Rambles, and erecting a Hotel and Cottages along the Bluff. Here one can come next Summer and enjoy the hospitalities of mine host of the "Cotocheset House", the drive along the sea side avenue, the beauties of woodland scenery and inland lakes, bathing in the waves that ripple on the beach at his feet, and feel the exhilaration of a sail on the Sound with the excitement thrown in of a bluefish tugging at the trailing line.

It would seem as if all the attractions which can be found in a country life are centered here — woods, lakes and sea fishing and bathing, and above all the glorious panorama of ocean unrolled and constantly on exhibition. The eye can never tire of watching its beauties by day, as its waves leap in the sunshine, bearing along the white sails of ships and schooners and the steamer trailing its pennon of smoke along the line where sky and water meet. At night the revolving eye of the distant lighthouse winks at him from its watery throne, and the murmuring of the sea and pines lulls him to slumber with their soothing duet. An avenue one hundred and fifty feet from the edge of the bluff and sixty feet in width is now being worked through the whole extent of this property, and drives through the woods and to the lakes are being constructed. The lakes are stocked with pickerel, black bass and perch, and pleasure boats for rowing and fishing will float on their smooth waters. Bathing houses will also be at hand in their season. The sea fishing for blue fish, scup, tautog, etc., cannot be excelled on the whole coast. This one feature alone has annually attracted many to the little village and many more have stayed away for lack of accommodations. That long felt want will now be supplied.

The "Cotocheset House" has for its foundation the stone taken from the site of the old Webster Mansion on Summer Street destroyed by the late great conflagration in Boston. Thus borne as it were on wings of flame, the foundation stones of Webster's old home rest by the sounding sea, whose music their master so loved to hear, and whose character is grand and unfathomable like his own.

For those seeking health as well as pleasure this locality is favorable. The East wind, so dreaded by invalids, blows from the land, and the South wind from the sea. The water being shallow for some distance out, is by many degrees warmer and safer than on those bold shores whose deep waters always strike an unhealthy chill to the bather and often bury the swimmer in their depths; and these may be an influence conducive to health in the balsamic odor of the Pines which stand in clusters of living green all over the property. The company is organized as the "Osterville Land Company." With ample means they intend to spare no effort to fully develop the beauties and natural advantages of this charming locality. They hope to induce many families to establish their Summer houses here. Their intention is to have a sale of lots in the Spring, and they feel confident that if the place is thoroughly viewed and inspected it will result in a sale of lots and the erection of cottages,

Seaview Avenue at the entrance to the Cotocheset House, looking east towards Craigville. c. 1880s.

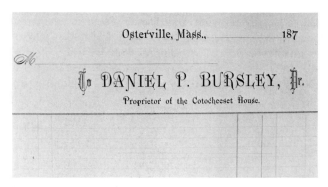

Captain Daniel P. Bursley, who held a contract with the Cotocheset House to operate his stage directly from the depot at West Barnstable to the Wianno hotel, also owned and maintained the hotel's stables a short distance away on Warren Avenue.

All that is left of a broadcast advertising the opening of the original Cotocheeset House at Wianno reads as follows:

This fine Hotel will open to the public on Wednesday, June 1_____, P.A. Roberts, — Manager, formerly proprietor of the Marlboro' Hotel, Boston, and the Waverly . . .

This favorite House has now been open for the reception of . . . become a favorite place of resort for those in pursuit of health and . . .

The House has been well patronised, necesitating (sic) additions and i . . have been made. Cottages on the grounds have also been occupied, and will . . . coming season.

The advantages of the place are many. The climate is uniform; the . . . less than ten degrees during the months of July and August. The Nor . . .

dreaded by invalids, flow from the land; the South and West winds from the . . .

The Hotel will be open for the reception of guests from June 13 to Septe . . . if found necessary.

The above sketch and verses are taken from a leaf in the Hotel Register: The verses read as follows:
Goot py! kind friends, goot py!
Und, if you blease, dond cry, —
We dond could helped dot, — must get away!
We like dese rolling seas,
Und dose salt-water breeze,
Und dos schrub oak-pine drees
Und dot nice COT-O-CHEES-
et house vas a goot blace to stay, —
A leedle vile longer, any vay!

But goot py, shents und ladies,
Und dose schweet, lofely babies,
Und dot nice fishes blue,
Und dem schmall scuppies too, —
Goot py! farewell! adieu!

Farewell dose crokay balls,
Dot nice long ten-pin halls,
Dot leedle pond close py;
Dose cooks und udder fry,
Dose waiter-girls (dot brings a sigh),
Good py! goot-py! g-o-o-t py!

Dot landlord man of dat hotel,
Oh! he was treat us awful well;
We dond forgot dot man in quite a spell, —
But den, Farewell, — farewell!

The last dings dot we got to zay
Is, we coom pack some udder day.
Ven dot next year got round we may
Got sooner here and longer stay;
But sure, the matter vas, we MUST GO 'VAY!

P.S. Dose huckleberry bugs dot bite
Dem fellers dond was quite all right.

SEACOAST CLUB

234

Mrs. Hill's Cottage. This cottage was located immediately to the left of the Town Landing at the head of Wianno Avenue. The end of Wianno Pier is visible at right. c. 1880s.

Bathing Pavillion at the Cotocheset Hotel which is now the Wianno Club. c. 1890.

January 15, 1884

Arrangements have been made and contracts let for the building of a new wharf at the beach. To Ira L. Hinckley is awarded the contract of furnishing piles; J. K. & B. Sears of Hyannis will furnish lumber and Nelson H. Bearse will superintend the construction of it.

Cotocheset House Burned

July 19, 1887

The quiet of the little village of Wianno beach, Osterville, was changed Sunday to that of a more romantic scene. About 6 o'clock in the morning fire was discovered issuing from a room in the third floor by two waiters, Lizzie Small and Hattie Lovell. At that time, the occupants of the Cotocheset House were asleep. They were soon aroused however, and as but very little air was stirring at that time, the guests had considerable time to remove their personal effects before the fire made much progress. All of the neighboring cottages turned out and rendered all possible assistance. The guests were cheerfully given accommodations in the cottages nearby. In less than two hours the large building was burned to the ground. About 80 per cent of all the household and personal effects were saved and the principal loss was on the third floor where but little was removed.

The Cotocheset House, under the able management of Mrs. Granville Ames, was never doing the business as it was at the present time. Every room was occupied and engaged until the close of the

Seaview Avenue looking west from beyond the Cotocheset House. c. 1900.

Wianno Pier at the foot of Wianno Avenue. c. 1900.

Wianno Pier at the foot of Wianno Avenue. c. 1900.

season. During the progress of the fire, everything seemed quiet, as it were, but very little excitement prevailed and everybody escaped without a single accident, something very unusual at such a time.

Mrs. Ames, with her usual tact and enterprise, lost no time, and before the fire was extinguished had carpenters at work erecting a new dining hall, and the business is to proceed without any interruption. During all this excitement a sumptuous repast was provided underneath a tent at promptly 2 o'clock, the usual Sunday hour of which the Patriot correspondent partook.

The Cotocheset House was owned by J. C. Stevens of Boston, who will undoubtedly erect at once a larger hotel here. The loss is estimated at about $25,000. The building was well covered by insurance, and Mrs. Ames' property, partially.

November 1, 1887

Work is being pushed forward upon the new hotel at the beach by a large force of workmen.

January 24, 1888

The masons are intending to commence plastering the new Hotel at the beach today (Tuesday).

March 6, 1888

We have received plans of the new Cotocheset House at Osterville and from them we learn what a really fine structure it is to be when completed. Mrs. Ames is deserving of all that the company is providing her and in her hands the new hotel will be even more popular — if it is possible — than the old house.

July 17, 1888

The new hotel built by the Cotocheset Co. on Wianno Beach at Osterville is completed and is now filled with company.

The house occupies a space of about 160 x 75 feet; was built under the direct management of the company, who employed Mr. M. C. Waterhouse of Bourne as superintendent of construction, on the site of the original Cotocheset House destroyed by fire on a Sunday morning in July last.

The unparalleled success of Mrs. Granville Ames as a hotel manager, and the popularity gained during her administration of affairs of the old Cotocheset, brought to her assistance after the fire substantial friends, ready and willing to aid in again putting her in possession of a summer resort at Wianno Beach. The work of clearing up the ruins was commenced immediately, and a stock company was formed with Henry W. Wellington of Boston as president, and Geo. H. Phelps of Boston, William Lloyd Garrison, Jr., of Boston, J.

Wianno Club — Summer of 1986.

G. Holland of Brooklyn and F. T. Jones of Boston, as directors. The stock was at once subscribed among the principal summer residents at the beach. Plans were secured and as early as September work was begun in earnest on the new house. A contract was made with Messrs. John Hinckley & Son of Barnstable to furnish the building materials, and before the site was fairly cleared the first cargo of lumber was on the spot. Since that time the work has been pushed with vigor and now there stands one of the finest appointed hotels in southeastern Massachusetts. Taste and adaptability have been studied in design and arrangements throughout, and an inspection of the house shows that there is not an undesirable room in it — all are of fair size, light, airy and neatly and cosily furnished. A transom over each door with a patented adjustable fastening gives good ventilation, and large windows in each room afford plenty of light and an unobstructed view of the surroundings.

The house is finished in oil throughout, there being no paint about the inside building. The wainscoting is of whitewood with trimmings of same and North Carolina pine. The grand staircase is finely finished with oiled maple stairposts and balusters and yellow pine treads. The appearance on entering the main entrance is at once pleasing and strikes the eye of the visitor with its beautiful finish and tasty arrangement.

Connected with the house is a laundry, stable, etc., all supplied by the complete system of water works which supply the main building. The house is lighted throughout with gas, manufactured on the premises, and the kitchens are provided with heated tables and dressers, and the most approved cooking arrangements. In fact, nothing is wanting that is usually found in this department of a first-class appointed hotel.

A Post-Office, named Wianno, has been established at the hotel, and is in the charge of Miss Jennie Hinckley, who is Postmistress.

The cost of the hotel with furnishings has been between $45,000 and $50,000, and there can be accommodated with the cottages connected with the house between 200 and 300 guests.

It is no surprise that this house is now taxed to its fullest capacity to accommodate its patrons. It is now full and so are all its cottages, and the season is one of the liveliest ever experienced at Wianno, and we congratulate Mrs. Ames on the auspicious opening of the new Cotocheset.

In this connection it will not be out of place to mention some of the most prominent cottages at the beach. Among them are H. W. Scoville of Waterbury, Ct.; C. B. Prescott and family of Newton; W. M. Sands and family of New York; W. H. Allen and family of Cincinnati; H. W. Wellington and family of Boston; Mrs. E. B. Chace and family of Valley Falls, R.I.; W. A. Dictrick and family of Covington, Ky.; Dr. Edward Tatum and family of Philadelphia; George H. Phelps and family of Boston.

The situation of the Cotocheset is one of the finest. It stands on a bluff above the beach, which affords the best of bathing facilities, and fronts a beautiful pine grove of large trees. Seashore and country are so closely combined that it is hard to realize that by passing through the spacious halls of the house one can choose for a stroll the white sand beach of the seashore or the shady lanes and walks leading through beautiful woods that will compare with many inland spots far better known to tourists. Such are some of the advantages of this resort and it is no wonder that the very best of our business and professional men have pitched their tent upon this spot.

From the bluff one has a splendid view of the Sound all dotted over with sails of every size, and the steamships of the various lines between the centres of trade. Within one hundred feet of the bluff runs a nicely laid out street, either side of which is lined by the finest cottages to be found at any summer resort in the country. Playgrounds, swings, lawn tennis courts, bathing houses, boats, and every facility for taking comfort are most invitingly close at hand. The entire grounds are beautifully shaded, and being constantly fanned by the pure cool and invigorating breezes from off the Sound can never be uncomfortably warm, even in the very hottest weather. Beautiful drives, over the finest roads in this part of the state, are accessible in all directions. Fishing and boating of the finest order are to be secured here, and the beach for bathing, especially for children, is unsurpassed. At this point the water is but little affected by the tides which make bathing and boating possible at any stage of the tide.

What more is needed to make this spot a paradise to the weary and careworn?

Those who planned and laid out this spot hoped to make an ideal summer resort, and they have succeeded so far as is possible. They purchased the entire section known as Wianno Beach and by their judicious handling, its exclusiveness has been kept up, and the social status of the community maintained to the highest degree. It is exclusive in as far that the projectors desired that no one should locate there but what was acceptable to those already there; and in this they have succeeded. The result is that in no corresponding area in town is found so great a value in taxable property, and every new cottage adds additional value to the town, and beauty and life to the locality. Long may the growth continue and the dwellers reap their full proportion of comfort and happiness.

July 31, 1888

Mrs. Ames of Cotocheset House gave a ball for the benefit of Village Improvement Society on Friday evening. About $40.00 was raised.

August 17, 1888

A party from the Cotocheset House went out with Mr. Adams on Saturday and caught four large sharks, one of them six feet long and weighed 200 lbs.

October 2, 1888

The Post Office at Wianno is closed for the season. Most of the guests have left the hotel. Nearly all the cottages are closed. The inclemency of the weather has made rather a short season.

February 19, 1889

Several thousand dollars are being expended upon the Cotocheset House in alterations and improvements.

May 14, 1889

State Inspector Coon was in town last week, whose duty it is to look after the safety of buildings under the direction of the state department of inspection, and examined the Cotocheset House.

He was very much pleased with the new house and pronounced it the finest seaside hotel he had inspected, and also spoke in very flattering terms of Mrs. Ames, the proprietor and manager.

July 23, 1889
The Cotocheset House is full to overflowing.

March 18, 1890
Mrs. Ames of the Cotocheset House has contracted for 300 tons of ice to be delivered at West Barnstable depot from Tilton, N.H. Four carloads arrived on Friday morning. Good demand for teams. The "Fish Co." have ordered 125 tons.

July 1, 1890
Most of the cottages at the Beach are now occupied. Guests are arriving daily at the Cotocheset House.

January 6, 1891
News was received here on Friday of the death of Mrs. James Tolman of Boston, for a number of years a summer resident of Wianno.

April 14, 1891
The wind and tide of last week did a considerable amount of damage at Wianno beach, destroying nearly all the bathing houses, washing away part of the bank and tearing down the bulkheads erected for the preservation of the bank.

May 5, 1891
Mr. Hollingsworth of Boston has recently been at Wianno and has had his lot at the beach nicely cleared up and we hope to see a fine cottage soon, as one more addition to our summer residences.

June 2, 1891
The Post Office at Wianno opened June 1st. Miss Jennie L. Hinckley, the Postmistress, having resigned, Mrs. T. H. Ames has been appointed Postmistress. Miss Genie M. Lovell will act as assistant.

August 4, 1891
J. A. Guyer, the Hyannis jeweler, has another invoice of souvenir spoons and among them a lot with "Wianno" on them.

December 8, 1891
Mr. Tiffany of New York spent Saturday and Sunday at his cottage, "The Cones," at Wianno. Mr. Charles Daniel has been enlarging and repairing the cottage, grading the lawn and putting it into very nice shape.

February 9, 1892
We have received the sad intelligence of the death at Brooklyn, Feb. 3rd, of Mrs. Christine (Chaplin) Brush, the well-known author and artist. Mrs. Brush was the wife of Rev. Alfred Brush of New Utrecht, N.Y., and the daughter of the late Jeremiah Chaplin of Boston. Her family was the first to make a summer home in Osterville and identified themselves with all the best interests of our little village.

May 10, 1892
Wianno Beach and the avenue are the busiest and liveliest places in the village just now. There is a small army of people engaged there at present. Carpenters, masons, painters, men who are cleaning up the grounds around the cottages, paper hangers, housecleaners, all combined, make it a busy place just now.

June 5, 1894
J. Mott Hallowell, Esq., Medford, is boarding at Owen Lewis' for a few days.

August 7, 1894
Wianno. — 57 guests arrived August. 1st, the largest number on record.

August 14, 1894
Wianno — 88 transients have taken dinner at the Cotocheset since Aug. 2.

October 16, 1894
Mr. Marcus Hollingsworth is to have a house built at Wianno.

April 22, 1895
The new steel windmill, erected by parties from Boston at Wianno Beach for Mr. H. D. Tiffany, fell down on Friday; cause, a flaw in one of the steel braces. The same parties are erecting another in its place.

Commemorative demitasse cup and saucer featuring the new Cotocheset House. c. 1900s.

July 8, 1895

The Cotocheset, under the management of Mrs. T. H. Ames, is nearly full of guests.

Mr. William Lloyd Garrison of Brookline occupies the very pretty Bay View cottage. He has leased the Edgewood to Mr. John F. Brown.

Mr. and Mrs. William H. Wellington, Miss Anna F. Wellington, Mr. Stanwood Wellington, Mrs. Franklin H. Elms, of Boston, Mrs. W. H. Blodgett, Miss Blodgett, of Newton, are recent arrivals at the Cotocheset.

Miss H. B. Tolman has opened Green Lodge.

Mr. H. W. Wellington, of Newton, who has just returned from California, has arrived with his family at his summer home.

Mr. Cross, of Baltimore, has arrived at his very pretty new cottage, built this spring on the cliff. He has as guests Dr. and Mrs. Babcock, of Baltimore.

"Old Hundred" is occupied by Mr. Frederick Harris.

Mr. H. D. Tiffany is at the Cones for the season.

Mr. H. W. Scoville, of Waterbury, Conn., has arrived at Comfort cottage, Mr. W. L. Allen, of Newton, at Sunset Lodge, and Mrs. Dennis at the Hallowell cottage.

October 7, 1895

"The Cotocheset" closed the summer season of 1895 Tuesday, Oct. 1st and Mrs. Ames left for her winter home Thursday, Oct. 3rd. The season has been very successful, more guests having remained through September than ever before, the average being fifty-four. Several of the cottages have been closed for the winter but the majority intend keeping open until the middle of Oct.

April 6, 1896

Messrs. Fritz and Olin Talbot of Longwood are at Mrs. T. H. Ames'.

April 20, 1896

Messrs. F. W. Parsons and Mark Hollingsworth of Boston are here looking after their cottages at Wianno.

December 14, 1896

A dandelion in full bloom was picked near the shore at Wianno by Miss Isabel Boult, Dec. 7th.

April 12, 1897

Alfred Jones Esq., of Boston, was here the past week, superintending the work on several windmills, partially erected last fall, and looking over the other Wianno property of which he is manager.

May 31, 1897

The "Cotocheset House" is open for the summer and guests are already here. Capt. Daniel P. Bursley has opened the Cotocheset stable. Several cottages are occupied and more to be very soon. Wianno is waking from her long winter sleep and preparing for the unusually big season before her.

June 21, 1897

During the storm of Tuesday, 17th, the lightning struck "The Cotocheset" near the desk in the office, entering where the telephone wire is connected. The shock was felt all around and frightened some, but no serious damage was done. The horse of Mr. John W. Williams, Jr., which was standing at the rear of the Hotel became frightened and ran for some distance, leaving the broken wagon on the Avenue.

September 11, 1899

Not a little excitement prevailed early Sunday evening, Sept. 3rd, when the Church bells rang a fire alarm. It was soon discovered that the town "dump" near Wianno was on fire, but with the quick response of nearly every man in the village the flames were soon under control. Fortunately it was discovered in season to prevent a conflagration that would have swept the village.

November 20, 1899

New York parties have just purchased of Mr. Joseph Stevens of Boston a parcel of land known as Picnic Grove at Wianno Beach. The lot contains about twenty acres, and it is reported that a large hotel will be erected in the near future.

July 23, 1900

About forty Cotocheset guests assembled in the hotel parlors Thursday evening at eight o'clock to play progressive euchre. There were six tables, six sitting at each table. It was one of the most enjoyable evenings that the guests of the Cotocheset have had this season.

November 26, 1900

Mr. and Mrs. Harris of Springfield, with Mr. Frasier, architect, of Boston, have been down making arrangements for their new cottage which is soon to be erected on the site of their old one, well-known as "Old Hundred." This cottage is to be moved to a lot on Wianno Avenue, in the rear of East Bay Lodge.

November 26, 1900

Mrs. Halliday's cottage is soon to be erected in the village on the bluff in the rear of Mrs. Ames' cottage. Mr. Paine has this work in his charge, and Mr. Joseph Tallman, the mason, work for both cottages.

June 8, 1903

Quite a number of cottages at Wianno are open for the season. The Cotocheset and Wianno Post Office opened June 1st. Work on the new Episcopal Church on the avenue is progressing rapidly.

July 3, 1905

There will be a regatta under the auspices of the Wianno Yacht Club tomorrow at 11 A.M.

Wianno Yacht Club

February 27, 1906

The Wianno Yacht Club membership since the close of the Racing Season of 1905 have held various meetings at the Clubhouse at Wianno, Mass., and at Boston. There is a general desire among the membership to make the Racing Season of 1906 an exceptionally interesting and successful one, and it is particularly desired by the members of the Club that a more general interest and participation in the races of the club shall take place among the Nantucket and Vineyard Sound community.

With this in view the Club has amended its by-laws and conditions of membership and inaugurated what has been termed "Yachting Members," the object being to enable those primarily interested in the racing of boats to become members of the Club at a nominal admission fee and nominal annual dues.

Like all other clubs, yachts to compete in the Club races must be steered by Club members. Heretofore those not members of the Club could only participate in the open or invitation races, and the above class of membership has been established in the hope that many not now connected with the Club will become yachting members, so that they can join in the Club races and sail their boats.

The Racing Rules of the Club have been so modified as to provide for classes such that are suitable for the Cape catboats, as well as the modern and more expensive craft.

Wianno — Cape Cod

Night on Wianno's shore. The sombre pines
Lifted their branches to the ebon sky
Like sable plumes — the silent stars
Looked down upon the waters of the bay
As sentinels upon a sleeping world.
When Lo! Above Hyannis' distant light
The full moon arose. In its wake
It left a trail of crimson and of gold
Across the ripples of the restless sea.
The midnight breeze, from far away
A wonderer, tireless in its flight,
Lingered a moment in its course,
Whispered this message — and was gone.

The Message

Behold! Yon flaming Orb — The ocean's ebb and
    flow
The myriad worlds that move through endless
    space
A universe controlled by Law — bespeaking Mind,
Purpose and Thought in all created things.
And cease to doubt, there is a power supreme
That rules all life, and which will bring
Perfection — out of everything.
                    Written by Wm. J. Seaver
                    August 5, 1906

July 27, 1908

A special policeman, Mr. Murphy, an ex-member of the Boston Force, has been appointed by the Town of Barnstable for Wianno.

June 3, 1913

The teamsters are very busy at present carting furniture for the new cottages at Wianno head.

April 12, 1915

Mrs. Thankful Ames is here and getting the Cotocheset House ready for summer.

November 29, 1915

Work has begun on Mr. Crossett's house at the beach and it is considered one of the largest houses built in that locality.

January 31, 1916

It is rumored that the Cotocheset hotel has been sold to a stock company, and that it will be improved.

Hotel Changes Hands

February 14, 1916

Agreements have been signed recently whereby parties representing the summer colony at Osterville and Wianno have purchased all the property of the Cotocheset Company.

It is proposed to change the Wianno Yacht Club to the Wianno Club. The Cotocheset Hotel will be used as the clubhouse and will be the center of the athletic and social activities of the community.

It is reported that about $50,000 worth of stock will be issued to finance the proposition.

Extensive alterations and renovations are already under way, including a new dining room on the oceanfront and a large ballroom. Twenty-one new bathrooms are being installed, also electric lights, room telephones, and steam heating, as the house is to be open all the year.

Land has been acquired for an 18-hole golf course, the construction of which is to be started immediately.

The clubhouse will be under the management of Robert P. Peckett of "Peckett's on Sugar Hill," Franconia, N.H., who will divide his time between the two places.

The club membership will be enlarged to take in a limited number of friends of the present members.

It is expected that the clubhouse will be ready by the 15th of June, and many requests for rooms are being received. It is proposed to make this a family club.

The executive committee includes E. E. Blodgett, chairman; W. B. H. Dowse, commodore; Horace L. Bearse, vice-commodore, H. B. Day, treasurer; Thomas F. Baxter, George S. Baldwin, and William Garrison, Jr.

January 7, 1918

The Wianno icehouses have been filled with good ice seven inches thick.

November 15, 1920

While excavating the ground in Garrison's grove, recently purchased by Mr. Wm. P. Halliday, several skeletons of Indians have been found. This is quite a curiosity to both the young and old, and seems to prove that this place was once the burying ground of the Indians.

December 27, 1928

The Wianno Club is having its auto parking space enlarged. In the spring the added space will be paved.

When golf at Wianno commenced, the club house was built on the corner of Seaview Avenue and what is now West Street. The building is now a private home; the architectural configuration is easily recognized.

Wianno Post Office — Biggest little Post Office in the whole wide world.

Miss Bertha West, Wianno postmistress for nearly a quarter of a century, October, 1922 to July, 1947.

The Biggest Little Post Office
In the Whole Wide World

Wianno, one of the most popular and exclusive summer colonies on Cape Cod, has been served since 1887 by "The Biggest Little Post Office in the World." Throughout the sixty years of its existence this office has had the unusual distinction of never having had a male postmaster. The guilding factor has always been a woman, and serving the public as an efficient arm of a vital government bureau has proven to be a matter of unique ingenuity throughout the history of this particular office.

Service to the summer colony started in July of 1887 under the mistressship of Jennie L. Hinckley, daughter of the Osterville postmaster, George H. Hinckley. The post office was established in the famous predecessor of the Wianno Club, known as the Cotocheset House. Private boxes were not to be had, and the residents received their mail much in the manner of a modern army post. The postmistress would sort the mail and at an appointed hour the patrons would assemble in the hotel and a reading of the names was held, each receiving his or her mail in alphabetical turn.

With the Wianno office not yet established as a "class" office the mail was delivered there more or less by virtue of generosity. The Osterville office received its delivery from the stage coach line, operated by Captain Bursley, running from West Barnstable to Osterville. Miss Hinckley met the coach in Osterville, and "rode the mail" to the Cotocheset House. Later she carried it in her own horse drawn dog-cart.

Sometime later the government authorized the hotel to have individual boxes for the mail, and these were installed in the hotel office.

During the summer of 1887, however, the Cotocheset House was destroyed by fire, and this forced the moving of the post office to an adjacent lot where it was housed in the Wayside cottage. Here it remained until a small building was erected to facilitate postal service. This same building was later moved to its present location, and is still in use.

Initially a fourth class post office, it has risen in ranks to one of third class. During the sixty years the office has had four postmistresses, Miss Hinckley serving from 1887 to 1891; T. H. Ames from 1891 to 1915; Sarah H. Boult from 1915 to 1922, and the present postmistress Miss Bertha West has been serving since October, 1922.

Five of the former clerks in the office were participants in World War II, one of whom was a casualty and one a prisoner of war in Germany.

Many of the patrons of the post office are second and third generations of notable families who have been served by this tiny office. Such notable persons as Andrew Adie, Francis W. Bird, Charles Sumner Bird, Edward E. Blodgett, Horace L. Bearse, Rev. Maltbie D. Babcock, Alfred Jones, Horace Frazer, Chief Justice F. Delano Putnam, E. A. Carter, J. S. Coffin, R. E. Paine, John T. Underwood of Underwood Typewriters Henry B. Day, William E. Jones, George Briggs, Frederick Harris, J. Mott Hallowell, Judge Richard Cross, W. L. Garrison, son of the famous abolitionist, and many others may be counted among the patrons of this, "The Biggest Little Post Office in the World", and possessor of one of the most colorful histories in postal annuls.

Bertha West Retires
Wianno Postmaster

Miss Bertha West, who recently retired as postmaster of the Wianno post-office, is deserving of a special tribute. Her long years of service—24 years, 8 months—alone prove the value of her services; but, it seems, she has given unusual quality of service.

From an interview with the editor, we quote Mrs. Louis Burlingham, of Wianno, as expressing tribute to Miss West for rendering splendid service in the face of serious health handicaps. Indeed, Mrs. Burlingham said Miss West performed an unbelievable job, it was so very well done. As a patron of the post-office herself she could speak for the patrons, who always found Miss West cheery and accommodating and who enjoyed her perfect service.

The Wianno post-office is open only in the summer from June 1 to September 30 and has grown from an office in name only in the old Cotocheset House in 1887 to a building of its own. There it is known today as the biggest "little" post-office in the world.

Wianno — A Retrospective Glance

Wianno lies about a mile to the south of Osterville Village, and was known to the old time native as "The Beach" or "The Cliffs." Observed from a fishing boat there was seen an undulating line of sandy bluffs twenty to forty feet above sea level with an inviting white beach at their base extending for a few miles in gentle curves. These headlands carried a well developed growth of picturesque pitch pines interspersed with occasional patches of oaks. The whole elevation fronted the south with a perfect exposure. An observer from the wooded bank-top looked out upon a wide, but relatively shallow, expanse of the Atlantic known locally as Vineyard Sound. To the southwest rose in dim outline the island of Martha's Vineyard. To the northeast was sharply defined the graceful and bending line of the Craigville and Hyannisport shore which lent to the view a restful limitation and pleasantly contrasting band of color.

Behind the Wianno frontage, snug in deep pine woods, were a group of three clear fresh-water ponds where black bass, striped perch and pickerel were plentiful. And in the sound, bluefish ran in generous schools in constant pursuit of the menhaden, and were the principal attraction for sportsmen who came to that region in its primitive years.

Prior to 1873 the ocean frontage bore only a casual relation to the village of Osterville although two weatherbeaten fish houses stood above high water mark on the beach opposite the head of what is now called Eel River, and is actually a narrow finger of West Bay. Legend tells us that Uncle John Bates used one of these structures for his fishing activities on bay and ocean, and reports his annual mowing of the salt hay at the bay head. Uncle Isaac Hodges utilized another for equally prosaic but productive purposes. Good fresh water was obtained by sinking shallow wells on the upper beach level. And on one of the nearby tongues of land protruding into West Bay, salt hay was gathered by Uncle Worthington Crosby, a picturesque member of the boat-building family that was to make the Cape Catboat a household word for three generations.

A new chapter opened for this region in 1873 when the Osterville Land Company, composed of Boston business men, took out a State Charter in May of that year. Influenced by the successful real estate development at Cottage City on Martha's Vineyard, they purchased an extensive acreage lying between East and West Bay, and the land was carefully mapped and plotted in lots, as set forth in the still authoritative plan drawn by Granger and Hobart, Engineers, in November, 1873. Visions of profitable operations in shore real estate were, however, rudely dissipated by the sudden panic which shook the banking world in that disastrous year, and it was not until five more years had passed that the enterprise regained new and effective momentum.

The Cotocheset House (adopting a name that occurred as early as 1658 in a deed given by the Indians to the proprietors of Barnstable) had been erected in a sightly pine grove commanding the waterfront as a focal point of the land development scheme. It had proved unprofitable during the depression period although Erastus Scudder of Osterville and Daniel P. Bursley of West Barnstable struggled manfully as successive managers. But it was not until the summer of 1878 that the hotel squared away for a long and successful voyage under the intelligent direction of Mrs. Granville Ames of Osterville, a woman of exceptional character and competence.

Thirty-eight years later the Cotocheset Property was sold to the Wianno Club, its capital stock being purchased at $100 a share. This purchase included the hotel building which had replaced the original structure of 1873 that burned to the ground July 17, 1887. The purchasers remodelled the building developing it into an adequate modern clubhouse, which is one of the best equipped establishments of its kind on the New England seaboard. In its earlier phase the Cotocheset House had catered primarily to guests from Greater Boston, New York and Philadelphia, and finally to families from most of the larger cities as far west as Cleveland, Chicago and Detroit.

Alongside the hotel there had grown up a steadily expanding cottage community which has flourished for more than sixty years. Henry W. Wellington, a Boston Merchant, was the first to build there a summer home which he occupied in 1876. At his passing a friend described him as "the founder and patriarch of the small colony on the lovely shore of the Cape bound together by a common sympathy and common aim." To this nest of summer pioneers came the writer's parents in 1878, which led to their building a cottage a year later.

The summer life of those days faced the waterfront. Bathing was the great daily rite for young and old, with the clan assembling just before noon. A quiet ocean with no undertow, and no treacherous and sudden deeps, with water registering close to 70 degrees Fahrenheit made bathing safe and delightful. The writer can recall no case of accidental drowning over a period of more than fifty years. Children soon became amphibious, naturally graduating into accomplished swimmers and competent and clever sailors. Terrestrial pursuits included bicycling, bowling, tennis, with weekend evenings of charades and informal dancing; and each season the Osterville baseball team, made up of both villagers and visitors, played the local nines of Cotuit, Craigville, Hyannis, Sandwich and Yarmouth.

These were the days of sand roads and horse-drawn rigs, of cotton window screens, oil lamps, hand pumps, and no plumbing. Mosquitoes swarmed, woodticks thrived in the long beach grass, and horseflies drank the blood of quadrupeds like winged ogres. Clothing fortunately was decidedly unconventional, but stout and lasting. And in bathing, the matrons wore costumes befitting an Eskimo.

The mature social life centered primarily about the cottage of Mrs. Elizabeth Buffum Chace, for many years chancellor of Brown University. Lectures, musicales, teas and dramatics were the order of the day, and guests with special gifts or reputation lent variety to these occasions. The Rev. Moncure D. Conway, a distinguished liberal clergyman, for many years the occupant of a popular London pulpit, took an active and stimulating part. Among the well-known figures of the day the actor Joseph Jefferson, who, with his family, joined for a time the cottage community, lent the charm of a rare personality to the social life. He was adept with rod and reel, and in company with Grover Cleveland fished the secluded fresh water ponds with results that are embalmed in local legend.

The ocean fishing, then so rewarding, was a daily attraction to all comers. The skipper John Freeman Adams with his catboat the "Chip," and later the "Florence," and Capt. Nelson H. Bearse of East Bay with the "Curlew" and the "Mischief" were at the pier each morning. With skill and caution they served their patrons, taking them to the Beacon, to Bishop and Clerks lighthouse, or to the fishing grounds near Horseshoe Shoal. By daylight and by moonlight sailing parties skirted those pleasant shores or made a bolder journey to Cottage City or Edgartown, or to Nantucket with its quaint and appealing sense of detachment. And the West Bay Skippers took parties to Tallman's Oyster house on "The Narrows" to enjoy the unequalled shellfish of Cotuit.

The relations between the summer visitors and the village community have ever been cordial and cooperative. The Osterville Free Library, founded in 1881, was one of the earliest expressions of goodwill on the part of the newcomers toward their Cape neighbors, and stands as a continuing bond between them. Honesty, kindliness, and straightforwardness have been outstanding traits among the Osterville folk, and these characteristics have done much to encourage the steady development of the summer colony.

William Bradford Homer Dowse   Fanny Lee Dowse

September 9, 1895

Mr. Dowse of Cincinnati has bought of Messrs. Stevens & Parsons a tract of land on East Bay and adjoining, embracing the lumber yard and the "Dry Island," and will have a house put up there this fall.

April 20, 1896

A large house is being built on Dry Island, East Bay, by contractor Chester Bearse for Mr. Dowse of Boston.

September 11, 1899

Mr. Dowse has also closed his residence on Dry Island and with his family returned to the city.

August 7, 1905

The pony team of Mr. Dowse collided with a heavier team on Main Street Wednesday, overturning the smaller and spilling out three young ladies without injury. This collision startled Mr. I. Crocker's horse at the store and he ran into the Baptist Church yard, breaking the lamp post, and stopping when tangled in one of the trees.

Residence of William Bradford Homer Dowse. Destroyed in the Hurricane of 1944. This is now the site of the bath house at Dowse's Beach. c. 1910.

Boardwalk leading to the residence of William Bradford Homer Dowse at Wianno. c. 1920.

April 26, 1928

In the death of William Bradford Homer Dowse, who died suddenly at the Phillips House, Mass. Gen. Hospital, the past week, Osterville loses another old time summer resident and the fifth of heads of families who were the founders of the summer colony at Wianno Beach, now famed as one of the most popular summer resorts in the country. Mr. Dowse was a great lover of this place and owned a summer home here where he spent what time he could aside from his extremely busy life as a lawyer and his manufacturing interests in this country and abroad. He was long president of the Home Market Club and was affiliated with a vast number of clubs, societies and philanthropic movements. As the representative of Gov. Coolidge in the tercentenary celebration of the sailing of the Pilgrim Fathers in England and Holland, he was received in audience by the Queen of Holland. As the Deputy Governor of the Commonwealth he was feted and honored by receptions and various festivities at the University of Leyden. The beautiful library in Sherborn and the memorial erected to the Soldiers of Sherborn who died in the various wars of the United States from 1674 to date are a monument to his generosity to his native town. Among the many clubs of which he was president and director was the Wianno Club of this village. In his passing the world has lost a great industrial leader, a man of brilliant intellect and great activity. The hearts of Osterville people sadden when we think of so many sudden deaths the past three months of those who have done so much towards the building up of our village in the past. He leaves a wife, Fanny Lee Dowse, three daughters, Mrs. Franklyn D. Putnam, Miss Margaret Dowse and Mrs. Sinclair Weeks, to whom is extended sympathy in their bereavement.

Watercolor painted in 1890s. Note schooner at left of Dry Island and the hunting blind under the hill. When the home of W. B. H. Dowse was destroyed in the 1944 hurricane, the bath house at Dowse's Beach replaced it on this rise.

George H. Phelps.
Mr. Phelps worked at and managed George Frost & Co., clothing manufacturers, Boston.

Melissa (Frost) Phelps.
Mrs. Phelps was the daughter of George Frost who founded George Frost & Co., Boston.

Parents of Margery and Marie Phelps. Margery Phelps married Francis Bird in 1912.

Death of F. W. Bird

August 12, 1918

Francis W. Bird of Walpole, son of Charles Sumner Bird, died Friday morning at the Massachusetts General Hospital after a brief illness. Mr. Bird underwent an operation which was followed by pneumonia, causing his death.

Mr. Bird was born in Walpole in 1881, was graduated from Harvard University in 1904 and from the Harvard Law School two years later. He served for three years as assistant United States district attorney for the southern district of New York. He had charge of the investigation of the sugar fraud in Louisiana for the Department of Justice, and was also engaged in studying the customs service of the country, with a view of approving the collection of customs duties and a reformation of the service.

His work in this line attracted the attention of high Treasury officials and on March 11, 1911, he

Mr. and Mrs. Francis Bird — 1912. Flower Girl — Margery Fay, niece to Mrs. Bird.

was appointed by President Taft United States Appraiser at New York City, one of the most important offices in the custom service of the country. He resigned this place in June, 1912, to engage in the Progressive movement, and was one of Col. Roosevelt's most enthusiastic supporters for the nomination against President Taft. That same year he was married to Margery Willard Phelps, daughter of Mr. and Mrs. George H. Phelps. Three children were born to them.

In December, 191?, he bought the Boston Evening Record and Daily Advertiser, which he edited until some months ago, when he disposed of his interests in both papers.

October 4, 1928

The death of Mrs. Melissa Frost Phelps, wife of the late George H. Phelps of Boston, came as a surprise and regret to many. Mrs. Phelps had been in failing health for some time. The end came peacefully at her home in Jamaica Plain, Sept. 24. Mr. Phelps passed away in 1914. They owned a beautiful summer home at Wianno and spent many years here where they were well known among the summer colony. Since his death she has not spent much time here. She leaves two daughters, Mrs. Henry Fay of Brookline and Mrs. Francis Bird of East Walpole.

Wianno Waterfront — c. 1885. The Chace cottage, later Blodgett cottage, was located immediately west of the town landing at the head of Wianno Avenue, on Sea View Avenue. The house was destroyed in the Hurricane of 1944.

247

A gathering of some early Wianno families.

Left to right, back row of four, standing: Mrs. Mary Tolman, Mr. James Tolman, Arnold B. Chace, and Mrs. John Wyman; middle row, Madam Elizabeth Chace, Mrs. Arnold B. Chace, Arthur Wyman, Mr. John Wyman; children seated on ground: Malcolm Chace, Bessie Carter, Richard Tolman, Daisy Chace, and Maud Chace. c. 1885.

Cotocheset Club Pier — 1885.
1. Helen Jones. 2. Mr. Alfred Jones 3. Mrs. Alfred Jones 4. Laura Jones 5. Eugene Shippen 6. Lucretia Hallowell 7. Carl Davis 8. Fannie Baldwin 9. Bessie Horton 10. ? 11. Jessie Ormsbee 12. ? 13. Ernest Walton 14. Evelyn Smally 15. Lucy Davis 16. Agnes Garrison 17. Bessie Walton 18. Margaret Swan 19. Richard Hallowell 20. ? Holland 21. ? 22. ? 23. Billy Garrison 24. Billy Moran 25. Frank Hallowell 26. J. Mott Hallowell 27. Lois Howe 28. Frank Garrison.

Two Hallowell boys, seated on the steps of a Sea View Avenue cottage, talking with actor, Mr. Joseph Jefferson (1829-1905). The two boys standing have not been identified. c. 1885.

Residence of R. E. Paine at Wianno. Built by Daniel Bros. on the waterfront at the head of Parker Road, the house was torn down c. 1935.

May 8, 1899

The fine summer residence of Mr. Frank A. Day, Sr. at Wianno, which has been in the process of building during the last few months, is completed, and is now being furnished by Eagleston Bros. of Hyannis. This is one of the most spacious and ornamental structures at the beach and reflects great credit upon the contractor and builder, Mr. Ira L. Hinckley of this village.

Mr. and Mrs. Frank A. Day, Sr. Mr. Day was an investment banker with R. L. Day & Co.

September 9, 1895

Mr. H. B. Day of Newton has purchased some land from W. L. Garrison at Wianno and is going to build there this year.

Henry B. Day and his wife, Julia (Stevens) Day. Their Wianno home on Sea View Avenue is no longer standing. He was a banker affiliated with Day Trust Company which later became New England Merchants' Bank, and is now the Bank of New England.

The George Ernest Briggs Family — c. 1915. Left to right: Effie (Backer) Briggs holding Elizabeth, Barbara, George Ernest Briggs holding Sara. Mr. Briggs was president of Lexington Lumber Company. George Ernest Briggs was the son of Rev. Thomas Briggs, pastor at Osterville Baptist Church in the late 1870s.

"Saucy Top" is believed to be the first house built west of Eel River on Sea View Avenue. The home of George Ernest Briggs, it is owned in 1988 by Mrs. Richard S. Taylor, a granddaughter. c. 1900s.

Eel River — c. 1910.

Eel River — 1986. Taken from approximately the same spot near the home of Mr. Roger Wellington on Garrison's Point, looking south towards Sea View Avenue.

Sea View Avenue — c. 1910. Looking east, the head of Eel River is on left — Nantucket Sound at right.

November 18, 1879

The foundation is being laid for a new house for Wm. Lloyd Garrison, Jr., of Boston, near the Hotel. The stock is to be got out of Maine. Mr. Garrison was here last week.

October 3, 1882

Another new house at the beach for Mr. Wm. L. Garrison is being built.

December 4, 1888

Mr. Charles Daniel is building a cottage for Mr. William Lloyd Garrison at the beach.

May 21, 1889

Mr. William Lloyd Garrison, wife and son, W. L. Garrison, Jr., spent Saturday and Sunday at "Edgewood," their new cottage at Wianno.

April 3, 1899

Mr. W. L. Garrison and family, of Boston, are at Pine Cottage.

---

*Note concerning the Garrison Family: Charles Garrison, son of William Lloyd Garrison, Jr., married Margaret Minot Carret.

George Naylor Talbot   Florence (Dyer) Talbot

George N. Talbot

Mrs. Ruth Plimpton of Wianno, daughter of Dr. Fritz Talbot, has supplied the following family history. "My grandfather, George N. Talbot, lived in Brookline, Mass., and ran a dry goods business in Fall River, called Bradley's. His son Stanley took over that business, and his son Rudolph developed the Talbot Store in Boston. Father and his brothers and sisters had a wonderful childhood in Osterville and were full of pranks. The police

used to chase them down the Wianno Club pier and they would jump off and swim away.

"My mother, Beatrice Bill, met Father while visiting his sister, Ruth Talbot, down here. After they were married and visiting in Osterville, Mother took a long walk by herself one day, and came back and told Father that she had discovered the most beautiful point of land where you could see spectacular sunsets. She urged him to come and see the point which is now the "Land's End" we live on.

"I am not sure when my grandparents, George and Florence Talbot, first came to Osterville, nor whether they bought or built what is now Manter Hall."

Fritz Bradley Talbot

December 29, 1927

Dr. Fritz B. Talbot of Wianno visited the school building on Tuesday and gave each child definite corrections and suggestions in posture. Dr. Talbot has offered prizes for the best posture and the greatest improvement in posture during the year. Another test will be given at the close of the year.

July 3, 1930

Dr. Fritz Talbot has arrived from New York with a 55-foot yacht. The family is here for the summer.

Hi Ga Ho —
(Hinkle-Gaff-Holmes)

September 13, 1887

Mr. D. H. J. Holmes of Cincinnati has recently bought of Russell Marston a tract of land adjoining Centerville River and extending back to the County road, intending another year to erect several cottages thereon. Mr. H. has also purchased some 15 acres adjoining, of Capt. C. A. Lovell.

November 1, 1887

Rumor that three large cottages are soon to be erected upon the land recently bought of Mr. Holmes of Cincinnati, of Capt. C. A. Lovell. Contractors and architects have been down to view the place, also workmen have commenced preparing the grounds.

January 24, 1888

Capt. W. H. Bearse is having the grounds of Messrs. Holmes & Co. cleared; and put in good order for three large houses to be built the coming season. A fine road has been graded through the premises by David J. Coleman, Esq. The place bids fair to be a very attractive one. Two hundred and fifty thousand bricks have been bought and are now being drawn to the premises. Also, a large quantity of stone for building purposes.

May 1, 1888

The contract has been made for the building of the two summer residences at Osterville for Mr. T. T. and M. C. Gaff of Cincinnati. Messrs. John Hinckley and Son are to furnish the building material and will hire the help. It is said these places will cost not far from $12,000 each.

June 16, 1891

The Mesrs. Gaffs and Holmes are at their summer residences and our village is enlivened by their presence, and their fine equipages are often seen on our streets.

May 23, 1898

Messrs. C. M. Hinkle and T. T. Gaff, with their families, are at their homes at the Bluffs for the summer.

November 7, 1898

Extensive alterations and improvements are in progress at the Holmes Cottage at the "Bluffs." Mr. Chester Bearse of Centerville is in charge.

November 26, 1900

Schooner Maggie, Capt. Richard Hardy, is at Scudder's Wharf with a load of crushed stone for the Gaff-Hinkle Estate.

April 1, 1901

It is with sadness that we learn of the death of Mrs. J. W. Gaff. For many years she has spent the summer months in Osterville, and by her kindness and generosity has made many warm friends, who will sincerely mourn her death. She has been quite feeble for several years, and was spending the winter in Florida, where she died.

November 6, 1906

Mr. Gordon Shillito, who usually spends his summers at this place, died of heart trouble at the home of his brother, Stewart Shillito, in Cincinnati Nov. 3rd. Mr. Shillito was a retired member of the large dry goods firm of John Shillito & Co., Cincinnati, and had lived in Paris most of the time since 1882.

January 22, 1923

Thomas T. Gaff, for many years a summer resident of Osterville, owning one of the finest estates in the village, died on Wednesday last at the Hotel Lenox in Boston. Mr. Gaff was born in Aurora, Indiana, in 1855 and graduated from Harvard in 1876. For the past 25 years he had made his home in Washington, D.C. He was vice-president of the Nile, Bement, Pond Tool Mfg. Co. Mr. Gaff is survived by his wife and two sisters, Mrs. C. M. Hinkle and Mrs. Daniel Holmes, both of whom have residences here adjoining his.

June 24, 1926

Mrs. Hinkle and daughter Jean have arrived at their summer home at the Bluffs.

Thomas T. Gaff residence, built in 1887.

Home of Charles Hinkle, built about 1896. He was from Cincinnati, Ohio, and was in the bookbinding business.

Mary (Gaff) Hinkle, wife of the late Charles M. Hinkle, died in 1939. She was the daughter of James W. and Rachel C. Gaff. The family built their first home in Osterville in 1887.

Families of Hinkle, Gaff, Holmes, Shillito. Standing, l. to r., Daniel Holmes, Dickie (Gaff) Holmes, Zaidee Gaff, Thomas Gaff, Jane Shillito, Charles Hinkle, Mary (Gaff) Hinkle, Mary Shillito, Gordon Shillito. Seated, l. to r., Rachel Holmes, Grandmother Rachel Gaff, Violet Shillito, Polly Holmes (held by her grandmother). Foreground, l. to r., Elsie Holmes and Zaidee Gaff. c. 1888.

The Crew building the Thomas Gaff Home (the first on the Bluffs in Osterville) — c. 1887. Workmen: 1. Willie Harlow 2. ? 3. Gus Nickerson 4. Bert Coleman 5. ? 6. Nelson Hallett 7. E. Ladd 8. Chester Bearse 9. ? 10. George Whitford 11. Harry Tallman 12. Joseph Tallman, Sr. 13. Sylvester Whelden 14. Nelson Lewis 15. ?.

Hinkle Bridge built about 1906-07 spanned Centerville River and crossed to Long Beach. The bridge was dismantled in 1974.

Bumps River Bridge

An account of the Sales of the working of the Road and Making the Bridge over the river from Centerville to Osterville, September 25, 1840.

Lot No.	Description		
1	Sold to Gorham Crosby, 40 rods		$ 5.00
2	Sold to Gorham Crosby		28.70
3	Bridge 125 feet to Edward Thatcher		300.00
4	Marsh to Moses Sturgis 14½ rods	$3	43.50
5	Marsh to Moses Sturgis 9 rods	$2.65	23.85
6	Road to Moses Sturgis 30 rods	.30	9.00
7	Road to Asa Bliss 39 rods	.12½	4.87½
8	Road to Asa Bliss 33 rods	.12½	2.75
9	Road to Asa Bliss 30 rods	.12½	3.75
10	Road to Stephen C. Nye 42 rods	1.00	42.00
11	Road to Stephen C. Nye 42 rods	1.00	42.00
12	Road to Stephen C. Nye 30 rods	.17½	5.25
13	Road to Asa Bliss 36 rods	.12½	4.50
14	Road to Asa Bliss 40 rods	.15	6.00
15	Road to Moses Sturgis 40 rods	.10	4.00
16	Road to Asa Bliss 23 rods	.12	2.75
17	Road to Asa Bliss 35 rods	.20	7.00
			$492.93½

Bumps River Bridge, c. 1885. Looking west towards Osterville.

Seapuit

November 29, 1892

Mr. F. Parsons was in town last week, looking at lands lying near and adjoining Ishams and Middle Ponds, with a view to purchasing for western parties, if he can do so satisfactorily.

July 20, 1896

Lumber is being carted to Seapuit Golf Links, where a new club house is to be built soon.

February 14, 1898

An ice house is being built at the Seapuit Golf Links, and report says a hotel is soon to be erected in that vicinity.

March 14, 1898

Work has commenced on the new hotel at Seapuit Golf Links. Mr. Ira L. Hinckley of this village has the contract.

March 27, 1899

A party of twenty came down from the city to spend Saturday and Sunday at Seapuit Club House and play golf. Sunday was especially fine for the day.

February 8, 1904

Mr. F. W. Parsons left this week for a trip South, visiting in Florida, Georgia and other places. Mr. and Mrs. Joshua Merrill, Jr., of Dedham, are at Seapuitt Inn during his absence.

November 3, 1927

Ralph Williams and Maurice Allen won gross and net honors at the Seapuit Club last weekend. Maurice Allen was low net, finishing 18 holes in 74. Ralph Williams and Henry Whiteley had a hard battle for the gross honors. Both finishing with a 90 in the morning, they were compelled to play another round in the afternoon. They were even up on the ninth tee and Williams had the best chance to win until Whiteley sank a 15-foot putt, evening up the game again. On the next round Whiteley's putting saved him from defeat until Williams made a 3 against Whiteley's 6 on the 4th hole. They fought hard all the way in, finishing 43 and 45 in favor of Williams. Both boys played a good game of golf and will clash again next weekend in an open elimination contest.

A Foursome's Scorecard — Labor Day Weekend — 1936.

Putting in front of the head house at Seapuit Links. The two caddies are left, William Whiteley, and right, Karl Chadwick. c. 1913.

The Seapuit Club, which had nearly 50 rooms, was razed in
1932.

St. Mary's Island from Seapuit Club with North Bay, Grand
Island, and Cotuit Narrows in the background. c. 1910.

Gateway to causeway leading to St. Mary's Island. c. 1910.

Index of Subjects

258

259

Sponsors

A

Mr. & Mrs. Francis J. Allen
Mrs. Elizabeth L. Alward
Mr. Neil F. Ames
Mr. Rodney W. Ames
Mr. Walcott R. Ames
Mrs. Marilyn S. Anderson — NY
Mrs. Frank Andres
Mrs. Ruth Arenovski
Mrs. Gertrude S. Atwood

B

Mrs. Marshall E. Baker — DE
Mr. & Mrs. Charles B. Barclay — PA
Mr. Norman Barrett
Mr. George W. Bartlett
Mr. & Mrs. William Bates — AZ
Earl & Alice Batson
Mrs. Carol Ames Beggs
Mr. & Mrs. Edwin Bennett
Mr. Kenneth H. Benoit — FL
Mr. Walter E. Bianchi
Mrs. Florence Whiteley Binkewicz
Mr. Paul Birmingham
Mr. & Mrs. Stanley C. Bodell — RI
Mrs. Sara Briggs Bolton
Mrs. Joann Ames Borsari
Mr. & Mrs. Norman Boucher
Alys B. Bownes — PA
Mr. William R. Brennan, Jr.
Mr. Harrison P. Bridge
Mrs. Bettie K. Brophy
Mr. William L. Brown
Mrs. R. Buffum — FL
Mrs. Hope M. Burke
Mrs. Jean Scudder Burrill

C

Mr. & Mrs. Louis W. Cabot
Mr. & Mrs. John M. Cammett — NY
Mr. & Mrs. Stuart H. Cammett, Jr. — MI
Mrs. Rachel Daniel Campana
Cape Cod Bank & Trust Company
Warren & Evelyn Carstensen
Mrs. Mary Scudder Case — CT
Mr. & Mrs. William N. Chase
Leslie Cheek — VA
Mr. & Mrs. Albert L. Chesbro
David & Priscilla Chesbro
Mrs. Grace Crocker Chesbro
Bob & Mary Ann Gresh Chisholm — SC
Donald & Doris Chisholm
Donald & Sally Coleman Chisholm
Stephen & Shawn Chisholm — PA
Mrs. Joanne Begg Chope
Mr. Roy E. Christensen
Mr. & Mrs. Arthur F. Clark
Dr. & Mrs. Robert B. Clarke
Mr. & Mrs. David Cole
Mr. & Mrs. Charles Coleman — CT
Miss Katherine C. Cotter
Capt. George K. Coyne, Jr., USN — VA
Mr. Frederick C. Crawford — OH
Alexander Addison Crosby
Miss Ann W. Crosby
Mr. & Mrs. Bradford A. Crosby

Mr. Britton W. Crosby
Charles Addison & Melissa Crosby
Mr. & Mrs. Chester Ames Crosby, Sr.
Chester A., Jr., & Patricia W. Crosby
Chester A. III, & Katrina Crosby
David & Barbara Crosby
Mrs. Edward M. Crosby
Luke, Daniel, and Grace Crosby
Mrs. Katherine Daniel Crowe
Mrs. John Cunningham — CT
Mr. Charles Ford Curran
Dr. & Mrs. David Curtis
Mr. Joseph W. Cusack
Mrs. Vivian E. Cushing

D

Mr. & Mrs. Kenneth D. Daley
Mr. C. Mitchell Daniel — IA
Miss Nancy Daniel
Sr. Marion Agnes - Daniel S.M.B.T.
Mrs. Betty K. Davis — PA
Mrs. Eleanor Whiteley Davis — FL
Mr. & Mrs. Holbrook R. Davis
Mr. & Mrs. Nathanael V. Davis
Mr. & Mrs. Frank A. Day
Ernest & Grace DeWitt
Mrs. Marie Adams Scudder DeWitt
Mrs. Anne Bell Dias
Walter & Joan Crosby Dottridge
Mr. & Mrs. Robert J. Doyle — TX
Mrs. Carolyn A. Dwyer — TX

E

Mr. & Mrs. George P. Edmonds, Jr.
Mrs. Rosamond J. Fuller-Ellis
Mrs. Jane Eshbaugh
Mrs. Jane Daniel Everett

F

Mr. Paul Fair
Dr. & Mrs. Patrick Falco
Mr. & Mrs. T. M. Farley — NJ
Mr. Robert A. Farrell
Mrs. Edna Murray Farrington
Mrs. Richard R. Flood
Mrs. Peter M. Folger — CA
Mrs. Heywood Fox — CT
Ms. Mary Della Adams Frechette
Mr. Frank and Leone French
Mr. & Mrs. Gerard A. Fulham
Mr. David G. Fuller, Jr. — FL
Mr. & Mrs. Edmund T. Fuller
Mr. Henry Crocker Fuller — NY
Lt. Col. Melvyn W. Fuller (Ret.), VT

G

John & Marion Gaide — NY
Mrs. Jeannette Hallett Gallaher
Mrs. Frederick A. Gilbert
Mrs. Evelyn C. Williams Goff — ID
Mr. & Mrs. Robert J. Gonnella
Mr. Cecil I. Goodspeed
Mrs. Lee R. Gowans
Mr. & Mrs. Richard H. Grant, Jr. — OH
Mrs. Geraldine Coffin Gresh
Mr. & Mrs. William Gresh
Mr. & Mrs. Richard A. Grey
Mrs. Beverly Whiteley Griffin
Mr. & Mrs. John M. Groff

H

Mr. & Mrs. Andrew P. Hall
Mrs. Cyril S. Hall
Mr. & Mrs. Delton Crosby Hall
Mrs. Josephine Crosby Hallett — FL
Miss Catherine J. Hansberry
Mrs. Joanne Cammett Hansen — NY
Mr. & Mrs. Warren E. Hansen
Mr. & Mrs. Donald Harding
Ann & Bob Harmon
Dr. & Mrs. Charles C. Haskell
Dr. Richard J. Haskell
Michael A. & Gail Nemetz-Haussmann
Mr. Donald S. Hawkins — NJ
Mr. & Mrs. Richard Henderson
Walton & Alberta Hinckley
Mr. James Gaff Hinkle
Mrs. Edward O. Hobday — DE
Mrs. E. Manning Hodges — NM
Mr. Frank W. Hodges — RI
Mr. & Mrs. Phelps Holloway
Mrs. Ruth H. Holloway — FL
Mrs. Louise Holly
Mr. & Mrs. Townsend Hornor
Mr. & Mrs. William Humphreys, III
Hyannis Public Library

I

James & Barbara Ingram
David & Nancy Irish

J

Mrs. Henry B. Jackson
Sara Jarabek — FL
Mrs. Michael D. Joly
Mr. & Mrs. George D. Jones

K

Mr. & Mrs. Robert Kahelin
Mr. & Mrs. Paul F. Kalat
Mr. & Mrs. Paul D. Kaneb
Mr. & Mrs. Joseph Keller
Mrs. Mary Wilson Kelley — IN
Mrs. Candace Kelley
Mr. & Mrs. Walter S. Kiebach — FL
Mr. Peter D. Kiernan — NY
Mr. George B. Kilborne
Mr. R. Stewart Kilborne — GA
Mrs. Edith M. Kiley
Mrs. Audrey Killion

L

Richard & Mary Law
Mr. C. Eldon Lawson
Mr. & Mrs. Robert Lebel
Mr. James H. Lemon, Jr. — DC
Leonard Insurance Agency
Ms. Andrea Leonard
Mrs. Burleigh D. Leonard
Mr. & Mrs. Willis H. Leonard
Mr. & Mrs. George Lewis — NJ
Mr. Jim Lewis — SC
Mr. & Mrs. Clifton Linnell
Mr. & Mrs. Lane Lovell
Mr. & Mrs. Richard Hallett Lovell
K. Prescott Low
Mr. Charles S. Lymneos

Sponsors

M

Mr. Hugh F. MacColl
Mr. Norman A. MacColl — RI
Mrs. Judith Leonard MacCready — CA
Mr. William K. Mackey
Mr. & Mrs. Charles B. MacLean
Mrs. Ann Ames Madden
Miss Mary Madden — NM
Mrs. Brenda Ames Mazzeo
Mr. James A. McCarthy
Mr. & Mrs. William F. McIntyre, Jr.
Gaile McShane
Mr. & Mrs. Paul Mellon — VA
Mr. Felix A. Mirando, Jr.
Mr. & Mrs. Joseph Monteforte
Mrs. Cameron Morris, Jr.
Mr. Harold N. Munger, Jr.

N

Mrs. Louise Ames Nickerson
Neil & Gail Nightingale
Mr. Lee Nute

O

Mr. & Mrs. Bruce S. Old
Mr. William B. O'Keefe

P

Mr. Stanton C. Parker — TX
Mr. Stuart C. Pate
Joseph & Elizabeth Pattison
Lee Payton
Mrs. Gretchen Riedell Perry
Mr. & Mrs. Robert A. Pemberton
Mrs. Jeannie Pessano — NJ
Charles and Carole Pieper
Mr. Gerry S. Pierce — NY
Mrs. Patricia A. Whiteley Pond — ME
Mrs. Andrew Whiteley-Post — CA
Mrs. Margaret Post — TX
Mrs. Vera Purchler — NY

R

Mrs. Carl F. Riedell (Ethel Parker)
Mrs. Kathleen Burlingame Roberti
Mrs. Jonathan C. Roche
Mr. David Rockwood
Rogers & Marney, Inc.
Mrs. Isobel Rogers
Mrs. Shirley Lewis Rogers
Mr. & Mrs. George Rowland
Mr. Lindsay Russell
Mr. & Mrs. Joseph N. Russo, III
Mr. Paul Mark Ryan

S

Mr. and Mrs. B. Francis Saul — MD
Mrs. Lucinda Ames Savery
Cynthia Lewis Sawyer — IL
Mr. & Mrs. John T. Scandlen
Ernest and Dorothy Schatz
Mr. & Mrs. Theodore A. Schilling
Mrs. George Schumann — CT
Mr. & Mrs. Davis H. Scudder
Mr. & Mrs. Herbert F. Scudder
Mr. & Mrs. Howard H. Scudder
Mr. Scott Morgan Scudder
Mr. Winthrop Davis Scudder
Mrs. Isabel Lewis Shaw — FL
Mr. & Mrs. John F. Shields
Mr. & Mrs. Richard S. Shreve
Mr. & Mrs. Robert F. Sims — FL
Ralph and Pauline Chadwick Smith
Mr. & Mrs. Joseph J. Sousa
Mr. & Mrs. W. Frederick Spence
Mr. & Mrs. Peter M. Standish — PA
Mr. & Mrs. David. B. Starck
Mrs. H. L. Steinberg — PA
Mr. & Mrs. Richard Stimets
Sturgis Library
Mr. & Mrs. Leslie C. Sutherland
Mrs. Allen N. Sweeny
Mrs. Jo Daniel Swift

T

Mrs. Richard S. Taylor — CA
Tele-Rental Video
Mr. David B. Temple
Mr. & Mrs. John B. Tew
Mr. & Mrs. Philip Thibodeau
Luciann P. Thompson — FL
Mrs. Emily Crocker Toolas
Mrs. Theodore R. Turner, Sr.

V

Mrs. James Burlingame Veinotte — MI
Mrs. Judith Vellone

W

Mrs. Marjorie Walsh
Mrs. Howard E. Way — MD
Mr. George B. Week — FL
Mr. & Mrs. Roger U. Wellington
Mr. & Mrs. Paul Wheaton — NY
Mrs. Betty Whiteley Wheeler — SC
Mr. & Mrs. William F. Whitcomb — PA
Mr. Allen J. White
Mrs. Adele Burlingame Whitehead
Mr. & Mrs. H. Alfred Whiteley, Jr.
Mrs. Elmer Scudder Whiteley
Mr. James F. Whiteley
Mr. Neil H. Whiteley
Mr. & Mrs. Philip E. Whiteley
William & Evelyn Whiteley
Dr. George & Jean Wild
Mrs. D. Forbes Will
Mr. & Mrs. Albert G. Williams
Mr. & Mrs. Earle C. Williams
Mr. & Mrs. Louis P. Williams — OH
Mrs. Emily Crosby Woodward
Mr. & Mrs. James Wright
Mr. & Mrs. Frederick Wrightson

Z

Dr. & Mrs. Richard Zeigler